Lessons of War

Lessons of War

by

William A. Keim

RIVERCROSS PUBLISHING, INC.
Orlando

ISBN: 1-58141-083-2

Library of Congress Control Number: 2003092179

Dedicated

to
Marybelle Chase Keim

Without her encouragement, support, and loving presence in my
life, this work would never have been completed

Table of Contents

Foreword

This book is written, not for the 40 million people whose lives were taken from them in World War II, but rather for those who saw war firsthand and who survived to begin again. For millions who belonged to a generation set in despair, there was no alternative but to take the lessons learned and reconstruct themselves into individuals, determined not merely to survive, but to prevail. This book is about lessons learned.

Lessons of War

Prologue

I turned my head slightly away from the conference table so that I could study the bird that had just arrived in the tree outside my office window. It was a small bird, probably a sparrow. It had a tiny stick in its mouth. After several nervous darts of its head it flew away.

Slowly I turned back to view the assembly of faculty members who had asked to see me about salary conditions. The young man at the far end of the table was their spokesman, our drama and speech teacher, chosen no doubt for his power of persuasion. He had begun the familiar argument about salary schedules in similar colleges, his voice rising and falling for dramatic impact. I wasn't listening. For years I had listened to and had been a part of a group or groups just like this one. His colleagues eagerly followed his words, nodding their heads at the right moments not unlike nervous sparrows. Instead, I looked at the backs of my hands. Others around the table sighed comfortably thinking that I was absorbed in thought about what their leader was saying.

I glanced up as the voice became lower in pitch. The speaker had just gotten to the part about family expense and community involvement. I swiveled my chair to the left just enough to allow me to look out the window again. This time I saw the crisp blueness of the sky and the faint fuzz of spring green, which was just beginning to show on the little hill just yards away from the building. Air rippled the little hill as I watched. Suddenly a candy wrapper blew into view and stuck on a bouquet of new grass stems. The piece of wrinkled paper struggled to get away. Twisting back and forth in the wind it remained fast, working its way deeper into the base of the stems. Finally as though it knew and accepted its fate, it shuddered one last time and lay still. Out of the reach of the living wind, it would die, its molecules would dissolve into the soil of the little hill, perhaps somehow to become a part of the tree to someday be cut down and be processed again into paper. Maybe decades in the future it would be a reborn candy wrapper and resume its windy journey across the land to become entangled in another patch of grass on another hillock upon which would grow a little tree. Could this lesson be what I had been trying to remember?

Captured by this momentary thought, I barely heard the droning voice off my bad right ear. Years ago I had learned to turn my head to the left in order to tune down noise created by teenagers and to turn off people who had little or nothing to say. My bad ear, with a serious decibel loss, was a gift given to me by a German artilleryman who one dark night near Saverne, France, yanked a lanyard and sent me, for free, a subtle control over my own sense of hearing.

I looked closely at the little hill outside my window, trying to focus through my new bifocals on the tiny slip of new grass. There was something out there that called to me, trying to nudge a memory back to my screen, something that seemed very important. I had watched that little hill for almost a year now. I had seen it in all weather, all times of the day and even at night when the light cast a softened shadow on it from the nearby Student Center. The hill changed, I had noted; it was sometimes distant, unconcerned. Sometimes, as now, it seemed alive, beckoning, insistent as though it struggled beneath the blowing grass to speak to me.

I stared, vaguely aware that there were others present in the room with me. Suddenly without warning, I knew at last what I was seeing. I had missed the point of the hill all year. A fine electric shock flowed up my back, through my neck and into my head. The hill was not outside a window on a college campus. It was, instead, a hill near a line of trees just outside Butzbach on the Mannheim plain of Germany.

Sitting straight in my chair, I quickly slipped back into those final days of fire and storm and with a rush of recognition, I saw a young soldier lying on the close side of the hill. He was on his back, a piece of fresh grass in his mouth, head resting within his helmet. He was relaxed, knees up, hands behind his neck watching the few bright cumulus clouds streaming by overhead in the blue sky. There was no sound but the soft wind that caressed the soldier's field jacket, moving the collar flap back and forth—I was that youth.

It was a simple reconaissance patrol. One short squad detailed to check the hills beyond the factory where the company was to be housed. No sweat. The war was nearly over. There had been no sign of an armed enemy for two days, all of the planes were ours and M company had leapfrogged through our position that morning moving over to Wetzlar to secure the road junction there. We had simply taken a walk, reached our stop line near the edge of the trees, and were resting before we started the hike back to Butzbach. All eight of us were silent, scattered around on the little hill, some dozing in the warm sun among the newly awakened spring insects, others gazing around, occupied with his own thoughts.

I moved my back slightly around a small stone, trying to get more comfortable. Suddenly amidst the lazy relaxation there was a faint but familiar chunking sound followed within seconds by a loud crashing bang. Cordite fumes came with a shower of dirt as the first mortar shell registered on us about one hundred yards back across the field we had just crossed.

The second crash was closer and louder, coming from behind us as we all sat up to stare without belief at the spot where the first round had struck the meadow.

"Down," I screamed.

I flung myself into the ground, the little hill, which moments before seemed so peaceful, had now become an exposed target. The third round was the final register followed quickly by several rounds fired for effect.

This is crazy, I thought. I yelled at the top of my voice, "Not now! Don't kill me! The war's over! I'm going home dammit! Stop! Stop!"

The earth thumped and shuddered. Each burst shattered my ears until I could hear nothing, only the shock of blast that tore at my head and back. Gasping for air in the charged smoke and heat, I lost contact with myself. Time was frozen.

Slowly I regained some sense only to find myself moving deeper and deeper into pain. There were still no worldly sounds, only excruciating pressure and pain in my ears and lungs.

Struggling to come back to consciousness in the floating silence, I forced my eyes open only to find myself watching a tiny black bug, inches from my eyes. Fascinated by the insect and not fully aware of where I was, I studied it closely in the ringing silence of my head. The bug was methodically exploring a stem of grass. Moving all of its legs, it ascended the sprig from the stem to the tip, antenna sweeping, stopping to confirm now and then. With incredible balance it swung its little body over the tip of the grass stem and started down the other side, busy with its insect audit. I closed my eyes, only vaguely aware that my face was pressed into the ground. I smelled the earth, rich and dank from winter's moistures. I felt dirt in my mouth. I chewed. It had a wonderful taste.

As awareness returned, I found that I was on my feet, running. As though I was in a terror filled dream I ran toward the far woods, neither hearing nor seeing. I probably fell but I was unaware of it. The line of trees kept getting farther away until suddenly it crashed into me knocking me sidewise onto fallen branches.

Four of us, weaponless, made it to the woods. Gasping for air, I looked back to see four motionless brown bundles, one blackened, on fire and smoldering. The earth was pocked with brown spots around and on my little hill.

Somehow, from a great distance a voice called to me as I stared at the hill. "Dr. Keim. Dr. Keim, are you all right?"

There was a voice in the room speaking to me as from an echo until it registered precise sound. The tobacco brown spots disappeared from the little hill outside my window as I quickly returned to my conference table. Swinging around in my chair, I snapped, "Of course I'm all right. I am thinking that what Linke is saying makes a lot of sense."

Amid a stirring of approval among the committee members, I looked at Mr. Linke. He beamed at me and went on talking.

Again I did not listen, instead I looked closely at him. His fashionably styled haircut cost him a lot of dollars. His teeth were even and white from careful expensive bending by a skilled orthodontist. He was handsome, strong, an early tan from hours on a tennis court added to his groom and poise. The marks of careful nutrition, planned by the family pediatrician were clearly evident. He was modern American youth. Confident, beautiful.

He was getting to the good part. The part about quality education.

"Young man," I thought, "have you ever been so scared that you didn't even know who you were? Have you ever known terror so real that you lost the ability to control your own body functions? Have you ever dreamed once about a strafing airplane or of a Tiger tank about to run you down from behind? Have you ever awakened at night sweating and sobbing from distorted visions of horrors that never go away?"

Mr. Linke concluded his remarks. The committee left after extracting from me the traditional promise to give consideration to what had been said. They were jovial, congratulating their spokesman for his presentation.

When they were all gone, I swung my chair in silence to face the window and a little fearfully I looked at the hill. It was again green with new grass. The wind had died and the scene was without motion. The bird came back to the tree, this time with a little string in its mouth, its head darting from side to side. It flew away in the late afternoon light making the branch jiggle in the calm air.

That night after my wife and sons had gone to bed, I sat robed at the desk in my study. The pool of light from the circular desk lamp isolated me from the rest of the darkened room. I could hear the final snapping of the fire cooling in the fireplace against the far wall. I rested my chin on cupped hands and looked again across the short expanse of mahogany veneer to the picture of my great grandfather in the silver frame. His tintype stare watched me with its usual hostility, handlebar moustache bristling, arrogance commanding his stiff pose. He was my dead end in a three year search for my ancestors. I knew only that he was an only son and that he had one son named Henry, that Henry had only one son named William and that my father named his only son after himself. I was the only son of an only son of an only son of an only son. A very thin thread of genetic possibility and random chance had put me at this desk in the middle of the night looking into the photographed eyes of the first Keim in my ancestral line to become an American. His name was Joseph and his citizenship certificate, dated October 20, 1864, hung on the wall in the darkness beyond my left shoulder. As I had so many times in the past, I said, "Joseph, who were you? Did you ever laugh? Were you ever afraid? Why didn't you leave at least one written word so that I might know you? What were the things that made you you? Did you ever do anything interesting? You were a child once, how did you become a man? Were you satisfied with yourself? When you did, did you really care?"

As I sat there in the puzzled silence of the darkened room, it came to me that I partially understood what the little hill had been trying to tell me that afternoon. Two hundred years from now perhaps some descendent of mine would wonder about me. Someone might ask, "Who was this boy from a poor family who had grown to be a college president?"

With that thought fresh in my mind, I reached quickly into my desk and pulled out a file folder marked "Photographs." Spreading the snapshots within the pool of light I saw that I had before me a chronology of myself peering out from a wide variety of glossy shapes and sizes. Most of the faces were smiling in the fashion of snapshots. Some were already turning a brown color. Here was my first picture, a tiny baby bundled in blankets and propped against a soft cushion. Next, a sober first grader at a school desk, arms folded, a blackboard in the background with little paper turkeys along its border. Billy, thin, undernourished. Picture taken at Thanksgiving in 1930; my father had been out of work for more than a year; we had been on the county welfare rolls for fourteen months.

A series of pictures, young friends, white duck pants, arms around each other's shoulders. I am the only one without a belt. Me shooting my bow and arrow. A poignant picture of me and my sister together with our mongrel dog, Brownie. Brownie was to be run over by a car on Noble's Lane a few weeks later.

Better times in junior high school. My father has a job as a director of a boys' orphanage. Me standing on the front steps of the orphanage in a brand new short leather jacket, smiling, long pants with the crease sewn into them. A series of high school and vacation pictures, Idaho,

17

Canada. Standing on a dock in a loose pullover sweater holding a thirteen pound catfish, which I had caught, legs in laced up high top hunting boots, whipcord riding breeches. Rimless glasses by now. High school graduation, California.

Then curiously the pictures stop smiling. Now they are in uniform, holding weapons, looking grim. One good one, standing next to a truck in Butzbach, holding a cigarette, tanned, body hard and lean, taken on the morning before the patrol and the little hill. One smudged print standing shirtless next to a squad tent on Okinawa—the last picture ever taken of me in uniform.

College graduation, series of pictures teaching, counseling, administrating, growing older, fatter. Picture of me with my first child, Carolyn. Snap of me at the helm of the Gracie S., Sterling Hayden's schooner. Standing beside 37 Yankee the day I soloed at Fullerton Airport, hand on the motionless propellor, grinning. College professor, college president.

I spread them all out in accurate chronological order. Those few pictures from birth to middle age told the graphic story of becoming somebody. I wondered to myself, "What will the last picture ever taken of me look like? Am I looking at it now?" I questioned.

Fascinated, I looked at the series, particularly at the little boy sitting at the battered desk in the first grade. I compared it closely with the recent picture of me sitting at my desk in the president's office. I studied them, side by side.

"Is this the same person? Is it possible for this thin little kid to grow up to be this grey middle-aged man and still be the same? If he has changed, how has he changed? What changed him?"

I let my eyes sweep back and forth across the glossy surfaces searching for clues. Seeing a full life time spread out this way was revealing. Pondering, I arrived at last to the central question.

"Was there a place and time in my life, which I could positively identify as a major turning point? A point of time unlike all others?"

I keep seeing the child, the son, the brother, the husband, the father, the student, the adventurer, the teacher, the soldier.

Then, almost as though I were merely confirming what I had known all along, I carefully picked up the picture of the young man with the pistol on his hip standing next to a truck outside a little town in Germany in the spring of 1945. I knew then that I had in my hand what I had been searching for for a long time. It was simple. There had been only one period of time in my life that had been so involved, so totally different from all other periods. That segment of my life had had an enormous effect on what I had become. Without those few years I might have become a grocery clerk, a criminal, a laborer. I know that I would never have finished college nor would I have ever gone into teaching.

I held the print by the edges and studied the face. My mind drifted, without chronology, through those three years of time. World War II, the greatest, most prolonged, costliest, bloodiest war. I had played a miniscule part in that war. However, I was a little different. I had fought in both hemispheres, against the Germans and then during the bloody end of the war against the Japanese on Okinawa. Not too many American soldiers had done that.

But in the playing of my part, I had become a person. I had become me. The war had been the single most important turning point in my life, just as it must have been for the many other young men who had lived through it.

Putting down the snapshot, I looked at the photograph of Joseph and said aloud, "Some day, great grandfather, someone will read what I am going to write, they will know about me. They will know about me during that period of my life when I set my values and became what I remained for the rest of my years on this earth. They will know what I thought, what I saw, and how, during that time, I felt about the world and the people around me. Perhaps they won't care, but right now, I do."

A distant dog barked in the chill of the spring night, as I pulled a yellow pad from my desk and began to write the story, which follows:

CHAPTER 1

INDUCTION

Once during my lifetime I was a soldier serving in the United States Army. This experience took place during World War II and from March 1943 until January 1946 I was on active service as a volunteer enlisted man. Looking back on those days from the comfort of over 50 years I can reflect on the war, the part I played in it and the profound effect that it has had on my life. The war was unquestionably the most important long term single event of my youth and perhaps in telling of it I will better explain the kind of person that I have become. I seldom think of the war anymore and I have never participated in veteran organizations or displayed publicly my affiliation with the Army. I suspect that very few people with whom I work even know that at one time in my life I was a soldier.

There is no easy way to explain the attraction of war to many of the youth of the early 30's and 40's. As a nation we had suffered a crippling Depression following World War I and isolationism accompanying the decline of the Depression produced a sense of martyrdom for those who had sacrificed in the trenches of 1917–1918. The earlier "lost generation" of writers, Hemingway, Faulkner, Graves, Sassoon, and Wilfred, described these sacrifices as individuals caught in the global events beyond their control, and there was an almost poetic attractiveness in the death of these heroic figures. Great films appeared, "Wings," "All Quiet on the Western Front" and "Farewell to Arms." The children of the late 20's and the 30's played these war scenes over and over and watched carefully the fathers and uncles who could not bring themselves to talk about "The Great War." There was a mystery about it. There seemed to be no conscious effort to indoctrinate the youth. Paradoxically there appeared to be a determined effort in the

30's to teach children peace rather than war. It was the case in my home and I believe it was the case in the homes of my playmates. But the VFW and the American Legion parades on Armistice Day were exciting and the heroes of young boys were aviators and soldiers. Even Charles Lindberg in 1927 was an Army aviator and was promoted to Colonel after his epic Atlantic solo flight. The League of Nations was dull and the Depression was uninteresting to children. I felt cheated that the war was over and that I had missed the opportunity to do my duty for my country and for my flag.

Neighborhood games revolved around war in general and World War I in particular. We young boys actually spent a part of summer digging a battlefield on the mountainous slag heap from a nearby coal mine. Trenches, shell holes and dugouts, were built and mock battles were held sometimes with 20 or 30 youths engaged. The mine company finally put a stop to it but there was a great summer of playing heroes. The Germans always lost. I was about 11 years of age at the time, our family was destitute and on welfare because during the Depression my father was out of work for almost three years. When he finally did get a job on the other side of Pittsburgh, we moved to an apartment and I started junior high school. I rode my bicycle, played softball, ran on the school track team and was a perfectly normal boy. My great personal joy, however, was model airplanes and I tolerated school each day in order to go home to my basement apartment private workshop and work on my models. I sold magazines and had a newspaper route in order to buy airplane kits. Most of my models were fighter planes and of course, my heroes were fighter pilots of World War I. On Halloween my costume was that of a soldier and I'll never forget the night that my father brought home a real coal bucket German helmet from the war. It was my greatest treasure and I kept it for years until it was stolen.

War was not an obsession with me, however, and I had many other interests, including girls as I graduated to high school and the world moved closer to a resumption of global conflict. In 1939 when I was a sophomore in high school, war between Germany, England and France broke out. America for the most part was avidly against participating and a great "stay out of foreign wars" attitude swept the nation. I thought that it was a little cowardly but it was also somewhat appealing and fashionable to oppose war.

Little by little, however, we were drawn into it and by 1940 when my family and I moved to California, our entry into the war seemed inevitable.

There is no way I can adequately describe my feelings when on Sunday, December 7, 1941, the Japanese attacked Pearl Harbor. I was driving a soldier friend of the family into Los Angeles from Bellflower when the radio in the car interrupted its normal broadcast to announce the stunning news. We drove quickly to our friend's unit, a radar installation in downtown Los Angeles, and I returned home as quickly as I could to share the excitement not only with my family but with my friends. Pearl Harbor? Where was it? The Japanese? I thought we were being drawn into a war with Germany and that the so-called Japanese empire was no possible threat to us. It was very confusing and the radio reports were very vague and contradictory. Few people knew anything about Pearl Harbor or even the Philippines. Names of islands and exotic places were announced on the radio, but most people had to go to world maps, encyclopedias and atlases trying to locate such places. That Sunday was, in some respects, like an exciting holiday. Army trucks appeared on the highways and anti-aircraft units began to dig emplacements around Douglas and North American aircraft factories in Long Beach and Downey, near our home. Finally an appeal went out over the local radio stations asking people not to drive around watching the Army units prepare for an implied immediate attack. Conditions were chaotic but very exciting.

On December 8 the entire student body of the high school sat in the auditorium and listened to President Roosevelt tell the nation of the extreme damage at Pearl Harbor and to ask the combined Congress for a declaration of war. It was a memorable and dramatic moment, which I shall never forget. I sat with my fellow seniors experiencing many emotions: outrage at the Japanese, pride in our President and in our country, a resolve to punish all enemies and a disturbing fatalistic thought that the festering wishes of my youth were being fulfilled. Another thought came to my mind, which was to come true: "There are actually young men present in this room who will die as a result of what the President is saying." I was thrilled by all of it.

The next few months were like a dream. I wanted to be brave and enlist, but my mother was sick with the thought of my going into the Army and most of my friends decided to remain in school to finish their senior year. I finally decided to stay with my friends but we were all impatient to become part of the great national urge to punish an enemy. We thought that the Japanese and Nazi were perfect enemies, easily discernible, the little yellow man and the Nazi with his brutality and his comic swasticas were instantly seized upon as symbols. They were the "enemy." Anyone could see that.

California and the rest of the West coast had a problem, however, because there was a large Japanese-American population living among us. A sizeable part of our senior class was of Japanese descent and when the government order came to relocate all of these people and their families into internment camps, there were mixed feelings. I wrote an editorial for the school newspaper expressing the anguish that we were feeling and when the Japanese-Americans left we were without most of our school leadership, athletes and good friends.

Signs appeared in local stores that proclaimed, "Don't be a sap, a Jap is a Jap." It was a dark period for our nation and some of us were very disturbed about it even at the time.

In June of 1942, just before I graduated from high school, I turned 18 and had to register for the draft. My plan was to wait until I was drafted and take my chances. During the summer of 1942 I worked in an oil field and then took a job in a defense plant making parachutes. When the college fall semester rolled around, my two best friends and I enrolled in a community college and I started on a degree in pre-architecture because I didn't know what else to do and it seemed interesting.

In November of 1942, I joined the College Enlisted Reserve Corps, which promised extended college deferments and a commission later. By so doing I lost my draft status and was then classified as a volunteer. Three months later the Enlisted Corps was activated and I received a notice to report to Fort McArthur in San Pedro for induction into the armed services.

The war itself was not going well in late 1942 and early 1943 and by then I was quite happy in college and doing better in my studies than I had ever done before in school. I was not reluctant to join the service but I was beginning to see that by being one of 14 million servicemen, I was probably not going to have such a personal effect on the outcome of the war after all. Of course we were going to eventually win, so who needed me to disrupt my life, leave my girlfriend and my social interests to become another G.I.?

The whole thing became very real for me when on the morning of my induction, my mother fell apart and cried as my father drove me to the college campus to catch the school bus to Fort McArthur. I was very touched by the reaction of my mother and with the very expensive watch that my father gave to me as a going away gift, our stiff upper lip was shattered, the ground fell away from under me and I sensed that I was truly being separated from my family.

The heroes of my youth, the excitement of the past war year, the growing dread of being separated from those whom I loved were all intensified in my mind that day as our group of Reserve Corps members boarded the bus at the college. The band played; the cheerleaders did their routine; a little patriotic speech was given by the dean of the college and I was at last off to the war.

Fort McArthur in San Pedro had been built prior to 1920 as a series of coastal defense batteries with a permanent garrison installation. It had become an induction and processing center for Southern California and although I didn't know it at the time, three long years would pass before I would return to Ft. McArthur to be declassified and returned to civilian life. The day our bus load of reservists entered the main gate to unload us in a large paved parking lot area, however, was to mark a formalized period of imprisonment for me. As the gate closed behind us, I knew from that moment on, my freedom of movement would be authorized by someone else.

We unloaded to our first command, "Line up, shut up, stand at attention!" I did my best to appear soldierly but I must confess that we were a rag tailed group and I felt a little foolish and giggled a little.

The first step was a long, complicated confused roll call of some 200 recruits who had arrived in other buses and had joined our little band. It was revealed to me at the roll call that all noncoms in the U.S. Army would pronounce my name Keem and the red faced Corporal had to shout it several times before I even knew he meant me. I was embarrassed and a little shaken when he make a mark next to my name. Many others in the larger group had the same problem, however, and by the time we got through the experience, everyone was feeling better. I was amused at some of the young men who had really difficult names and who could not believe that the word being yelled over and over was really a name of someone.

The next step in the induction process was lunch and I couldn't believe that either. It occurred to me that I was going to miss my mother a great deal.

Soldiers were telling us rules, reminding us that we were in the Army, attempting to assemble us into marching groups and answering questions such as, "Will we be able to go home tonight?"

We spent the afternoon being assigned bunk beds in barracks, getting our hair cut close to our scalps and filling out forms. We were all anxious to get our uniforms because there were rumors that after three days we would get passes for the weekend. The college group as an entity had long ago been disassembled as we learned the Army's penchant for alphabetizing. I found myself with a group of strangers whose names all began with either a J or a K. It was my first experience with loneliness but we were all too excited to notice it much and when at the end of the second day we were issued equipment and uniforms, most of the depression disappeared. I was surprised at the care with which the uniforms were fitted. Tailors fitted each man and if alterations were required, the man was given a tag with instructions to pick up the garment the next day. Particular care was given to the fitting of the dress uniform. As I recall, I was issued two pairs of shoes, a raincoat, a topcoat, two scratchy wool shirts, three sets of underwear (shorts only), six pairs of sox, and two sets of fatigues. The fatigues were ugly blue things that no one bothered to fit and I believe came in three sizes, small, medium, and large. Actually all sizes were large, some were just larger than others. A floppy blue hat was issued along with the fatigues but within a few weeks, we were to be seen in ugly green pants, jackets and a less shapeless hat. In addition we received two blankets, two pair of wool pants, two caps, a dress blouse, plus two identical barracks bags marked "A" and "B." Why they were marked this way was a mystery to me, which was to continue until the bags were replaced in 1944 by one larger duffle bag with a shoulder strap and handle. At no time during my Army life did anyone explain why I had two barracks bags nor did I ever receive instruction that certain items went only in bag A or bag B. There were other mysteries about the Army also.

For instance, we were assembled at 10:00 p.m. at night and marched off to take our Army aptitude tests. Some of the men were feeling very happy since they had spent the evening at the P.X. drinking beer but most of us were simply exhausted after a day of marching, physical exercises, and being on work detail, moving piles of lumber from one place to another. It seemed a strange time to take the tests, which would be the single most important factor in placing a person in training. It was common rumor that low scores meant the Infantry or worse. Anyway by 1:00 a.m. we were through and struggled back to the barracks only to be awakened at 5:30 for reveille and a swell Army breakfast of powdered eggs or something.

The rumor regarding passes was true, so early Saturday afternoon we all rushed to the main gate for the pay phones that were located there. After a long wait my Dad picked me up. I was very proud of my uniform, and incidently of my father who drove up in his Army staff car, which the Red Cross had assigned to him. He was in his Army officer's uniform that Red Cross directors were required to wear and together we looked very professional. My new friends were very impressed thinking that he was probably a General. We were all so new in the service that we had not yet learned how to distinguish rank, and the staff car painted in Army olive drab was very effective.

The next few days were harder to take. There were rumors that casualties had been so high in the Pacific that the entire post of inductees was to be transferred to the Marines as replacements. We also heard that we were all to be assigned to the Infantry. We were issued our soldier's handbooks and spent hours reading and practicing the rules of the U.S. Army. I learned that there were many things, which you must memorize word for word: your serial number, guard instructions, different kinds of poison gases and how to recognize the odors of each, first aid, how to address the company commander, etc., etc.

I was astonished at the physical condition of some of the inductees. Many were very frail, some were obese and most were physically unable to perform the rigorous demands of the hours of group calesthentics that we were subjected to each day. I enjoyed the physical aspect of the training. I had been playing baseball since I was 12 and had been on both the high school and college track team and while not a very muscular person, I was, by Army standards, in good physical condition. However, the days began to seem longer as the novelty of being a soldier wore off and my fellow sufferers began to complain and to look for ways to avoid work assignments. I remember an older man in our group who had done a hitch in the regular Army. We all regarded him with awe and respect although he seldom spoke and never appeared for calesthentics, work details or any roll call that I can recall. He simply ignored the entire process and appeared only when it was to his advantage. He never missed a meal nor did he ever spend a night in his bunk.

It wasn't long before we began to wear out the piles of lumber moving them around from location to location and finally back to where they had been in the first place. Just about the time we were to start over again, we were each scheduled for an interview out of which was to grow our assignment and training. By this time I was wiser and convinced that I needed to look out for myself if I was to survive the war. My father, with his many service contacts, had discovered that a new unit of cartographers was to be developed and assigned to the Los Angeles area. During phone conversations he told me what to say in the interview and I practiced saying map-making words and giving the impression that I was at least a trainable cartographer. This was difficult since I knew virtually nothing about the subject. I was supposed to ask to be assigned to this new unit and my father and I both believed that with his influence it had all been arranged. Everyone winked at one another and I waited for the interview. It was not long in coming. I sat in a room with a hundred or so other inductees and soon the name "Keem" was shouted from one of the cubicles along the wall. I went in and sat down in front of a desk behind which sat one of the most implacable human beings I had ever seen. At first I thought that he was dead. However, he stared at me while I stumbled through my cartographer's speech. I resisted winking at him when I was through; instead I just smiled at him knowingly.

After watching me for a few moments, he sighed audibly and told me my test scores and that I was being assigned to the Ordnance Department. Much to my surprise I had high scores in both math and comprehension, but I left his office trying to figure out what he meant by what he had said. I thought that Ordnance was fixing trucks and I hardly even knew how to change a tire.

Two days later we were told to put everything we owned into our A and B bags and to fall out in the company street at 9:00 a.m. Between the interview and this announcement, I had talked to my father on the phone and he had insisted that I should not worry, that everything would be all right. I was not worried, instead I began practicing my map-making words again.

When we were all assembled in the company street, the Sergeant began reading names, training stations and points of departure. Many of the young men were assigned to Ft. Ord, California, lined up and marched off to trains waiting on sidings within the camp. Several other smaller groups went in trucks to other destinations. Finally there were only four or five of us left standing next to our A and B bags, looking nervously at one another. At last he called Keem and I learned that my Army career *would* be spent as an Ordnance soldier. He told the few of us left in the company street that we would embark in a few hours for the Aberdeen Proving Grounds in Maryland.

A very chilling bitterness took hold of me. The games were over. The fun and novelty had ceased. The stories about Army life were true. They didn't care, they just didn't care and it was very unfair. I was choking with anger with a tight sickness in my stomach as I hefted my A and B bags and walked with my companions to the train. It was a long hike, we had to stop every few hundred feet to get our breath and the Corporal in charge of our party would not tell us anything or allow us to stop and make phone calls. We arrived at the train, were boarded and told to sit down and stay there. The Corporal gave me a large brown sealed envelope with our records and a mimeographed copy of our orders. I was apparently in charge of the detail with instructions that if any member of the small group did not show up as specified, I would be court-martialled. The orders listed five names, serial numbers and our destination at the 1st Ordnance Training Battalion of the Ordnance School at Aberdeen Proving Grounds in Maryland. My heart sank as I noticed we were to report there by the fastest possible means immediately. We sat together on that train until almost 5:00 p.m. without food or any indication that we were ever going to depart. Other groups of men arrived from time to time filling the six or seven cars. None seemed to be going to Maryland, however.

At last we were told by a bored and unresponsive Corporal to disembark and go to the mess hall for dinner. Most of us made a beeline for a telephone instead. I was very bitter and when I got my father on the phone, I'm afraid that I made him feel bad that he hadn't been able to reverse a decision of the U.S. Government. At least my family knew that I was on my way to Maryland, so I reboarded the train and nursed my adolescent despair.

It sounds impossible now to believe the level of anguish that I experienced on that day, but I had never been away from home in my life, not even to a summer camp. I thought that I would die among these insensitive strangers, some of whom acted as though they were on a vacation trip of some sort. I was sick about leaving my home. Finally, there was activity, doors banged, a civilian conductor came through the car, and by 9:00 p.m. in total darkness the train moved silently out of Fort McArthur. We moved slowly through Los Angeles and stopped in Pasadena sometime during the night to pick up another group of inductees on their way to Aberdeen.

We slept in our seats and by morning of the next day, we were stopped on the pass out of San Bernardino while the train engines were changed for the trip across the country. We were allowed out of the cars briefly and I will always remember looking down the pass at the hazed mountains behind Los Angeles. These ranges of mountains are similar to a Japanese painting of morning, very beautiful, soothing and consoling.

The trip from California to Maryland took seven days. It was uncomfortable but it was an important personal passage for me. During these days and tear filled nights, I passed from the innocence of childhood and the romanticism of adolescence into the beginning world of the adult. It was painful but it was life. When I stepped off the train at Aberdeen station in Maryland with my orders and my charges all accounted for, it was with more a sense of adventure to come and with less a sense of having been betrayed. That interminable train trip had been a gateway point in my life.

CHAPTER II

BASIC TRAINING

I was soon told that being in the Ordnance was not a disgrace; it was an honor. Besides fixing trucks, the Ordnance Department of the Army was responsible for the selection, experimentation and maintenance of all the material used by the Army. It was made up of skilled technicians, scientists and inventors. Although no one mentioned it, it also had thousands of men with lesser skills and thousands with no skills at all.

I was assigned to the 3rd Platoon, Company B of the 1st Ordnance Training Battalion. Our Sergeant was a crusty gravel voiced Army man named Sgt. Dow. I still remember him as a stereotype of a training Sergeant and my six weeks with him during basic training is still as an important memory to me as the war, which was to follow. He was tough but in many ways he loved us all and took personal pride in the platoon and in our accomplishments. We had other noncommissioned and commissioned officers, but I don't remember any of them even though our squad leaders were with us through all of the training. I only remember Sgt. Dow and to this day I could not say the name Dow without the prefix Sergeant.

Aberdeen Proving Grounds was enormous. I never saw the entire camp since it extended for miles and included artillery ranges and extensive tank and vehicle testing grounds, rifle ranges, forests, swamps and I believe even several airstrips.

That part of Maryland was then a beautiful low lying rolling forest area with many streams, which mostly emptied into Chesapeake Bay.

Every Army in the world apparently believes that its soldiers must be up and functioning by dawn. Consequently, morning roll calls are invariably conducted in considerable darkness. They certainly were in Aberdeen.

At 5:30 a.m. a whistle would blow and the lights in the barracks would be turned on. No gentle voice urging you to awaken, no period of transition allowing you to reluctantly pass from sleep to awareness. This was the Army and at a certain time you were to be *awake*. From the first morning when the whistle blew and lights came on absolutely shattering my sleep, the man in the bed next to mine said, "I'll get a job tomorrow, Mother." For six weeks he said that, every day but Sunday, when we were allowed to sleep until 7:00. At first it was funny and then boring and then finally maddening. Those around him could easily have killed him within four weeks. I sometimes have a vision of him as an old man still saying it every morning and I'm sure that if there is a day of resurrection, he will peer over the edge of his grave and shout, "I'll get a job tomorrow, Mother."

There were also some fine and memorable people. One such person was Don Holt, who had boarded the train in Pasadena, and with whom I was able to spend almost my entire Army career. He was an older man, nearly 30, and was called "Dad" and "Pop" by everyone. Although he had never been to college, he was witty, sensitive, intelligent, well-read and had a brilliant mind. I saw his Army service record once and his I.Q. was listed as 160. He had one flaw, however. He was a compulsive gambler.

He helped me a great deal by keeping my intellectual and creative curiosity alive during a period of time when neither of these characteristics were considered as virtues.

The mornings began with reveille of course and this consisted of a Battalion assembly at 6:00 a.m. with all companies facing the parade ground, which was perhaps a ten acre quadrangle around which the battalion barracks stood. In the cool morning darkness it was at first a fiasco as each squad leader had to shout a report to each platoon leader, who in turn reported to each company commander that all men were present and accounted for. Sometimes, at first, individuals weren't present or accounted for and then the confusion, in the dark, of reporting the person's name and rank caused innumerable delays around the battalion perimeter. After each company was ready, the four company commanders represented by a Sergeant, since no officer was present that early in the morning, had to shout to the Battalion officer of the day, in the darkness, in proper sequence of course, that his company was present or accounted for, or that so many men were absent and not accounted for. At first it was not uncommon for this procedure to take 20 or 30 minutes to complete. The time spent, of course, came out of breakfast time, since the next formation was scheduled for 7:30 a.m.

All in all it was the worst possible way to start out a day and one of the best ways to make enemies was to be late for roll call and cost people their breakfast time.

After roll call we went to breakfast. The Battalion had one mess hall for approximately 1,000 men. I can't recall whether we had staggered times for eating but I don't think so. I remember long double lines and a rather efficient system of serving on metal trays. The food was very good—bacon and fried eggs, potatoes, toast, sausage, milk, coffee and all you could eat. An officer was stationed at the exit to make sure that no food was wasted and he personally supervised the scraping of leftovers from the trays. There were large garbage cans at the mess hall exit and before you turned in your empty tray to the collecting point, it was necessary to personally scrape all remaining food into the garbage can under the eye of this officer. There was a sign over the serving line that stated, "Take all you want but eat all you take."

Men were turned back to eat leftover food if the officer deemed that there was wastage. Some of the men were finicky eaters or took something that they discovered they didn't like and some of the ingenious methods of getting rid of unwanted food while appearing at the garbage cans was sometimes very amusing and often innovative. No one seemed to care about coffee wastage so the procedure was to use the undrunk coffee in your cup to wash uneaten scraps from the tray by pouring what was left in the cup across the tilted tray. By carefully saving less than an inch of coffee in the bottom of the cup a person could fill it with unwanted food giving the impression that the cup was almost full of unusable coffee. By being quick the inspecting officer would miss the fact that globs of food cascaded across the tray.

We all dressed in those large green fatigues during basic training. We were also issued additional equipment on our first day. I was fascinated by the Army equipment even though it all had been used over and over by preceding training units and none of it was new. We were issued packs, shelter halfs, tent pegs, cartridge belts, first aid packets, canteens, canteen cups with mess gear, helmet liners, leggings, gas masks, blankets and a 1903 Springfield bolt action rifle.

I had always loved guns and rifles. My father and I had hunted together in Bedford County in Pennsylvania as soon as I was able to handle a shotgun and I owned at home a .22 target rifle and a .410 gauge shotgun. I was familiar with firearms, regarded them as potentially dangerous and knew the safety precautions that were necessary in order to use them as an effective weapon.

I was really astonished to discover how many of the new soldiers had never handled a gun, couldn't load one and had no notion whatever as to how to aim and fire the thing. We spent many hours in rifle training. We learned how to strip and clean these old World War I rifles, how to handle them, how to use the slings in the different firing positions and spent countless hours in practice dry run firing sessions. Small squads would sit around on the parade ground pulling triggers on empty chambers. Sometimes the combined snickering of bolts and the clicking of firing pins created a tremendous racket.

The basic training of an Ordnance soldier in World War II was different from that of a combat infantryman. Our soldiering time frame was shorter because we were all to be assigned to additional technical training, which was to follow the basics of physical conditioning, weapons, drill, first aid, map reading and all of the killing and survival techniques required of a service soldier. We were considered service troops and training was split between soldiering and technical knowledge. Our basic training lasted six weeks, whereas a combat training program covered a span of 12 weeks. During the soldiering training, we worked and trained six days a week, often quitting around noon on Saturday and never, as I remember, did we train on Sundays.

We were given a complete medical examination and scheduled individually for dental appointments. Like many of the children of the Depression years, I had been plagued with improperly cared for teeth. But I received excellent dental care in the Army. For the first time in my life I had good teeth and the dentists even managed to save two teeth that I had thought would need to be extracted. During dental appointment time we were excused from the regular training sessions. Perhaps the healthiest time of my life was spent during basic training in the Army. What with good medical care, an excellent balanced diet, constant physical exercise and a regular sleep schedule, I gained weight, hardened muscle tone and felt great. I was never sick; as a matter of fact I was only on sick call two or three times during my three years in the Army and on those occasions I was overseas.

The training itself was outdated. The world had been at modern war for five years and combat circumstances had turned to air power and armoured forces as major battle conditions. Mobility and in-depth infantry tactics seemed to have replaced the stagnant trench strategies of World War I, yet one trained hard out of old manuals that favored "over the top" mentality. It bothered me that I was being trained in "no man's land" squad drills and that my single action bolt rifle was first issued in 1903. Even I knew better than that.

Poison gas drill was a good example of this outdated process. We were required to memorize the types of gases used during World War I, how to recognize the various types such as phosgene, which smelled like mown hay, and we practiced the standard drill for putting on masks. There was one actual exercise where we, with our masks on, were led into a small bunker and tear gas was released. As a demonstration of the effectiveness of our gas masks we were then instructed to lift the side of the face piece and take a sniff. The result was predictable when too many of the men inhaled too much of the gas and then broke for the small door trying to get out into the fresh air. By the time we were all outside everyone was gasping and crying. Everyone but me that is; I didn't take a sniff of the damned gas, because I knew my mask was working.

To my knowledge there was never an authenticated case of poison gas having been used in World War II. It wasn't that kind of war and from the number of American gas masks thrown away overseas everyone seemed to have known it but the top commanders. In all fairness, the horrors of gas in the earlier war never left the conscious minds of the planners, and the gas training was a precautionary measure. None could predict what the enemy would do if the war went against him. The Germans, Italians and Japanese all threw their masks away also. They weren't all that sure of us either and had also been trained in measures against gas attacks. Improved American masks were developed in 1944-45 and you could tell which outfits had been issued the new mask by the countless numbers of them in ditches, under bushes and scattered in fields where they had been discarded by advancing troops.

We also did exercises in the field in squad, platoon, and company field maneuvers. Hand signals and aircraft panel markers were used to tell where to go and what to do. This training was obviously useful and we paid attention to it pretty carefully. I liked map reading and because of my good sense of direction, I was often used as a scout to examine and report on terrain. There were three of us in the platoon who did this very well and I really enjoyed moving Indian like through the fields and forests to scout out enemy positions and report his disposition of troops. We often worked with the other platoons taking turns being the enemy forces. It was a safe game reminiscent of the warrior games of my childhood.

As part of our physical conditioning, which made up at least half of our basic training, we were required to run a combat course. This included climbing ropes, crawling through tunnels, walking narrow planks, leaping water holes, hurtling over wooden wall barriers and running. I liked this also. It was a competitive event and I often won it against other members of the platoon. Some of the older men in their late 20's or early 30's could never complete the course and were subject to a lot of friendly American style ridicule. We also had a calesthentics period each day but I did not like these sessions very much. I didn't mind the exercise but I did object to the punitive way in which some of the leaders conducted them. It was transformed into a torture session and I believe some of the exercises often did more harm than good.

There were no Blacks in our battalion because the Army segregated them in World War II and most were assigned to the Quartermaster Corps under the command of white officers. I understand that in the closing period of the war some Black units were used in combat and that there were even some Black pilot officers in the Air Corps. I was never near any of them except those who were quartermaster soldiers.

We saw hate films called "Know Your Enemy," which depicted the German as an inhuman Hun and the Japanese as a subhuman monster. These films were well made and were carefully cut from uncensored combat footage and newsreel shots. They were remarkable pieces of propaganda and because each contained uncensored combat film clips, plus the fact that each was titled "classified, only for the Armed Services," there was an assumed element of truth to them. In fact, each segment was blatant propaganda to make us hate our enemy.

In addition to the "Know Your Enemy" series we saw many excellent training films on weapons, first aid and other aspects of soldiering. However, our favorite was a film that we called the "Mickey Mouse" film. It was about the horrors of venereal disease and for most of the young men it was a revelation of sorts. In spite of our bravado I trust that the majority of the recruits were very unfamiliar with sex. I know that at the time I subscribed to the morality of the day, which dictated that pre or extramarital sex was uncommon, illegal and immoral. The V.D. film had us on the edge of our seats, however, goggle-eyed, trying to learn how to do it rather than learn why *not* to do it. Penicillin had not yet been introduced as a treatment for venereal disease and the Army had a serious problem of treating what was then an incurable illness. The Army technique was to use simple scare tactics laced with punishment. If you contracted the disease, you were hospitalized without pay, lost your rank and privileges and your family was notified of your condition. The latter was enough to keep most of the men thinking about it.

There was also an elaborate education program on the use of prophalactics as a preventative, and squad demonstrations conducted by a Corporal with a broomstick were hilarious and memorable. Army regulations required that every soldier receive these instructions and see the "Mickey Mouse" film periodically so that in the end we became very familiar with the subject.

There was one other humiliation that we endured periodically and that was the medical inspection imposed to make sure that no one was hiding V.D. For a reason known only to the Army there was a special uniform combination worn to these inspections and anyone seeing the formation dressed in that manner knew immediately where it was going and what it would be doing when it got there. A platoon marching in raincoats and helmet liners drew hoots and jeers from everyone else nearby. The raincoats were huge of course and trousers were not worn so that a formation with flashing white legs, flapping raincoats and the incongruous helmet liner presented a unique picture known only to those who ever served in the Army during the war. The medical examination was brief but tops on the humiliation scale. The object was for the medical inspector, usually an enlisted medical orderly of dubious sexual preference, to see for himself whether you were hiding a venereal infection deep within your urinary tract. This process required that you squeeze your own penis in such a way that if there was an infection it would be apparent to this deeply interested second party. Coming from a generation that took a dim view of a young man squeezing anyone's genitals, including his own, the experience was repulsive and some-times strangely disturbing. "Skin it back and milk it down" were the instructions given at the moment of truth. During some of the more obtuse moments of my life I have thought that the expression itself might be a fitting epitaph for my tombstone but better judgment is beginning to prevail and I think I'll just go with dates.

We trained hard for four weeks and even the old men were begin-ning to shape up and not fall out so often on the long 10 and 20 mile forced marches.

Luckily I was only on K.P. once during basic training and pulled garbage detail only twice. I will not comment on these experiences beyond noting that they were as bad as anything I had ever heard about them.

An event that we all looked forward to was firing on the rifle range. A great deal of preparation was given over to this magic day. I must have squeezed the trigger on an empty chamber 3,000 times before I ever saw a bullet. We were never issued live ammunition, of course, since it was considered too dangerous by the training command.

We were told over and over by Sgt. Dow that it was a long tradition that each man in his training platoon qualified on the range. He hinted darkly that to disgrace his platoon by not qualifying was to disgrace him personally. This concept was unthinkable to us and it was clear that it was a good deal less unthinkable to Sgt. Dow. We all began squeezing our triggers whenever we had the chance.

To qualify on the range meant that a minimum number of points had to be scored by hitting the graduated target with just so many bullets from different firing positions. I have forgotten just how many points were required but I think the distance to the target was 100 yards.

If you met the minimum score you were awarded a marksman medal. If you did better you were an expert and the top scores were given sharpshooter medals. For the platoon to meet Sgt. Dow's stan-dards, we all had to earn at least a marksman's medal.

Finally the day arrived. We cleaned our weapons and climbed into trucks for the dusty drive over dirt roads to the firing ranges miles away. We were excited and even sang songs. When we arrived at the range, we were met by a very solemn group of range officers and non-coms. There were no smiles, only many rules, mostly about range safety. Naturally we practiced the rules before we were allowed to do the real thing. We were set into teams of four and learned that two men worked the individually numbered targets in the butts while the other two members of the team fired the rifles, one at a time. As a man fired, his companion acted as a coach and spotter for him until he was finished and then they reversed roles. Safety was the theme of the range and most of us were terrified, not of the target or rifle, but rather of the range officer and his roving band of tyrannical assistants.

When the actual moment arrived for the first shot to be fired, the shooter gingerly placed a single round of live ammunition in his rifle from the prone position and waited for the word from the range officer. There was absolute silence as the officer called, "Ready on the right, ready on the left, ready on the firing line—commence firing." The first crack of the old Springfield had for us, what must have been the reaction of the first shell fired on Fort Sumter. The moment was electric and we all had the feeling that we were present at a great moment in history. The crescendo was soon deafening, as 50 rifles began systematically banging away at the targets across the range. The coach and spotter for each rifleman handed him one round at a time, only after the target had been marked following each shot. The spotter's job was to shout out the score and record it on the official record. He sat, stood or lay at right angles to the rifleman depending on the firing position.

In the target butts there was fantastic activity. Each target was counterbalanced with another target. Each target was numbered with a large bullet riddled numeral, which stood on the flat ground in front of the butts, and immediately below the target. The number corresponded with the numbered position on the firing line, but the problem in the butts was in trying to determine when your particular rifleman had fired on the target. We watched the dirt hill behind the target for dust spurts, which would signify that a shot into or at our target had been made, but the method was not all that foolproof, especially at first, when the firing was erratic and it was not uncommon for rifleman number 22 to be deliberately putting holes in target 24 or 25. There was only one field phone in the pits and one on the firing line to serve 50 targets. I remember that when the firing started, the two of us energetically and dutifully ran our target up and down for at least five rounds before the phone rang to tell us that our shooter hadn't started firing yet. I began to wonder whether or not America really *was* going to win the war.

We had a long pole with a flat 6″ metal disk attached to the end of it. It was white on one side and black on the other. The procedure was to run up the target and then place the disk over the bullet hole so that the rifleman and his spotter could see where the bullet had gone and theoretically adjust his shots for better accuracy. If the white disk was used, it showed clearly against the black bullseye; the black of course was used for other scores on the white target areas. We also had a red flag on a long pole called "Maggie's drawers" that indicated a clear miss of the whole target.

The red flag was used a lot. Our black and white marker disk already had several bullet holes in it from previous use, which was interesting, but by the time we had finished our stint in the target pits, I was convinced that everything and everybody in the whole state of Maryland was probably sporting at least one bullet hole.

After each shot was fired, we had to paste a little piece of paper over the hole to make the target intact again for the next shot—white paper for white areas and black for bullseyes. We were very busy, flinching at richochettes, coughing in the shower of dirt, pasting, marking hits, running up targets and waving flags. My companion laconically suggested that if the Army only realized it, they could run a broom up his posterior and he could sweep up while he was doing everything else.

We learned the really important lesson about Army target shooting that day. The lesson was called the 30 calibre pencil, and it saved many a man from disgrace and shame. It takes no imagination to realize that one could promote a lasting friendship with the rifle team if one covered up a wide shot and ran a pencil through the bullseye. This understanding between teams was very clear and marked one of the highest levels of communication between men that I ever encountered in the Army. The pencil was left at the target and as the target team went to the rifle firing line to take its turn, there was a mutual understanding that all four men were going to qualify that memorable day.

When it was finally my turn to fire, I was really confident. After all, I had squeezed my trigger thousands of times, and besides that I had winged my father with my 410 gauge shotgun one day shooting at a wild turkey—got them both firing from the hip. Even though they both had jumped around a lot and it had been the first time I had ever heard my father curse, I had at the time, considered it a difficult shot to make.

I was ready, and at the signal to fire, I thoughtfully laid my sights on the center of the target and squeezed off my first live round as a soldier of democracy. My first and immediate reaction was that the rifle had exploded and that my shoulder had been blown away. My second reaction came when I realized that the cloud of dust halfway between me and the target was mine. I tried to smile at my spotter but he looked very nervous and was busy moving back a few feet—Maggie's drawers.

When I was finally finished with my qualifying round, I was grateful that it was over and that the target crew had found the pencil. I barely qualified as a marksman. My spotter did very little better than I had done but by then he was so shaken that I had to coax him into firing at all.

One other memorable event occurred at the range that day. We finished our allotted rounds from the prone position, had moved into the sitting position, and were dutifully listening to the command, "Ready on the right, ready on the left" when the unthinkable happened. The range officer had just announced, "Ready on the left" when a rifle shot broke the silence. Everyone froze as the echo of that shot faded away; everyone but the range officer that is. He leaned far out the tower and screamed, "Who fired that shot?"

I have never felt sorrier for a fellow human being than I did for the small young man at the end of the range who held up his hand. The officer flew out of the tower, sputtering and yelling. I feared for HIS life; I had never seen a man turn that red before.

"Bring that man to me," he shrieked.

A political assassin would have received less abuse and chewing out than that poor unfortunate creature received that day.

The incident was apparently somewhat commonplace in the Army, because afterward I never heard anyone break wind without some high pitched voice inquiring, "Who fired that shot?"

At last it was over. After picking up all of our empty cartridges, we silently boarded the trucks, went back to the barracks and cleaned our weapons far into the evening hours. I had at first loved that rifle but after firing it, it was just like another personal inarticulate enemy of mine. The next morning at roll call the announcement was made and it was no surprise to us, to Sgt. Dow, or to the pencils that *every* man in his platoon had qualified as at least a marksman. We cheered in the dark. The Germans and Japanese should have also cheered that day, because they certainly were in no danger from Company B, 1st Ordinance Training Battalion of Aberdeen, Maryland.

About half way through basic training, platoons took turns on post guard duty. We were each assigned a 24 hour period during which we were to actually guard parts of the Proving Grounds. Naturally we practiced this for hours and learned the General Orders. There were ten of them that had to be memorized. I still remember General Order #1. "I will walk my post in a military manner, keeping always on the alert and observing everything that takes place within sight or hearing."

A rather large responsibility I thought, but the other nine were just as general and concluded with the order, "I will call the Sergeant of the Guard in all cases not covered by instructions."

The benefit of the General Orders to the guard was that it gave him something to do while being on guard duty. To try to memorize and keep them straight was a forbidding task when at any time an officer might conceivably jump out from behind a bush and shout, "What is General Order number six, soldier?" We practiced the proper form for being posted, being relieved, and most importantly how to address the officer of the Guard. The Army put a lot of emphasis on how an enlisted man should address an officer and when everyone knew the procedures and proper words to be spoken, it seemed to give a lot of comfort to those in command.

We were finally ready and one afternoon around four o'clock in the afternoon, trucks picked us up along with our gear. We were taken to the South part of the post where there were miles of warehouses, which were presumably a primary target for the enemy 3,000 miles away. We were assigned guard barracks and bunks and it was solemnly announced that for the next 24 hours the safety and security of the Proving Grounds was our responsibility. We were impressed.

A Corporal posted a duty roster and we saw that each man had four hours on guard duty, and eight hours off, which meant that each of us would walk his post in a military manner for two four hour stints during the next 24 hours. It was forbidden to leave the barracks except for meals, but even then we were marched to and from those meals in formation.

The evening seemed long but I finally got to sleep about an hour before someone awakened me to go on duty. It was very dark, there was no coffee, our uniform consisted of a field jacket, empty cartridge belt, canteen, helmet liner, gas mask, leggins, and rifle. We received our instructions, which were: know your general orders, your Army serial number, your rifle serial number. There was to be no sitting down, no slouching, no smoking and no talking to other guards. After a close personal inspection, we were marched off to take our posts. It was an interesting exercise because the detail of 10 men had to march to each designated guard post, be challenged, relieve the old guard, repeat special instructions and post a new man. The new guard took his place from the front of the detail and the old guard fell in at the end of the line as we all marched by. It took over an hour. Naturally, I was the last guard to be placed out on the periphery of our guard area among some very dark warehouses. The man I relieved said nothing, simply adding his footsteps to those of the detail, the marching steps of which gradually faded away. The Corporal's flashlight swinging back and forth to the rhythm of the group was the last thing I saw in the cool summer night. "My God," I thought, "I am alone, guarding this United States installation from an imminent parachute attack, or worse, from shadowy saboteurs, carrying poison phosgene gas, who will mount their attack on Washington from these important warehouses!"

After awhile I calmed down a little. The realization that I had an empty rifle, no ammunition and no means to signal for help in *any* event gave me the confidence that surely the Army wouldn't place its faith in an unarmed man as the last barrier between itself and the enemy.

The thought, however, troubled me as I recalled the experiences that I had encountered so far with the military mind. "Hell, yes, they would!" I concluded that I had better act like a guard and began walking my post in a military manner, keeping always, etc., etc.

My post was a straight line between two warehouses, which were about a block in length, and after my eyes adjusted somewhat to the pitch darkness, I found that I could negotiate the walk back and forth without falling too many times over the pipes, boxes and lumber that were scattered around in an abandoned fashion.

I reviewed the general orders in my mind and after what seemed like two hours or so I glanced at the luminous dial on my watch. Twenty minutes had elapsed since I had started. I shook the watch, *it was* running. After another interminable period, I discovered that I was getting tired of guard duty and that the warehouses were empty. I reasoned that there were probably guards between each row of warehouses so I took to extending my turns at the end of my building hoping to catch sight of one of the guards as he completed his turn. There weren't any guards. There wasn't anything. In fact I was alone in the world with the only sounds being made by me when I fell down over a piece of wire or ran headlong into a box and backed away cursing. If there were parachutists and saboteurs, they must have wondered what in hell was going on between those two empty buildings. They would have heard long periods of silence punctuated by a crash, followed by loud cursing.

At last the four hours were over. I had seen no one, nor had I been attacked. I made sure that I was on the spot where I was to be relieved so that no time would be wasted in getting me out of that treacherous alleyway. One of my knees was bleeding and I thought I could feel that my two front teeth were a little loose.

A half hour went by and I was still standing there. No guard detail, no welcome flashlight, no relief in sight. I began to feel a little uneasy but quickly dismissed the notion that Aberdeen Proving Grounds had been captured and that I was the only American still alive. Surely, I would have heard *something*.

It was now 6:30 a.m. and the sun was coming up. The warehouses were not merely empty, they had been abandoned and were falling down! I thought it out. There had been a guard when I had arrived so it must be a guard post. Someone *must* know that I am here, I reasoned, and they're just late in making the rounds. Anyway it was a good deal easier picking my way through the obstacles in the light, so I resumed my guard duty. I was tired and irritable. I'm always irritable in the morning anyway but after walking back and forth with an empty rifle for seven and a half hours, the word irritable began to be insufficient to describe my feelings. I took to muttering, and finally to yelling unrelenting obscenities. This helped a little, but not much.

41

Finally, after eight hours the guard detail appeared and I was relieved. Luckily by now the Corporal of the Guard had a truck and I was able to ride back to the guardhouse. I'm not sure that I could have made it otherwise.

When I entered the guard room, the Sergeant sitting at the desk looked startled. Then a broad grin spread across his face and he said, "Oh yes, *you're* the one. I wondered why we had a man left over on the last shift."

I thought seriously about killing him but then realized that I was unarmed.

Of course someone woke me up three hours later to go back out there to do my second shift. My name and serial number were clearly typed on the duty roster. I went on guard duty silently without even trying to explain it to anyone.

During the last week of basic training we went on maneuvers, which required camping out for two nights. This exercise was meant to give the battalion experience in living outside and to test what we had learned about battlefield survival. The area selected for the exercise was one of the many peninsulas that jutted out into the upper Chesapeake Bay. It was fairly wild country with only one or two dirt roads running through it. Company areas were marked out on a map; we were instructed once again on everything we had learned, and a convoy of trucks was assigned to transport us to what was called the bivouac area. We made up full field packs, checked our gear and sat out in the company street waiting for the convoy. Some of us noticed that the wind was picking up and that low clouds were scudding across a darkening sky. The clouds weren't the usual summer storm cumulus that frequently appeared in the blue skies of Maryland. These clouds had a funny greenish tinge to them and were travelling very rapidly. I made sure that my raincoat was rolled on top of my pack where it was supposed to be. In about two hours the trucks arrived and it was no surprise to any of us to see that they were all uncovered and opened to the elements. As we loaded, the first hard drops of rain arrived. Raincoats appeared during a concentrated period of groans and complaints. As the line of trucks drove out through the main post gate, the rain increased in intensity. It took two hours to reach the bivouac area.

By then we were soaked through, Army issue raincoats being made of a blotter like material that was calculated to withstand anything but water. I really believe that they had been designed to collect moisture in desert areas. Later in the war, good quality weatherized ponchos were issued that could be used for all sorts of things but in the summer of 1943 the raincoats were good only for V.D. examinations in mild weather. The Sergeants and Corporals were all riding in the dry truck cabs, of course, so that when we arrived in what was now a driving rain, they were dry and even cheerful enough to yell at us because our rifles were getting wet. I must admit that not many of us had thought about keeping his rifle dry rather than himself. We lined up in platoons along the muddy road and as the trucks disappeared in the rain, we felt a sudden sodden loneliness. However, even the Captain who appeared in a covered jeep seemed sure that our first task was to get out of the rain. He yelled this brilliant order to Sergeant Dow and sped off down the road in a shower of mud and spinning wheels. We never saw him again during the entire time of the bivouac.

Each platoon then formed a single line along the road and "counted off in two's" starting at one end of the line with the number one. Each man took his turn by shouting one or two as the sequence was repeated over and over down the line. If the man on your left was one, you were two and the man on your right was one and so forth. At first I thought that this was some clever code way to make it stop raining but as it turned out, it was simply the Army's way to select a tent partner for you.

The Sergeant then announced that we now all had a number, either one or two. However, he soon discovered that several men had already forgotten his number. Many arguments broke out. Sgt. Dow turned almost as red as the firing range officer and finally ended up making us do it all over again. By this time there had been some men moving around in line and almost everyone had a different number the second time through. We did it several times and each time the man on the far end of the line had a different number. Even the noncoms began to see that something was wrong. It was incredible. Here we were standing in a heavy, wind-driven rain trying to decide if we were either a "one" or a "two." It was funny and soon some of us were giggling a little as everyone leaned forward each time to see if the end man got the same number twice in a row. Some, I thought, began laughing with an edge of hysteria that I considered a little unhealthy and more than a little unsettling.

Finally after a half dozen tries, the laughing died down and we became very sober and serious about what was happening to us. Why *couldn't* we do this? Rain or not, there was no excuse for sixty men not to be able to count off in two's. For thousands of years, soldiers had been counting off, and now in the rain at Aberdeen Proving Grounds, the world was to see the first platoon in history that couldn't count off in two's. However, we did solve it. Sgt. Dow called us to strict parade attention and then personally, with his Corporals following him, stood in front of each soaking wet man while that man repeated his appropriate number. It didn't take long to discover the culprit. There was one man who reacted in a strange way to counting off. When the man next to him shouted one, he repeated the word and also shouted one.

I really hadn't considered that there were people in the world who didn't know the proper sequencing of one and two.

Finally we all agreed to the fact that we were either a "one" or "two" and then were told that the "ones" would pair up with the "twos" and together we would put up our tents. The Army field manual calls for a regimented way of doing this so that all the little tents are in perfect rows with exact spacing between them. The rain and the forested area precluded this scheme, so we were merely instructed to find a good spot nearby and put up our pup tents. I found what I thought was a likeable number "one" young man named John and we agreed to pair up and share a tent.

We each had in our field pack a shelter half (emphasis on half), a collapsible tent pole about two and one-half feet long (emphasis on collapsible), five wooden tent pegs and a short length of clothesline type rope. When I was first issued the tent pegs, I got no smiles whatever when I asked the supply Sergeant if they were to be used for fighting vampires.

Shelter halves are marvelous but tricky. Each shelter half is identical but by reversing one of the halves, they fit together with metal buttons and by using total pegs, poles, and ropes you were supposed to be able to construct a two man tent about three feet high and seven feet long. The tricky part was finding a partner who hadn't lost his pegs, pole or rope. Another tricky part was the need for a piece of flat dry ground since there was no bottom or floor to the tent.

I am convinced that Maryland, as a state, was created out of all the ravines and ridges that were left over after Virginia, Delaware, and Pennsylvania had made their choice of terrain. The name, Maryland, is probably a colonial synonym for "leftovers."

John and I got the tent up only to discover that water ran directly into our shelter. We dug ditches, which would have outclassed European castle moats, but these became roaring channels of muddy water that emptied directly into our tent. We then concluded that we were probably in a stream bed, took down the marvelous but tricky shelter and sought higher ground. I believe that we were halfway to the Allegheny Mountains in Pennsylvania when we blundered into the Company "C" bivouac area and were turned back by a sullen but determined Sergeant.

Returning to our own area, we settled on a little hill under an oak tree and as darkness began to fall, we hammered pegs and stretched wet rope into some semblance of a two man shelter. By now the wind was blowing the rain directly into our faces, the oak tree was groaning and creaking like an old man, and for the first of many times to come in the future the word "desertion" occurred to me.

John and I stuffed all of our gear into the pup tent. Packs, rifles, blankets, gas masks and overcoats went in before we made the discovery that there was no room for us. In absolute frustration we literally cursed our way into the mass of equipment and for the first time in over six hours we were out of the direct rain. I emphasize direct rain because it soon became obvious that the term shelter, as used by the Army, was a very poor use of the word. Psychology teaches us that one of man's basic drives is shelter, but on that black, windswept night under a confused and complaining oak tree, we had very little of it.

In the first place, our shelter halves had been used for many years by training troops and they were as sheer as the sails of the Ancient Mariner. In the second place, shelter halves were apparently made out of the same material used in the making of Army raincoats.

We found a candle and lit it but the dripping water soon put it out. There we were, crammed together with equipment stacked on top of us, lying on our backs with water falling steadily on our faces. I put my helmet liner firmly over my face but it was like being *inside* a drum. I discovered that by sticking out my tongue I could lift up the bottom edge of the liner so that the noise was not so deafening but my tongue soon dried out and the irony of having my tongue being the only thing about me that was dry was too much, even for me. I let the liner slam down and tried to pretend that I was the tympani section of the L.A. Philharmonic. Everything seemed under control until I began to imagine that the drumming was the music to the "William Tell Overture." Try as I would, I couldn't get it out of my mind until John under his own helmet liner covering his face, said quietly, "It sounds like 'Red Sails in the Sunset,' doesn't it?"

I finally convinced him it was really the "William Tell Overture" and we both began singing along with it. "Dum ditty dum, ditty dum, dum dum." It was insane. Soaking wet, cold, lying painfully on our backs on the roots of an old tree humming the "William Tell Overture!"

During the interminable night, most of our tent pegs loosened in the mud and the gale force wind did the rest. By morning our so-called shelter was whipping around us and in that wet grey dawn, the knowledge that almost all of the company tents were down did little to lift our spirits. I never spent a worse night and I felt and am certain that I looked like a very old prune.

We were told later that it was a hurricane, which swept the Chesapeake area that early summer, but I never did check to see whether or not that was an official definition. I only know that next to a typoon, which I was to experience years later on Okinawa, it was certainly the worst rain storm I had ever seen.

The morning came like a very bad hangover for all of us and as we stumbled around trying to locate our equipment, retrieve tents and straighten our backs, Sgt. Dow called a platoon formation. Astonishing as it seemed under the conditions, he read to the company the duty roster and posted it on a wet makeshift bulletin board. We were to reorganize our camp, chlorinate our drinking water, post perimeter guards, watch out for enemy aircraft, and be alert for gas attacks. The instructions barely filtered through our consciousness as the wind and rain drove so hard against us that we had trouble standing up, let alone keeping a platoon formation.

We were given cold wet food from the back of a weapons carrier truck and went back to trying to sort out our belongings. We found all but two of our tent pegs but the biting wind driven cold rain made it all but impossible to make a sensible camp. After looking around awhile, John and I decided to remain where we were even though sleeping on roots and rocks was all but impossible as we had learned the night before. In spite of it all, we put up the shelter tent, hammering in the pegs with our folding shovels until they were more or less securely fastened into the ground. We dug a drainage ditch, stowed our gear and made our way back to the duty roster just in time to fall in for another company formation. About half of our platoon was still thrashing around in the brush and trees, so being available, we were assigned to perimeter guard. I groaned a little at going back on guard duty but without warehouses to watch, the prospects of guard seemed a little brighter. At least I didn't have to go back into that damned tent.

I must say that the weather actually let up a little by mid morning. It never stopped raining altogether but the wind died down accompanied by a studied cheerfulness in the company.

I got my rifle out of the tent, empty of course since I was going on guard duty, and in due time I was taken out to a muddy road intersection in the forest and told to guard it.

"Remember," the Corporal said, "these are simulated combat conditions so guard this post as though you were within sight and sound of the enemy."

He gave me the password and countersign, told me I would be relieved in four hours and disappeared down the road with the remaining guard detail.

The area was heavily forested and in the absence of wind and in the protection of the trees it was fairly dry. I moved back into the trees out of sight behind some bushes and began guarding the intersection. Nothing happened except that I actually began to dry out a little. My body heat not being dissipated by the wind went to work and within an hour or so I really began to feel dry and almost warm. I sat on a log, lit a cigarette and watched the squirrels. It reminded me of my hunting days.

In two hours, however, the sky became dark again with returning storm clouds and I could barely see the tops of the pine trees that had begun whistling as the wind returned. I hardly had time to get under better cover when the rain returned with stinging persistence.

At the same time I heard the grinding of a vehicle, which was approaching the intersection, so I unslung my empty rifle and moved a little closer to the road junction. Soon headlights appeared down the track and I realized that indeed it was getting very dark. As the vehicle came closer, I could see that it was a jeep. The rain was a silver sheet of water reflected through the headlights. I waited until the jeep was almost at the intersection before I shouted, "Halt!" The jeep slid to a stop as I moved closer to it through the bushes, my rifle pointed directly at the two people in the front seats. One of them was a Lieutenant from our training company, a young effete sort of man, newly commissioned and not well liked by anyone.

I shouted from my cover in the bushes, "Get out of that jeep and give me the password."

The lieutenant was furious. He did not want to get out of the jeep and into the rain.

"What is your name soldier?" he shouted.

"Get out of that jeep, Lieutenant and give me the password," I repeated as evenly as possible.

With a great display of annoyance, he scrambled out of the jeep and started off toward me in the forest.

"Halt!" I said, beginning to enjoy the scene a little. "The password, Lieutenant."

He stood in the mud and driving rain trying to control himself with rather poor results. "Why aren't you guarding your post soldier?" he shouted hysterically, "I'll court-martial you for this!"

"I *am* guarding this post, sir," I replied, "I'm guarding it under combat conditions as I was instructed to do and no fool would stand in the middle of an intersection in combat."

He was silent as he digested what was apparently a new idea to him.

"The password, sir, if you please," I repeated.

He told me the password. I gave the countersign and after asking me to repeat all 10 general orders, which I did without error, he lurched back into the jeep as it drove away in the darkness. Although I enjoyed the encounter, I was afraid that I would pay for it when I got back to camp. I did.

As soon as I was relieved, I was told to report to Sgt. Dow. I hurried to his tent, which was a large six man squad tent set up as an orderly room with sleeping space for him and the three squad Corporals. It even had flooring in it. He made me stand at attention, dripping water, while he finished reading something. At last he looked up and said, "Keem, don't be a smart ass with our company officers. It comes back on me and I don't like it. Is there any questions?"

47

I knew better than to justify what had happened, and I was well aware that when Sgt. Dow said, "*Is* there any questions," he meant that there *were* no questions. I tried to look sufficiently chastised and replied, "No, Sergeant, no questions."

Then he did a curious thing. He actually tried to smile a little but I think it hurt his face in the attempt. He restored his face quickly and growled, "Good work, that *is* the way to guard a road junction in combat. Now get the hell out of here."

I returned to my pup tent, soaking wet again, only to discover that it was full of water and that the wind had blown down one end of the shelter half collapsing one of our collapsible tent poles.

John had not returned from guard duty, so I struggled to put everything in order and crawled into the damned thing, mud, water, and all.

Having been on guard duty at noon, I had missed what had passed for lunch, so I just lay there, wet to the skin, my boots covered with inches of mud, doing a solo of the "William Tell Overture."

The two man tent was almost big enough for one person so I enjoyed the luxury until my companion returned in the afternoon in a black mood and every bit as wet as I was.

Incredibly we were called out in the late afternoon for extended order drill and to practice against air attacks. The storm was apparently reaching peak conditions as we marched down the road looking for enemy aircraft. If marching in columns of two, when attacked by enemy aircraft we were to run off the road, throw ourselves under bushes, into ravines, depressions in the ground, and fire our rifles at the airplane. We were told with solemn wisdom not to jump in the roadside ditch because enemy pilots liked to strafe roadside ditches. After a normally dry simulated air attack it sometimes took a long time to get our column back on the road since some men took it seriously and ran until they found appropriate cover. There were, of course, no airplanes flying around in a hurricane so we responded to a shout from the head of the column, "Aircraft," and took off for cover. In a rainstorm, however, the exercise was simply absurd. By the time we returned to our bivouac area, no one was even remotely dry nor was anyone not covered with Maryland mud.

The day became night and there was an understandable absence of joking or even laughing. It was as though a certain breaking point had been reached and that everyone knew it. It was no longer a game. It was no longer training or novelty. It was stupidity.

Supper was cold wet rations out of the visiting weapons carrier and after receiving the food, everyone crawled into his shelter for another miserable night. It had now been raining for over 36 hours. I drank some chlorinated water, gagged on it and marveled at the Army mentality, which dictated that we chlorinate perfectly good drinking water so that we could get used to its unpleasant taste. It was like shooting yourself a little, so you would know ahead of time how it felt if you were ever actually wounded. Finally even the training command realized that the bivouac was a reenactment of Civil War General Burnside's mud march, so around midnight a convoy of trucks arrived to return us to the camp and to warm and dry barracks. We simply wrapped everything up in our tents to be sorted out later, boarded the open trucks and drove back to camp arriving about 3 a.m. I never saw anything as welcome as that cot in the comfort of the dry barracks. Before we fell into an exhausted sleep, Sgt. Dow came around to tell us that the gracious company commander, whom we had not seen in 36 hours, was going to excuse us from standing reville. We could sleep until 7:30!

After four weeks of basic training, everyone was eligible for a weekend pass. This meant that by mid afternoon on Saturday, we could leave the post and return by reville on Monday morning. Most of us accepted the pass, of course, because it meant a different kind of freedom even if most of us had nowhere to go. Most of us didn't even know where Aberdeen was located in Maryland, so the planning about where to go was speculative and men familiar with the area were listened to with awesome attention as they explained train schedules and distances to nearby cities. We discovered that Baltimore was the closest city requiring less than a two hour train ride. Four of us decided to go to the big city on our first weekend pass.

After regular field equipment and personal inspection on Saturday, we rushed through lunch and prepared ourselves for the big event. We put on our class A summer dress uniforms, called sun tans, consisting of a light colored buff pair of pants, a matching shirt and necktie, which for some reason was to be tucked *inside* the shirt between the second and third buttons, polished shoes and a field cap that topped off the supposedly military appearance. However, to us, we looked all the world like light brown gas station attendants. Crowding into the orderly room we were instructed to line up in front of Sgt. Dow. After much pushing and shoving we presented ourselves one at a time for the final inspection before we could receive a pass. Each man was scrutinized front and back by the Sergeant. He checked clothes, length of hair, fingernails, asked to see a clean handkerchief and then gave each man who passed the inspection a little yellow wallet sized pass and a prophalactic kit. The pass explained who a person was, what unit he belonged to and in no uncertain terms it spelled out when he was to return to his unit. The pass was signed by a Captain, no less, and Sgt. Dow explained that to lose that little yellow card was tantamount to desertion, disloyalty and treason. We were all very impressed with the sudden personal responsibility, which we had, to that wallet sized piece of cardboard.

The prophalactic or "pro" kit was another matter. It consisted of two tubes of ointment with instructions, a little cloth bag with a draw string on it and one condom or "rubber" as they were affectionately called. The rubber was an ubiquitous invention and in the next years I was to see it used for uncounted purposes that reached far beyond the imagination of its creator. Designed to cover the standard male sex organ during intercourse, it was also a perfect size for covering the muzzle end of an M-1 infantry rifle during inclement weather. It kept out dirt, water, snow and of course, prevented the rifle from getting the dreaded veneral disease.

Rubbers made nice balloon decorations at parties and could be used to carry limited quantities of wine. They made satisfactory containers for urine during emergencies and with the end cut off made an excellent waterproof protective sleeve to cover a bandaged finger. Used to cover dog tags, a rubber could prevent telltale clattering of metal, although slices of gas mask hose were much more effective in keeping down unwanted dog tag noise. Rubbers made handy pocket coin purses, especially in a foreign country where cheap light aluminum coins were used. It was neither uncommon or apparently the least bit embarrassing to anyone to see a G.I. pay for an item in France or England by extracting coins from his flexible white rubber pocket purse.

The various uses of the pro kit were without end and only the imagination of the average American civilian soldier set the limits on how he made use of any of the material and equipment issued to him during the course of his service time.

Finally the four of us passed inspection and stood ready to be greeted by the grateful civilian population, which we assumed was waiting eagerly outside the main gate to greet us as heroes. I learned important lessons on my first Army pass. During World War II, almost everyone seemed to be in service. Most people seen in public in centers of population were either soldiers, sailors or marines. Cities, train stations, streets, restaurants, bars and movie theaters were full of servicemen and most civilians were distrustful and frightened of them. The people who worked in restaurants, bars, train stations, etc. were tired of the boisterousness and rudeness of servicemen, most of whom came from far away places and were ignorant of local traditions and acceptable regional mores.

However, at the beginning of the war, a new class of people had suddenly been thrust onto the center stage of public life. It was a class that was dressed in a uniform and instantly recognizable as different, but signaled respect and admiration from all others who were not. Respect was called for because this new, but temporary class, was performing a dangerous task for the country. The admiration lasted for awhile, but as the novelty wore off, and as the civilian population learned that there were rascals within this specially created group, the results were predictable. There were exceptions, I'm sure, but I have been on pass in large cities in 1943-1944 and I found, for the most part, a hostile environment, which only accented the problem and forced service men to congregate together for psychological, if not physical support. Servicemen's clubs were popular, overcrowded, and curiously unsatisfying to the lone serviceman looking for an open and honest relationship in a new city.

I tried to visit a museum once in New York City, but was treated with insulting skepticism by the museum guards and so shunned by civilian visitors to the museum that I left confused and bitter about my status in society. Walking along a residential street on a hot summer night in Baltimore, I was picked up by a police patrol who would not believe that I was just taking a walk as I had done a thousand times as a youth in Pittsburgh. I was taken downtown to the train station, turned over to the military police and warned to be careful where I went in the city in the future. I had done nothing wrong except to be in uniform.

Being on general pass was seldom fun no matter where you were. There were memorable exceptions when the choice of companions or the place of destination was either off the beaten path or involved private transportation or previous arrangements with specific civilians. But for the solitary serviceman just looking in a strange city, it was a relief getting back to the barracks and to the familiar routine. This is not to say that we didn't come off any pass full of lies about conquests and wondrous adventures usually involving a grateful young lady in distress. It was accepted that no one had his pro kit when he returned from pass. It had, of course, been *used.* I suspect that even today one can find traces of thousands and thousands of unopened and unused pro kits that were secretly thrown out of the train windows on the late night run from Baltimore to Aberdeen. To return to the post with a pro kit was an unwritten disgrace not to be suffered by anyone. To all appearances we were very worldly and wise, when in reality we were, as the civilian soldiers of WWII, probably the largest collection of liars ever assembled on the North American continent.

On weekends when passes were not available we inevitably did two things. First, we slept in on Sunday; secondly, we spent time at the rather large enlisted men's recreation building on the post. Saturday morning for garrison and training troops was a regular day always highlighted by a late morning or before noon inspection. Sometimes it was a full inspection, which included the barracks as well as an inspection of personal equipment and the individual. If the inspection was good and the company commander deemed it appropriate, Saturday afternoon and all day Sunday were days of rest, relaxation and recreation if you could find it. If the inspection was not good, Saturday afternoon, along with the threat of losing Sunday was spent recleaning the barracks, equipment and personnel. This loss of Saturday only happened once to us during the early weeks of basic training. From then on, everyone worked hard not to be the sad sack who had a speck of dust in his rifle barrel or who allowed discernible dirt to be found between the cracks in the floorboards around his bed. It was hell to be among the men who cost his platoon their weekends of freedom. Behind each bed was a shelf with a wooden pole suspended beneath it. The shelf was for specified items such as helmet liner, garrison cap, mess kit, gas masks, etc.

On the wooden pole there were a number of specified coat hangers, two inches apart, to be measured with a ruler by some inspecting officers, and an absolute order in which articles of clothing were to be buttoned and hung from the coat hangers: raincoat, overcoat, fatigues, blouse, field jacket, cotton shirts, O.D. shirts, trousers, cotton and trousers, wool.

At the foot of each bed was a footlocker in which articles of clothing and permitted items were kept. The footlocker had a removable shelf in it, which was tipped at a precise angle to enable the inspecting officer to see all of the articles in the shelf and under it. Underwear, socks, handkerchiefs, all folded in a special way with the folded edge in the correct direction were on display. Writing kits, soldiers' manuals, pictures of loved ones, bibles, and sewing kits were allowable if properly stored in the footlocker. Shoes, aligned perfectly and well polished were placed under the bed. The laces, of course, were to be untwisted and tied in an appropriate manner.

The bed itself, as though it were an unforgiveable symbol of the civilian lack of discipline and extravagance, received special attention. The Army hated beds. Men could be made to look alike, to respond as though a group were one individual; equipment could be made into identical units. Everyone and everything could be made into a universal and uniform unit, except a bed with a man sleeping in it. Beds were different. It was almost as though when a man slept, he escaped uniformity and became himself again. The irony of it was lost on the Army that merely hated sleeping because each man did it differently.

I am convinced that somewhere in history there are records of generals who experimented with methods by which all soldiers were made to sleep at attention. A barracks full of sleeping men was so unmilitary, so rumpled. It was an affront to the military mind.

The only recourse that the Army had to this terrible contradiction to its system was to forcefully attack the bed itself at inspections when no one was in it. All energies were unmercifully directed toward this inanimate object. If it could not behave during the night, it could, by God, be made to demonstrate its devotion to uniformity during daylight hours!!

Consequently, we were trained and retrained in the proper making of beds. I swear that I left basic training knowing more about bed making than I did about killing the enemy. The bed became the focus for inspections. Rulers were used to make sure that all corners of a standard blanket were folded precisely the same. All Army blankets had a large U.S. woven into them and on inspection days we would stretch a string across the beds the length of the barracks to make sure that these symbols were absolutely aligned with one another. Sheets and blankets had to be stretched to a drumhead tauntness. It was a rule that an inspecting officer must be able to "bounce" a coin off the rigidity of the blanket. I can't recall whether or not the coin had to bounce to a certain height, but it probably not only had to bounce at least six inches, but was also required to stay in the air until permitted to fall back by the inspecting officer.

If we could have somehow consolidated all of the anger, hatred and violence that the Army directed toward the bed, and redirected the collective energy toward the enemy, the war could have been shortened by years. The only thing I'm sure of is that German, Japanese and Italian officers were no doubt very busy bouncing Marks, Yen and Lira off beds in distant places.

The crowning evidence of this irrational hatred of the bed was expressed so eloquently in military jargonese after each inspection. Following the inspection we were kept in the barracks until the official results were posted on the bulletin board. These results told us whether we were to be released for the weekend. Some men received demerits for certain atrocities committed against the system and they were singled out for special punishment, such as extra K.P. duty or the withholding of an earned weekend pass. If their crime was serious enough, or if there were many demerits issued, the entire barracks was punished.

There was a category of demerit posted on the bulletin board that expressed the Army's disapproval of the bed. The category was "bed be not neat." It was a shameful thing to have your name appear under this demerit heading. Most of us shunned these named individuals simply because we could not bring ourselves to associate with a scoundrel whose bed be not neat. As a matter of truth, we actually had a man who, working hours on Friday evening getting ready for the Saturday inspection, would actually sleep on the floor next to his bed rather than have the proclamation "Bed be not neat" leveled against him on Saturday!

Once a good inspection was over, we were faced with a dilemma, did we sit on the bed? unlace the shoes? put the raincoat at the other end of the pole? put footlockers in the order that we preferred? or did we go sit on the barrack's steps and leave everything exactly the way it was supposed to be?

I suddenly understood why my mother used to say, "Stay out of the house. I just cleaned it!" A person should not tamper with perfection, not just to demonstrate something trivial like being a human being.

Without passes, most of us would drift off to the Post Exchange (PX), where we could buy 3.2 beer, cokes, candy and listen to twanging music on the jukebox while our perfect barracks collected microscopic dust particles. A PX was invented by a man looking for the quickest way to boredom. He reached his objective with the standardized Army PX. A person could fall into a coma sitting at a table with a group of other people who all looked alike and who had nothing to talk about except an inspection. It raised an interesting point, however, and that was the extreme level of difficulty of human communication that newly drafted civilians had with one another during basic training. At first there was an impulse to talk about oneself to others. This changed very rapidly as it became obvious that resentments, prejudices and regional differences could turn people away from one another. Skills in group dynamics and knowledge of human relationships was sadly lacking in the 1940's. I soon learned not to tell anyone that I had ever been to college. I had no notion that well over 90 percent of my platoon not only had never been to college but that they considered it unmanly to attend school at all.

The last thing anyone ever confessed to one another was that he had come straight out of school into the Army. I once looked through our training records one night when I was assigned all night orderly room duty as punishment for my bed being *almost* not neat. I was dismayed to discover that over half of the men had never completed high school and that there were less than 20 of us out of 160 who had any college at all. Achievement scores were not impressive. The average was 110. We had men with scores of 68 and one individual in the platoon who had scored 22 on the standardized test. It turned out that he was illiterate, could not read or write and had watched other men marking squares and did the same in an indiscriminate manner. That he scored at all was a remarkable testimony to the law of probability, but he was one of several men that I encountered in WWII who could not read or write. For the most part, these men were shy, courteous and hesitantly friendly.

Many of the other recruits were not. We had several men who were unbelievably crude, boisterous and were bullies. They played cruel jokes on the younger men and harassed all persons outside their small circle of similar men. I tried to avoid them.

I guess the one single determinant to self grouping in the Army was by region. If you were from California, you spent what time you could with others from California. This state system seemed to be satisfying, as it seemed to preserve a psychological base for the individual and provided for some commonality of experience, however vague. "Where are you from?" was always the first question asked of a new man.

It seems strange today but in the 1940's regional loyalty was very strong and population mobility that developed following the war had not yet achieved its impact on the nation. People were born in one place and lived there as their parents and grandparents had done before them.

Within the state groups, there also developed a subtle, almost secret, grouping of individuals based on intellect. While there was no overt attempt to screen acquaintances, it was normal for guarded friendships to develop among the few of us who had entered the service from college. We tended to walk to the PX together, gather in the barracks together and to share family stories and finally reveal the inevitable picture of the girl back home. Everyone had a girl back home. Several of the men had wives back home. One or two even had their wives join them in Maryland. There were no government housing provisions for enlisted men to have wives, so opportunistic citizens of the small town of Aberdeen rented space to many of these women who waited patiently for the few passes that would periodically release their husbands for a few hours. I went into town with a friend once to visit his wife and was dismayed to find her living in the rear of a garage with blankets stretched on a clothesline to provide some privacy. There were no kitchen or bath facilities, so I presumed that she used those in the house. They were paying $25 a month for space in the garage and paid it during the time when her husband was earning $21 a month as a Private in the Army of the United States.

Basic training progressed so rapidly with so much to do that the thought of forming lasting friendships seemed not only unnecessary but also unwise. We were constantly reminded throughout basic training that following the basics of soldiering, each of us would be assigned to a specialized branch of the Ordnance Department for our technical training. This technical training was to prepare us for our final use to the Army and following the training, each of us would be assigned as replacements in field units scattered around the world. The uncertainty of what was to become of us as individuals set a tone for forming friendships, the theme being, "Why bother, this is only basic training and I'll never see these people again once I start into the real war."

During the long weeks of squeezing triggers and penises, we were oriented concerning the Ordnance schools. These were schools that provided training in auto mechanics, weapons, heavy and light combat vehicles, fire control and supply.

Our platoon visited some of these schools that were scattered around the huge Proving Grounds. Some of the training seemed very interesting, although I became concerned that I would be assigned to auto mechanics and twisting greasy wrenches seemed very unglamourous and noncombative to me. I hoped for small arms maintenance in spite of my experience with the Springfield on the rifle range. I reasoned that if I could just get my hands on a machine gun, I was bound to hit something.

We took written tests to determine our interests and I tried to give the answers that would be most apt to see me assigned to small arms.

Finally a day arrived toward the end of the six weeks of basic training when certain men who were deemed to have certain leadership abilities were selected to perform for the company officers. I was astonished to read *my* name on the bulletin board as one chosen for this group because those who passed the performance test would remain at Aberdeen as permanent training command cadre' with the rank of Corporal.

The test was right out of the book, a predictable exercise in military logic. I was ordered to appear at company headquarters in summer dress uniform at precisely 9:15 a.m. on the following Friday. Sgt. Dow told our small assembled group to brush up on general orders, military courtesy and, "For God's sake, when the Captain asks you a question, *speak up!*"

I appeared as ordered along with the others at 9:15 a.m., spotless, scrubbed, knowledgeable and absolutely terrified. At 10:20 the Captain and two other company officers arrived, rushed through the orderly room without a glance in our direction and entered his private office. I was still standing 30 minutes later because I didn't want to wrinkle myself by sitting down. At last the 1st Sergeant nodded to me to enter the Captain's office. As I was about to knock on the door as prescribed by military code, the Sgt. growled, "Speak up when you're in there."

I entered the arena. The room was larger than I imagined that it would be. The Captain, flanked by two Lieutenants, sat on the far side behind a table shuffling papers. I took the prescribed steps into the room, stood at glittering attention, saluted and shouted, "Sir, Private Keim, William 19183291, reporting to the Company Commander as ordered!"

I held the salute. I had to hold the salute until the Company Commander returned it. Holding the salute was a rule of God. I must say something about my salute. My career in the armed forces was ultimately and directly affected by a wild pitch thrown by Tony Esposito across the street from Liberty School on Ellsworth Avenue in Pittsburgh when I was 16 years of age. The ball glanced off my mitt and broke my ring finger on my right hand. The knuckle was never properly set; consequently my ring finger droops down almost an inch when my hand is held as straight as I can make it. It is still like that and except for burning it picking up coffee pots, I never notice it much anymore.

However, on that morning trying out for the team, you would have thought that my inability to hold my fingers in a perfectly straight line while saluting was tantamount to cursing the flag.

I had to admit, after seeing myself in the barracks mirror, that I *did* look like I was holding an imaginary pair of binoculars in my right hand when I was saluting. I tended to curl all of my fingers to match the broken one. I stood there saluting while the officers tried to figure out whether or not I was deliberately breaking a rule. Finally the Captain, a swarthy short man, rose, came around the table, walked up to me and with his face inches from mine said, "What's wrong with your fingers, soldier?"

Terrified because I had never been that close to an officer before, I shouted into his face, "Tony Esposito!"

The Captain took several steps backwards, blinked twice and asked incredulously, "What?"

I immediately realized that of all the words I could have said, none would have caused me more trouble than the two words that I had chosen. Still saluting, I stumbled through an explanation of a baseball and an Italian kid whom I could have cheerfully killed at that moment.

The openmouthed Captain, closed his mouth, returned to his chair, shuffled the papers again and finally begrugingly returned my salute. I dropped my numb right arm.

"At ease," he said.

I snapped to the prescribed position, noticing that the Lieutenant tapping a pencil on the table edge, was the same man whom I had encountered while guarding the rainy intersection on bivouac. I don't think he recognized me, although I was almost certain that he was tapping out the "William Tell Overture" with his pencil. He switched to tapping his front teeth with the pencil, which didn't seem to surprise his colleagues or break the rhythm of the overture.

They all looked at me. I looked at them. The Lieutenant put down his pencil, leaned back in his chair and said, "Private Keem," his eyes flickered for a moment as though he remembered something but he shook his head slightly and continued, "Keem, you are on guard duty." He glanced sideways at the Captain, smug, confident, "There is a fence next to your guard post." The Captain stopped reading my file and looked interested, "A civilian lady lies badly injured on the other side of the fence." With the mention of the word, civilian, the other Lieutenant looked interested.

"It is an isolated guard post beyond the call of the next guard, or of the Sgt. of the guard."

Even I looked interested.

The questioning officer leaned forward, elbows on the table and in a cunning manner asked, "What would you do?"

I looked at them one at a time. Slowly and consciously something happened to me. I was no longer terrified of these men. I thought of the rifle range and of the 1903 Springfields, the old worn-out World War I equipment, the bivouac, the leaky tent, the toothbrushes used to clean the floor under the bed, of someone cutting off all my hair. I thought of my bed not being neat, of the utter loneliness of the intimate strangers with whom I lived. I remembered the garbage detail, the heat, the V.D. inspections, the early morning roll calls, the mindlessness of it all and I even, for a moment, thought of a blanket hanging on a sagging clothesline at the back of someone's garage.

"Well soldier, *What would you do?*"

I looked directly into his eyes and said quietly and seriously, "Why, I'd let the dumb son-of-a-bitch die, sir."

They all stared at me transfixed, then slowly and together they removed their elbows from the table. The stony silence was at last broken by the Captain who was noticeably paler.

Clearing his throat, he said, "Give me a command, Private."

"Sir?" I asked.

"Give me a command as though you were addressing a *company* at drill!"

He said it in an exasperated manner.

Again I looked closely at these men, one not much older than I, separated from me by a class system, which I had been taught did not exist in America. There they sat, in their stunningly creased uniforms, brass polished, bars glittering, wearing clothes of a quality that I was forbidden to wear, comfortable low cut shoes and all of them bearing the authority over men's lives like a tailored glove.

I *gave* the Captain a command. It was at the absolute top of my voice. I literally screamed for them and for me, *"Fall-out!"*

I can recall only one time in my life that I ever yelled louder. On the other occasion I had hit my thumb with a ballpeen hammer while trying to straighten out a metal garbage can lid that I had just run over with my car.

I startled the three officers. All were actually and visibly shaken. As the Captain dismissed me, I noticed that the bivouac Lieutenant's eyes narrowed in a sudden spasm of recognition. As a final tribute to them, I raised my hand in my snappiest salute, four fingers as straight as possible because I had also noticed while practicing before the mirror, that when I really straightened my hand, my broken ring finger looked a lot like an upside down obscene gesture. The effort was lost on them, but I didn't care. I didn't care in the least.

None too gently I closed the door behind me. Striding through the orderly room through a shocked group of prospective Corporals and a wide-eyed first Sergeant, I turned and said as I reached the outer door, "Don't forget to speak up when you go in there."

I ran back to the Company B area, raced up the steps of the barracks two at a time, hurried down the second floor aisle and deliriously *jumped* on my neat bed. For the first time in almost three months I laughed out loud. Still laughing, I tore off my tie, jumped up and moved all of my coat hangers out of line, kicked my shoes under the bed, threw myself back on the bed, put my hands behind my head and grinned at my frozen faced companions who stared at me as though I had gone completely mad.

I didn't mind, for in that one glorious moment I knew that the United States Army could NOT defeat me and that I would ultimately survive the experience.

CHAPTER III

FIRE CONTROL SCHOOL

Saturday, the day following my performance test was our last day in the training battalion. At 9:00 a.m. we were all packed, in our dress uniforms, each accompanied by his "A" and "B" bag standing in company formation waiting to be assigned to the next phase of our training, the technical schools.

The Army, in its lust for theatrics, never lost an opportunity to turn a simple exercise into a suspenseful and punishing pageant. Rather than post the information on the bulletin board, the Company Commander, reading from a clipboard, announced the name of the school to the entire company and then one by one, in alphabetical order of course, mispronounced the names of the individuals assigned to each technical training unit. To heighten the drama, as each man's name was called, he fell out of formation and boarded the appropriate truck waiting to take him away. This caused exaggerated delays as men struggling with their bags moved out of formation, some amidst catcalls or congratulations from their friends.

As each school's roster was completed, it took time to reestablish order back in the company. The longer the delay the more satisfaction it seemed to give the Captain. He knew very well that the anxiety level of the remaining men was at a high level risk so he took deliberate delight in making the calling of the names last as long as possible.

The automotive school went by without my name being called; so did supply, weapons and combat vehicles.

I began to feel a familiar numbness as I realized that there were only five of us left standing in the company area. It was Ft. McArthur all over again, only this time it was bound to be worse. Finally the Captain looked up from his clipboard and stared directly at me. For

one horrifying moment, I thought, "My God, of course, letting the civilian die was the *right* answer."

He then smiled and said, "The next man has been chosen to join
this training company as a member of our regular cadre'." Pausing to
let this sink in, he shouted, "Private Jarwaski, front and center!"

As this misguided individual broke into a wide grin and presented
himself in front of the Captain, I heaved a sigh of relief. Jarwaski was
recognized by everyone as being dumb. He would no doubt make an
excellent addition to the cadre'. The Captain made a big production out
of personally presenting Corporal stripes to Jarwaski amid shouts and
smirks from the other cadre' noncoms. In spite of it all I was a little
envious. Six weeks in basic training had taught us all the value of the
special privileges that went with rank. Sgt. Dow seemed unaffected by
it all. The high jinks with Jarwaski was over at last and I was convinced
that there only remained the final dramatic moment when the four of
us would be sent to the stockade or assigned to permanent K.P.

I suppose that if I counted all of the surprises of my life the one
that occurred then was the greatest I ever experienced. I could never
have dreamed that it would happen and have seldom been less com-
posed that I was when the Company Commander addressed the remaining four of us. He called our names, Barker, Holt, Keem and
Marston. He glanced at me.

"These men will report to the Fire Control school to receive special
training in electronic gun directors. They will transfer from this training
company with the rank of Corporal, T/5."

Dramatically, the Captain handed his clipboard to the bivouac
Lieutenant and pausing for a moment said, "Men, this has never hap-
pened in this company before. I can only tell you that it is very irregular
to transfer from a training battalion to an Ordnance school with rank.
You have been carefully chosen for an important training assignment.
Good luck to you."

Perhaps it was the shock, the joy, the relief, or a combination of
them all, but for a fleeting moment I really believed that he meant it.

We were then informed by one of the suddenly unfriendly noncoms handing us our special orders that since the fire control school
was only "a little ways" over on the post, we were to walk to it. We
swung our bags over our shoulders and clutching our orders in our
hands, we staggered down past the chapel towards the fire control
barracks area. It turned out to be about one-half mile away. To add to
our discomfort as soon as we reached the boundary of training company
"B", it began to rain. It didn't matter. I was a *Corporal*. Only three
months in the Army and already I was a *Corporal*. I kept looking at the
mimeographed orders. It was true. We all talked and yelled, really
excited, four wet soldiers, delirious with joy, lurching down the company street to the fire control training company orderly room.

We checked in with the Sergeant who seemed unimpressed and were assigned to adjoining bunks in the same barracks. It being Saturday afternoon by then, no one was around so we just organized our gear, dried out and talked. Fire control, what was that? What kind of fire control? Putting out fires? Hadn't the Captain said electronics? What was that? We soon learned that our backgrounds were dissimilar, two had been to college, two had not. We came from different parts of the country with different interests. We had one thing in common however, none of us knew *anything* about electronics or fire control.

One of the first things we did, of course, was to race over to the closest P.X. to show the clerk our orders and to buy our stripes and sew them on. We put them on our shirts, coats, fatigues, and field jackets. We finally concluded that raincoats were not proper for stripes, since none of us could remember ever having seen rank on a raincoat.

The next thing was to call home. In 1943 a phone call on Saturday from Maryland to California could take anywhere from two to four hours to complete. Special rates were given to servicemen calling from military posts, but the actual time spent on the phone was strictly limited to three minutes.

Even though it was still raining, we put on our field jackets, distaining the raincoats in favor of displaying our exalted rank, and walked to the enlisted men's recreation center about six blocks away. We placed our calls with the volunteer lady and waited for the connection along with about 100 other men who were waiting to get through. As soon as the proper connection was completed, your name was announced over the public address system and you were sent to one of about a dozen numbered phone booths to await the final buzz, which would signify that your party was on the line. All long distance phone calls were completed in this manner from all Army posts. I never saw it done differently. Of course it was during days that preceded direct dialing. The phone call home on that particular day was an exciting one. My mother, of course, did not understand what a Corporal was; she only knew that Hitler had been one and presumed that I was being put in charge of the Army. My father was astonished because he assumed that everyone would recognize, as he had done a long time ago, that I was not too bright. But they were appropriately pleased.

The clerk in the orderly room could tell us nothing in response to our many questions, only that we were to report to a specified Major at the fire control school on Monday morning at 9:00 a.m. He gave us directions to the permanent fire control school buildings and we talked through most of the night in excited anticipation.

The Major was very solemn, punctual but grim. There were about ten of us in a standard classroom with tablet armchairs, blackboard and lecturn. Before the Major arrived, we learned that the other six men had arrived from field units, one from as far away as a camp in Alabama. Everyone was at least a Corporal and one man from Pennsylvania was a Staff Sergeant.

As soon as we all settled down, the small bespectacled Major began our orientation with a carefully worded speech about national security and secrecy. Although he mentioned the severe laws that governed security during wartime, the presentation was not threatening. He simply told us that we had been carefully selected to learn theory and maintenance on a new highly secret electronic anti-aircraft gun director. It was called the M-9. We would also learn about a developing model, the M-10. The course would take 16 weeks and when we completed it each of us would be one of only a few men who knew how to maintain and service this piece of equipment. He was polite and didn't shout. He then took us to a large closed room about the size of a gymnasium. In one corner was a huge mounted 90mm anti-aircraft gun. On the other side of the room were several pieces of large cabinet sized equipment connected by cable to the gun. With the help of several men dressed in white laboratory coats, the Major demonstrated how the gun could be aimed by moving the rotating handles on an optical electrically controlled gunsight mounted on a pedestal in the far corner. It was truly amazing to see this large anti-aircraft gun swing swiftly from position to position with no one near it. The Major said the M-9 was accurate to within 100 feet at altitudes beyond eight miles. We were all wide-eyed. The demonstration was impressive. It began to look as though the 1903 Springfield rifle was replaced by something a little more sophisticated.

Returning to the same small classroom where we had received our original orientation, the Major introduced us to two Sergeants who were to be our instructors. Both of the Sergeants had been college mathematics instructors and were in their late 30's or early 40's. When the Major left, it became clear that both Sergeants were deadly serious about the review of algebra, geometry, trigonometry and calculus, which was to be their part of the training program. We had two weeks for the review. I was not alarmed, having taken all four aspects of math in either high school or college, but several of the men, including the Staff Sergeant, were badly shaken by the news as we learned during a short ten minute smoking break.

In fact one member of the group barely knew his multiplication tables. He had been assigned by mistake from the field and was returned to his unit the next day, following a debriefing by the sympathetic Major. Two other men, including the Staff Sergeant, failed the two week review and were dropped from the group leaving, by then, only six of us to go on into the electronics part of the course.

On the Monday of the third week we were issued two black 8 1/2 by 11 notebooks. "Confidential" was written in large letters on the covers of each. Each book was numbered and we were required to sign for our respective copies. The experience of having something both personal and confidential was, to say the least, a very unique one. To lose the book or even to show it to someone not qualified to see it was treasonous and covered by the laws of espionage. No one laughed. The first book was theory as was the second and finally the third volume, which we received later in the course, dealt with the installation and maintenance of the M-9.

The classes were at first exciting and interesting. That we were a special privileged little group was known by everyone in our barracks. When it became apparent that none of us would be required to pull guard duty or K.P. or stand any company formations other than reveille, the rest of the company shunned us. They were mostly opticians being trained in the maintenance of optical fire control equipment. We didn't mind in the least being treated as an elitist group. Not only was it a great change from basic training but we were afforded at least a modicum of privacy and we were attending classes in the one building of the fire control school that was air-conditioned. This fact alone in the humid Maryland summer of 1943 was enough reason for the rest of the company to shun us.

We worked hard. There was little time for my mind to wander while struggling with tracing circuits, coming to grips with positive and negative, considering the effect of variable condensers, pondering the mathematics, and allowing for fuse setting time and wind drift. My work notebooks had very few "Doodlings" in the margins, a characteristic that has always masked my penchant for art and reveals my boredom with most school work. I was not bored; for the first time in my young life, I was motivated to learn because I did not want to fail. I also believed that the secret work, which I was doing, was actually going to be important to winning the war and I marveled at my earlier desire to be assigned to something as insignificant as weapons school.

Finally after eight weeks of study in classrooms, we were turned loose on the actual M-9 and shown the prototype of the M-10. Bell Telephone Laboratories was prime contractor on both models and we worked for part of the time under the direction of the Bell civilian technicians who had first demonstrated the director to us. It was exciting to work in a large air-conditioned laboratory with serious instructors who were obviously the best men available in the country. Determination and pride became part of what we were doing.

The final series of examinations, both written and practical, were nerve-wracking. We were cautioned that we had to pass them or we could still fail the course. We studied together in the evenings in the barracks and a new companionship grew among the four of us who had come from basic training. A sense of purpose, which the cynicism of later years would never affect, bound us together. It was one of the closest relationships that I ever formed with other men. The memory of it is dug into my mind and I'm very sorry that I have never experienced it again in my lifetime. Combat brings a closeness to those who survive but this closeness within our group seemed more personal because at the time in our youth we were sharing a danger more serious to human survival than a mere physical fear. We were in constant intellectual danger. Stretching our minds amid strangers, we faced a lonely annihilation on a plane that was to remain a mystery to our families and loved ones. Forbidden to discuss the training with anyone, we were people who shared with one another the fear of failing. We knew what was at stake. No one would ever know what we had gone through if we did, at the last minute, fail. People would only presume that we had been unsuccessful in a simple training program at Aberdeen and consequently unworthy.

The experience was not simply failing English literature or Spanish 1. This was failing our war effort, our nation and our families. More important, this was the extreme extension of the most serious concern of modern man, fear of failing oneself. We loved one another for we shared the unspoken knowledge that each of us harbored this deep concern.

Somewhat to my surprise, I breezed through the written examinations, which we all admitted were simple and not too difficult. However, the practical examination was known to be more of a problem. We were held in a classroom while one of the instructors went into the laboratory and deliberately caused a malfunction in one of the components of the M-9. Our task, to be solved individually, was to repair the malfunction and restore the gun director to working order. A time limit of four hours was set for each person to make the necessary repairs. We were encouraged to use our workbooks and were to be allowed full use of all of the electronic testing equipment in the lab. There were thousands of circuits, hundreds of vacuum tubes, servomotors, cables, power sources and full components, which could be fused, broken or caused to malfunction because of a simple improper contact. The task was enormous. In order to remind us that, in spite of the special treatment of the past ten weeks, we were still in the Army, the selection for sequence in the test was to be made on the basis of the alphabet.

There were six of us in the section. Barker went first, then Holt followed by me and the rest of the group. On Wednesday of the last week of training, George Barker entered the laboratory at 8:00 a.m. The rest of us waited. In an hour he had not returned, two hours, three hours and finally the wall clock crept up to the noon hour. Our Sergeant appeared and told us to go to chow. He was uncommunicative and as we walked toward the mess hall we were entirely silent. We were worried. George was a good student. If *he* was having trouble, none of us could do it. The meal was an experience in solemn behavior in the presence of what we considered a hostile environment. We had grown tired of pushing our food around on the steel trays and were smoking cigarettes when George Barker walked into the mess hall. He was smiling and waved to us as he went over to the mess line to get his food. We were not only relieved to see him but were very impatient to talk to him. He came over with a full tray of food, sat down and just grinned at us.

"Jesus, George, what happened?" someone shouted at last.

"You won't believe it," he said. "The Sergeant put it out of order and it took all of the Bell people to repair the damned thing!"

It turned out that the Sergeant in charge had recalibrated the main computer and this had caused a major burnout of the electro-servos between the tracker and the gun. The civilians finally solved the problem, replaced the servos, chewed out the Sergeant and sent George to lunch. Barker was elated. The result was that he had been given a passing grade on the test. We concluded that this had been done rather than reveal to the military that the Sergeant had screwed up.

Holt was next. Don Holt was an extremely intelligent and resourceful person so that it was no surprise to see him return within an hour with a satisfied expression on his genial face. "No problem," he stated, "I saw the trouble right away when I opened the first panel on the computer."

"What are you saying?" I asked.

"Well, hell," he replied, "I could see where the dust had been disturbed on the first zero set and knew that someone had removed a tube."

He added, "I didn't want to give away my private scientific research methods, so I fooled around checking out the whole system and then went back after an hour and replaced the tube."

"Someone did a good job on one of the tube connectors," he added seriously. "The tube looked O.K., but a tiny cut had been made in the base to keep the circuit from working. If I hadn't seen the dust smear, I'd have never found it in a week.

My heart sank but I didn't have long to think about it before the Sergeant opened the door and motioned me to follow him into the lab.

"Corporal," he said significantly, "do the best you can. If you get stuck, call me."

With that he withdrew.

Staring at the M-9, I sincerely believed that I was looking at one of the real secret weapons in the arsenal of democracy, a multimillion dollar marvel of technology. The fate of mankind hung on my ability to give meticulous accuracy to this slumbering, wounded creature.

I squared my shoulders, walked to the main power panel and threw the switch. Although I had expected the sounds of a celestial choir, there was nothing but a flicker on the main dial. It worked. I walked to the power rectifier that transformed AC current into proper DC voltages, which were needed in order to run the motors and supply a governable system of power to the various components. It was in order. Next the computer and the adjusting panel. There were 28 separate amplifiers in the computer, each of which had to be calibrated separately in a prescribed sequence to insure accuracy. If one was not set with extreme accuracy, all amplifiers in the remaining sequence would be off. A very slight error in calibrating the 1st zero set would compound into errors that would cause the shell to miss the target by a thousand feet or more.

It took me two hours to check out the whole system: the rectifier, computer, tracker and altitude converter. Except for an obviously misset parallex calculation between the gun and the tracker, the system worked perfectly. Resetting the parallex adjustment, I rechecked the entire system and after two and one half hours of work, summoned the Sergeant by phone to check over my work. He did, pronounced it satisfactory, congratulated me and left the room to alert the remaining section members that they would complete the tests the next day.

I gathered my workbooks and my tools together, shut down the system and as I reached to turn out the lights in my lab, I could not resist an impulse to smile at the M-9. Together we had proved that I could be successful in a highly competitive enterprise. It was the very first experience in my life in conquering an intellectual problem all by myself, one that gave me great personal satisfaction.

That gun director had helped build within me a cornerstone of confidence in my own intellectual ability. Perhaps the Army regarded the investment in my training as a problematical use of money, but to me completing the course and receiving the certificate as a qualified maintenance man was a milestone in my life.

I took one more look at the marvelous sleepy beast, still warm in the darkened room and flicked off the lab light.

Turning to leave, I was not to know that during the rest of the war and throughout the rest of my life, I was never again to set eyes on another M-9 electronically controlled gun director.

The next day both Barston and Patterson passed the test. We were finished with technical school.

Early on Saturday, I was awakened by Holt who was smiling broadly, a condition that for him was unfamiliar at that time of the day.

"Your section 8 came through," I mumbled.

Still smiling, he said, "Go look at the bulletin board."

In spite of my pleading, he would tell me nothing. He just sat on his bunk and smiled. I struggled into my clothes, cursing him continuously until I found my boots. I went into the company street to find a crowd around the company bulletin board. There were groans, back pounding and cheers. It was clear that the field assignments had been posted.

Forcing my way through the group, I found my name on the third page under the heading, fire control. For the second time since I entered Aberdeen six months previously, I was astonished at my success. There it was. Two names, mine and Holt's, both posted to an Ordnance regiment at Santa Anita, California.

"My God," I yelled, "Pasadena, that's only 15 miles from my home."

My impulsive announcement was met with jeers and curses from the others reading the bulletin boards, but as I pushed my way through the crowd, I couldn't care less what they thought, for I was blessed. There surely *was* a God who was looking out for bright and good young men.

Holt and I celebrated that night at the P.X., for he also lived near Pasadena. Throughout our drunkenness, which lasted far into the night, we told and retold the stories of our days of training. We concluded that never were there two better friends nor had anyone ever seen two more lucky people. Everything that had happened since we entered the Army had come into crystal focus as we agreed loudly, that up until now, it had been merely a mistake. Now finally, as field soldiers, we were recognized for our worth and rewarded for our endeavors. It was a happy evening.

The phone calls were made the next day in spite of splitting headaches and grassy tongues. We were on our way home.

Aberdeen Interlude—1972

It was a sweltering Sunday afternoon driving from Philadelphia to Washington, D.C., on Interstate 95. The humidity was uncommonly high even for the East coast in August, but as we glided along in air-conditioned comfort in our late model car, we were insulated from the oppressive heat. In fact it was only by observing that farm animals were grouped inactively in what shade they could find did we notice at all that it was hot outside. There was no breeze, trees seemed depressed, stunned by the heat. I was reaching over to replace a tape in the stereo system when I saw the green overhead sign on the freeway announcing the turnoff to Aberdeen. We had decided earlier that we would interrupt our journey and visit the little town. Gliding down the banked concrete off-ramp, we entered the outskirts. The town had changed in 30 years, but strangely it had remained unchanged. Fast food services, new apartment buildings, a revitalized business center had failed to hide from the knowledgeable observer that the section of town near the old railroad depot was the same. This one-sided section of street behind the station was exactly the same. Even the newly painted railroad station with its carefully resurfaced platform built around attractive planters could not disguise this tiny place, which had been a part of my life.

We had intended just to drive through the town, but seeing the large sign on the other side of the tracks giving directions to Aberdeen Proving Grounds caused me, out of curiosity, to turn toward the Army base. Rumbling across the new multi-track intersection, we drove to the main gate. They had either moved the gate closer to town or the long drunken walks back to camp in the middle of the night had been the result of coordination problems rather than distance. We were at the gate almost at once. There were four traffic lanes leading into and out of the camp, all passing through a newly built attractive brick and stone entrance. My thought was to reach the gate and then turn around and proceed back to the interstate, but a strange nostalgia came over me.

I stopped the car about fifty feet short of the gate as I realized that the emotion that I was experiencing was not an affection for the camp but rather a feeling of camaraderie with the lone soldier guarding the entrance to the post. He watched us with an inquisitive look rather than with any apparent alarm. Finally he held up his hand in a half wave and smiled at me. Astonished, I smiled back and drove ahead to the entrance.

Rolling down the window caused us to gasp as the summer heat rolled into the car and instantly defeated our air-conditioned environmental system. Still smiling, the very young man stepped over to the car and leaned down to me. I looked up at him, standing silhouetted against the sun, smiling in the heat. I looked at his summer uniform, which was immaculate, creased, his tie firmly placed between the 2nd and 3rd buttons, his web belt in the correct hip position, side arm in just the right place, white helmet liner squarely positioned above two slightly amused but terribly young eyes.

I fought a desire to ask, "Are you walking your post in a military manner, keeping always on the alert and observing everything taking place within sight or hearing?"

Instead I stammered nervously, "This is crazy, but I trained here in World War II and I was wondering if there is any chance at all for us to be allowed to go on the post for a few minutes?"

I grinned while trying my best not to look like a parachutist or a saboteur. The grey hair and 30 pounds excess weight were bound to help give the impression that I was a solid middle class, middle-aged veteran, representing no danger to the United States government. I hoped that it would anyway. Before I could search for some absolute identification, which I presumed I would be required to produce, the young man said, "Why of course, sir, the post is open to visitors all day on Sunday."

I was totally disarmed. Since my years of service as an enlisted man, I have never been comfortable when anyone addressed me as *sir*. It is a heritage belonging only to those who have been an enlisted man during their youth but it persists. To this day, I flinch a little and hear intonations of insolence and challenge in every *sir* directed toward me. I know what to listen for.

This soldier was being polite, however. He was not using the word as a weapon. He actually meant it as a courtesy.

I was also chagrined that I wasn't smart enough to realize that, of course, the post was open to visitors. The big war, after all, had been over for nearly thirty years and all military installations were open to civilian traffic. They always had been in peacetime. I had been on several Air Force and Navy bases to visit air shows, museums, and ships. I had even been conducted on a tour of a missile installation once.

But before I could apologize, the guard produced a post map and a pamphlet that explained the Ordnance department and its mission.

"Do we need a pass?" I asked numbly. "No, sir, just follow the signs and we would appreciate it very much if you would park only in designated places and observe speed limits," he replied.

I looked at him closely again. So very young, so very poised. Stepping back from the car, he motioned us through the gate and said, "If you need directions, just ask anyone. Have a nice visit."

Smiling in return, I rolled up the window, grateful to escape the heat, put the car in gear and slowly passed once more onto the sacred soil of Aberdeen Proving Grounds.

I didn't use the map. I didn't need it. I drove directly to the Command of Company B, 1st Ordnance Training Battalion. I even took the back way, forgoing the main road, which I knew took a circuitous route to my destination as we drove that short distance. I did notice, however, that a museum and tracked vehicle park had been built on the site of the dental clinic, but everything else seemed to be in place, exactly as I had remembered it.

There were some minor exceptions. The buildings were white instead of olive drab and things seemed closer together and smaller after 30 years. Of course they were, I reasoned, I had spent six months here on foot, seldom in a vehicle of any kind. Walking always makes distances seem greater.

Swinging around the silent chapel, I braked to a halt. Leaning on the steering wheel, I gazed into the battalion training area. It was not only deserted, it was evidently abandoned. For some reason I could not bring myself to drive a car into that scene. We left the car and walked through the dizzying heat out onto the dry dusty parade ground.

My wife remained silent, sensing that the flood of memories were entirely mine. Not wishing to intrude, she stood to one side as I slowly turned in a circle gazing at the ramshackle and rundown area.

The oblong parade ground was much smaller than I had remembered. I tried to imagine that I could hear the snickering of bolts and the ghostly cry through the morning darkness, "Company B all present or accounted for, *sir!"*

But I could not hear the sounds. I could not feel the excitement of those moments. Instead I felt only the angry heat tearing at my head and shoulders. I felt at once very old and very used.

Turning to the right, I saw the company orderly room, a separate small building and the scene of my "tryout" for a company cadre position. This building was no classic scene of triumph, it was only a pathetic, boarded up little building, badly in need of repair. The mess hall, delapidated, past its time, doors hanging crazily on broken hinges. Completing the circle, I walked to the building that had housed the 3rd platoon of Company B. Boarded up, cracked paint peeling, crumbling sidewalk broken and intersticed with weeds, brown dry from the summer heat.

Why was this building not still shining from the inspections of the past? Did we not do it well? I had scrubbed the floors with a toothbrush, seeking to dislodge specks of dirt from the space between the boards. I felt betrayed. It is a cruel and mortal lesson to learn, but standing there in the steaming heat, unconsciously standing a little straighter, trying without success to tighten my stomach muscles, I learned with a rush that time is, after all, a continuum. Thomas Wolfe had said, "You can't go home again." He didn't just mean that it had changed; he meant that it simply wasn't there any longer. What does change, I wondered? Do we change or does the physical place change? The answer was clear. *Everything* changes because it must. There is no option, there is no way to depress the passing of time, atomic particles erode and owe no allegiance to any mortal or to any place. The past is *in* the past. I walked completely around the barracks, shuffling slowly, kicking up dust and trampling down clumps of weeds. Irritated insects swarmed and settled again in the heat buzzing their tiny curses at being disturbed. The countless former generations of their very ancesters had left specs on my gear years before. Disgusting specs to be erased before the inspecting officer soiled even a tip of his omnipotent white glove.

I stopped once more in front of the barracks and looked at it one time unconsciously noting the work that must be done. I knew then that I was looking at this building for the last time. I would never return to this place again.

We walked back to the car in some silence. I turned on the air-conditioner, grateful for the cold stream of air across my knuckles gripping the steering wheel. As I looked back at the company area, I could not help but be deeply moved. In many ways my adult life had begun on this uninspiring little piece of ground. As a mere youth I had fought despair, loneliness and humiliation at this place. I had overcome them all right here.

I could not speak.

We drove deeper into the post past scores of buildings, but I could not find the fire control training center. I watched for it in a detached sort of way. The school had probably been replaced by several large beautiful technical buildings that no doubt housed fire control apparatus far more sophisticated than the M-9 or M-10. Today my early primitive computer controlled fire directors would probably be considered antiquated curiosities.

I thought however that in the bowels of one of the buildings, perhaps in a darkened storage area there sits the M-9, still warm, smelling of sweet oil and heated electrical circuits, caring for itself. Stirring occasionally into activity, alone, clucking, calibrating its own zero sets and whispering confidentially to its computer circuits that once, in time, it had been a dreaded secret weapon against the enemies of democracy.

We found the recreation building next to the water tower. It was larger, additions having been built on the back of the structure, but essentially it was the same. My wife was pleased to see the building from which I had made those important phone calls in those days before we were married. We stayed in the car and talked about the excitement of those few phone calls. I began to feel better.

We then visited the museum and the tracked vehicle park, which contained captured tanks and other tracked vehicles from past wars. A huge 60 ton German tiger tank dominated the rows of parked vehicles. Many tanks have been developed since World War II, faster, more sophisticated, costlier, but in my mind, there has never been a tank conceived to equal the functional brutality and beauty of the fearsome tiger. Its long 88mm gun barrel, incredible armour plate and wide metal tracks all blend to give it a commanding presence of its own. No soldier who served in the European theatre of operations during World War II can never look at a German tiger without awe and fear. The very word, tiger, no longer means a beautiful stripped cat to us. It means a cold clutch in the pit of the stomach and an overpowering desire to press oneself beneath the protective crust of the earth.

There it stood, buttoned up, as though it were carefully watching the stream of visitors going by, tolerating the small boys who ignored the "keep off" sign to climb on its squat flanks and heavy turret. It was easy to imagine that the crew was still inside, black uniforms, headsets on. Powerful Maybach engine rumbling, shriek of metal as the monster moves a little on its tracks, the commander correcting his position for the next crack of the 88. The gun loader ready to pass another round of armor piercing shell to the marvelously accurate gun layer—all waiting for the precise moment to fire. I remembered the British adage, "He who has not fought the German, does not know war."

We moved away from the danger, my heart pumping in spite of myself. "It must be the heat," I said to no one in particular.

As we left Aberdeen Proving Grounds, I consciously and formally saluted the boy-guard on the gate. Smiling a little as though he was used to grey-haired men saluting him, he came to smart attention and, as though on parade, returned my salute.

In spite of myself, tears sprang to my eyes, not for him, not for me, but for all times that once had been.

CHAPTER IV

FIELD TRAINING

The train trip back to California was ponderously slow with interminable waits in large cities. The coaches were standard but of course not air-conditioned and we suffered terribly from the late summer heat. In all it took 10 days and nights to cross the country, every foot of it in discomfort laced with the homecoming excitement, which gripped me throughout the whole trip.

We finally arrived at the San Bernardino pass and once again I stood beside the train looking over the Los Angeles basin with its incredible layers of purple mountains to the north and west. I realized that I was a different person than I had been when only five short months ago I had stood at this exact spot filled with bitterness, fright and despair. In the intervening months I had grown into a man. The feeling was satisfying and as the donkey engines arrived to take the train down the torturous pass, I climbed up into the coach with physical ease and with a sense of purpose that I had never known before in my 19 years.

We descended into the Los Angeles basin in early evening light, arriving at the Santa Anita siding around midnight. Assigned to transient barracks for the night, I found time, after dumping my gear on a bed, to make a phone call from a pay station near our company area. It was a thrill to deposit my nickel and to dial my home. It was a local call.

My parents were also thrilled that I had arrived, but were a little less than enthusiastic that I had awakened them in the middle of the night. My parents, like most of their generation, distrusted telegrams and telephones. Both of them were absolutely convinced that either device brought only bad news, particularly if the telephone rang anytime after the sun went down. A telegram was just bad news anytime.

74

We had been at Santa Anita for about four weeks, drilling, exercising and behaving like post soldiers when the rumor was spread that we were leaving. By then I had established a neat pattern of going on pass every night, had talked my father into giving me his car and gasoline ration book, and had my mother retailoring all of my Army uniforms. She even did my laundry on weekends. I was the only soldier in the company with ironed shorts. Needless to say, I did not want to leave. The rumor persisted, of course, and eventually became fact.

However, during our last week at in Southern California, we were called upon to march in a special war bond parade in Los Angeles. It was to be a battalion parade and all four companies were to be involved. With the endless practicing company drill and polishing our equipment, we gradually came to hate the notion of a parade. At first being in a parade seemed exciting but as the extra time of preparation began to mount, the whole idea seemed about as thrilling as a V.D. inspection.

In addition, all weekend passes were cancelled since the event was scheduled for Saturday afternoon and the battalion commander wanted every man to be in the parade. Cancelling passes did very little to make us feel better. On the morning of the eventful day, we assembled as a battalion in a park on the outskirts of Los Angeles. There our battalion commander, a former Sergeant in World War I who had become a car salesman and had been turned into a Lt. Colonel, spoke through a loud speaker to the entire battalion. It was perhaps the most remarkable speech I have ever heard. The speech seemed like a pre-parade and pep talk at first but soon turned into a diatribe about income taxes and concluded with the admonition, "Remember men, never buy a used car without looking under the floor mat!"

While a thousand men stood silently trying to figure out what that statement had to do with the parade, or for that matter, what floor mats had to do with anything else, the battalion adjutant, sensing the drama of the moment, sprang to the microphone and shouted, "Give 'em hell!"

From that moment on, the parade itself had nowhere to go but up. We formed the battalion and marched out of the park with the Colonel and his exhuberant adjutant leading us in a brand new jeep.

The adjutant was standing up backward in the back seat of the jeep to give the battalion inspiration and as the Corporal driver shot forward with spinning wheels, the poor adjutant did a perfect cartwheel over the spare tire onto the street. He was agile for an older man, however, and leaping to his feet, he chased after the jeep holding his hands to his forehead. The Colonel was sitting in the front seat staring implacably straight ahead and of course the driver, who knew very well what had happened, pretended he didn't see the bleeding wild man chasing after them.

The Colonel was probably still thinking about the floor mat.

It soon became obvious to everyone that where we started from was a hell of a long ways from Los Angeles. By noon we could actually see the city hall in the center of the city, but it took an agonizingly long time before it began to get closer. We were all getting tired and looking more like a large band of sweating street urchins, we finally arrived at our assigned parade starting position. We were about an hour late. The Colonel arrived ten minutes later, having been lost in East Los Angeles for over two hours. We never did see the adjutant again, although in 1953, I thought that I saw a man who looked a lot like him chasing a car in Compton. It was probably someone else.

Regrouping and straightening ourselves out, we started off on the two mile parade route. By then the sun was blazing hot and there was an ominous silence along the sidewalks. It became clear that no one had come out to see this fearless band of warriors or that the Colonel had not had the right day for the parade. Unperturbed, California drivers whizzed by us on all sides honking and yelling at us and incredulously, a streetcar forced its way through the mass of marching men. With great alacrity and sound judgment, we allowed the clanging streetcar to pass, simply forming up again as it proceeded ahead of the column. We began to feel the need to form a British defense square in order to protect ourselves but miracuously a military band began to play up ahead and as we rounded a corner we found ourselves actually marching in the parade.

We had been warned about slipping on the streetcar tracks but no one had mentioned the large metal plates that marked pedestrian streetcar loading zones. These metal and concrete protubrances were maliciously placed at the end of every other block or so to make safety islands for people waiting to board streetcars. The plates stuck up from the street about six inches. We became aware of the problem when one whole file of K company disappeared from the parade in front of us in a tangle of men, helmet liners, carbines and curses. The man in front of me fell down four times and was bleeding from the mouth by the time the parade was over. I only fell once, breaking the stock of my carbine in two places. As a crowning insult when we arrived at a near empty reviewing stand, a loud speaker explained that we were part of a parachute regiment on our way to the Pacific theatre of operations. There were only about twenty people in the reviewing stands. I cannot remember seeing anyone else along the parade route watching the parade. However, there was one dog barking from an alleyway, but I think the men falling down scared it away. The parade was over at last as trucks arrived to take us back to the park from which we had marched six hours before. We could have used those trucks in the morning. We were all given a bologna sandwich and a Coke in the park and counted our casualties from the streetcar markers. Casualties were heavy. Missing teeth, broken equipment, lost helmet liners, skinned knees and elbows and bleeding noses marked our bruised and suffering company.

We were instantly suspicious when the Colonel and his driver drove up in the jeep. Incredibly, the Commander was very happy, congratulated us all for a splendid little parade and then fell heavily backwards into his seat as the driver suddenly shot out of the park again with spinning wheels. We had the feeling that the Colonel had not finished saying all that he had wanted to say. However, our company gave a great spontaneous ringing cheer, not for the Colonel, but for the driver.

I only saw that Colonel two or three times more during the entire war and each time he seemed to be deep in thought about some perplexing problem probably having to do with used cars. Following the parade, he was ever after known to the battalion as "Old Floor Mat."

The Corporal driver, having become an expert in the first aid treatment of whiplash, was promoted to Sergeant several weeks later.

During our stay at Santa Anita I was made plans and training noncom for the company. My responsibilities included scheduling weekly training sessions for the 200 men. The training included calesthentics, map reading, closed and open order drill, gas mask exercises, aircraft identification and in general, advanced preparation for overseas assignment. Lt. Bond, our platoon officer, supervised my work and approved all schedules. He had been a jeweler before the war and tended to look at everyone as a potential for owning a broken watch. He was also very formal with absolutely no sense of humor or any understanding of human interaction. He detested cursing and I have seen a man stand in front of him, in deep puzzlement for minutes trying to put a sentence together without using the word, "fuck."

The training was a farce. We had to cover certain material, which was dictated to us by a battalion staff officer who had apparently been a school teacher before becoming a "jackass." Each company had a plans and training noncommissioned officer and we had briefings with this officer on a regularly scheduled basis. One day he announced that every man in the battalion would take a written test at the conclusion of each training module. He wanted to be able to certify to the Colonel that every single man in the battalion was qualified in advanced training. He made it very clear to us that each of us had company responsibility as plans and training noncom and was personally responsible that each man in his company was certifiable. We looked at one another knowingly as he shuffled papers and patted his pockets as though he was looking for a piece of chalk.

From then on we gave tests to our company on every subject from battlefield survival to aircraft identification. Since I was personally responsible for each man passing the written test, I devised a testing system based on the "30 calibre" pencil principle. I would assemble a platoon, usually sitting in the company street, pass out answer sheets and read the multiple choice questions to them. The method of getting everyone through the test was in the reading of the choices that were given as possible answers to the question. A sample question would be:

Question: How can you tell if an airplane is a Japanese Betty Bomber?

Answers: Choose one.

a. It says "Made in Japan" on the tail.

b. It has a cigar shaped fuselage.

c. The pilot speaks Japanese.

Incredible as it may seem, without some help, half of the platoon would have selected the wrong answer.

I would read the answers, watch the frowns of concentration and the gnawing on pencil stubs while what intellect there was struggled with disquieting wide-eyed panic. The whole platoon would watch me closely and when I had their full attention, I would say slowly, enunciating each word, "I want you to *bee* careful of this question."

One by one the face of each man would light up in varying degree of recognition and then each would carefully mark "B" on the answer sheet. A few would miss it.

Eventually every man in my company qualified on every test. Some of the less sophisticated members of the group had to take the test two or three times before passing it. But every one of them were eventually certified to the batallion jackass.

I felt like Sergeant Dow with his marksman medals.

Toward the end of October, our company engaged in some field training in the California foothills near San Dimas Canyon. We had some wonderful fun that ended in an absolute disaster.

The first and second platoon of the company were not informed that the third platoon was to act as an enemy force, but were simply informed that the third was being sent ahead a day prior to the exercise to prepare the camp for the entire company.

The third platoon was issued made up German uniforms complete with insignia and was equipped with booby traps, smoke bombs and land mines. The mines were charged with moderate sized firecrackers.

The enemy force arrived at the bivouac area before we knew our mission and with great glee, Captain Smart explained how we were to fade into the hills at dusk, mine the roads, and sweep down on the 1st and 2nd platoon in camp around midnight. Since it was close to Halloween, we all thought that the idea was really a fine one and we took great delight in strutting around yelling "Heil Hitler" and other famous Germanic phrases. Instead we should have been studying a map while there was still some daylight.

At the time we had a new second Lieutenant platoon officer named Jarvis who was fresh from an ROTC program in New Mexico. He was insufferable. He had been a voice music major in college, believing himself to be a future operatic star. He sang arias constantly and carried around with him one of those ceramic caricatures of a Mexican bandit, which he addressed as "Pancho." They had an interesting relationship together, because the ugly little figure, however implacable, clearly served as a blue blanket for a troubled and lonely man.

Around dusk, the new Lieutenant assembled the three squads, which made up the third platoon, and in the presence of Pancho, spread out a map on the dusty road in a grove of sycamore trees. In the lengthening evening shadows we were fascinated by the tactics that we were to use in our night raid on our unsuspecting companions who were to arrive soon to camp in this very grove. Our 1st squad was to hide to the West and wait until the 1st and 2nd platoons arrived with their trucks. They were to wait until the camp was secure and then mine the road into the grove to prevent escape from the anticipated panic of the surprise attack.

Second squad was to move South and East through the hills to link up with my squad, the 3rd, which was to move to the North and East in a large semicircle to join 2nd squad and swoop down on the sleeping camp. The signal for the attack was to be three blank rifle shots from Jarvis. Once in position 2nd and 3rd squads were to set off a smoke bomb to signal their arrival at the designated location in the hills. We all stared at the only map. Sixty heads turned and looked at Pancho who was holding down a corner of the map. He was unperturbed, as usual, so we took this for a sign that the attack by the three squads was a brilliant piece of battle tactics. We checked our watches, figuring four hours to get into position. We were required by Jarvis to repeat our orders including the fact that the 1st squad was to attack back up the road from the West once the other two squads had begun their assault from the East. Jarvis would accompany the 1st squad on the road and supervise the mining. As squad leader of the 3rd squad, I was handed a compass as was the other squad Corporal who was to lead his men to the South and East and join my group in the hills, which were now deep in purple shadows.

At this dramatic moment, Jarvis had us give a final check of our equipment and then for reasons known only to Pancho, he had us group around him while he sang, "Give me some men who are stouthearted men . . ." from "Naughty Marietta."

Even though some unfeeling clod giggled, the moment was somehow hauntingly touching—sixty men next to Pancho standing in a beautiful grove of sycamore trees in a ravine on a cool autumn evening in California about to launch an attack reminiscent of Jackson's flank move around the Yankees at Chancellorsville. Even Pancho seemed impressed.

The last echoes of Jarvis' cracking voice had faded up the ravine when we heard the far off noise of the trucks of 1st and 2nd platoon grinding their way up the dirt road to the campground. Like Indians we faded silently North, South and West.

My squad of twenty men with me in front and the second in command in the rear as prescribed by the squad field training manual began the sweeping curve ascent of the foothills of the ravine.

Although I had lived in California for a number of years, I had never been in San Dimas Canyon nor in any other canyon for that matter. We soon learned that climbing out of a ravine in thick head-high chapperal bushes is very difficult to do. It is a lot like climbing a wall covered with cardboard handholds, which either come loose or slap you in the face when you touch them.

It was getting dark but we managed to clear the first series of cliffs.

With an important flourish, I removed my Army issue compass from its web cover to check our direction. The squad gathered around to study the compass. Only then did I discover that it was brand new and still covered with Cosmoline, an Army substance invented by either the cruelest or the greatest comedian of all times. A thick grease used to cover metal, Cosmoline hardened in a saddistic manner in a matter of a few weeks and absolutely defied removal except by the dogged persistence with a sharp blade or a special chemical wash that was never, never made available to members of the U.S. Army.

We stood there while I scraped and chipped away at the damnable stuff trying to clean the glass so that I could see the luminous dial in the rapidly fading light.

I was soon dismayed to discover the second oversight. Luminous dials only work if they are first exposed to light for a period of time. I obviously had a World War I Army issue compass, which had been a stranger to any light at all since 1918. The luminous dial did not luminate. We had no flashlights and Lt. Jarvis had solemnly warned us against striking a match lest an enemy aircraft gliding silently at 40,000 feet would see it and drop a bomb directly on us.

I squatted behind some chapperal and struck a match anyway. We were headed in the right direction but before the match went out I noticed how brown and crackling the dry tufts of grass and bushes were.

We headed North in single file climbing up and up toward a faintly visible skyline. Stars appeared. It began to get chilly, although we noticed the cold only when we stopped our sweating and cursing climb. I glanced at my watch, which had a usable luminous dial, and was alarmed to discover that it was already after 10:30! We were supposed to be in position with the second squad in only an hour and a half and we, according to my calculations, had not even reached the point where we were to turn East for the linkup. I made my first command decision. Disregarding the arguments, counter suggestions and references to my beloved mother's ancestral background, I headed the column East following a ridge, which dropped sharply downward at a right angle to the direction we had been following. It was easier walking anyway.

Several minutes later I was glancing at my watch when suddenly a flashlight appeared ten feet in front of me shining directly into my eyes. I was astounded and stood there shielding my face with my arm. A voice behind the light said, "Whadya want?"

Vaguely conscious that the squad was bunched in a tight circle behind me, I replied, "Whadya *you* want?"

At once the light went out and I could hear voices that sounded curiously flat as though coming from across a body of water.

The light came on again moving slowly from one squad member to another. I was a little nervous as the light flickered across German insignia and swastica arm bands. The voice ordered, "You fellows, come on over here."

We took two steps only to discover in astonishment that we were on a concrete surface that seemed quite wide. Slowly it dawned on me. San Dimas Canyon had a reservoir dam built in it. It was part of the water supply for Los Angeles and I had sat through a boring discussion in school about the water supply system for the Los Angeles basin two years before.

I stepped forward in the flashlight's beam trying very hard not to look like a saboteur. Dressed as an armed German soldier, this was hard to do, even in the dark.

"See here," I said, "we have to cross the dam to get to the other side."

It must have sounded like a chicken joke because someone behind me laughed out loud.

The light went out immediately and incredibly the voice from the darkness said, "Oh, O.K. go ahead."

Single file, twenty German soldiers, carrying weapons and smoke bombs, crossed the dam without challenge or apparently even another curious glance. The memory of that brilliant piece of security work was to remain in my thoughts for a long time. There was no question in anyone's mind that the destruction of the major San Dimas Canyon dam would cause enormous loss of life and property in the Los Angeles basin. Why, during wartime, the security of this vital reservoir was entrusted to two idiots with flashlights will remain a mystery to me and to the other members of the 3rd squad.

We cleared the dam and after checking my watch, we struck off to the East, climbing again, in the wild hope of meeting the 2nd squad in the hills above the sycamore grove. It was 11:30 by now. I imagined that we were probably one or two miles from our assault position with very difficult terrain to negotiate. My companions were beginning to grumble about the pace I was setting. Then to my complete astonishment we blundered into the 2nd squad sitting among the chapperal. They were also exhausted, sweating and lacking much enthusiasm for a downhill attack in the pitch darkness.

Corporal Johnson, leader of the 2nd squad, was anxious to set off the smoke bomb signalling that we were in position. This puzzled me a little since I was almost positive that we were not in position but rather a mile or so farther North than we were supposed to be. Not only that, but for the first time it occurred to some of us that smoke was not going to be seen on this dark night anyway.

At 12:00 we set off the smoke. *Of course* it couldn't be seen. *We* couldn't see it even though we all began choking and coughing as we stood there in the middle of it. Even though we had found a flat rock upon which to set the bomb, some stray sparks had caused a small grass fire, which we stamped out right away. Having lived in California, I was acutely aware of fire hazard in the tinder dry hills. It all seemed secure, however, as the last of the infernal smoke disappeared in the cooling night air. A small hill breeze had come up, which made the night more comfortable, and with the activity caused by the smoke, some enthusiasm was beginning to return to the group. We spread out in silence waiting for the three rifle shots. At 12:35 we still had heard nothing except some irregularly spaced muffled thuds coming from a far distance off our left flank. At 12:45 Johnson and I decided on a plan. We would move closer and see what was going on. Not wanting to lose track of forty men trying to move though the many ravined terrain, we moved out in two squad columns in single file. He and I took the lead point in each column as we moved cautiously and carefully forward to the West. After a half hour or so I talked him into turning in a Southerly direction because I was convinced that we were headed back for the dam and would miss the grove completely.

There was no noise whatever as we finally found the grove. Trucks were parked throughout the camp area and the squad tents were all silent. It was clearly an unsuspecting campground ready to be surprised. We had not even seen perimeter guards. However, I was still a little edgy about the 1st squad, which was to have attacked up the West road at midnight. There was no sign of them.

Johnson and I, in whispered conversation, decided to spread out our two squads on the North and then while he led them on a sweep through the camp I would start up one of the trucks, drive around inside the tent area causing confusion and attracting attention by blowing the horn and throwing smoke grenades.

I gave him ten minutes to get into position and then went for a truck. The silence was eerie in the camp as I cautiously opened the door of a nearby six by six ready to mount the cab and start out on my mission.

At once there was a tremendous, firey explosion in my face. Someone hiding on the floor of the truck cab had fired a rifle directly over my head. Just as suddenly every truck in the camp switched on its lights and the 1st and 2nd platoon poured out of the vehicles to surround and capture all of us. We had been totally taken in by the ambush. There was great laughter and jeering from the successful platoons, although I heard very little of it through the ringing in my ears caused by the blank cartridge fired so close to my head.

We then learned that someone had "tipped off" the rest of the company that 3rd platoon was planning the little surprise. It took no imagination at all for them to plan a little counteraction of their own. It turned out that our tipster was a Corporal in the supply room who handled the issuing of our German uniforms. He could not resist telling the story to someone and before we had ever arrived at San Dimas, 1st and 2nd platoons had had their own plan ready.

Our first squad had been observed by the rest of the company but had been allowed to mine the road and withdraw. A careful trap had been prepared to capture them at their start line but it was never sprung. It wasn't necessary. Jarvis himself had stepped on four of the freshly buried mines as the squad came back up the road to attack the camp. The muffled thuds that we had heard from the hills were all from Jarvis, as dirt, rocks and dust were blown up his pantlegs in some sort of ironic revenge. He was easily captured and was resting nicely in the company headquarters tent. Pancho was with him.

By this time the sky was lightening to the East but it had a funny orange glow to it. I looked at my watch and saw immediately that it was certainly not the sun coming up at 3:00 a.m. I hurried over to the headquarters tent, which was marked by the company flag, and the jeep parked in front of it. Entering, I informed the Captain that we had a fire in the hills. I did not tell him that I suspected that our brief grass fire had probably been fanned into flame again by the night wind. In fact I never told anyone that story, nor did any other member of 2nd or 3rd squad ever reveal that we had probably started a major brush fire with an unobservable smoke bomb.

I was a little excited because I knew that the grove was in danger and I also knew of the horrors of a California hill fire.

Lt. Jarvis, covered with dust and looking a little sheepish, was sitting on a cot in the tent cleaning his friend Pancho with his handkerchief. The Lt. was humming an Italian aria of some sort when I began yelling about the fire. He immediately leaped to his feet and sprinted for the jeep. Clutching Pancho he shouted that he was going out to the main road to phone the fire department. Captain Smart called the company together and organized us into a fire fighting line. We passed out what tools we had from the trucks: shovels, axes and a few picks. These, plus our own entrenching tools, gave all of us at least some means to build a fire stop. By this time we could see quite clearly in the grove from the orange glow in the sky and it was easy to see the line of flames on the hill about a mile East of us. As we started off for the fire, we were treated to eight more muffled thuds as Jarvis managed somehow to drive over all of the remaining mines as he roared off to the West to look for help. We were never to see him again.

We managed, with the help of the forest service fire brigade, to stop the fire after it had consumed several acres of brush. We were lucky that the wind had died and that the fire had started on the West side of an isolated hillock surrounded by creek beds. We were lucky. Jarvis wasn't so lucky.

As we gathered the next morning in the smokey grove, covered with sweat streaked dirt, we learned from the forest ranger that as the Lt. had made his dash for the main road, he had met the fire truck coming in. The firemen had correctly run this madman off the narrow dirt road. Intent on getting to the fire, they had no time for a dust covered person screaming and waving a small ceramic Mexican bandit at them. Lt. Jarvis had driven noisily over the steep bank of a dry creek bed turning the jeep over and breaking both of his legs. The ranger had taken him to the hospital in San Dimas.

"Do you know what he did on the way to the hospital?" the ranger asked.

Without hesitation, we all said, "He sang."

Puzzled, the ranger asked, "How did you know that?"

We shrugged and walked away to the trucks that were ready to take us back to Santa Anita.

"Not only that," the ranger shouted at us, "but he wouldn't let go of the ugly statue he had, took it into the operating room with him!"

I don't know if Lt. Jarvis ever made it to the war, but I do know that everytime in Europe if we heard a muffled thud from the distance, *someone* would say, "There goes Jarvis."

By that evening we were all painfully aware that, almost without exception, every man in the company was infected with poison oak. We were a mass of welts and blisters and were covered with an itchy rash. When I awakened the next morning I could not open my eyes; my eyelids were so stuck together with caked mucous that I had to literally pry my eyes open with my fingers.

We streaked calomine lotion all over us. Some of the men were even hospitalized for several weeks. I only know that I have since never been so uncomfortable in my life as I was for several days and scratching nights. All in all the San Dimas Canyon exercise provided our company with memories that lasted for years.

CHAPTER V

ADVANCED TRAINING

It was late in November 1943 when we received word that the battalion was to be shipped to Camp Forrest, Tennessee, for some rigorous field training. This seemed incredible to us since we assumed we were training in California so that we could be sent into the Pacific to fight the Japanese. None of us could imagine what the hills of Tennessee had to do with the island hopping warfare that was underway in the West. We went anyway. I said my goodbyes, gave the car back to my relieved father, picked up my laundry from my uncomplaining mother and packed my gear.

Those of us from Southern California left Santa Anita with great reluctance. It had been a good four months for us all.

Two companies of the battalion boarded a troop train that arrived outside the camp early one morning and started out for the San Bernardino pass. This time, however, the train was a special one made up of elongated reconverted boxcars that were filled with bunk beds. Each car held about eighty men since the beds were made of metal stancions with four beds to a rack. The beds were constructed crosswise in the car making you lie at a right angle to the direction in which the train was travelling. This was thrilling since we were constantly being thrown out of our beds onto the floor as the train jerked its way across the country. The men in the top bunks took a fearful and serious beating. One even broke his wrist in Albuquerque when the train made a sudden stop. The floor of the car was, of course, made of iron. There was a narrow passageway at the foot of the bunks that ran the length of the car. At first we kept the sliding doors open most of the time sitting in the doorway with our feet dangling outside the car enjoying the pleasant November Southwest. It was not too hot and we had a good relaxing time until some officer decided that the troop train looked unsightly and we were not allowed in the doorways. There were also some whispered suggestions that some lurking spy might see soldiers on the train and make a direct report to Adolph Hitler. Since most 1943 railroad traffic in the United States was of some military significance, it seemed hard to believe that a report even to Hitler, of two companies of an Ordnance battalion would alter the outcome of the war. Post war research has since indicated that enemy spy activity on the North American continent was practically nonexistent and terribly amateurish at best. By the time we arrived in New Mexico, however, we were all tucked neatly inside the boxcars, bored to death. Reading was a favorite pastime with plenty of the new paperback books, which were available to us for the first time. Our other activity was waiting for chow. There was a mess car in the center of the train and three times a day, on schedule, each carload of men would troop through the narrow passageway of the other cars to get to the mess car. Banging our mess kits on other men's bunks, we would be greeted with jeers and curses, particularly if those occupants had not eaten yet. There seemed to be a very complicated, rotating schedule worked out to feed the hundreds of men on the train. Sergeants were mostly red faced from shouting instructions at what seemed to be an endless, roving band of men with mess gear. The entire scheme was complicated by the fact that once you picked up your food, you had to return to your own car to eat it. To do this inevitably resulted in meeting the next group fighting their way to the mess car to pick up their food. Passageways and doorways between cars were very narrow, since the management objective was to get as much usable space for soldiers and as little as possible for comfort, convenience or for roving back and forth on the train. All of this in a jerking train making innumerable and often, what seemed to be, sadistic stops.

Our food was not very good. Perhaps our cooks were unfamiliar with a moveable feast but it was among the worst food I was ever served in the Army. Poorly prepared, often stone cold by the time we got back to our bunks to eat it, the meals, nevertheless, were the only diversion during the trip.

We had coffee at every meal. Scalding hot coffee presented a particular problem to every soldier in World War II. It was not really the awful coffee itself that presented the problem, but rather the container out of which we were to drink the bitter stuff.

Every soldier had a canteen. This canteen was carried in a lightly padded cloth cover that hung from the web waist belt, which also carried a first aid kit and ammunition. The canteen for obvious weight reasons was made of aluminum and while it did decrease weight, it provided a water container that froze its contents in the winter and punished us with a nice drink of hot water during the summer. Some clever engineer had also designed a drinking cup in which the canteen itself fitted. The canteen was slightly kidney shaped to fit the hip when being carried and of course the cup, which held about a half pint of liquid, was also kidney shaped. The cup was also made of aluminum with a rather thickly rolled lip all around it. By taking the cup off the bottom of the canteen we had for ourselves a basic drinking container. However, this same clever engineer, seeking absolutes, had designed a folding metal alloy handle that swung away from the bottom of the cup and locked into place with a sliding metal clip near the lip of the cup.

The problem that this created was obvious and would have been anticipated with anyone with even a little sense. The aluminum cup, once bent or dented, as they all soon became, provided a very insecure base for the sliding lock on the handle. By keeping one's thumb on the rolled aluminum lip, it was possible to prevent the lock from slipping, but once filled with scalding coffee, no person responsive to third degree burns could keep his thumb on a rapidly heating piece of aluminum for very long. Consequently, there was a lot of hurrying to put the cup down before the pain became unbearable. Those who didn't make it released their thumbs. The act of letting go was usually accompanied by an agonizing cry, followed by cursing when the cup collapsed against the handle and dumped the scalding coffee on the floor, the crotch or on anyone else unfortunate to be nearby at the time.

This sequence was repeated a thousand times as men attempted to make it back to a bunk against the constant flow of people trying to reach the mess car. If he made it back to his own car, the man was subject to the second serious fault of the magic aluminum cup. It appeared that the hidden function of the rolled aluminum lip was to collect all of the heat from any liquid, which was poured into the cup. The effect was similar to pressing a red hot curved piece of metal against the lips. The result was painful but often humorous. Most soldiers, particularly new ones, could be identified by the almost permanent smile that was burned into the corners of their lips. We looked like the happiest and most contented soldiers on earth, thanks to the wonders of an aluminum cup.

Some men finally filed off the thick aluminum lip but this merely gave them a destructive thin smile. I thought that without the thick lip burn, the smile looked more like a sneer, particularly when it only burned one side of the mouth. However, as the war progressed the aluminum cups were replaced by a stamped alloy one without a rolled lip, and the older cups became a collector's item, which signified that a man had been in the Army in the old burn days.

Except for chow, the trip was mostly uneventful. However, as we crossed the Mississippi and headed North into Tennessee, it began to get noticeably colder. On the fifth day there was some excitement as someone, peering through a small window in the mess car, saw some remnants of snow on the ground. There were many men who had never seen snow before and the sight was the major topic of conversation until we arrived late at night on a R.R. siding at Camp Forrest.

Camp Forrest was named after Bedford Forrest, the famous Civil War Confederate Cavalry General. I think it was named after him to punish him for fighting against the Union. Apparently they had to name it after someone and after looking the camp over carefully, someone suggested the most hated name in memory, Bedford Forrest.

It seemed to be mostly swampland dotted with Southern pines and a cloying mud, which must have been shipped from Flanders or from the ridges around Verdun. There were many warehouses, railroad spur lines and a baffling system of unconnected dirt roads, which were able to support heavy vehicles only in cold weather. The only interesting feature of the camp was the fact that it was a center for German prisoners of war who had been captured in Africa. These were men from the famous Africa Corps of General Rommel, the desert fox, and were considered elite troops. It was our first contact with the enemy.

The Germans were used as a labor force in what can only be described as an exercise in moving materials from one warehouse to another and then back again. We were, of course, curious to see these supermen and we noncoms vied for the opportunity to supervise the work details that used the Germans.

After we were settled at Camp Forrest for about a week, during which we exercised daily, went on short forced marches, had inspections, and checked out the little nearby town of Tullahoma, I got my opportunity.

I took a truck to the PW camp to pick up ten POW's to help move some boxes from warehouse A to warehouse B. The compound was set a little away from the main operational center of the camp and was surrounded by a high barbed wire fence with guard towers on each corner. Driving up to the gate, I announced my intentions and handed a surly Corporal my requisition for the prisoners. He directed me inside with a backhand wave at small groups of men assembled in the center of the PW cage. Several other trucks were picking up and loading men.

Before I could get very far a Sergeant wearing a pistol stopped me, took my requisition and then shouted some words in German. I stayed in the truck but could hear the scraping and banging coming from the rear as men boarded the open truck behind me. The Sergeant waved me out with a neat forehand after I had signed the papers signifying, I guessed, that I was now the proud but responsible owner of ten genuine Nazi's.

It was about 9:00 in the morning when we arrived at warehouse A, a short distance from the prisoner compound and predictably very close to warehouse B.

Backing into a loading dock, I turned off the engine, climbed down from the cab and walked back to have my first confrontation with the enemies of the American way of life.

I don't know what I had expected to see. I had never seen real foreigners before, even though I had grown up with the children of immigrants in Pittsburgh. The thought struck me for the first time that I was unarmed! What if they jumped me? Maybe these ten men had been planning this breakout for weeks, waiting only for the opportunity to kill with their bare hands or with weapons that they had cleverly made out of cardboard or sticks. I had heard how inventive and calculating Germans could be. After all, I had seen "Why We Fight." After climbing the steps to the loading dock, I realized that I had no option but to brazen it out. I cautiously walked to the truck, keeping in mind that, in case of attack, I could jump down from the dock and run like hell.

There were ten men sitting silently on the benches in the back of the truck, five on each side. They wore U.S. Army fatigues, just like me. The only difference was that on each leg, front and back, a large white P and W had been stenciled. The same held true for the jacket, front and back, it said, PW. Some of the Germans were wearing the shapeless U.S. Army fatigue caps, one or two of them wore faded pointed caps from the Africa Corps.

I stood at the back of the truck while we stared at one another. I tried to look stern but merciful. They looked bored, several looked slightly amused. For the most part they were tough looking guys. All of them were a good deal older than I.

It was amazing for if it hadn't been for their distinctive clothes, they looked just like everyone I had ever seen before. Some with glasses, thin, fat, brown eyes, blue eyes. Perhaps it was the age of these men, but they struck me, in a way I could not explain, as looking like schoolteachers.

Stepping back, I looked up and down the dock for someone to tell me what we were supposed to do. I had been told to find Sergeant Warner and report to him with my prisoners. There was no one on the dock and the only open door to the warehouse was about 100 feet away. I waited. The Germans waited. No one spoke. I practiced looking more stern and less merciful. I lit a cigarette, threw away the match with clear contempt, drew in a lung full of smoke in my best imitation of Humphrey Bogart, coughed, gagged, jumped around, bent over trying to breathe. Tears came to my eyes as I tried to draw in some air. Out of the corner of my bleary eye, I could see that some of the Germans were smiling.

Finally with a great wheezy gasp of air and one final convulsive explosive cough, I was able to breathe again. Looking at the cigarette with obvious disgust, I threw it away muttering, "Bad cigarette."

We waited in silence for about fifteen minutes while the POW's sat comfortably in the truck and while I struggled to regain my composure. I thought about moving the truck but there was no place I could move it except to another deserted dock space. I walked up and down importantly until at last one of the Germans who was wearing a peaked Africa Corps cap sighed audibly, leaned back on the bench and said calmly in perfect English, "Corporal, Sergeant Warner's office is through that door."

He pointed in the direction of the open door down the dock. I glared at him after partially recovering from my astonishment. "I know THAT!" I shouted a little hysterically.

He nodded and sighed again. After what I thought was the appropriate length of time to reestablish myself, I looked at my watch in exasperation and started off in the direction of the open door to the warehouse.

I had gone about halfway when I realized that I was walking away from my charges, leaving them to escape or to put into operation their clever plan for taking over Camp Forrest. I was committed; however, I couldn't go back. Instead I started walking sidewise like a crab watching the doorway and watching the truck. None of the Germans in the truck were watching me, they were talking quietly to one another.

Reaching the doorway, I peered inside hoping to see Sergeant Warner. Instead I saw only another POW sitting on a bench well inside the door. The fairly darkened warehouse was full of boxes and crates, but there was no one there to talk to except a Nazi soldier.

I hesitated in the doorway, uncertain. I needed to find Warner but I also felt compelled to watch the truck. Army trucks had no keys by this time, merely a switch, someone having figured out that the war might easily be lost while we all tried to find the right key to over two million trucks. Conscious, however, that any one of the Germans in the truck could easily jump down, drive off with the damned thing and take over the camp, I could see myself explaining this to the camp commander.

Contemplating this fact, I was startled when the POW sitting on the bench shouted, "Hey, Corporal, Warner's down there."

He pointed down a narrow aisle between two rows of stacked crates.

I took the risk, resisted the impulse to ask the POW to watch the truck for me, and quickly started down the aisle. No Warner. After going about what seemed like a block, I came to two absorbed POW's standing between the crates looking at something that one of them was

90

holding in his hand. Their backs were turned to me and they were speaking earnestly to one another.

Because of the narrowness of the aisle, I could not pass without some sort of contact. I came up behind them and cleared my throat to get their attention. They both turned to face me and I almost had a heart attack. The object, which the one was holding, was a U.S. Army issue Colt .45 automatic pistol. It was pointed directly at my stomach. I froze. There I stood in a darkened warehouse, seeing the enemy for the first time in my life, being killed. Before I could say a word the one with the pistol said, "Geladen?"

I could not speak; my tongue was stuck to my teeth. "Geladen?" he repeated.

A hoarse croak escaped from my mouth as I tried to imagine what the German words were for "I surrender, for Christ's sake, don't shoot!"

Apparently there was something about my face that eventually communicated to them that I was either going to faint, scream or urinate in my pants. The one with the gun looked down at his hand holding the gun and laughing, patted my shoulder and flipped the .45 expertly, handing me the pistol butt first. With trembling hand, I grabbed the gun in good Bogart private eye style and waving it at both of them, backed off a few feet in a half crouch.

"Hands up!" I shouted.

They were puzzled.

"Vas ist los?" the gun handler asked.

"Put your fucking hands up!" I screamed, "You're all under arrest!"

When I heard the words I was saying, I burst into laughter. The Germans seemed confused. However, laughing was probably the only thing I could have done at the moment to save us all from further embarrassment.

In a moment we all three laughed. I pretended that I had been joking and playfully spun the pistol on my finger. Naturally it came to a stop pointing at me. The Germans glanced at one another, rolling their eyes in mock despair. At that moment, Sergeant Warner appeared with a clipboard and six or eight POW's trailing after him. Standing there with the pistol pointed at myself, I said, "Sergeant, what do you want me to do?"

He looked at me carefully out of flintlike eyes and grunted, "Pull the trigger."

I waited for some slight sign of humor. There was none. I sheepishly handed the gun to him muttering something about taking it from the two Germans. Turning away from me, he said a few words in German to the POW's who had followed him. They all laughed. Facing me again, he asked sarcastically, "Where is your work detail, Corporal?"

At that moment I realized that I had completely forgotten the detail in the truck. Without a word I turned and ran for the doorway, which looked to be about a mile away. Bursting through it and skidding to a stop at the very edge of the dock, I looked quickly to see whether the truck was still there.

It was there with my ten charges sitting, relaxed and talking to one another. I waved for them to come over to me at the doorway and by the time they arrived, I was getting my breath back well enough to look stern but somewhat merciful again.

We went inside the warehouse and reported to Sergeant Warner who said for us to sit on the benches until he needed us. My POW's were already sitting on the benches but the English speaking one moved over to make space for me to join him. He was of medium height, but thin, with a weathered face and grey close cropped hair showing at the edges of his cap. We sat there for almost two hours. His name was Franz. To my astonishment, I learned that indeed he had been a school-teacher from Stuttgart. He had been in the Army for four years, was himself a Corporal and had not heard from or about his family for over a year. He was married with three children. He was a nice guy but said that he believed that Germany was really winning the war and that we Americans were being fed lies and propaganda about the way battles were going. He reached inside his shirt and brought out a copy of the Army newspaper, "Stars and Stripes." It was the latest issue, which I had not yet seen. On the front page was a report of the Russian front and of the German collapse around Stalingrad. He flatly stated that these were lies, that the German Army had already captured Moscow and the Russians were being pursued into Siberia. I looked closely at the battle map and article. It looked real enough to me. However, there was something very chilling in the confidence that the German displayed. His English was perfect and at the time, I had no doubt but that he absolutely believed that what he was saying was true. Even though there were aerial photographs of destroyed targets, he discounted the stories of the bombing raids on Germany. He seemed a little less sure of the falseness of these stories, however, and I remembered that his family was in Stuttgart.

"What is your name, Corporal?" he asked.

I told him and he replied that he knew some Keims near Freiberg on the Rhine River. We chatted about my ancestors who came from Bavaria; he seemed very interested and spoke of the religious persecution in the area about the time my great grandfather immigrated in 1850. He seemed glad to be a teacher again. Finally he leaned close to me and said softly, "You know, Wilhelm, you Americans are being used by the British, you should not be fighting us Germans—together Germany and America should be fighting the Russians."

I must have looked a little bit surprised, but he went on, "Mark my words, the day will come when the United States will have to fight the Communists!"

Then he said, almost to himself, "Americans and Germans are very much alike, our religion, our governments, our economy—the real danger to the world is Communism."

I looked closely at this enemy schoolteacher sitting next to me on a wooden bench in Camp Forrest, Tennessee. He seemed confident, but I could see that he was frightened about himself and his family. I realized then that he *knew* Germany was going to lose the war. I realized that with his final comments, he knew that Moscow had not been captured and that the German Army really was being thrown back at Stalingrad. He was a lonely and desperate man. As he put his face in his hands, I touched his German arm and tried to console him.

"It will be O.K., Franz," I said awkwardly. "If they ever do bomb Stuttgart, surely the people will be moved out into the country."

I certainly didn't know anything of the sort; I didn't even know at the time where Stuttgart was or even if there was countryside around it. Looking hopefully at me, he raised his head and asked expectantly, "Oh, do you think so?"

When I nodded, he quickly added, "Of course they will, the government wouldn't keep them inside the city, not women and children. My wife is a seamstress—she could live on a farm and help. The children are young but strong—they could help."

He paused, looking down closely at the stenciled P and W on his thighs. I could see tears at the corners of his eyes.

Warner appeared from around the crates and said gruffly as he entered his office, "Corporal, take these men back to the cage, I don't need them today."

When I stopped the truck in the compound, after a careful count of prisoners at the gate, I stepped to the rear in spite of the armed Sergeant who was trying to wave me away. As Franz jumped from the truck, he stopped in front of me briefly to smile shyly and say, "Good luck, Wilhelm, may you survive this terrible war."

"And luck to you, Franz," I replied.

I meant it.

That night in the P.X., I sat nursing a 3.2 beer trying to sort out in my mind what I had seen and heard that day. My friend, Holt, sat in silence with me for awhile and finally asked, "Now what the hell's the matter with you? You look like you think we're going to lose the war."

"Holt," I yelled over the self pitying twanging country music coming out of the jukebox, "I need to talk to you!"

"Let's get out of here," he shouted moving from the battered table.

We went outside and sat in the dark on the side steps of the P.X. The music faded somewhat into the distance. We weren't drunk. I told the whole story to him while he sat listening carefully to my feelings and reactions. He was a good listener and having a friend like him with whom I could discuss my most inner feelings, was not only unusual in the Army but it saved my mind for me. When I had finished, he said quietly, "I thought it was me. I worked with some of them today and it bothered me a great deal also."

"Let's remember," he added, "these guys were part of the old German Army, they were fighting in the desert with Rommel and simply can't believe that the war is going against them. They remember the golden conquest days of 1939."

"Also," he added, "for hundreds of years Germans have hated the Russians. World War I and the rise of Communism haven't helped at all. A German will say anything to get support against a Russian. They're desperately afraid of them."

I thought that over for awhile, but I also thought of Franz, the older Corporal from the African Corps, crying out of fear for his wife and children.

I sighed and said softly, "I only know that I met the enemy today, and he is us."

We walked back to the barracks in the growing chill of the dark November night. Neither of us had much more to say to one another.

The days at Camp Forrest were busy days. From the intensity of the training it was clear that we were getting ready to go to the war zone. We now assumed that since we were training under winter conditions that we were probably going to leave Tennessee and embark for England. We marched, exercised, ran combat courses and trained over again in poison gas drill. The November winter began to settle among the trees and an occasional snow flurry was no longer an oddity.

In the spring our battalion was moved from San Diego to the Pomona Fairgrounds, site of the Los Angeles county fair, where we took up our final physical conditioning prior to staging for overseas. It was rigorous and demanding. Some of the older men were transferred when it was decided that they could not maintain the pace. Any physical disabilities became apparent following a twenty mile forced march with 65 pounds of equipment to carry. Even though I thrived on the sheer torture of it, I had to admit that sometimes my legs and back hurt painfully when I lay on my cot following a forced march.

We cleaned brand new equipment, brought the battalion up to its assigned table of organization strength with replacements and waited for the orders to move.

Incredibly when the move orders finally came, we discovered that we were going to New Jersey for embarkation out of New York. It was to be my fifth interminable train ride across the country in slightly over a year of active service.

Again it was the San Bernardino pass at twilight, by now a familiar sight, this time with a slight difference, however. This time I might, headed as we were to the great war to the East, just possibly never to return to the pass again.

Standing beside the halted train, several of us gazed out over the great misty Los Angeles plain, each quiet with his thoughts kept to himself. In my mind there was but one thought. I might die as a result of where I was going. The thought was not the childhood game of detached fascination with death. The made-up, but never believed, secretly thrilling imagining of what it is like to be dead, the scene viewed in the child mind as though he were a spectator, not a participant. My thought was a straight, clean thought; I might actually die.

I was sobered as I stood there, arms folded across my chest in the canyon chill of the early evening breeze coming up the slope from San Bernardino. I was the last to climb the steps into the train when the harried conductor shouted for us to board, and as I did so, I turned and took one last look back at the smudged basin, which was the living place for the people I loved. I felt them there, all of them. I could see my father sitting in the living room reading the paper, glasses on the end of his nose; my mother polishing the kitchen after dinner; my sister in her room combing her long blond hair and getting ready for the inevitable date. They did not know that I was on this train, at this place, going to New Jersey. But I knew, and as the door crashed shut in the train vestibule, I lifted my hand in a slight signal to them all that I was off to a war from which I might not return.

CHAPTER VI

THE CONVOY

We boarded a Liberty ship troop transport bound for England in the spring of 1944. During our short stay at Camp Dix, New Jersey, a staging camp for the port of embarkation, we trained in climbing down nets into smaller boats. The exercise was conducted in order to provide the troops with the experience in the process of abandoning ship and included demonstrations in survival in fuel oil and gasoline burning on the surface of the water. A large concrete lined lake had been constructed with the side of a simulated troopship sitting in it. We climbed down the net ladders a few at a time and then jumped into landing craft with full equipment plus life jackets. It was awkward and somehow meaningless, since none of us could imagine that if torpedoed, we would dutifully collect our packs, rifles, gas masks, helmets and entrancing tools before trying to jump onto a small pitching life raft in the middle of the Atlantic Ocean. The drills for fire were conducted by having a group of well trained men swim under water, which had gasoline burning on its surface. Staging troops sat on bleachers and observed while an officer, using a public address system, explained the procedure. A man in the demonstration would surface in the flames and by vigorous splashing, clear the fire away from his face long enough to breathe and to submerge quickly again. The area of fire was usually a few square yards and the gasoline would soon burn off the surface. None of us was really convinced by the demonstration since we all knew that tankers at sea disgorged millions of gallons of fuel over a surface that could easily extend for a mile or more. We recognized that few men, if any, could sustain the surface and submerge routine for any extended period of time. The Army did want us to know, however, that it was humanly possible to survive water fire. The demonstration and abandon ship drill were apparently part of a psychological effort to give the troops some comfort and a feeling of safety while crossing the enemy infested sea lanes.

We also did close drill, exercised, took a few short forced marches in the rolling hills of New Jersey, and of course were inspected several times for venereal disease. The battalion was at Camp Dix for about two weeks before we were ordered to maximum security, not allowed off the post and cautioned closely about secrecy. Mail was carefully censored and phone calls were not allowed. After three days of this total isolation, we boarded a train one spring evening that took us to a large empty warehouse on the Jersey waterfront. Once there, we were ordered to sit in lettered sections, squads, platoons and companies together. Each man was given a number, which was chalked on the front of his helmet by a group of boarding officers, who took great pains to check each man's identification dog tags before the number was applied. We were warned not to smudge the number or move from our positions, which would put us out of numerical sequence. All numbers were checked twice while we sat on the cement floor, surrounded by our belongings.

The lighted warehouse was very old with high riveted steel rafters covered by corregated rusting iron. Large doors led outside to a dock area, which was a beehive of blazing light activity during the night.

The sounds of rumbling winches, groaning cranes, and shouting men all filtered into the warehouse where 2,000 men sat on the floor with an important number marked on each head. The night was a long one, a few men tried to sing but the excitement of being a part of the drama of the gigantic effort to move masses of men and equipment to war was so overwhelming that mostly we sat in silence or in subdued conversation. Rumors were wild; we were going on an aircraft carrier, we were really going on a large submarine; we weren't going at all but being recalled to Santa Anita in California. I actually started the California rumor myself as a joke but was not surprised to have it whispered back to me by a man in M company when I visited the makeshift latrine two hours later.

Our company clerk, with great assurance, swore that he had seen the orders, which could take us through the Panama Canal and on to Hawaii. Only a few men slept. At about 4:00 a.m. we were whistled into the company and battalion formation. Again our numbers were checked for sequence. Everyone was present and in proper order. Even the company officers were numbered, the lowest number for Company L, which was 118, was chalked on Captain Smart's helmet. The officers were required to sit on the floor in numerical sequence with their men even though one or two of them seemed uncomfortable. After the company check of numbers, we found ourselves standing, our equipment hanging on us, our duffle bags stacked in front of each man ready to be slung over the shoulder. The troopship boarding officers continued to confer near one of the doors leading to the dockside area. Sheaves of papers on clipboards were flipped over and over as final checks were made and sums were totalled and rechecked. We stood for almost two hours after the boarding officers unexpectantly left the warehouse. We were, of course, not allowed to sit on our duffle bags nor were we permitted to leave the formation. The Major in charge of the boarding team, using a public address system, had made it very clear that no one was to sit on anything or leave his assigned mathematical position. After about an hour of standing with nothing happening, the drama of the occasion began to wear a little thin. Groans and complaints began to be heard from the battalion standing in formation in the warehouse. Two thousand men began to express some form of hostility. We had water in our canteens but had been instructed that no man was to board the troop transport without a full canteen of water. Most of us, now knowing what might happen if his canteen "be not full" when he approached the gangplank, resisted the need for water. There were many men, on the other hand, who freely drank their water. We had no food, nor had anyone from the boarding team even mentioned food. At 6:00 a.m. the Major and his entourage strode importantly to the front of the battalion and announced that we would again check our numbers.

This incredible announcement was greeted with hoots, jeers and profanity from the battalion. Even some of our officers joined in because of their own discomfort and frustration. A process of enlisted men disapproval had developed during the war years among the civilian soldiers. It was both explicit and effective. If there was displeasure over inefficiency, stupidity or an unpopular order, someone from the group would shout out the number 48! This person was usually undetected since this particular process of disapproval was practiced only in large groups, such as company formation. Once "48" was heard, the entire company or group would shout in unison "49!" and again "50!" in cadence. The numbers were followed by everyone yelling at the top of his voice, "Some shit!" The word "some" was elongated into *so-om-m-m-e,* so as to give explosive emphasis to "shit," which was barked out to complete the rhythm of the sequence. "48, 49, 50, *somme* shit" was a very popular expression in the American civilian Army of World War II and it was heard very often.

If there ever was an occasion to use the chant, it was in the warehouse after six hours of sitting on cement and standing in formation and then having numbers checked for the fourth time. The chant was used with thunderous effect by an entire battalion making the corregated roof thrum and echo.

Our battalion commander, "Old Floor Mat," was horrified by this mutinous behavior, of course. He signalled the company commanders to silence the men and we quickly became quiet. No one could really care since our point had been made and we all felt a little better for having made it. Undaunted, although a little unnerved by the incident, the boarding officers, some looking up at the warehouse roof from time to time as though to reassure themselves that it was going to stay there, made their fourth number check. It took thirty more minutes as the teams canvassed all four companies at the same time. It could have been worse, the Major could have made the check all by himself.

At last a whistle was blown; we were called to attention, ordered to shoulder our duffle bags and in single file, beginning with number one, "Old Floor Mat" himself, we went single file out into the beautiful spring morning onto the loading dock.

To our surprise the ship that we were to board was right outside the door to the warehouse. A single gangway lead from the dock up to the deck of what looked to be a very huge boat. It seemed like the side of a building to those of us who had never been on an ocean going vessel before.

As each man stepped on the gangplank, an officer checked the helmet number against a roster. He called out the last name, "Keem."

I replied, as I had been instructed to do with my rank, first name and Army serial number. I was then allowed to walk up the gangplank to be met at the top by another officer who repeated the exercise and then waved me to a line of sailors who formed a gauntlet leading to an entrance down into the hold of the ship. Struggling as I was with my equipment and dufflebag, I had little time to notice very much about the ship except that the deck seemed very cluttered with cables, hatch covers, crates and cardboard trash.

Stumbling along behind the man ahead of me, I heard them say to one of the sailors, "Is it always this rough on the ocean?"

There was no movement of the ship at all, of course, and while I laughed, the crew member seemed to think that it was not at all funny.

When I reached the gangway ladder that lead into the hold, I almost fell over the high step that separates all deck area from any entrance into the interior of a ship. For a newcomer to ocean travel, it was a surprise common to all to find doorways that required stepping through, so a sailor stood beside the entrance and dutifully caught each man by the arm before he could trip and pitch head first into the cavernous interior of the hold. The ladder down was very steep although there were narrow iron steps instead of rungs and the angle was more step-like instead of being similar to ladder rungs. I went down four separate levels into the hold of the ship growing more and more apprehensive as I realized that I was well below the water line, before a yawning sailor stopped my descent and laconically waved me toward a narrow passage leading to a doorway to another part of the interior of the vessel. By this time I had no notion as to whether I was going to the front or the back of the ship, the ladders having alternated in directions coming down. As it turned out, it was toward the bow, but it didn't matter anyway—we were below the water line.

At last I entered the compartment to which our company had been assigned and put down my duffle bag with relief. The compartment was really the fourth level of the forward hold of the Liberty ship. The floors, which were normally removable covers allowing access straight down from the open deck above for the loading of cargo, were sealed and the space that could be used for cargo was fitted with racks of bunks for troops. The cargo space of the ship then became four deck levels with bunks on each level. Our company was on the bottom level with three additional decks above us packed with soldiers of our battalion. Pack is the right word because our 2,000 man battalion plus part of an engineer regiment was transported across the Atlantic in this one ship. There were over 3,000 troops on board.

Bunks were stacked four high on each deck allowing no more than about eighteen inches between the bunks. The bunks themselves were made out of stretched canvas, which quickly sagged with any application of weight. At the time I weighed about 150 pounds but was unfortunate to have Lelly, my companion from Camp Forrest, occupy the canvas bunk immediately above me. He weighed in at about 190. Within hours I had the feeling that Lelly and I were sharing the same bunk. I solved the problem eventually by not attempting to turn over while sleeping. I couldn't have turned over anyway. Lelly's butt was on my stomach.

Our duffle bags and equipment had to be lashed to the end of our bunk space. Space was inadequate for this challenge but by shifting some of the extra clothing and personal items into our bunks we could cope. Absolutely nothing was allowed on the deck floor because it interfered with sweeping that we were told was done every day.

It was dark in the bottom of a ship below the water line. Light was provided on the bulkheads, that is, around the sides and ends of the compartment but no overhead light was available because of the construction problems in dealing with a theoretical open hold. The light that we received came from open bulbs covered by a heavy wire mesh. The lights were never all shut off, however, because of the imminent need to abandon ship without notice. No one ever explained how the thousands of men could climb those steep ladders in an emergency with any possibility of survival. Consequently, the compartment was generally quiet with young men who tried not to think of what death would be like trapped inside a dark iron tomb, drowning in panic.

When I found my assigned bunk, I discovered a life jacket on it. Made of grey cloth and stuffed with kapok, it was extremely bulky around the front of the body and the back of the neck with a cloth belt that came around from the back of the jacket and fastened with a simple metal snap lock. We immediately tried them on, parading around looking like turkeys the day before Thanksgiving. We were to learn shortly that we were to have our life jackets with us at all times while we were at sea; we were not to sit on them, nor were we to use them as pillows while sleeping. In other words the jacket was to be a constant annoyance and inconvenience at *all* times. Most men wore them because it was the easiest way to carry the damned thing around. However, few people fastened the belt so that in coming down the ladders, the loose metal fastener would make an insistent "clinking" sound as it struck each of the iron steps. My most compelling memory of passing from one continent to another on American troopship is one of a rhythmic "chink, chink, chink," of those belt buckles on the steps.

Nervousness caused by the ever present fear instilled by the knowledge of a possible watery death resulted in 3,000 men constantly flowing back and forth like the trapped animals, which we had become. The sound of the belt buckles never stopped, but like the trained ticking of a somber clock became the constant reminder of our mortality.

There was a latrine next to our compartment. It was the embodiment of functionality. The lack of privacy was typical of all military latrines but this one had an additional surprise in store for our company. While the ship was tied to the dock, the long trough like urinals, flushed constantly by seawater, were satisfactory. Once at sea, however, the pitching of the ship was to cause enormous urine and saltwater tidal waves that had nowhere to go but to cascade upon the men in the latrine and eventually to find their way into the compartment housing our company. Later, as seasick men staggered into the latrine to throw up in the urinal, they innocently added other body wastes into the sloshing mass of liquid that made its way inexorably into the troop compartment. After the first day at sea, the odor, which simply defeated every air molecule in the compartment, was sickening. The combination of urine, vomit and stopped up toilets, combined with the simple presence of 200 tightly confined, unbathed men made the experience of breathing a process of extreme self control.

The "clinking" of belt buckles, the experience of never being further than arm lengths away from another human being who was grimly frightened, and the horrendous odor of body waste created an extended voyage of tension and despair.

I have read that a 19th century slave ship could be smelled on the sea air while still out of sight over the horizon. There is, in my mind, no doubt but that the story is absolutely true.

We were fed twice a day, a late breakfast and an early dinner. The food was served in a stand up interior, no window mess hall, which our compartment visited at scheduled times. Metal trays and ceramic coffee mugs were provided for fairly good food and the worst coffee I ever tasted.

As seasickness increased on the restless waters of the spring Atlantic, there were fewer and fewer people in the mess hall but with the bulky life jackets the room seemed to be always crowded. Most men ate quickly in apprehensive silence.

During daylight hours we were to be permitted on the open deck with serious restrictions as to where we were allowed to be. We could not interfere with the merchant marine crew nor be in the way of the trained Navy gun crews who served the gun tubs, which were placed around the perimeter of the ship. Officers, of course, had special cabin space and had certain upper deck areas reserved for them. It was always with a deep bitterness that we enlisted men, jammed together like cattle in a small deck area, gazed up to the officer's deck to see one or two of them strolling in open space or leaning on the railing in relaxed comfort.

Seasickness was a problem. One of the men from Arkansas in the 1st squad became ill before we put to sea. He remained in his bunk throughout the voyage, never eating, growing constantly weaker from dehydration. His dilemma was apparently caused by his mental attitude. However, knowing this did not console him. The ship's medical team visited him occasionally with advice to get fresh air.

At least thirty to fifty percent of the troops on board were seasick at one time or another and I must admit that the sight of someone else throwing up under the conditions that we suffered on board did nothing to keep a carefully settled stomach from joining in. I was never seasick but like most others the fear of death and the sickness of the omnipresent tension was never completely gone from my mind.

I threw my heavy gear on my bunk just moments before Radich passed the word that we would chow down in ten minutes. There was time enough to look around a little, try on the life jacket and argue with Lelly about who was to get what space for the storage of duffle bags. We ate in a good mood, pleased with the quality of food and with what we all believed was the open ocean stability of the ship.

Having had little or no sleep during the night in the warehouse, most of us returned immediately to our bunks and fell into deep sleep. During the afternoon I was awakened by an enormous shuddering of the ship. I knew at once that we were sinking as did many others who began to cry out, some still asleep. We were not sinking, of course, as we soon discovered. The ship had merely started up its engines. The shuddering was to become an all too familiar sensation for the next interminable days, shattering our earlier confidence, which we had expressed when we were on a stable platform. Men looked at one another with silent apprehension. We felt the iron cave in which we were encased move sidewise in a slipping manner.

Almost on signal, many of us, grabbing our life jackets, made for the ladders. If we were underway to the big war, we would at least see New York for the last time. Climbing the ladders to the open deck, we were surprised and a little angry to discover the doors guarded by an armed guard who would not let us out on deck. Returning to our compartment we were met by Lt. Harding, the only company officer who ever came into our living area during the entire voyage. He told us that for security reasons no soldiers were allowed on deck during the departure of troopships. Spies could be lurking on docks, bridges and in tall buildings supposedly with the power to signal enemy submarines lying in wait to torpedo prizes like us. We listened in awed silence and felt the thickness of fear that filled the darkened compartment and left a metallic taste in the back of the throat.

One by one we returned to our bunks. The ship shuddered in a rhythmic fashion as a slight roll began to accompany the subtle forward motion of the vessel. In the dimness we lay in whispered conversations, each man in his own way fighting back the ugly signals of approaching death. A few old jokes and chants were called out by the company comedians but these were received by a lack of response. Finally all conversation stopped. Men drifted off into sleep while others like me stared in the semi-darkness, startled to discover that in the silence one could actually hear the hissing sound of water as it moved along the sides of the ship.

I thought of this particular ship. Made in a shipyard in a matter of weeks, it was called a liberty ship. Workers had swarmed like insects across its hull, sections had been welded together in workshops and then boldly lifted into place to be in turn welded to other sections. Fitters, riveters, electricians, plumbers, woodworkers and finally painters, working around the clock, had assembled this marvelous piece of technology like a jigsaw puzzle. This marvel was the epitome of the American industrial genius. No challenge had been too great for the industrial giant, which was America. I tried very hard to be proud and impressed but at no time in my life have I ever wished harder to be someplace else other than during my time on that troopship. Even Camp Forrest seemed like a pleasant summer camp compared to the experience.

I was awakened by Holt who was shaking me by the shoulder. "Hey, Keim," he said, "let's go to chow."

I looked at him for moments, realizing that the ship was not only rolling from side to side but that it seemed also to be bucking forward and backwards. Holt was holding on to the metal frame of my bunk to keep himself from falling. In the dimness I could see his face. He was smiling.

"You are the craziest bastard I ever knew," I said at last. I added, "Don't you know that we are in the process of dying?"

Still smiling, he replied slowly, "Hell, yes, let's go to chow first, then we'll die."

I kicked my way out of the bunk and in a rare show of emotion, I put my hand on his shoulder pretending to help myself down from the bunk.

He was never one for any display of emotion but this time instead of gently pulling away as he had done in the past, he just nodded in recognition of the fact that if we were to survive this voyage we would need one another. We stood beside the bunks, unsmiling, for several moments.

Together we went to chow. The mess hall was thick with heat and the pitch and roll of the ship was much more noticeable in the crowded and noisy dining area. Cups slid around on the stand up tables. Coffee spilled. Soon men began bolting through the doors to be sick in the corridors just outside the mess hall. One man never made it to the door. Looking at the glutinous mass on my tray, which had been identified as "hash" by one of the Negro servers, I began to have serious misgivings about my alarmed stomach. Looking up at Holt, I discovered that he too was having some difficulty with his resolve. We both nodded and without a word dumped our food in a nauseating garbage container before we left the steam and stench of the mess hall to make our way back down to the compartment.

"Chink, chink," went our belt buckles.

The hold somehow seemed cooler in comparison to the heat of the mess hall. There was an omnipresent card game going on in one of the darkened rows between the bunks. Subdued yelling and cursing could be heard as cards were slapped down on the deck to break flushes or to destroy a developing straight. The light was poor so there were many arguments among the players. Gambling was forbidden in the Army but I witnessed more of it in the service than I ever saw on the Las Vegas strip on a good night. Knowing Holt's compulsion for cards and dice, I quickly led him away from the scene suggesting that instead of joining the game that we try to get up on deck.

"You go ahead, I'll be up in a minute," he said, licking his lips.

"Be careful, Don," I replied turning to leave.

"Hey, Keim," he called before I could reach the compartment ladder. I stopped and turned, hoping that he had changed his mind. He hadn't, however, instead he grinned and said, "Don't die without me."

When I reached the doorway leading to the deck, I was astonished to discover that it was lashed open and unguarded. I quickly passed through it to the outside air. My first impression was one of fresh wind and cleanliness. My second impression was one of intense beauty. Having never been on the open sea before, I was at once exhilerated by the immensity of the sky and by the almost purified feeling that came in the presence of the sea itself.

Rushing across an almost deserted deck, I found a short strip of railing between two stacks of deck liferafts. It was late afternoon with the sun going down behind us. By leaning over the rail, I could see ahead to the blue black sky coming up from the East. Turning quickly I could see the side wake of our ship swirling slightly as it deepened from white to blue green. I was startled to discover that we were surrounded by other ships. We were, of course, in a convoy but I had assumed that we would not form into one until we were well at sea and here we were barely out of the port of New York and had already joined another twenty ships that were all headed East in four stately columns. I stood at the railing for over two hours with all of the human spirit that was in me reaching out to make contact with the overwhelming spirit of the discovery of the sea. Fascinated, I watched the waves pass the sides of the high ship. I would pick out a point as we moved through the water and watch it as it transferred its energy field along the towering side of our ship. I repeated the experience of watching a spot dozens of times. Birds wheeled and veered in the fading light. The sky became darker and blazing stars began to appear in the East. A loud speaker shattered my thoughts for a moment as it proclaimed that blackout procedures were now in effect. The announcement was followed by a bustle of activity as civilian sailors slammed porthole covers shut, dogged them down and dropped thick canvas covers over passageway entrances.

"The smoking lamp is out," stated the no nonsense loud speaker.

I stripped my cigarette and dropped the crumbs over the side, watching in vain to see if I could follow the travels of the tiny roll of paper as it traversed the length of the ship. I began to get cold and I was grateful for the kapok life preserver, which was of some use as insulation against the cold. Reluctant to leave my secluded little shelter, I merely rested my arms on the railing and drank the sweetness of the air in the absolute beauty of sea and sky. Claustrophobic fears began to drain from my mind. Fascinated, I noticed the flecks of phosphorescence in the water, tiny creatures disturbed for an instant by this mighty iron behemoth bound for war. In my wonderous mood, I pondered the insignificance and the idiocy of man in the face of the momentum of this awesome nature. Here we were with our tiny, meaningless warsome venture scraping against the grain of the dignity of the universe. Somehow seen in this perspective, my own life and the possibility of death seemed not quite so important. It was important, of course, but even during frightened reflective times like these, I, like all the others, while knowing about death, could not really believe that one of those brown bundles flecked with red could ever actually be me. Only later did I understand that only by the merest of chance did I remain alive and that in fact I *could* be one of those bleeding bundles. The fear that

I felt on the troopship was a generalized sort of fear, still far removed from the sad knowledge soon to come that death was as real as life and just as arbitrary.

Watching the water, I became aware that many men now crowded the deck. Murmurs of appreciation for the open sky could be heard and soon I noticed that the flow of men was moving toward the bow of the ship. I left my private world and joined the shuffling crowd that moved along in the darkness cracking ankles on unfamiliar deck obstructions. Mild curses and familiar accusations punctuated a strange warmth of comradeship that seemed to envelop all of us as we moved along. From the man next to me, I learned that a fairly famous singer was on board with the engineers unit and that he was going to do some songs on the forward hatch near the bow. I had several of his records at home and had been impressed by his talent for the contemporary popular music of the times. We found places to sit on the deck and in the growing clarity of simple starlight, we could see the vocalist who, with no musical accompaniment, sang several beautiful lilting ballads for our pleasure. His accompaniment was only the swishing of the sea and the throbbing of the living ship. The stars pitched and rolled. The freshening wind felt wonderful. The deck plates thrummed comfortably and for minutes it seemed impossible to believe that we were in the slightest danger.

For his last number he sang "I'll Be Seeing You," a wartime song of the promise of return. Several hundred silent men whose lives were joined together on a tiny chip of iron, pitching and yawing on the face of the deep, black and unconcerned Atlantic Ocean wept to themselves. It was a poignant moment and when he finished, his beautiful tenor voice trailing across the water to an echoed silence, we just sat for many minutes without moving, watching the rolling stars.

During the night we were apparently joined by two other groups of ships for in the early morning light, we could see through the mist that the convoy had now doubled in size. Our ship was near one edge of the convoy itself in the second row about halfway back in our column. This made it difficult to see the entire convoy as the ships wallowed along at the speed of the slowest ship in the fleet. Pitching up and down it was impossible to see everything at one time. I doubt if anyone on board, except for the ship's officers, ever knew just how large the convoy was. We were freighters, tankers and some other vessels of undetermined design; many flew flags of different nations. We were accompanied by two baby flattops, flying British flags. These aircraft carriers were Liberty ships that had been converted to catapult launch capability and carried only two or three expendable spitfires to be used against submarines. The carriers could not recover their planes on the very small decks so, in theory, the pilot would ditch next to the carrier and only he would be plucked from the ocean, abandoning his aircraft after having sunk the submarine.

There were also several destroyers and light cruisers that circled the convoy in a constantly moving protective screen. The destroyer, blowing black smoke, could move at spectacular speeds and it was great fun to watch them slide by the columns like lean grey watchdogs, bounding along with signal blinkers flashing, mothering their group of slow retarded children with silent but loving attention.

The convoy was silent. Separation of several hundreds of yards between ships and columns eliminated communication except by the use of signal flags and lamps. During the daylight hours the ships maintained position through visual sighting but it was not uncommon for ships to drift or stray out of their assigned spot during the blacked out night. We experienced one near collision at night when the sailor who was on our ship's bow lookout went to sleep and we came within fifty feet of crashing into the tanker just ahead of us in our column. If a soldier who was walking the night deck because he couldn't sleep hadn't awakened the lookout in time, we might all have perished.

The most dangerous times for submarine attack were the early morning and evening hours. During these times each day the crew was on alert, the gun tubs were manned and all troops stood by to try to abandon ship should it become necessary. There was a tenseness during these few hours each day, which was unmatched at any other time. When our destroyer escort was off our flank we felt better but often the protective screen would race off to the other edges of the convoy leaving us with a deep sense of vulnerability. Imagined torpedo tracks were seen, periscopes that were not there were sighted and reported, and everyone on board was afraid. It was a curious contradiction to experience fear during the period of the day, which was often the most serene and beautiful times on the ocean. The mornings were generally calm with occasional mists or fog that was burned off by a probing cyclopic sun. As the sun disappeared into fresh morning sky, the convoy, coming as it did from the mantle of darkness, would seem to be unbelievably visible. The ships, strung out of position because of the problems of the nighttime steering, seemed taller in the water, each broadcasting an incredible clarity in the clear bright morning sunlight. During both the morning and evening watch period, troops crowded the deck, partly out of fear of being trapped below in the event that a torpedo found its way to the ship, partly out of the excitement and drama generated by the fear itself, but mostly I think out of a sort of appreciation for the crystaline beauty of the moment.

The evening alert was often set against a dazzling cumulus cloud sunset with long rays of the sun radiating up to the sky and down to the ocean. During one particular beautiful sunset, I heard a man say,

"You almost expect big block letters to come up on the horizon and say *the end.*" On these occasions, one could sense an almost physical lessening of tension as the sun disappeared behind us and the great expanse of sky gradually turned to a protective black.

We practiced abandon ship drills but they were an exercise in pure theory. It was impossible to get all the men on deck at one time. There were too many of us to line up by life rafts and railings, and the life boats were reserved for the merchant marines and gun crews anyway. We simply gathered our gear on klaxon signals, put on our life jackets and those of us who could not get to the deck stood in line on the ladders and in the compartments. When the drill was over we were told by loud speaker to return to our compartments. The 3,000 "chink-chink-chinks" were deafening, almost obscuring the noise of curses, grumbling, complaints and the appropriate chant, "48-49-50." Looking up four flights of zigzag ladders crowded with men and knowing that on the three inner decks above us there were more men ready to fight their way onto the steps, gave us the impression that only the crew in the superstructure had any hope of ever abandoning that ship and getting off alive. There was little comfort in the abandon ship drill.

We seldom talked to the civilian merchant marines who were the crew of the vessel. They were very busy, going from one job to another, perhaps indifferent to the thousands and thousands of troops that they had seen on their many voyages. We also distained speaking to them. They were, we had been conditioned to believe, very successful draft dodgers who had succeeded in staying out of the service by taking a high paying job on a merchant ship. Rumors were that a seaman made over $400 a month. At the time I was making slightly over $50 a month as a Sergeant in the Army. This feeling about the merchant marines gradually diminished on the voyage. Most of us came to understand that what they did was to risk their lives in a very definite way. I knew one thing; no amount of money would have ever gotten me to voluntarily take the place of one of those tight lipped, hollow eyed merchant seamen.

The convoy, in spite of its slowness, hobby-horsed its agonizing way across the Atlantic Ocean without incident. We heard thudding depth charges being dropped once near the front of the convoy but were never told whether it was a real submarine scare, just a Navy practice, or Lt. Jarvis. In fact, we were never told anything, not even our destination. Loud speakers told us what to do but I do not recollect that any usable information ever emanated from that hateful device.

Rumors about our destination were, of course, passed around like a well-worn but familiar garment, embellished as suited the teller and reembellished again by the listener who hastened to become the reteller.

We were going to Africa, to England, to the Mediterranean, to Iceland, to South Africa, even to Russia as an attack force. It often

108

seemed that the more bizarre the story, the more insistent became the teller. One could almost learn to judge reasonableness and truth by observing the intensity of the teller. The greater the insistence and sincerity, the greater the probability that the person was lying. We had one fellow, however, who was a complete enigma. His name was Senson; he had red hair, and he came from the Bronx. He was the epitome of the "dead pan" and the actual physical transformation that came over his face when he was telling something confidential was frightening to watch. He was also one of those apparently nearsighted individuals who had to stand very close to a person in order to see him. The close proximity of a person who was doing a Dr. Jekyll number was always unsettling. Senson would walk up so that his face was within an inch or two of mine and say, "Ju hear?"

"No, Senson, I have not heard," I would reply, trying, without success to back away from him. He would follow, stepping on my toes. Once I had said to him in exasperation, "Senson, if we're going to dance, you've *got* to let me lead. I don't know your steps."

Unperturbed, he would calculate that he had my wide-eyed attention and then he would transform. Remaining quiet, sometimes holding my arm in a claw-like grip so that I would not get away, he would narrow his eyes until they were almost closed. His long reddish eyelashes would caress his high cheek bones as he adjusted his face into one of absolute deathlike composure. Not a muscle twitched, not a vein throbbed, no pulse could be detected. He would then whisper in a hollow prophet-like voice through lips that appeared closed around a mouth, which did not move. It was eerie to watch. Even his throat did not move when he spoke. The first time he transformed for me, I looked behind him, convinced that he had someone back there performing a ventriloquist act. Senson certainly looked like a wooden dummy. However, it was hard not to believe this apparition even when he told you the most impossible rumors. There was something of a spirit world about him, as though he was possessed by a higher authority who was using him to spread wisdom and truth.

Late one night there was a red glow on the horizon behind us. The next morning we were told by one of the Navy gunners that a tanker, with mechanical troubles, had dropped back out of the convoy and apparently had been sunk by a prowling submarine. It was a sobering incident and we treated the merchant sailors with a little more respect as they hurried through their duties with no show of expression on their faces.

Two days later the freighter in the next column off our left flank began to flutter flags in a great show of agitation as it dropped out of the column and fell behind the convoy rows. It too was having mechanical trouble and the convoy had no option but to go on without her.

There was a moving moment as all of the ships in the convoy in a simple sign of farewell blew their steam whistles. The flat wailing echo of countless whistles and horns cracked back and forth across the surface of the heaving ocean in a sad goodbye to a dying companion. Men could be seen standing resolutely on the deck of the dead vessel as it seemed to slide down and away from us. One man near the bow of the stricken ship waved a tiny white hand, perhaps to a friend or perhaps as a goodbye to life as the freighter wallowed from the convoy. It was soon gone from sight to a fate that we did not want to think about.

One sunny afternoon I worked my way forward and undetected, stood at the very front of the ship. The unmanned gun tub towered over my head behind me but I leaned on the absolute prow of the troopship, buffeted by the strong clean wind that virtually howled out of the sea to assault my impertinence. It was exhilerating but also frightening. The up and down movement was exaggerated to the extreme from this position, as occasionally we crashed into the surface of the water as the ship plunged downward. Salt spray cascaded onto me, feeling fresh in its coldness.

Turning to leave, I noticed on the gunnel next to the anchor port a small bronze plaque that piqued my curiosity. Kneeling down to it, I read, "To the American LST 541, the best friend the enemy ever had, Operation Torch, 1942."

Puzzled by the plaque, I found a merchant marine next to the forward hatch who was willing to answer my questions. As he worked coiling some line, he growled, "That damned LST almost sunk us off the Africa Coast as we were unloading troops."

"Was it at night?" I asked.

"Hell, no. Broad daylight. The son of a bitch came off the beach and hit us head on. We took a lot of water."

I followed with another question, "Did the LST sink?"

"No such luck. The dumb bastard backed away and hotfooted it out of there. The skipper got his number though and that Lt.J.G. commanding the tub got a real chewing out."

He looked out over the ocean for a minute and with a far away look on his face said softly, "We did get a few good days in Southhampton out of it though, took us a week to get up the coast with full pumps and about four days leave while they worked her over in dry dock. Yeah," he added, "that old 541 boat was a real piss cutter."

I was to remember the conversation several weeks later in what was for me one of the most incredible coincidences of the war.

After twelve days of steaming Northeast, during which time we became almost used to the smells, the sounds and the fear, we came within sight of the Irish coast. British aircraft began to appear in the sky regularly and the tension lessened among the crew and the gunners

110

as covers were put over the guns and lashed down. We waved to the low flying RAF planes as they roared by the convoy at mast level. We had made it. The ships in the convoy scattered, some going North, some South and a few of us headed around Northern Ireland and made steam for Scotland. Whistles and horns were blown and in the shelter of the headlands where the seas were calmer, we could even hear some faint cheering from crews of other ships who knew that one more safe voyage had been made.

There was much activity on the ship as we passed down through the Irish Sea on our way to the city of Glasgow. Two other troop freighters and a tanker accompanied us in company with one of our beloved destroyers from our convoy screen. Every four hours or so an RAF flying boat would skim along with us, dipping its wings in salute and showing flickering signal lamps. Seeing the bright colorful roundels of the RAF gave us all a tremendous boost of confidence and a twinge of comradeship with the British. We felt that the British had been fighting for almost five years and that they knew how to protect convoys. Being in British waters, in the physical presence of real fighting veterans somehow made us all feel more secure and gave us a feeling that, at last, we were really a part of the war. Certainly the sight of the green coastlines after those twelve days on the open ocean created a sense of joviality. There was lighthearted pushing and shoving, jokes were heard, and for the first time in all those days, laughter could be heard in all of the compartments of the ship.

We cleaned up. For almost two weeks we had been left alone—few inspections, no pressure to keep absolute track of everything, and very little encouragement to keep things clean. We were in a good mood, however, so arguments over who had whose gear were plentiful but not serious. I never did find my gas mask, which was too bad since I had a nice supply of smoking tobacco stuffed inside the face piece. We sorted out the gear, put on our cleanest fatigues, swept out the compartment on the orders of the merchant marines and waited impatiently to get off the ship.

Finally we slid into a vast harbor filled with ships, dropped anchor about a mile from land, and waited. In about an hour, during which the troops crowded the deck anxious for a glimpse of Scotland, a small motorboat approached the side of the ship with a civilian in a flapping black raincoat, standing precariously on the small open deck in front of the open cockpit.

With a throaty roar the motor boat reversed its engine, nearly pitching the raincoated man over the prow. The small boat came to a stop directly below some of us who were crowded at the rail between the life rafts.

Taking some folded papers out of his raincoat pocket, the man studied them for several moments before looking up at us. Cupping his hands around his mouth he shouted up to those of us at the railing in a thick Scottish accent, "What's the name of your ship, laddie?"

Incredulous, we all stared down at this blowing raincoat that housed the accented voice. No one answered him. We were transfixed by this foreign devil from another world. We stared at him. He repeated the question to a mute audience. Flustered by our silence, he was about to speak to his pilot when a bullhorn from the bridge above us metallically boomed out the name of the ship.

Consulting his papers, after shuffling through them a few times, the raincoat, still cupping his hands shouted docking information up to the bridge. After being acknowledged, the motor boat sped away to the next ship, the raincoat streaming behind the man who, at all times, seemed on the verge of pitching over the side of the careening little boat. Apparently he was the harbormaster for Glasgow, Scotland, giving personal directions to the hundreds of vessels in the harbor.

After several hours we weighed anchor and picked our way through the maze of ships in the port. Arriving at what appeared to be the heaviest concentration of vessels, we found ourselves steaming slowly up the Firth of Clyde, the river that empties into Galway Bay. After two hours of picking our way through the maze of traffic, we tied up to a dock and all watched with extreme interest the Scottish dockworkers scrambling to make the ship fast and to put a gangplank in place. The instant that it was in position, a ship's officer bounded down the gangplank. He carried a briefcase and disappeared into a glass enclosed office near the dock warehouse.

In a holiday mood we crowded the decks, hanging over the railing to watch the bustle of activity next to our ship on the docks. Several workers, curious about us, stopped to watch, exchanging banter with one or two of the more vocal Americans. There was suddenly a roar of approval from the entire ship as two women came out of the warehouse office, stopping to look up at a full boatload of Yanks. Appreciative whistles and catcalls caused the two of them to stand close together while they giggled and feigned lack of interest in the noise cascading down on them from the decks above. They were nicely dressed in street clothes although neither was wearing stockings; silk or rayon was scarce in wartime. One of the women, rather heavily built, was clearly older than the other. In fact they appeared almost to be mother and daughter. The younger was actually quite pretty. After two weeks of not seeing a female, the reaction of the troops was ribald but predictable. The shouting of propositions intermingled with obscene suggestions began to be heard over the general bedlam. Some of us began to feel a little uneasy about what the dock workers would think, but the male Scotch workers laughed at the comments. None of them seemed at all alarmed that a boatload of Americans were practically seducing their women in their presence.

Suddenly without warning, the older woman reached down and with a quick jerk pulled the skirt of the younger woman up to her waist. There was a unanimous gasp at the sight of panties and the lovely legs of a pretty female. The gasp was followed by a thunderous roar from the throats of 2,000 sex starved young men.

Several people ran out of the warehouse, the ship's officers vaulted out of the glass enclosed office and workers stretched their necks on the next docks to see what was going on.

I once read that when the trench mines were set off near Ypres, Belgium, during World War I, the sound could be heard in England. I don't know what the decibel count was that day on the River Clyde, but I had a sudden vision of a Belgian farmer looking up from his work in the fields and saying, in Flemish, of course, "What the hell was that?"

Without embarrassment the two women who never stopped laughing, waved to us and disappeared into one of the warehouses. Our introduction to the female Britain was over.

Concorde Interlude—1979

In the late summer of 1978 my first wife of 32 years died a lingering death and I found myself alone in the world. Our children had grown and had departed along their own pathways. Following her death, I continued my professional career, which included much convention travel and dialogue with colleagues. Much to my delight I became reacquainted with a remarkable woman whom I had known previously while teaching at a university in Virginia. We had been friends and were soon in love with one another. In the late spring of 1979 we were married and decided to honeymoon in France.

We arrived one hour late at National Airport in the District of Columbia on flight 402 out of Kansas City. Traffic had been heavy, putting us in a holding pattern over Maryland, while we impatiently studied our watches convinced that we would arrive too late. We had a connecting flight on Air France Concorde, flight 054 out of Dulles leaving at 1:15 p.m. Our Kansas City plane touched down at National at 11:50. Unless we were very lucky getting a fast cab, we were going to miss the flight that we had planned for over four months.

Rushing up the passenger ramp, we were astonished to find a petite lady in a powder blue suit holding a clipboard sign that read, "Keim, Concorde flight." Stumbling through introductions as we hurried toward the baggage carousal, we learned that a limousine was waiting to take us the twelve miles or so to our Concorde flight at Dulles. Snatching up our bags with the help of our guide, we ran to the Ambassador limousine to be whisked up the George Washington Parkway, arriving at Dulles Airport with thirty minutes to spare before our Concorde was scheduled to depart.

The pressure on takeoff was quite noticeable. We were pressed back into our seats as the birdlike Concorde, standing high on its wheels thundered down runway one eight at Dulles to catapult itself into an early afternoon cloudless sky. We soon reached 31,000 feet at subsonic speed before the French Captain spoke to us over the cabin speaker. He spoke in French, Spanish and then finally in English to tell us that since the United States forbid supersonic speed over the continental limits, we would attain Mach speed after we had gone to 60,000 feet beyond the North American shoreline. A friendly cabin steward delivered dinner menus to us and took our cocktail order. Before the drinks arrived in crystal goblets, we could feel the Concorde accelerate into its climb. Gazing out the very small window panel, we saw the shoreline disappear behind us. There was then a surge of speed that had no accompanying sound since we had passed Mach 1. We were simply outracing our own sound. The silence was eerie but the busy preparation for dinner was reassuring. Stewards hurried to place colorful linen tablecloths on each folddown individual serving tray. Silver and crystal were unobtrusively put in position without disturbance as we sipped our second cocktail and watched with fascination as the Mach digital readout panel blinked on the cabin bulkhead. At Mach 1.5 there was some exhuberance from the passengers. As the digits moved to 1.7-1.8 there was a stirring of anticipation among the occupants, most of whom were European business executives. At Mach 2, there was a faint cheer heard as congratulations were passed between the very few humans on the planet who had ever achieved a speed twice that of sound. Dinner arrived at Mach 2.02. The meter settled comfortably at this reading to remain relatively unchanged and unnoticed during the remainder of the flight.

The steward poured a very good Magis Chambertin from a linen wrapped bottle as we ate Howard a la Parisenne followed by quail with grapes. The Paupiette de Sole Archiduc was superb as was the remainder of the seven course dinner, which was topped off with a delicious chestnut mousse.

Sipping Grand Marnier, I watched the darkening sky coming up from the East. We had been in the air less than two hours but the Concorde had already passed through four time zones. Because of our altitude at 60,000 feet and the growing darkness, I could barely see the ocean below us. I studied the water trying to make out wave patterns or current stretch marks. As I gazed down, unexpectedly Norman Corwin's lines about the Atlantic came to my mind. "The bones of how many good men lie below."

I thought of a stricken freighter that fell away from a convoy so many years before. "Are their bones down there?" I wondered.

How long does it take for bones, under tons of pressure, to dissolve? Surely after 36 years of erosion, marine life and water pressure, there can be little left of even the ship except a few scraps of corroded iron and other unidentified debris, perhaps half covered with silt, swaying slightly against a tugging current. At that icy depth there would be no light, no sound except for the angry snarling and clicking of crustaceans. I felt the hair crawl on the nape of my neck. I shuddered involuntarily.

The moonless sky was now totally dark. The ocean could not be seen, even in the faint glow of increasing starlight. The bright cabin was quiet as passengers, satiated by the excellent cuisine and after-dinner brandy and liqueurs, settled comfortably in their cradlelike arm chairs. A few slept. Catching the eye of the cabin steward, I held up my empty Grand Marnier glass. He hurried to fill it. I settled back, savoring the flavor and aroma of the exquisite liqueur.

Turning my head slightly, I traced with my eyes as I had done so often before the beautiful lines of the cheekbones of my bride. Her eyes were closed in contentment, a slight smile on her lovely face. The thought of icy death below faded. Suddenly, as I gazed with love at this warm woman in the cabin, as though coming from far away silence, I heard very faintly, "Chink, chink, chink."

Startled, I quickly turned to the small window and pressed my face against the thickened double plastic, straining to hear and see. There was nothing; I saw only my own reflection in the window. An aging, grey-haired man, who looked like my father, stared back at me over the cobalt curvature of the earth.

Again, "Chink, chink, chink," this time louder, more insistent.

A rush of emotion, tinged with fear, enveloped me. The sound meant something to me. I could not immediately identify what it meant. However, I felt that it came from the bowels of the ocean eight miles beneath me and that the sound came from the past.

"Chink, chink, chink." A tightness of my back beginning at the bottom of my spine held me rigid in my seat. I am not a superstitious man but it came to me that what I was hearing was the clattering of an unfastened life jacket belt buckle striking the iron steps of a troopship. I was genuinely afraid.

Numbly, I watched the steward silently fill the china coffee cup of the passenger who sat across the aisle from us. Transfixed, I watched the man pick up his silver spoon to stir sugar into his coffee. Clearly puzzled by my unexpected attention, he smiled vaguely as he stirred.

"Chink, chink, chink," went his cup. We both smiled at one another; I with a deep flood of relief.

As the Mach meter unwound, I could see the lights on the coast of France far below. Within minutes the slim aircraft kissed its wheels on the runway of Charles de Gaulle Airport, North of Paris. Total time of flight 054 from Washington, D.C. to Paris, France—three hours and thirty-three minutes. We stepped onto the soil of Europe, eager to begin our honeymoon adventures.

CHAPTER VII

ENGLAND

Near dusk and in a drizzling rain, we were loaded aboard a train. The train backed onto the dock and we crowded into dark dirty compartments of what appeared to be second class coaches from a regular passenger train. Six men to a compartment with only K rations for food, no place to stretch out and sleep. We were excited, of course, by the prospects of seeing Britain, so there was much laughing and joke making. At dark, however, officers came through the train instructing us that under penalty of severe punishment, no one was to raise the window shades or any of the windows. We were in a strict blackout war zone. No lights were to be seen, nor any clue given that this was a troop train.

Solemnly we were told that our destination could not be revealed, but we were headed South. South meant to everyone that we were going where the action was. The magic word, London, was whispered around from compartment to compartment, at which time the man sitting next to me put on his helmet, trying to do it casually so that no one would notice how scared he had become. The massive German bombing raids on London were over by the Summer of 44, but the hated V-1 buzz bombs were still wracking damage on London and other major Channel cities. There was even an occasional aircraft bombing raid intending to harass and probably sent by the Germans to assess damage from the unmanned flying bombs.

As the train slid slowly away from the dock, there was a noticeable decrease in the level of levity. We quickly commented on the contrast between the British train smooth start as compared to the jerking, neck snapping start of its American counterpart. Once under way, we settled back with our curtains drawn seeking what small comfort there was in the cramped quarters. With my feet stretched out on the seat between the men opposite me, I soon fell into a pattern of dozing and wakefulness. The clicking of the train wheels plus the smoothness of acceleration and declaration was very conducive to falling asleep.

We ate our rations, drank water from our canteens, smoked countless cigarettes, discussed rumors, told lies about women and passed the night in a fairly quiet but excited holiday mood. Only once in the darkened unlit coach did I awake to discover that the others were all asleep at the same time. With some guilt, I slid the curtain aside and peeked out at England. We were traveling through what seemed to be farmland, although there were no lights to be seen anywhere. Only the starlight gave any significance at all to the scene but I thought that I could see clusters of buildings, lines of trees, and an occasional patch of forest. The land was rather flat, reminding me a lot of parts of the Midwest. There were no cars, trucks or even people, which was no surprise, as a quick glance at my luminous watch told me that it was 3:30 a.m. I closed the curtain and slipped back into a dreamless sleep.

All the next day we travelled across the English countryside cocoon-like inside our curtained train. More K rations were distributed along with the caution not to open the curtains nor to give any sign whatever that we were a troop train.

Somehow the warning seemed more sensible than it had when we were being spasmotically jerked across the Arizona desert. There were very few delays in our continuous trip. We would sit briefly on a siding while another train took the right of way, but these stops were only minutes long. The British railway system, even in wartime, was very efficient, apparently timed to the second.

In the early evening dusk we stopped. By stealing a peek, we could see that we were in a railway station that seemed to be near a moderately sized town. Our inside compartment door crashed open and Sergeant Otter yelled, "Get your gear together, we're here."

Shortly thereafter, we got off the train and formed up on the station platform under the indifferent gaze of several civilian travelers who did not seem to realize that we had come to save their country for them. Their boredom with us bordered on impatience, for they seemed more interested in train schedules than in expressing their gratitude. Soon we were hustled off the platform into a line of closed six-by trucks in the growing darkness. Men, in their curiosity to see something, argued and in some cases pushed and shoved to get the end seats, so that they could see out of the back of the truck.

"We don't have far to go," growled Otter, "so get in there, sit down and shut up."

Within ten minutes we had rumbled through a post gate, past guards who didn't even look at the trucks as they rolled by. Arriving at what appeared to be the parade ground, we jumped down from the trucks with all of our gear and lined up in loose company and battalion formation. By now it was pitch dark, no lights could be seen anywhere. Even the trucks, as they departed back toward the post gate, showed only thin slit-like blackout lights.

As the noise and feeble lights of the trucks faded away, a voice shouted to us from the night. "Welcome. Welcome to Warminster, England."

The voice coming to us from the pitch black belonged to one of our battalion officers who had been sent on ahead of the battalion several days before to make arrangements for our arrival. He had apparently shipped out of New Jersey in a prior convoy or had managed a flight across the Atlantic with the Air Corps. In any event, he was listened to with great attention for he was now a veteran of the English scene.

He told us briefly of the camp, that it had been a British Forces training camp but had been reassigned to the U.S. Army as a base ordnance depot. The voice assured us that no buzz bombs had ever arrived at Warminster since it was located in South Central England nearly one hundred miles from London. Astonishingly, there were groans of disappointment from some of the men at this announcement. We were very new to the war.

As we stood there in the darkness, listening to a disembodied voice, shivering a little in the chilly summer night, we heard a faint beginning sound of thunder. The sound increased in intensity so that the voice was forced to stop in midsentence. Finally someone from within the formation yelled with great excitement, "Bombers!"

Our battalion officer shouted above the mounting sound, "It's all right, men, there's an English airfield not far from here; they go over every night on their way to Germany."

We were hypnotized by the sound that soon grew into an absolute crescendo of noise. Stars blinked off and on as the shadowy forms passed in front of them in a great wheeling arc, marking the formation's flight path to the European continent.

Finally, as the sound began to diminish, a few faint cheers could be heard from the assembled battalion. The moment was so stirring that most of us felt a twinge of envy for the crews of the planes, which were on their way to strike a real blow against the enemy. These were no planes on a training flight. This was an honest to God combat mission, fully armed and carrying tons of bombs, hundreds of men.

When the excitement had died down, the voice from the darkness continued its instructions. Finished at last, we were all assigned Quonset huts, and guides with guarded flashlights took us in small groups to our quarters.

A Quonset hut is like a large corrugated tin can, which has been sliced in half length-wise and placed on a foundation slab on the ground so that people could shelter inside the created metal curve. The ends were sealed to provide doorways and three windows were pierced on each side of the curve to get some light inside. They were wired for electricity and potbellied stoves gave heat for the hut. Each housed about twenty men. Although ugly, Quonset huts were the backbone of field life throughout the war, both overseas and in the United States. Only permanent camps, which I had seen in the U.S. such as Aberdeen and Camp Forrest, were equipped with wooden barracks that looked like shoeboxes. England, we were to learn, seemed virtually covered with Quonset huts.

The hut for third squad was equipped with bunks and blankets. Heat from an oil fed stove at both ends made the hut a home.

We went to bed almost immediately just to stretch out at last in a genuine sleeping position. After two weeks of crowded canvas racks and seat cushions on railroad trains, we were grateful to just lie there on our backs with blankets pulled up under our chins and talk quietly back and forth. One by one the men dropped off to sleep until after an hour or so the hut was silent. I looked up without seeing the curved ceiling in the darkness, feeling the excitement of being in England, wondering what tomorrow would bring. I thought of home, not with pain but rather with some sense of pride. Here I was, in the war, at last. What would they think if they knew where I was? What time was it in California anyway? Probably about noon. My home seemed very far away.

As my mind jumped back and forth from home to Warminster, England, I was startled to hear someone speak quietly in the darkness, "They're comin' back."

It was George who spoke, He had great ears and before anyone else had heard the subtle throbbing of hundreds of engines, he had picked up the sound lying in his bunk. Soon everyone was awake, lying quietly, listening to the returning thunder. The metal of the hut thrummed a little as the planes swung in their arc overhead. Some of the engines were coughing and missing in their measured cadence. Perhaps it was because of the thickness of the metal roof or maybe just my imagination, but the thunder did not seem so loud, nor was it as prolonged, as it had seemed to me when the planes had headed out earlier in the evening. The sound faded away to a murmur, finally returning the hut to an echoing sort of silence. After a short pause, someone said in the darkness, "Those poor bastards."

Warminster, England, was a lovely little town of slightly over 50,000 in population. Nestled in a valley below rolling farmland, it provided civilization to a series of road junctions and intersecting railway lines. A busy canal connected Warminster with a network of commerce. Its townspeople were courteous but preoccupied, almost as though the war was, after all, the personal business of the thousands of American, Canadian and British soldiers who either drifted through the shopping and drinking centers of the city or who pursued their duties in marching columns or traffic convoys. Civilians, concentrating on their own lives, passed silently through and among the military environment, eyes averted, scurrying about Warminster intent upon their personal endeavors. Shopkeepers were wary of the Yankee soldier but happy to sell him goods from their meager supply of wartime items, sometimes at inflated prices. The bars or pubs, of course, did the most business, selling warm beer, stout and a variety of gin and scotch to the comparatively rich Americans. We were rich. On the average, an American soldier received ten times as much money a month as his British counterpart. Resentment and bitterness over this disparity marked many arguments and fights between the Yanks and the Limeys. Often, after a few drinks, sometimes involving English women, an argument over money would be settled outside on the cobblestone street. Black eyes and bruises were common sights at reveille each morning, particularly on Monday morning following a weekend of drinking.

Americans were regarded by the British as heavy drinkers and womanizers. My experience would lead me to believe that this generalization was more or less accurate. Further, many Britishers thought of us as crude, loud and insensitive. Again, their observation of the behavior of many, if not most Americans, was accurate. Much of the apparent dissatisfaction that surfaced between the two cultures was due to the newness of the interchange. Foreign travel in the 30's and 40's was financially beyond the middle class of America so that there had been very little opportunity for the two nations to enjoy a broad interchange of people. In my battalion of over 2,000 men, I knew of only two who had ever been to England before. Both of the men were older senior officers.

Low cost airfare and transatlantic flying was yet to be practical. The jet engine, let alone supersonic flight, was still on the drawing boards in the spring of 1944. The European tour was conducted by ocean going luxury liner in the early part of the 20th century at such cost as to be prohibitive for the average working man of either culture. This now meant that two cultures, dissimilar in many ways were thrown together under the adverse conditions of war. The British saw us as braggarts. We, in our ignorance, saw ourselves as once again winning a war for them as our fathers had done in 1918. These conditions of derision and distain from the Americans created an overall atmosphere of distrust.

Attempts were made by higher ups to minimize this feeling, the basic premise being that allied soldiers, fighting side by side should at least be friendly toward one another. Later, I was to read a surrender pamphlet dropped by a German plane over our lines that played heavily on the theme of distrust. It read, "Yanks, why are you here fighting a war for the British?"

We were shown a film about the British people, their heritage, their links with America and their sacrifices and determination in defense of democracy and justice. It was a good film, made especially for those who regarded the British with distrust because of their apparent differences. Then in a stroke of absolute brilliance, we were shown the film that the British had made to explain the Americans to their own troops. The effect was magical, going a long way toward creating, for us, a better base of understanding of the British.

In the first place, the film was funny. It showed an American football game and described the game as "an armored engagement," trying to describe differences in a witty, light vein. The film defended we Americans as honest, hardworking, family people with an identity and destiny all of our own. Emphasis was placed on our ability to gather our collective strength for national purposes. We were pictured as courageous, determined and capable people. The British audience was cautioned against thinking that Americans were all Chicago style gangsters or cowboys. Both of these stereotypes were produced by the American movie industry that swept the world in the 30's and 40's.

After seeing the film, we were impressed with ourselves, proud of our country, willing to be a little more tolerant toward others who could venture to really try to understand us. I can only believe that the attempt to reduce hostility between the two armed camps resulted in the British forces also viewing the film produced about themselves that we had seen.

The film was an intelligent use of audio-visual media to educate. It is not difficult to understand that one of the more positive changes to come out of World War II was the wholesale introduction of the motion picture projector into the classrooms of America. There was seldom a week that went by during the whole of our training, including our weeks in England, in which we did not view a film of some sort. The sixteen millimeter film, in a few short years, had become a recognized and respected tool in the collection of educational technology.

I soon bought a bicycle from a Sergeant who was being transferred, keeping it locked and chained to drainpipes, telephone poles and anything else to which I could secure this precious belonging. It was in poor condition, but a valuable item. As I recall, I paid over four times what it had sold for originally. I oiled it and cared for it as though it were a living pet. The leather seat was in shambles and the tires were absolutely irresponsible, made up mostly of patches and friction tape so thick that even on asphalt paving, it was like cycling on rough cobblestone. Regardless of the health of the contraption, I loved it and loved the relative freedom of circuit that it gave me. On Sundays, when it wasn't raining, I would take food and canteen into the countryside, trying to get as far away from the post as I could before having to turn back to make the main gate before the summer sun turned the hills behind the camp into a dusky purple. The farmland was beautiful and well cared for, mostly by older men or women and children. Even on Sunday, the fields were being earnestly worked, almost in a frenzy in the dazzling heat. Few people ever took the time to notice me thumping along on ruptured wheels, although sometimes I would join a small cluster of people sitting in shade to eat their noon meal. I was always welcomed by the non-city people who were genuinely curious about me and about my country so far beyond the sea. I was, for the most part, the only American that the farmers ever talked to. We shared what we had to eat, although I was almost always embarrassed to discover that what I had brought along for lunch was invariably food that they had not seen for years, if at all. In particular, I once shared a small can of peaches that was viewed with awe and reverence by three women and two small boys. The two boys, ages about ten or eleven, had never tasted peaches before in their lives.

As they devoured the entire contents, running small fingers along the inside of the can to lick the succulent juice, I was saddened by memories of the Depression years of my own youth. At twenty I had already spent over half of my life in war or in the despair of poverty. As I left the group on the bright Sunday afternoon, one of the women named Louise, the boys' mother, walked with me over to the stone wall to my friend, the bicycle. As I prepared to mount, she said to me with tears in the corners of her cornstalk eyes, "Yank, thank you for them peaches."

As I looked at her face, I realized that she was probably not much older than I. I saw the strain, the tightness of fright and concern around her mouth, the weathered skin on her forehead and the wisp of sultry blond hair straying beyond the tight cotton head covering. She was, or had been, a pretty woman.

"That's O.K., Mam," I replied, suddenly deciding on something. "Hey, I'll be back next Sunday with some more if you guys are still here to meet me."

Tears popped from her eyes and ran down her cheeks. We both pretended that we didn't notice.

"Why say, Yank, that would be real nice," she said softly, lips trembling.

As I jumped up on the high seat and cried out in pain, she added rather apologetically, "It's the war, you know, Yank. We don't get much food, it goes to you soldier boys, not that you don't deserve it, mind."

I pedalled away, feeling the heavy guilt that she had placed on my shoulders. All the next week, I stole food from the mess hall. When I arrived back on the farm for our picnic lunch, I was greeted with surprise and pleasure. I really don't think they had expected me to show up, although the two boys had been joined by a third child, a wispish girl with long scraggly blond hair. She was introduced to me as Katherine, a cousin who was visiting with the farm family over the weekend.

They sat in a circle on the grass under the welcome shade of a great oak tree and watched me as I took the items out of my knapsack and placed them in the center of the group within reach of everyone. With silent reverence, they watched me as I placed peaches, pears, chunks of white bread, packages of cooked meats and a jar of marmalade. I tried to joke as I put the cans, packages and jars on the grass, but it was an awkward moment for them. At last I was able to say to Louise, "Let's eat, Mam."

Very consciously, each can was opened with my little G.I. can opener and the peaches and pears were solemnly divided onto plates that the women provided. Care was taken to make sure that I had received my proper portion. I took care not to refuse the division. When the plates were filled and the food divided, Louise gave the signal to eat. I was surprised at the courtesy, restraint and politeness with which the children ate. They relished the marmalade and devoured the meat, bread and canned fruit. It was a marvelous picnic for everyone.

As we adults smoked my American cigarettes, the children ran off to play, thanking me one at a time for a "nice lunch," and telling me how full they were. As Louise, her friend, and I smoked and chatted, I noticed out of the corner of my eye that soon the little girl had broken off play and was standing behind the oak tree savagely eating the paper in which the meat had been wrapped. It was a moment of the war years that I will never forget. The British had been at war for six years before I arrived at that oak tree.

Our first Sergeant approached me one Friday afternoon while I was having a drink at the noncommissioned officer's club named Club FUBAR, which was an acronym for "Fucked Up Beyond All Recognition." The Sergeant was a large, gross man from Boston whom we called "Farmer," because of his size, the way he seemed to be following a horse when he walked, and his disposition and low level of imagination. He had been appointed First Sergeant when we had arrived in England presumably to whip the company into shape for the war, which we all thought we would soon enter. The Farmer was not well liked, not because we didn't want to be in soldierly form, but rather because of his overt favoritism, his crudeness and his vindictiveness against anyone with education. He had never spoken directly to me before that moment in Club FUBAR.

"Hey, Keem," he said, "I got a truck leavin' for Stroud, how 'bout you and me goin' Stroud fishin'?"

It was years later that I came to realize that in Boston, this might, just might, be considered a joke as a play on words for scrod fishing. At the time, however, I was so overwhelmed by his apparently friendly attention and not expecting to find the Farmer's arm around my shoulder, I sputtered, "Hell, yes, Sergeant, let's go."

I didn't even know what or where Stroud was nor had I any idea what he had in mind when he mentioned fishing. Stroud turned out to be a small town about thirty miles from Warminster. Stroud fishing turned out to be looking for girls.

It was late in the afternoon when we, along with a dozen other soldiers, climbed down from the truck onto the wet cobblestones of the city square of Stroud. "I'll be back at midnight!" the driver shouted as he clashed gears and rumbled off into the drizzling rain presumably to do some fishing of his own.

Caught without raincoats, the two of us shuffled along the main street until we found what looked like a pub. Opening the door, we entered into the heat and smell of a small town public drinking house. It was full of smoke and soldiers. We drove a wedge through the men at the end of the bar and yelling through the clamor, ordered some Scotch. The British did not use ice in their liquor, even the beer was served warm. It took getting used to, but once I became accustomed to it, it seemed natural, making a lot of sense. However, without the diluting effect of ice, the strength of the liquor remained full down to the last drop in the glass. Being only twenty, I was understandably quite drunk by the time I had finished my second glass. Both the Farmer and I were really feeling fine; he was telling me a complicated story about how he had been kicked out of high school because the principal was out to get him, when two women crowded into the mass of men right behind us. One of them, after looking around the room for a few moments, tapped me on the arm and asked boldly, "Hey Ducks, buy us a drink?"

Swaying slightly and trying desperately to get the woman's face into focus, I shouted, "You bet, baby!"

I expect that what I actually said, "Youb et blaby."

Whatever I said, it didn't seem to matter to either of them as they elbowed some space near the bar between the Farmer and me. Both were dressed in a blue ill fitting uniform that turned out to belong to the local bus company. One was tall and the other, with blond hair, was short. They were bus drivers just getting off work for the day.

Holding tightly to the edge of the bar with my elbows to keep from sliding to the floor, I leered at the shorter of the two and in my best man of the world manner kept up a peppy conversation, I think. The Farmer was talking all the time to the other bus driver, from time to time patting her shoulder. She seemed to be agreeing with him about something. The noise continued to roar in my ears, my eyes watered from the smoke and I seemed to be blinking a lot at an out of focus face as I gulped down the last of my third drink. I tentatively bit my lip a little. It was numb. So was the rest of my face. With my back to the bar, I tried to run my fingers through my hair, missing my entire head with my hand by at least six inches. The force of my gesture pirouetted me neatly around in a half circle so that I found myself facing the bar. I tried to put my elbows on the massive edge, but missed and struck my chin on the wet surface so hard that I knocked over my empty glass just inches from my eyes. With arms dangling at my sides, I stared, fascinated, at the shiny drops of liquid on the glass. Just as I started to giggle at the spectacle, I felt someone or something from very far away hitting me on the back. Thump. Thump. Thump.

"Wazzat?" I asked the glass, my chin still on the bar.

The glass said, "Come on, Ducks, we're going along to our digs."

It took me a few moments to figure it out but apparently the glass wanted me to go somewhere with it.

"That's curious," I thought, "I hardly even know this glass."

I giggled again, around and through a numb tongue.

Slowly the glass moved away from me. "Aw, come on glass, that's O.K." I apologized.

But there was something around my neck, pulling me up. Probably a brown boa constrictor, I reasoned, not too concerned. This thing around my neck was pulling me up and away from my friend, the glass. The brown snake around my throat tugged me until I was looking into two eyes.

"Two piss holes in the snow," I announced.

Voices, piercing yet very far away seemed to be following me as I floated away from the bar on what appeared to be my way to the door. In later life I was to be reminded of the way the door magically opened when I first rode into Mr. Toad's ride at Disneyland.

I could not locate my feet but didn't seem to need them anyway. I found myself in what seemed to be a very large cold room with some-one sprinkling water on my face.

"Wazzat?" I asked, vaguely conscious that I would probably need a better question if I were to go through life like that.

Something shrieked in my left ear, "Watch him! He's going to throw up!"

I thought I was going to laugh, but instead I threw up. God, did I throw up. I thought momentarily of Huntsville and of a white lightning jar, but the single random thought did not help my stomach at all. Eventually the Farmer helped me to my feet. In the fading light I could see vomit about halfway across the cobblestone street. In despair I sank to my knees again and resumed throwing up. Everything finally subsided and waving the Sergeant away, I struggled weakly to my feet.

I turned, facing the laughter behind me in the rain. The two bus drivers were standing there, giggling. The short one said, "Come on Ducks, let's go fuck."

It took awhile for her words to penetrate. I fumbled for a handkerchief and mopped my face trying to find a response. Here for the first time in my life was *the moment of truth.* However, I had not thought that it would happen like this. Somehow, candlelight and wine in a warm, cozy restaurant masked by words of love edged with tenderness was what I had had in mind. Instead, I found myself standing in a darkened strange little town in a drizzling rain, sick to my stomach, being asked in the crudest way possible, by an out of focus bus driver to go with her to fuck.

Before I could explain any of the incongruity to anyone, the Farmer pulled me away from the curb, jammed my cap on my head and the four of us started to walk away from the city square. Actually, they walked, the Farmer and the tall one; I staggered along with the short blond holding me up and warning me about curbs and the numerous steps that stuck out on the sidewalk from the flat fronted row houses. After we had gone three or four blocks, I began to feel a little better. The sobering cold air, drizzling rain, and the faintly disturbing thought that at last I was going to go to bed with a girl, all seemed to make my eyes focus better. I tried to look at my bus driver but it was, by this time, getting quite dark and I could make out only a shoulder high form that was still talking and laughing. Stopping for a moment to disengage my arms from hers. I said apologetically, "Hey, I'm O.K., sorry about being sick."

Releasing her grip on my arm, she replied, "That's O.K., Yank, just keep your pecker up and you'll do fine."

We turned. I walked along with her in semi-drunken silence trying to find some rationale that what was going to happen would be part of what I was looking for in life.

By the time we had climbed a rather steep hill and turned into one of the row houses, I had arrived at the universal conclusion that I have learned is reached by all members of either sex, "What the hell, how could it hurt?"

I never thought once of the Mickey Mouse film. The four of us crowded into a pitch black hallway that smelled of garbage and urine. Everyone but me seemed to be talking and laughing as we fumbled our way into what they had described on our way there as their "flat."

It was a single room with one naked light bulb hanging down from the center of the ceiling. When the light was switched on, the garish light flooded across a scene of indescribable filth and confusion. A greasy mattress covered with discarded bottles, cans, newspapers and clothing occupied the center of the floor. I looked around the room. I could see no windows, no closets, no pictures, no shelves, no furniture. Everything was on the floor in what appeared to be a pattern of random discard. Perhaps it was the light, but even the Farmer seemed perplexed and a little pale.

Unperturbed, the bus drivers began kicking things into corners, all the time laughing and talking to each other. Kicking the trash into new piles seemed only to stir up the odor a little more. My stomach began to remind me that it had requested a little kindness earlier in the evening, but before I could really think about it, the short driver took me by the hand and said, "Come on, Ducks, it's you and me upstairs to the bedroom!"

With that she dragged me over to a steep staircase, which I had not seen in a dark corner of the room. It was more a ladder than a staircase, but I dutifully climbed up behind her turning once to see the Farmer taking off his pants near the mattress on the floor. The woman with him was sitting on the mattress unlacing her heavy shoes. Coming up through a trapdoor in the floor, we left that scene and entered a smaller room, which was similar to an attic. The driver pulled a string on the light bulb hanging from the ceiling. The room was just as cluttered as the one downstairs but it did have a narrow bed in it along one wall. Throwing clothing and beer bottles from the bed onto the floor, she said in a matter of fact way, "Take your clothes off, Ducks."

I obediently fumbled with the buttons on my field jacket as she shrugged out of her bus driver's tunic. In the light of the low wattage bulb that was still swinging back and forth, she transformed from a shapeless mass of wool uniform into a young woman. I threw my jacket on a pile of garments and as I unbuttoned my shirt, I studied her out of the corner of my eye as she hurriedly undressed herself.

I was astonished. In the light, without her tunic, baggy pants and heavy boots, she looked almost lovely. Beyond my nervousness, I felt a very unfamiliar stirring of my animal senses. I gawked as she pulled a man's undershirt over her head and slipped out of her panties. Standing naked a few feet away, she tossed her head, put her hands on her hips and laughed at my confusion. "Hey Ducks, this is your first time, isn't it?"

"Of course not," I stammered, blushing through wounded pride, "I do this all the time," I added a little lamely.

I could not keep my eyes from staring at the round pinkness of her nipples on her pointed breasts. Nor could I stop glancing at her mound of pubic hair, the first real nude woman I had ever seen in my life. As I hopped on one foot trying to get my trousers over my G.I. boots, she came over to me and said, reaching for my pants, "Here Ducks, lemme help."

Ignoring my protest, she knelt down in front of me, face disturbingly close to my private parts, and began pulling on my trouser leg. Being on one foot at the time, I lost my balance and we tumbled together onto the scattered clothing on the floor.

As we lay there laughing, I felt the warmness of her breast on my arm. I also felt the urgency of the pressure of her arms and hands as they snaked around my back. I also felt what was happening to me personally. She felt it too and feigned surprise as she giggled harshly in my ear. The sequence of events was entirely new to me but I had sense enough to realize that I must finish taking my pants off at once.

Rolling over on my side I struggled impatiently trying to roll the damned things over my boots. As I was doing this, I noticed light out of the corner of my eye. The light was coming through a knothole in the floor from the room below. I looked through it as I began to pick savagely at my shoelaces. The hole was directly over the mattress below and while I could not see all of the two figures below I could see enough of them to be transfixed by what I saw. The Farmer was lying on top of the tall bus driver, she with her long legs holding him. His bare buttocks were moving in and out as he rhythmically thrust forward and backward. Never before in my life had I witnessed fornication. I was both revolted and fascinated by the spectacle. There was no sound from below, only the rhythm and the animal like white buttocks moving in the pool of light. I could see that the Farmer still had his shoes and socks on. I watched from my hidden vantage point and strangely stimulated until I realized that I was alone on the floor of the upstairs room. I sat up and silently untied my shoes, seeing that the girl had gone to the bed.

A strange sadness and sort of realization came over me and I felt the same as I had one day as a child when I tried to stop halfway down a slide but could not. The whole evening, from the bar to the street to the house had swept me along with it. I had made no effort to change anything. I had allowed the events to proceed, almost as though I had been a mere spectator.

With my shoes neatly lined up together on the floor in front of me, I sat for a moment pondering, struggling out of my residual drunkenness, trying to fathom what was happening. The questions were clear. Did I as a person have control over that part of me, which was only physical? Did I have a choice?

Standing up at last, naked, I went to the bed under the light bulb. I sat on the side of the bed and looked soberly at the girl stretched out on her back in a provocative pose. She *was* young, no older than I. I put my hand on the other side of her narrow waist, leaning closer to her. She smiled.

I believe that at that instant, I sobered up completely, because the girl with all of her female impact, suddenly came into sharp crystalline focus. Even with my shadow on her body from the bulb over my head, I could see that she was, like her surroundings, dirty. Her smile, looking more like a grimace now, revealed yellow jagged teeth, which may never have been brushed. There were dirt streaks along her neck and arms. Her matted hair was black at the roots from dirt. Her nostrils were clogged with yellow mucus and she smelled. I leaned over her, lightly kissing one of her erect nipples.

"Hurry up, Ducks, do you want to fuck or not?" she cried petulantly.

Moving my arm, I sat up again on the edge of the bed noting that the male animal part of me was certainly still ready for anything. I looked at the light streaming up through the knothole in the floor. I spread my fingers out on my knees studying them. I swept the incredible room with my eyes seeing the filth. I turned once again and looked at her angry, pouting face.

"Tell you what, *Ducks*," I said quietly, "thank you, but I don't believe that I do."

She was very angry and as I stood up and began putting on my clothes, she cursed me using words and phrases that I had not heard since my basic training days at Aberdeen. As I gathered up my jacket at last, I realized that she had become quiet. Starting down the steps, I saw that she had begun massaging her stiff nipples with her fingers. Her eyes were closed and she was moaning to herself, twisting her knees back and forth.

As I disappeared through the opening, I said softly, "Goodbye Ducks," without a glance.

I stepped around the mattress on the floor in the downstairs room, hurried through the dark steaming hallway and stepped out into the refreshing cold night air. I leaned my back against the closed door and took several deep deep breaths. I was happy and exhilerated. I looked down at my crotch and said, "Don't worry, fellows, there will be other times. Tonight the fishing in Stroud was poor; we had to throw that one back."

Groping my way down the hill in the thick darkness of blacked out Stroud, I eventually found my way to the square and after a long wait boarded the truck back to the camp. Most of us were there to climb drunkenly into the truck, although the Farmer did now show up in time. I never did know how he got back to Warminster. I only know that while I was to see him daily for the next six months, he was never to speak to me again.

After the first month at Warminster, it became obvious to our battalion and company officers that there were no electronic gun directors to be maintained. The men in our other units—artillery, optics, motor vehicles and small arms, were all kept busy at the business of the depot but the half dozen or so of the higher trained gun director technicians had nothing to do. The solution of this personnel vacuum was obvious, as I was soon to learn. Those of us without ordnance tasks to occupy us would be assigned to operation duties such as K.P., garbage detail or permanent post guard. The functional duties that kept up the administrative detail of the company had to be maintained and rather than rotate these duties among cadre who were involved in depot work, it was much simpler to assign these tasks on a permanent basis to those with nothing else to do. It did not seem to bother anyone that those with some of the highest level of training would be performing the most mundane tasks assignable. It was Army logic. No one should just sit around.

As ranking noncom, I was given my choice as either head garbage collector or as Sergeant of the guard. It was a terrible choice to make; my experiences at Aberdeen in both of these areas made it very difficult for me to determine which assignment would be worse. I finally decided on the guard detail. Much to my surprise, I learned that I would be one of three Sergeants whose responsibility would be the security of the entire depot. Each Sergeant worked a rotating eight hour shift and we were headquartered at the main gate leading onto the post. There were approximately thirty guards per shift under our separate command. I was issued white leggings, an MP arm band and a 45 calibre semiautomatic pistol.

I learned on my first shift that the posting and the returning of the perimeter guard around the depot was one of my major responsibilities. I was also responsible for the guardhouse and the prisoners in the camp stockade, a room adjoining the small one story brick guardhouse next to the main gate.

The most perplexing problem was trying to locate the men who were supposed to show up for guard duty from the various units operating the depot. On each shift there were a number of "extra" men named supernumeraries. These men were held in reserve in case of emergency, such as a posted guard becoming sick, being killed or more likely needing to go to the bathroom. It seldom worked that way.

Because all the units but mine used the rotating guard duty system, there were many incidents of abuse and lack of interest. Men reported who were drunk, unsoldierly, disoriented or just plain hostile over being put on guard detail. Live ammunition had to be issued to men who had never seen a loaded weapon except on a basic training rifle range. Hardly a shift would go by, day or night, that I did not hear the inevitable rifle shot from some quarter of our fenced in depot. I would jump in the jeep to race off to some far corner of the post only to find my guard sheepishly looking at his rifle. Most would make up an outrageous story of shadowy figures, suspected parachutists or strange noises. None of the stories ever proved to be true, of course. Every one of those live rounds was fired by mistake. One guard, adamant about his story of a figure trying to cross the wire fence in the night, had actually come very close to blowing off his own foot. The end of his shoe was gone, the bullet having missed his toes by a fraction of an inch.

Being Sergeant of the guard was a singular job, but it was also frustrating and more demanding than I had imagined. Each morning shift, as I was trying to assemble an inadequate number of disgruntled men for duty, I would take a minute to gaze longingly at the garbage truck that rumbled through the gate, its crew laughing and jeering, on its way to some mysterious dump near Warminster. Sometimes the truck, weaving and loaded with singing drunks, would not return until I was going off duty eight hours later.

If a man did not show up for guard duty or had to be sent back because he could not pass personal or equipment inspection, it was my duty to call his company CP and report it. Theoretically the First Sergeant of the company or the company clerk would then send another man. This never happened. At first I was very conscientious about the report, telephoning at once from the guardhouse after checking over my list of those who were to report. I soon learned to make do with what I had, because usually a laconic voice on the other end of the field phone would say, "I'll tell the Sergeant."

I would never hear from them again. On one occasion I did get a reaction, however. It was in town in my favorite pub, when a huge man, a very angry Private first class, surprised me at the bar by grabbing me by the throat and lifting me off the floor about a foot. Through watering eyes and while gasping for breath, I could hear him say, "Are you the stool pigeon who told my First Sergeant I ain't showed up for fucking guard duty?"

I sputtered while he went on, "You want your ass kicked, you do that again."

He put me down. I never did that again. On many a wet day or night, I stood guard at the main gate myself because there were not enough men to go around.

Early one afternoon, I was called away from my desk in the guardhouse by one of the two guards at the main gate. They had stopped a jeep with a British officer who did not have the proper pass with which to enter the post. As I walked over to the jeep, I could see the flash of red on the officer's cap that indicated that he was a senior staff officer. A closer look, followed by a salute, revealed him to be a General. He was furious at being held up at the gate and launched into a tirade over being treated like a common soldier.

131

Shifting uncomfortably from foot to foot, I waited for him to finish before I said, "Sir, my instructions are to allow no one on this post without a signed pass."

After some further sputtering and shouting, I slid into the jeep beside him and directed him to drive to the post headquarters. In a red faced rage he raced through the post, ignoring my one comment about depot speed limit. We slammed to a stop in front of the headquarters building, both of us jumping out of the vehicle at the same time. I ran ahead of him up the steps, threw open the door, yelled for attention to the startled clerks and junior officers inside and stood holding open the door for him as he swept inside. I waited for him on the steps. In a few minutes the door crashed open and my General, holding his valid pass delicately by his fingertips within an inch of my face said sarcastically, "Soldier, here is my bloody pass. I will now enter this bloody post!"

With that he went to the jeep, driving off, engine racing, without looking back or without an offer to drive me back to the guardhouse. A white faced American Captain stood behind me in the headquarters doorway watching him go. We both shrugged and I walked the half mile back to the main gate.

Later that day I was again called away from my desk by the guard. My General was leaving the post and had demanded to speak to me. As I approached the idling jeep, I was surprised to see the officer jump out and stride over to meet me. I gave him my best bent finger salute, noticing that the two guards on the gate moved away so as not to catch the flak and abuse that we all expected. Instead the Brigadier returned my salute and with a slight smile said, "Sergeant, I'm sorry that I was so nasty to you. I'm not used to Yanks who carry out their orders. Well done, lad."

With that he spun around, jumped back in the driver's seat and roared off through the gate. I was pleased to see that both of my guards gave him a snappy rifle salute as he left the post.

The only thing about guard duty, other than the fact that no one in my own company ever knew what I was doing or where I might be found most of the time, was that the camp bakery sent over a slab of freshly baked coffee cake every morning. On the evening shift there was an occasional large tray of sheet cake. The hot coffee roll was delicious, easily counted as among the best food I ever ate in the Army. It disappeared quickly, being divided among the guards near the guardhouse and shared with our only prisoner in the stockade, a pervert. He had been brought in one evening by the local constabulary of Warminster, charged with perversion involving a ten year old boy. Naturally he was shunned by everyone; we even refused to speak to him. After all he was an American soldier and shocking behavior such as that could not be understood, much less tolerated.

There was a small barred window set low in the wall between the stockade room and the guard room where my desk and phone were located. Sometimes out of the corner of my eye, I could see him watching me through the window, his head bent sideways as he stooped to look out. It was an eerie feeling because I was often alone in the outer room. I read the detailed civilian arrest report when he was brought in but could not believe the words I read. The description of what he had done with the little boy was so revolting, so disgusting that except for allowing someone to pass him a small piece of coffee cake once in awhile, I had nothing to do with him. I even tried to avoid looking at him, although once an hour I had to look through the window to make sure that he had not escaped. He was a small dark man from Philadelphia with a ferret-like face and straight black hair. We kept him in the stockade for four weeks before he was transferred somewhere else to stand trial in a British court. We were all relieved when he left and heard later that he was given a dishonorable discharge and sent back to the states.

The most interesting but often the most troublesome time on the main gate occurred Saturday night around midnight. It was then that passes expired and close to 500 men would begin to pour back onto the post. The main gate was the only gate through which personnel on foot were permitted to pass, so the tangle was severe as passes were checked. Sometimes an irksome junior officer would supervise the process, after making men line up so that passes could be checked against dog tags. These officers would appear without warning, usually having been assigned as post officer of the day who took their duties a little too seriously.

The great interest, however, on a normal night with the O.D. was to look at the men as they straggled back through the gate. Many were drunk, of course, a few being sick, some singing, most in small groups together. But occasionally a lone ashen faced man would walk up to me and with eyes darting from side to side would whisper, "Where's the pro station?"

I would direct him to the camp hospital and reflect on the Mickey Mouse film and on the small town of Stroud.

Men would come back bleeding from fights, many without caps, jackets or raincoats. Clothes of any kind were premium items in England, and you had to literally watch your hat and coat in any public gathering place. Also articles of clothing were prime gift and barter items often having been exchanged for some mysterious favor from some of the female population. There was even one hatless, barefooted man who appeared one night without even his shirt and even though there was a drizzling rain, I could see in the dim light, he was smiling. I have often wondered what adventure he had had that Saturday night in Warminster. Whatever it had been, it had cost the American taxpayer quite a lot.

By this time the fighting in France was reaching a fever pitch as forces around Caen and St. Lo were gathering to force a breakout. The airfield North of the camp presented a constant flow of aircraft on their way to strike the beach area and crippled planes trailing oily smoke were often seeing trying to make it back. Sometimes they didn't quite make it. There would be a muffled thud followed by a column of black smoke on the horizon beyond the hills. Green flares being shot from the planes were seen signifying that a plane had wounded aboard and was seeking a priority landing. It was a sobering time for us, the apprehension being magnified by the constant rumors that we were soon going to join the actual fighting on the continent. Time dragged on and we stayed in Warminster.

There was very little interchange between the Americans and the people of Warminster. I was sorry for this because my interest in the people went far beyond seeking physical relationships with the women who frequented the pubs looking for free drinks, money or field jackets. Except for the few farmers and their families with whom I had spoken on Sunday bicycle rides, I had been in England for six weeks and had not made a single British friend.

I took to going into town during the day when I was off Sergeant of the guard duty. Passes for me were no problem; one of the fringe benefits beyond the coffee cake, was a permanent pass when I was not on duty. The visits to the shopping market center of town were discouraging. People avoided American soldiers, averting their eyes, refusing to speak or to even answer questions or to give simple directions. Their response would be to push past and go on their way, hurrying to escape any contact from the foreign devils.

I caught on right away. Avoiding downtown, I began a rather systematic cultivation of the side streets and the many narrow lanes, which led to the areas of the city that were occupied by residences. At first this too was discouraging. Housewives calling children into the home when I approached was a common reaction to my lonely patrol. I was usually on foot since I had discovered that an American soldier in a residential area on a bicycle attracted unnecessary attention and suspicion. Apparently the populace believed that with the help of a local Bobby, they could outrun me if trouble developed, whereas a young man with wheels might present a stamina problem to someone chasing him on foot. In any event I learned that a quiet passage on the cracked and broken sidewalks of Warminster could often bring at least a nod from a passerby and once in a great while could evoke a smile and a short word of greeting.

I never attempted a conversation with any passerby, but rather, instead settled for simple eye contact. I smiled a lot at anyone who would just look at me. At first I worried about the seemingly pathetic nature of my desire to make a friend. More importantly I began to subscribe to the growing notion that there might just be something different about my mental balance since I was beginning to feel a satisfaction when a civilian just spoke to me. I would sit on my bunk in the Quonset hut and ponder the problem until the answer was acceptable. It appeared to be a simple loneliness to reach out of the military life into the past where I had been happy. Since leaving New Jersey, I had hardly spoken to a civilian, my life was almost totally occupied with men, orders and preparation for war. I had friends, of course, but like me their occupation was narrow and stifling.

One hot afternoon after a summer shower had made the steam swirl in patches on the softened asphalt, I blundered into a solution. Waiting for the heavy cooling rain to stop, I had stood under some elm trees near a gate entrance to a rather large house set back from the street along a curving driveway. Standing alone under the protection of the trees, I studied the house. Having had a year of prearchitectural courses in college, I had become familiar with and fascinated by buildings. It was a three story red brick structure of Georgian design with no porch, just a double casemented doorway, rigid but with a functional beauty, nicely balanced by triple dormers and straight line shuttered windows. Graceful trees framed the house across a grassy sweep of lawn. The words, "Manor House," came to my mind. As I was speculating on the age of the structure and wondering about its engineering problems, the door of the house opened and a British soldier stepped out into the lessening rain. Even at that distance I could tell he was British. Their uniforms were almost the same color as the American drill but a soldier of the Crown always carried his cap stuffed under the shoulder epaulet of his jacket. As this soldier pulled his cap loose, he turned and spoke to someone standing just inside the doorway. They said goodbye and he walked down the driveway toward where I was standing. He was tall and handsome. There was something about the deliberate way he walked, which said confidence. Striding down the driveway, he approached me as he withdrew a single cigarette from his tunic pocket.

"I say chap, have you a light?" he asked.

I fumbled all over myself trying to be helpful. The soldier smiled in quiet amusement as I finally found my Zippo lighter in my field jacket.

Exhaling smoke as I lit his cigarette for him, he said, "Thank you chap. Did you get wet from the rain?"

His manner of speaking was cultured but courteous, without the twang of the cockney or the nasal arrogance of the upper class. He was a Private in his Majesty's service but he was an educated young man. We made some small comments about the weather and then I asked, "Do you live in this lovely house?"

He laughed. "Heavens no," was the reply. "I'm from London, don't you know? That's Mrs. Martin's home. Go in if you like. Well chap, cheerio!"

With that he strode off down the street, heavy boots crunching on the still wet and steaming brick sidewalk.

I looked cautiously at the house, deciding impulsively to go up to the door. As I stood uncertainly before the brass knocker, I noticed a small neatly lettered framed sign to the right of the door. It read, "All Servicemen Are Welcome."

The door was opened by an elderly man in a black alpaca jacket who stood aside graciously and bowed as I entered a small paneled entrance hall. Taking my cap and field jacket, he motioned for me to pass through a thick blue velour drape that closed off the entrance from the rest of the house. I entered into one of the most elegant rooms I had ever seen. Oak paneling and wide board pegged floors gave a subtle warmth to the blue of the scattered deep carpets. A crystal chandelier hung over a heavy walnut table in the center of the large room. Portraits graced the walls. Over the great fireplace hung a large painting of a heavy nude woman in a gigantic gold frame. The light from an exhibitor's lamp over the piece was the only electric light that I could see in the room. The afternoon sun, refreshed from the rain, streamed past the velour drapes at the sides of the latticed windows.

Something stirred in my memory about the painting. I walked, almost on tiptoes over to the fireplace and stared up at the work. There it was, in the corner near the frame. The single word, Rubens.

I stepped back, my spine tingling. "My God," I whispered, "a real Rubens."

I was standing back from the fireplace, entranced by the painting when I heard a slight feminine cough off to the right of me.

Turning quickly, I saw a woman in her 40's, graceful, silver blond hair pulled back tightly around her oval face. She stood quietly in the doorway, hands clasped in front of her. She wore a white silk open necked blouse and a plaid skirt. Her eyes were as blue as the cerulean sky near the cherubs in the Rubens. She studied me for a moment before she smiled.

"Why, hello, how nice for you to drop by," her voice low, cultured. "Do you like the painting?" she asked as she walked closer to me.

I stood awkwardly on one foot and then the other. "Oh yes, Mam," I replied. "The Flemish arts are among my favorite, although I don't recall ever having seen a print of this particular work. Was it done about the middle of the 17th century?"

She was standing quite close to me by this time. She was almost as tall as I was. She studied me before answering my question. I could see a softness come into her wide and beautiful eyes. She smiled broadly.

"Well," she said taking my arm, "I can see that we need to have a long talk about Peter Paul Rubens and you."

Laughing a low sort of chuckle, she went on, "But first won't you join us? We were just about to have tea in the sun room."

Without waiting for my response, she guided me out of the large paneled room, down a short corridor and into a sunfilled room with all manner of green plants spaced against the walls. Large windows and a skylight drenched the white trimmed room with light. The floor was marble. In the center of the space not occupied by growing plants sat a white glass topped ornate iron table. On two chairs next to the table sat two British soldiers. They stared at me unsmiling as my hostess marched me over to them. They were enlisted men like myself, one a Private, the other a Corporal. Turning to me as the men stood up, "I'm so sorry. I'm Mrs. Martin. What is your name? You're a Sergeant, aren't you?" she said, glancing at my chevrons.

I stumbled through my name, resisting the impulse to mispronounce it. I felt somewhat embarrassed and completely out of place. Mrs. Martin then introduced me to the other soldiers who merely nodded without a word. We were all invited to be seated as the man in the alpaca jacket pushed a tea cart through a small disguised door that I had not seen when I had entered the room. As she poured tea she talked about prices and the scarcity of food. She did not chatter but spoke slowly and deliberately about the crush of the war on Warminster.

I glanced around at the room. Never in my life had I ever seen such a place. My life had been spent in small homes. I speculated that our entire home in Cannonsburg, Pennsylvania, would have fitted comfortably into this room. I couldn't help but think that I was fifteen years of age before I even had a room of my own and it would have fitted neatly onto the top of the tea cart.

"Do you like this sun room?" Mrs. Martin asked.

"Yes Mam," I replied. "It is a lovely large sun room."

Perhaps it was the unconscious emphasis that I had placed on the word, large, but I thought that I caught a flicker of shadow behind her eyes.

She added quickly, "Of course there are not so many women as lucky as I to have such a marvelous home."

The two other young men shifted slightly in their chairs. The one named Tom looked hard at me and said pointedly, "We don't see many Yanks in this part of Warminster."

"No, I expect not," I snapped. "Most of us are fighting the war."

I was beginning to be a little irritated by Tom and his friend and I guess intimidated by the opulence of my surroundings.

Everyone stiffened at my comment, but before the silence could become important, Mrs. Martin, with noticeable moisture in the corners of her eyes, quickly changed the subject to a discussion of the problems in keeping the plants alive during the winter months. The tensions went out of the three of us and we finished the tea. The little cakes were really delicious.

"Tom is Jason's son, you know," volunteered Mrs. Martin.

From the slight inclination of her head, I gathered that the black jacket was Tom's father, named Jason. Tom looked at me defiantly.

"Hey, that's really great, Tom," I said without much conviction.

Tom shot to his feet, jerking on the Corporal's arm.

"We must leave, Mrs. Martin, we know that you have had a busy day and that you must be tired."

He looked directly at me. I stood with them. I got the message. I was prepared to leave. She saw us to the door as I manipulated the space so that the Englishmen were outside on the steps while I was still in the entryway shrugging into my field jacket. She stood very close to me as I said, taking her proffered hand, "Thank you very much for the tea, the Rubens and the most wonderful time I have had since I left home."

I felt the pressure of her fingers on mine. "I enjoyed your visit. Do come back," she offered. "I mean that Sergeant," she added.

Looking directly into my eyes, she released my hand and smiling led me to the open door. I half waved as the door closed behind me.

When I reached the street, Tom and his companion were waiting for me. Tom was angry. He grabbed my arm, spinning me around so that I was between the two of them. The Corporal held my other arm behind me and Tom hissed in my face, "I ought to knock your bloody head off." Louder he said, "Stay away from here, you're not wanted at this house. She's a fine lady and we don't want you bloody Yanks fucking around here!" Shouting now, he finished, "Stay in town with the whores, where you bloody well belong!"

The Corporal released my arm and the two of them hurried down the sidewalk, the Corporal in earnest conversation with Tom, holding his arm, trying to quiet him down. As they turned into a side street, I straightened myself out and followed them into town but at a much slower pace. I did not want to catch up to them. I needed a drink.

An hour or so later as I was standing by myself at a bar on my second glass of gin, the Corporal slid in beside me, bought a warm beer and after downing most of it in one long swallow said, "I'm sorry, Sergeant, about that back there," he waved in the direction of the Martin house, finished the beer, wiped his mouth with the back of his hand and went on, "Tom's hotheaded, he's devoted to the Martins, his dad, granddad and God knows how many great granddads have served them for many years."

The barkeep brought us another round and we drank in silence for several minutes. "She's alone, you know," he said quietly. "He was shot down over the Channel in '40. Then she lost the boy on the Prince of Wales in '41.''

As he stared into his beer, I looked closely at him. Small, stocky little old Englishman, sick of war. I decided to tell him about myself. I talked while we drank together. I talked for over an hour. Although he wasn't a civilian, he was English, named Freddy and he listened politely as I tried to explain the loneliness of a civilian soldier in a foreign country. At first he was distant, almost embarrassed. He looked around from time to time as though he didn't want anyone to see me talking to him. I explained my early childhood, my family, my schools and my friends. I even showed him pictures from my wallet. He said the right things at the right time and when I had finally finished, I was flush with a warm feeling toward this human being who had served so well as a listener. He himself had become animated and friendly. It didn't surprise me to hear him tell me about himself. I also said the right things at the right times about his wallet pictures. We left the pub, arms around each others' shoulders and staggered down toward the post. I had made an enemy that day but had also made two friends.

The following Sunday, I waited impatiently until almost teatime and then knocked on the door of Mrs. Martin's house. Tom's father invited me in but when I asked to speak to her, he informed me that she was in London for the weekend. I joined several other British servicemen in the large room but they merely stared at me. After studying the Rubens for a while and idly flipping the pages of a few books on the library shelves, I thanked Tom's father and hurried back to my Quonset hut to nurse a savage feeling of disappointment. I could not explain it. This woman was old enough to be my mother. Her only son had died at sea, so she must be in her late 40's or early 50's. I was 20. But I kept seeing her in the doorway and the memory of her eyes and hair kept turning over and over in my mind.

I returned the next afternoon when I finished my guard shift but no one answered my repeated knocks. I went back to the pub to look for Freddy but he wasn't there, nor did he appear even though I anxiously watched the door until well into the evening as I stretched out a few warm drinks. I returned again to the camp, feeling betrayed and consumed by self pity and despair. I was so bitter that there were tears in my eyes. Finally I resolved that I would give her one more chance. I returned to the manor home on Saturday afternoon, determined that if she were not there, I would simply walk out of her life and leave her to nurse *her* despair at my leaving. Waiting for my knock to be answered, I practiced the message I would give the alpaca jacket, fully expecting that she would not be here. The message would be simple but poignant. It would burn in her memory forever. She would be very sorry that she had sent me to die in battle without even having been at home to wish me goodbye.

I was about to knock again when the door was opened not by the butler, but by Mrs. Martin herself. I stood there with my mouth open. Swallowing hard, I began to stammer as she cried, "Oh, Bill, I'm so glad to see you."

As she took my arm, a great flood of warmth swept over me. She had called me by my Christian name! Never before had she called me anything but Sergeant. I had not even thought that she had remembered my name.

We passed together into the empty large panelled room and under the light of the Rubens. She placed both hands on my shoulders. She was radiant and beautiful. Before I could put my arms around her, she said with wide eyes, "I've got to tell you the news."

Then she quickly released her hold on me and turning with hands clasped together in front of her like a little girl, she exclaimed, "They think he's alive! They believe that he is in a prisoner of war camp in China!"

She began pacing back and forth in front of the Rubens, nervous but as excited as a girl. Her movements were quick but graceful. She was clearly thrilled, releasing her joy in a flood of words, which I could barely follow. Apparently she had been in London on business, had stopped by the war office and had been informed that Jeffrey, her son, I presumed, had been reported by the Red Cross as having been picked up at sea and interred in a Japanese prisoner of war camp somewhere on the China mainland. Sometimes her eyes sparkled with tears but often she laughed out loud as the words tumbled in a torrent from her lips.

I could only interject a few monosyllables from time to time, "Great," or "Wonderful," I would say. After several minutes of pacing and talking, she swept me out of the room into a small room that I had not seen before. The room was a small library with walls of books and open shelves lined with trophies, cricket bats, fencing swords and framed photographs. French doors, open to the summer air, looked out over a well cared for lawn. The room was in the rear of the home looking into the backyard. Yard is an American term because this room looked out over a spacious estate and garden. There were no other buildings, telephone lines or homes to be seen, only verdant woods at the far end of the lawn.

We sat together on a small sofa facing the open doors. She continued to talk. "This was his favorite room, you know. Jason keeps it up but I have not been in here for two years!" She paused to look around in wonder.

"Can you imagine? Oh, how differently I feel about this room."

Suddenly she jumped to her feet and almost running, went to the mantel of the ever present fireplace to reach for a framed picture of a young man in a naval uniform. Looking at it searchingly for moments, she finally cried, "Oh my God."

With that she burst into racking tears, holding the picture to her breast with both arms around it.

I sat quietly, not wanting to intrude. I did not know what to do. I was a stranger taking part in a scene that made me feel inadequate. I did not know my lines. I had no experience with this. I only knew that I had to do something to help this most beautiful woman. I was a poor lower class boy from America presuming to help a wealthy, cultured lady from England who stood alone, just feet away from me, crying. Silently, I moved over behind her and put my arms around her, holding her and the picture.

"Mrs. Martin," I said twice.

The crying reduced slowly to sobs and then to a soft whimper or two followed by sniffling. She turned to take my proffered handker-chief, luckily it was new, the only clean one I had left in my barracks bag that morning. She dabbed at her eyes and then blew her nose with a loud unlikely sound. The noise was clearly a masculine "honk." We were startled by the sound that she had made and both of us burst into uncontrollable laughter. We laughed until the tears came. We were on the thin edge of hysteria by the time we sank back together on the sofa, gasping for air. As she sat up on the edge of the cushion to blow her nose again, she looked at me and we both exploded again into laughter. This time we laughed so hard that I was so weak that I could only flop my hands at my sides as I lay back on the small cushion.

With a great effort to control her composure, Mrs. Martin delicately dabbed at her nose with the handkerchief and smoothed her hair. Her face, still radiant and filled with happiness, was flushed. She looked out over the lawn, lips trembling a little so that I was sure that she was going to cry again. Instead, she stood up, straightened her shoulders and returned to the fireplace where she had placed the picture. This time she looked serenely at the smiling face. Turning to me again, she looked across the small space between us for many silent moments. She seemed older.

"I would like to talk about it." she stated. "Will you listen?"

It was a fascinating hour as she went from item to item in the room. Holding up trophies, pointing to photographs and even taking down a fencing foil to do a fair reposite' with it. She talked all of the time, describing how the trophy had been won, how the photograph had been taken, who was in it and what Jeffrey had been doing at the time. I could follow some of her description, but the jumbled chronology finally overcame my reason. I simply listened to each fragment of story and didn't try to fit it all together. It was very evident, however, that her son, Jeffrey, was and had been the very center of her life. By the time she had finished, it was getting quite dark, well beyond teatime and far beyond dinnertime for me. I had said very little during the period in which she had reconstructed a Jeffrey who was now alive again. She hadn't needed my comments, she had merely needed someone to be there with her.

As I walked back to the post in the cooling evening, I could not help but speculate over the similarity between my conversation with Freddy in the pub and Mrs. Martin's outpouring to me. These two events had been the same. Far different had been the stories, even further separated had been the characters in the stories. My story had been of a poor boy from blue collar America; Jeffery, a British Naval officer, had been wealthy, privately educated and by my standards, very pampered. However, we both had been loved and had lived our dissimilar childhoods in an arena of understanding, support and happiness.

Lying on my bunk in the dark Quonset hut that night I realized that my infaluation with Mrs. Martin had grown into a realization, which in turn had become a basic lesson. People, regardless of age, nationality or background are the same. Their needs are the same, their hopes are the same. As a twenty year old, about to enter battle, this realization was to affect how I saw my enemy.

A faint thrumming in the darkness, marking the return of the first bomb run over a German city, made the point very clear to me. There were airmen aboard that English craft, perhaps wounded, certainly exhausted from the fear that each had just experienced. But I thought, at this moment there is a *German* pilot, perhaps wounded, certainly exhausted from fear, fighting a shattered fighter plane into a turn for a final approach to his own landing strip. And behind each of these different crews, there is a family, a wife, a sweetheart, tight with private fears of their own.

For the first time since my arrival in England, I thought of the fear that each member of my own family must be experiencing. Fear for me. Would my mother keep my room locked forever if I died? I tried to imagine my mother as Mrs. Martin. Yes, my mother could, and would play Mrs. Martin's scene if she discovered that I had returned from the dead. There would not be so many trophies or photographs of important people but there were other things. Italian, German and Japanese mothers could and would also. We were all the same.

While I was in Warminster, I visited with Mrs. Martin twice more. She was polite, friendly and animated in her relationship with me, but I noticed, showed me exactly the same level of friendship that she offered to other servicemen who enjoyed her open hospitality. I drank tea, played cards and chess, read the books in the main library, spoke often to Jason, and continually enjoyed Peter Paul Rubens.

Mrs. Martin never spoke to me again about our late afternoon affair between her and her son, Jeffery. She was kind to me but treated me as though the day had never happened. I was never to see his favorite room again, nor did I ever see Tom or Corporal Freddy during my remaining days in England. When I closed the door behind me for the last time, after shaking her lovely warm hand and looking into her cornflower eyes, I knew that the important incident in my life was closed and that I would never visit the house again.

One day, during my off hours, I volunteered to drive one of six jeeps about fifty miles down to a staging area North of Southhampton. The jeeps were to be delivered to the motor pool officer at a large depot for shipment to France. A three-quarter ton weapons carrier was to accompany us so that we could have transportation back to Warminster. Each of us was given a map and we were instructed to proceed in convoy, lead by the weapons carrier.

We rolled out the gate at 11:00 a.m. on a warm overcast day. The sky was entirely covered by low clouds with patches of milky white light carried by the sun, which occasionally broke the hold of the low hanging cloud bank.

Driving a World War II jeep was fun. They handled beautifully. It was like driving a combination carnival bump car and a souped-up dragster. They were sensitive, responsive and powerful for their size. I always enjoyed driving a jeep; it reminded me of my college days and a Model A that I tried desperately without success to convert into a "Hot rod."

I particularly enjoyed the drive this day because I was alone and could enjoy the solitude as we rumbled through little villages that I had never seen before. By noon I was used to driving on the left side of the road from the left seat. At first the driving position that placed the driver next to the curb was very awkward, particularly when making right turns or navigating the constant circles, called "roundabouts" by the British, which are encountered in almost every town or village. But I had learned how to do it, speculating how peculiar it was going to be in the future returning to the wrong side of the road. In spite of all logic, the British continued to contend that the way they drove was the right way and that everyone else in the world was wrong by driving on the right instead of on the left.

I marvelled at the British mind but knew enough about history to think that there was not the remotest possibility that they would ever change. Their own comic devotion to their way of doing things is strong and remains one of the charms of the British people. For Americans, driving across England was difficult for another reason. There were very few direction signs or even signs that announced the name of a town. The reason was simple. All signs had been removed early in the war so as not to be of help to the Germans who were a real potential invader threat to the British Isles early in the war. A parachute force

143

dropped across a few miles of terrain could be kept virtually helpless if they didn't know exactly where *they* were. Consequently a lot of time was spent in roadside conversation with farmers and errant civilians on bicycles. The question, "How do I get to such and such town?" would, with slight variations, invariably be answered, "Quite right, straight ahead, bear left, to the second turning, straight till you come to where old Johnson's farm used to be. You can't miss it."

The phrase "you cawn't miss it!" became a common sarcastic call, back and forth among the American vehicles in England. No one who ever drove a truck for more than a few hundred yards was unfamiliar with the cry, "You cawn't miss it!"

Well, you bloody well *could* miss it and did, all the time. I expect that half of the gasoline used by the American forces in England was burned away while drivers tried in exasperation to understand directions and in looking for where Johnson's farm used to be.

This particular day was no exception to the rule of being lost most of the time. Within a few miles, the weapons carrier and the six jeeps were strung out and badly separated. The Army, of course, had specific intervals for vehicles in convoy. The spacing was a group defense against strafing, bombing, artillery or any other kind of enemy action. Unfortunately it was difficult to maintain the proper interval. Going through towns crowded with other traffic, civilian pedestrians, and thousands of bicycles, I became entangled in pedestrian traffic in a small village only to watch the jeep I had been following disappear around a corner. Within a few minutes it was out of sight. The jeep, which was supposed to be following me, was nowhere to be seen even though I pulled over on the shoulder of the highway and waited for ten minutes. Waiting was a mistake since it meant I could never catch the convoy ahead of me again. Unperturbed, I started driving myself at a leisurely pace, relieved not to be forced to follow convoy rules. I noticed that the clouds had become a sort of ground fog that restricted visibility to less than one hundred yards. As I pressed ahead, I realized that the map was useless in the weather conditions. However, I reasoned that if I could keep to what appeared to be the main road, I was bound to end up somewhere important such as where Johnson's farm used to be.

I had plenty of gas and driving the jeep, even in fog, was very pleasant. The fun ended almost at once as I came to an almost perfect fork in the road—one main highway leading to the right, another identical main road leading to the left. I sat at the fork motionless, trying to decide what I should do, as I cursed the concrete pedestal upon which once a very important directional sign had stood. The sun, obscured in the fog, couldn't even tell me whether I was going North or South. So I swung the jeep to the left onto a highway, which as far as I knew or at the moment cared, lead to the edge of the earth or beyond.

I sang to myself as I drove. I was isolated by the fog; I felt young, alive and beautiful. There was no other traffic in either direction. I watched from one side to the other, looking for anything that matched my mood. A good stone wall, a line of ordered trees whispering for attention through the mist, or a close stone home with a thick, damp thatched roof, a well loved garden of vegetables. The trip was euphoric and because of the limited visibility, I seemed suspended, as in a dream of my own.

I discovered that the road was ascending and that there were no longer clumps of trees or any sign of buildings. The country next to the road was moor-like with only rarely a snaking stone wall wafting off into the fog. However, as I climbed, the sky became lighter and there were patches of actual sunlight that sent shafts of golden light down through the cloud cover to make large spots of yellow green on the fields next to the road.

Suddenly, out of the fog, I approached a rather large parking area off to the left. Impulsively I swung into the vehicle park, which was empty for as long as I could see. I pulled over to the curb, stopped the jeep and turned off the ignition. The silence was total and awesome as I strained to hear any sound. I thought I heard a distant cowbell but I was not sure. I got out of the jeep and took a few steps beyond the curb before I came to a well worn dirt path that led from the parking area up a slight incline to disappear into the mist. Without thought for the security of my jeep, I unhesitantly followed the path up the hill. Peering ahead as I walked, I thought that I could see some structure looming up through the fog but it seemed broken and strangely scattered. I stopped and studied what I was seeing. As I tried to puzzle it out in the silence, the sky broke open slightly so that the scene before me softened into a cold yellow light and I knew suddenly where I was. I was standing at Stonehenge, which was at that time believed to be an ancient Druid temple.

I hurried along the path until I broke into a circle of massive stones. The effect was magic. I was absolutely alone in a now dazzling refracted light, in the center of legend. The colossal arranged upright stones in a huge circle were more than impressive. They were magnificent. Spaced apart, these pillar like blocks supported other lintel stones, which connected them in places to form a link between the uprights. Some were missing, a few were scattered around as though some giant child had flung his blocks in anger or petulance.

I sat on one of them, letting my senses drink in the mystery and enjoy the marvel of it all. I had read about Stonehenge, but had had no real idea where it was located in England, and had never even thought about it once since being stationed at Warminster.

What was Stonehenge? No one knew in 1944. It was an anthropological mystery. Historians could only guess that it had been built by

Druid priests. It appeared to be a temple of some sort, but what its significance was, was still speculation. There were dark tales of possible human sacrifices and the curious outer circle of buried white chalk pits was an additional puzzle. No one could explain the huge stones themselves or where they had come from since they did not appear to be indigenous to the region.

Stonehenge was to remain a comparative secret for thirty more years before it was theorized that it was simply a giant calendar. Early tribes, perhaps sun worshipers, had placed the blocks so that the openings between the stones marked the rise and setting of the sun and stars. But on this foggy day, this legendary piece of England was beautiful and it was entirely mine in the silent mist. Perhaps it was being there alone that marked the place and event as important to me. I only knew that up to that moment, I had never really experienced such a total feeling of human history.

By now the sun was breaking through in shorter intervals and the fog itself was burning away. As it did so, I could see that I was on a small hill overlooking open fields. It was mostly pasture land with a few strolling cows, heads down, eating.

I could see the jeep in the now visible parking lot about 300 yards away from the temple. It looked strange all by itself and somehow the contrast between the authority of Stonehenge and the tiny insect-like vehicle of modern war was startling.

I wondered what the priests of this place would have thought if they could have seen that jeep. Even more important was what would they have thought about the fact that it, and its driver, had come from the other side of the planet.

I took one last look around and feeling exhilarated by the experience, I hurried down the hill to the jeep.

I found the huge, sprawling depot with little trouble since I found that Stonehenge itself was marked on the military map, giving me a point of reference. I was the third jeep to arrive at the depot, but the others straggled in within an hour and the weapons carrier, our lead off vehicle, showed up last of all, two hours late. On our way back to Warminster in the back of the weapons carrier, one of the other jeep drivers asked, "Did any of you guys see them big rocks on the way down?"

No one had noticed Stonehenge but me, but I didn't admit to it. He grunted, "Man, them Limeys are crazy to build anything like that!" After a pause, he said aloud to no one in particular, "Damned thing don't even have a roof on it!"

CHAPTER VIII

DEPARTURE FROM ENGLAND

Our battalion of over 100 vehicles arrived at the blacked out staging area late in the evening. There was a cold rain falling through the salt air, which was blowing in from the Southwest on a strong gusting wind. We were told to stay in the trucks until directions could be obtained as to where we were to spend the night. Except for runners working their way through the long line of wet trucks with masked swinging flashlights, there was no movement. I had been assigned as a driver, so I was relatively dry and warm inside the closed cab. My companion, a Corporal from the 3rd squad, remained asleep, a condition he had maintained since leaving Warminster almost ten hours before. With the engine stopped, the silence was eerie. Only the wind, which intermittently slashed the rain against the windshield, brought with it the knowledge that time was passing.

I soon fell into an exhausted sleep, only to be jerked awake as my cab door was slammed open by a voice that yelled, "Stay in the trucks. Company L will assemble in the morning."

The door crashed shut, but I could hear the order being repeated at the back of the truck, followed by the groans and curses of tired, wet Army men. The shout, "48, 49, 50, Somme-Shit!" rang out, but drifted away into the chilling rain.

The wind buffeted us all through the long night; the rain never stopped. Around midnight or shortly thereafter, the Corporal awoke. After fourteen hours sleep, he was refreshed and talkative. We ate some K rations, talked quietly about women, discussed rumors about where we were going in France and drank some sour red wine, which he had kept in his aluminum canteen. The wine reminded me of the taste of the cod liver oil that children in the 30's were forced to take. Apparently

147

there had been some imaginative merchandising during the 30's that had stressed the magical and beneficial effects of the vitamins in cod liver oil on the young developing bodies of the children of America. Everyone whom I knew under the age of eighteen took the stuff, either in rubbery capsules or by the teaspoon. It tasted, of course, terrible. I don't believe that I stopped belching cod liver oil until I was well into my late 20's. Years later my youngest son was assigned a paper to write in his sixth grade history class, so naturally he came to his ancient father for information. He asked, "Dad, what was the one thing you remember most from your life in the olden days?"

I had replied without hesitation, "Cod liver oil!"

Puzzled by my answer, but determined to finish his assignment, he recorded my response and submitted the paper to his teacher.

She had been either very young or had recently arrived from some other planet where they had never heard of cod liver oil, because she had written in the margin in red ink, "Try not to be funny. This is a serious assignment."

His grade had been a C minus. I had given up trying to convince my son that I *had* been serious, but I'm sure that in order to really understand about cod liver oil, you would have had to swallow a gallon or two of it during your lifetime. Then you would have understood. Of course there was also castor oil, but I don't want to talk about that.

Toward morning, we noticed a steady flow of shadowy forms moving off to the right of the convoy, so we struggled into our raincoats and joined the stream. Our destination turned out to be a large blacked out mess hall with a set of double doors to keep the light from showing. The bright interior was actually painful to eyes that had been squinting through darkness for hours. Once we could see, however, we discovered that there were well over two hundred men, sitting at tables, sleeping on the dry cement floor, or talking quietly but earnestly with one another. The great discovery was that there were several large urns of hot coffee. We pushed our way through the mass of men and proceeded to burn smiles on our faces with the scalding but welcome liquid. There were no windows in the building, the sounds of the wind and rain could not be heard over the droning noise of conversation, snoring and occasional burst of excited laughter. There was a human isolation factor at work. We were all together as a group but seemed to be totally apart from the forces that had brought us together at this place and time, a microorganism blindly concerned with itself but unaware of the swirling universe around it.

It was a comforting sort of group camaraderie that we manufactured for ourselves and neither the Corporal or I ever once spoke about going back to the truck for our companions. We simply enjoyed the warm friendliness and mutual appreciation that we felt around us. Talk turned to the Channel crossing with its dangers. Cherbourg had been cleared, so we assumed we would disembark there. Where would we go? To the 1st, 9th or 3rd Army? The 1st and 9th together with the British and Canadians were moving toward Holland and Belgium along the coast of the continent. Patton's Third Army was striking toward Paris and the East. The 7th Army, under General Patch, was moving up the Rhone Valley along with the French 1st Army toward Alsace-Lorraine. During the summer, the 7th had surprised the world with its spectacular invasion of Southern France against demoralized German resistance.

The rumors were consistent; we were to join the 3rd Army near Paris. Some even speculated that arrangements had already been made for us to set up a Base Ordnance Depot in Paris itself. Excitement was high over the possibilities of being stationed in the blacked out City of Lights.

Sitting in the mess hall, many of us dug out our French phrase books and practiced pronunciation. Some scoffed at the idea, choosing instead to fall back on the notion that if the Frogs wanted to speak to us they had better learn English. After all, for the second time in two decades, the Yanks were again in Europe to save their asses.

The language drill was funny. Some of the men, by far most of them, had never spoken a foreign word in their lives and often the result of a virgin tongue strangling and sputtering over a simple French word was hilarious. "Bong Jur Madam Mausoly," became a standard phrase similar to, "You cawn't miss it!"

The phrase book itself was Army issue, along with some invasion currency that looked like soap coupons. We were each given about 150 francs, which was worth less than five dollars. We had been lectured earlier in Warminster about the absolute need to purchase things from the French. Great attention had been given to the punishment for looting, cheating, or stealing when dealing with our Allies. They might just as well have issued each man a bottle of wine because as it turned out the French had very little else to sell except table wine. Having been occupied by the Germans since 1939, who loved them not, there was precious little that remained in France, which was for sale. The exceptions, of course, were wine and women.

We had seen the Mickey Mouse film again and again. By now, however, we were not so impressed with it, even the part where a slender rod about the diameter of a coat hanger wire was inserted into the penis about eight inches, twisted to open hooks along the sides of the wire and then jerked out to open scar tissue, so that the urinary track could bleed freely. The very first time we had seen the film was the only time in my memory up to then that I had ever heard grown men scream. The thought of that hook studded wire being jerked out

149

of one's penis was just too much for the mind to accept. We had grown calloused, however. Many men had had sexual experiences in England without contracting V.D., so the general attitude had developed that the disease was not necessarily carried by *all* women, as the film would have had us believe. As a matter of fact, I only knew of two cases of the disease in our company during the war. Both men, one an officer, were transferred to a base hospital and were never seen again. Perhaps the development of the use of penicillin as a cure came in time to save them humiliation and embarrassment at home. I hope so, because I believe there were very few active young men in wartime who do not fall victim to the rationale, "I might as well do it. I may be dead tomorrow."

It was an easy way to justify doing something that one knew was wrong by the standards of the time. No one *really* believed that he would be dead tomorrow. I knew very few Americans who did not experience sex in some form or other during the war.

The phrase book was interesting and also sobering, for it not only contained normal words of greetings and commonly used conversational phrases, but there were also references to wounded men, enemy tanks, artillery and machine guns. How to ask for directions to hospitals and how to seek medical help were provided. Most of us concentrated on what to say to the Madam Mousaly, however, favoring peaceful pursuits, over the destruction of the Germans or the care of our dead and wounded.

It must have been toward morning, although being in the blacked out windowless building, it was impossible to tell, when the door crashed open to admit a flood of grey morning light, followed immediately by a red faced plump British officer. He stood in the doorway, hands on ample hips, swagger stick jiggling behind him in his hands, handlebar moustache bristling. He glared for several seconds before erupting in a torrent of curses. We stood or sat in awed openmouthed appreciation for his explosive vocabulary, which took bodily functions as its major theme. Cursing well is a true art form and our officer was an absolute professional in the art. I had never been chewed out so well or so precisely. When he finally subsided with a not too cultured reference to our origins, we all felt exorcised. The gist of what he had to say, once his shouts were analyzed, was that we were to have remained in the trucks as we had been ordered to do the night before. It seemed clear that unless we were to return *at once* to our assigned vehicle, we would be summarily executed, or worse. He stood aside with an icy stare as several hundred men stampeded for the door to burst out into the misty cold rain that continued to fall from low racing clouds. Everyone turned his face away from the British officer in an unconscious desire to remain anonymous in case of future identification check. There was no laughing or speaking among the men who scurried rodent-like up the hill to the immobile convoy, which stood train-like against the dark pearl colored sky. The field was cleared in minutes.

Jerking open my cab door, I discovered that my companion had beaten me up the hill by a few seconds. He was gasping for air, making gulping noises through his nose. Neither of us spoke for some time, merely filling the cab with gasping and coughing. I finally took my first opportunity to look around in the silver daylight. We were located on a windswept bluff overlooking an open sea. Our road was actually on a cliff that extended straight down several hundred feet into a green grey choppy ocean. It was my first ever view of the English Channel. The horizon could not be seen because of the rain and low clouds that joined white capped waves clashing together several hundred yards out in the water. The clouds seemed to be only a few feet above the top of the bluff upon which sat our isolated convoy, and the suddenly forbidden mess hall was the only building to be seen anywhere. It was built quite near the edge of the cliff. It appeared to be randomly placed, for there was no road to it, only man-made paths through the vegetation, coming and going so much like a giant spiderweb, having been woven by hundreds and thousands of feet. Perhaps it was the coffee or lack of sleep, but I felt tired, on the sick edge of nausea. The Corporal had fallen asleep. As near as I could tell, he hadn't even looked out of the window.

This lack of interest in the surroundings surprised me slightly, although I was to observe it in others during the coming weeks and months. There were so many Americans who seemed not to care about what was happening around them, nor to be even slightly interested in the country, the cultural changes, or even the topography in which they were fatally involved. It was almost as though each cherished the remnants of his individuality and guarded it against the world around him. He would not be influenced or intimidated by any outside force. He would remain isolated, secure. I knew some who never changed the time on their watches from what it had been in the hometown from which they had come. At eight o'clock in the evening, the watch proclaimed two o'clock in the afternoon in Albany, New York, and nothing could change that.

The Corporal snored softly as I looked around for some sign that we were about to move. There was nothing. We sat in the trucks for some time before I noticed some stir of activity down the line. Several people seemed to be moving from vehicle to vehicle giving instructions. At last a red faced MP banged on the side of our cab and shouted, "Get down to the mess hall in ten minutes. Take your mess gear."

We left immediately, of course, alerting the men in the rear of the truck over their curses and grumbling.

A steady stream of men shuffled along the spiderwebs, converging on the mess hall, mess gear banging with distinctive sounds that have only been heard in times of war. We hurried along, a little immersed by the numbers of men who threatened to fill the building before we could get there.

Inside we found coffee, powdered eggs, bacon, toast, orange marmalade and warmth. Once breakfast was over, there was an enormous impulse to linger amid the fresh rumors and the physical satisfaction that comes from a hot breakfast following a cold, desolate night. We sipped coffee, amid an increasing volume of excited voices and clamoring, which was a measure of our high-pitched feelings. We were about to embark to liberate the continent of Europe and even the dullest of intellects could not help but be moved by the critical and dramatic moment of truth.

Finally forced outside of the mess hall by angry junior officers, I breathed the cold misty air of the English Channel and knew that the importance of the moment would never fade from my memory. I was about to be part of the invasion force that had already gone down in history as one of the greatest single efforts of modern man. After a quick trip to the canvas sided latrine behind the mess hall, I climbed back up the hill to the truck, swinging my metal mess kit in a wide arc to dry it from the scalding hot water, which was present at each meal for cleaning utensils. This water was in a large garbage can. An oil fed portable heater, thrust into the can, caused the water to boil within a matter of minutes. Sometimes there were two containers of water, one for soaping and one for rinsing. If you could keep your hand out of the scalding hot liquid, it really did a good, almost sterilizing job on the metal mess kit. The kit itself was designed so that its lid, knife, fork, spoon and the infamous coffee cup, all slid down the folding handle of the main portion of the mess kit, making it possible to dip everything at once by holding onto the handle. The trouble was caused when the entire gear was dipped up and down a few times. Splashing and waves invariably brought cries of pain. It was not uncommon for the inevitable line of shuffling soldiers to come to a halt while some unfortunate searched for a wire so that he could retrieve his mess kit from the bottom of the garbage can where he had let it sink because he had had a low threshold of boiling water pain.

After breakfast we sat impatiently in the trucks for almost two hours. At last there was activity at the front of the convoy, a jeep sped by heading toward the rear of the vehicles, people began running back to their assigned trucks and engines began to roar. My own truck started up immediately and the company began slowly to move forward. We wound down off the bluff into a sizeable town that seemed entirely filled with military personnel and equipment. Truck, artillery and tank parks were crammed with equipment. There were lines of half tracks, ambulances, weapons carriers and jeeps. There were also mountains of boxes and gasoline drums, all stacked neatly, and all guarded by MP's. It was very impressive to drive past a carefully spaced line of over 100 thirty-four ton Sherman tanks—no match for the German 60 ton Tiger, but still impressive with each 75MM cannon in alignment. There was an enormous amount of activity in spite of the drizzly rain that had begun again. Each intersection of the civilian free town was commanded by a military policeman who rigorously directed steady streams of military vehicles, his white helmet, gloves and leggings easily visible to all.

Our convoy was directed through town to a large assembly point near the shore. There we were ordered out of the trucks into a long warehouse where once again our helmets were chalked with numbers and we were held in formation while our belongings and equipment were checked. By early afternoon we moved out of the warehouse into what had become a cold driving rain. Those of us who had been drivers were assigned back to our vehicles to drive them aboard the Landing Ship Tanks (LST) to which our company had been assigned. All previous passengers of the truck convoy were assembled near gangplanks that lead to the LST's. Since this type of ship, about 200 feet in length, was designed with a cavernous hold, capable of holding perhaps thirty or forty vehicles, it was flat bottomed without a keel, to allow it to literally run up on a beach. The bow of the ship opened, a ramp was lowered and tanks, trucks and artillery could be unloaded directly onto a shoreline, negating the need for piers or docks. There were interior decks, of course, for troops and living quarters for the crew. The LST was the workhorse of all invasions during World War II. There were over 3,000 of them used in the Normandy campaign.

As it approached a beach, the ship would drop stern anchors on long cables. When the unloading was complete, it would wait for a change in tide or simply pull itself off the beach on its own anchors, turn around and put out to sea again. It was armed, of course, with heavy concentration on antiaircraft armament. The landing ship tank was utilitarian in design but with its necessary flat bottom, it was not a very seaworthy or comfortable ship in open water. It behaved a lot like a large directionless cork.

As I turned my truck around and prepared to back into my assigned LST, I noticed the huge block black and white number painted on the bow, "541," It was the same LST that had rammed the troopship in which I had crossed the Atlantic. It seemed impossible to believe that of all the tank carriers in the war, I would encounter such an incredible coincidence.

Backing up the steep ramp and disappearing backwards into the deep hold gave one the impression of being swallowed backwards by some openmouthed monster. The interior was all metal, dank with moisture and very noisy. Throaty trucks, bucking their way amid waving arms and red faced loading officers, were carefully positioned and then chained to the floor from all four corners. Once my vehicle was locked in place, I hurried up a metal ladder to the deck above, struggling with my gear, eager to escape the noise and confusion of the hold.

I found my bunk in a small compartment with a dozen or so other men from my platoon. We were told over the speaker system that the mess hall was open and that we did not need our mess gear.

We picked our way up ladders and across an open deck to the rear of the ship where a disinterested sailor waved us toward the mess hall situated one deck below. The rain had stopped, the sun was beginning to show through broken clouds and we all were in a jovial mood. The mess hall did nothing to break up our high spirits, which was a pleasant surprise. The food was, by service standards, superb. The mess attendants, dressed in white, were not only courteous but were actually friendly. For lunch there was a choice of entrees, meat or chicken, with several vegetables to choose from and hot fresh rolls. There were two choices of dessert. Even the coffee served in the porcelain mugs was good! We were served on metal cafeteria trays, which provided for the food to be separated, something that a mess kit could not do. Real silverware provided a nice change from the huge spoons and clumsy forks that came with mess kits.

The man in front of me in line seemed not to be able to comprehend the choices. When asked whether he wanted roast beef or chicken, he paused, before stammering, "Could I have both?"

The steward smiled and gave him a generous helping of both. As my awed companion went down the line next to the gleaming stainless steel hot table, he repeated his question over and over until his tray was filled with every choice possible. He took both desserts. He also ate everything on his tray.

Faced with the best food we had had in over a year, we soon became almost jubilant. I repeated the Liberty Ship story to my friends who assumed good naturedly that I had made the whole thing up just to entertain them. However, one of the young men was a Catholic and when I had finished what I thought was the funny story, he very surreptitiously made the sign of the cross. That little sign unnerved me a little and I must admit that I never repeated the story again but rather spent my remaining time on the 541 watching for imminent collisions. The first one was not long in coming.

Following an excellent dinner with real ice cream for dessert, we all crowded on the deck under a bright evening sky to watch the crew cast off. As the LST backed away from the ramp, a faint but cautious cheer could be heard. Several other LST's were backing into the basin, turning to pick their way down the Channel to an apparent assembly point outside the harbor. There seemed to be some pecking order being observed about which ship preceded other ships in the line as we headed toward the outer limits of the Channel. In particular an LST, flying a Canadian flag off our starboard beam, began to churn water and ran directly ahead of us as though to cut us off from our mid Channel course. Sailors on both the 541 and the Canadian ship were shouting to one another, shaking their fists and exchanging obscene gestures. They continued to do this right up to the moment when, with a tremendous crash, we struck the Canadian a glancing blow about halfway along his port side. The railings and stanchions on both ships bent and buckled as we careened off one another amid shrieking steel and the sound of klaxons from both ships. We slid unevenly to a dead stop in the water. The Canadian continued on its course as one crew member on the stern gave a very clear obscene gesture in our direction. I glanced up at our bridge and saw a young white faced officer with his hands gripping the curved weather bridge railing. He seemed paralyzed until a crew member wearing a steel helmet touched him on the arm and said something in his ear. Whatever it was that was said galvanized the officer into action. He jumped back from the railing and disappeared into the wheelhouse. The sailor with the helmet could be seen shaking his head back and forth in apparent disbelief. He looked to heaven with his arms spread and then he too left the bridge for the wheelhouse directly behind him.

We returned to our loading ramp before dark, having cut an unnerving and erratic course back up the Channel, dodging the steady line of LST's heading for the assembly point. On the trip back, I noticed that everyone crowding the open deck was wearing his life jacket, carefully belted. During the night our sleep was continuously interrupted by the repair work on the starboard side. Loud banging and welding went on almost all night under the cover of a portable canvas cover that was used to preserve the blackout.

By breakfast time, the repairs were apparently completed to everyone's satisfaction and we slid down the Channel alone to greet the morning sun in the open sea. There were few other ships to be seen anywhere. We simply set out in the English Channel in pursuit of a convoy that was nowhere in sight.

The Channel is an interesting, most violent body of water. At its narrowest point between Dover and Le Havre, it is a little over twenty miles wide. But from Southampton to Normandy, it is about 100 miles of choppy water and powerful current.

Not formidable in terms of distance, a normal LST could make the crossing easily in the better part of a single day. In the 541, it took us six days.

For most of the human beings on board, including the crew, it was days of seasickness and misery. Not for me, however. I reasoned that with the kind of food being served three times a day, a man would have to be crazy to be throwing up. So I stayed on the open deck as much as possible, avoided the overheated interior of the ship and appeared first in the chow line at every meal. Sometimes I was the only one in line at the appointed time. Eating became a lonely experience, often in an almost deserted rocking mess hall. The food continued to be plentiful, excellent and appreciated. I gorged myself for six days, spent most of the daylight hours on deck, watched for ships flying the Canadian flag, and belched a lot. No one else knew it but I was on vacation.

We had only been out of Southampton for a few hours when the trouble began. Apparently the combination of open water, the motion of the flat bottomed boat along with the roll and yaw of the ungainly craft, shook loose a cable, perhaps one of the stern anchor ones. The cable trailing in the wake of old 541 had snaked itself around the rudder and the starboard propeller shaft, which brought the engines to a shuddering stop. We drifted in a nice graceful arc in the middle of the English Channel, rudder jammed to one side. As soon as we lost forward momentum, we stopped dead in the water bobbing like a piece of grey driftwood.

Bells rang, crewmen hurried to join the officers on the stern and all leaned far out over the railing and peered down into the hissing water. The silence was profound. Finally the Captain, who was a Lt. Junior Grade, straightened up with a sigh, turned and quickly walked away. As he passed me, I thought I saw tears in the young man's eyes. The only sound was the wind and the sea, as waves slapped the sides of the LST.

The moment was broken at last by one of the crew who said slowly and solemnly, "Holy shit."

His words seemed to sum it up for everyone. For three days we went up and down, rolled and yawed with an occasional near broaching of the ship in large swells that seemed to come from the Northeast with uncanny timing. We always seemed to have our worst moments when no one was near enough to anything to hold on to. As near as I could tell, I was the only person on board who wasn't seasick, although there were times when I had to be very, very careful not to think about pork or cod liver oil. During one of my solitary meals in the mess hall, a sudden orgiastic lurch of the ship emptied my food tray onto my lap and sent me spinning into a metal table, which was bolted to the floor. When I painfully worked my way back to my bunk, I must have smelled like a walking garbage pit, because I emptied the compartment of people in no time at all. Eventually they all stumbled back wiping mouths and glaring dolefully at me. I was not too popular with my sick companions.

Between meals I took to watching the crew on the stern, trying to entangle the cable. There were about six of them who worked very hard. Some were extremely courageous in going over the side on ropes with hacksaws to try to cut the troublesome entanglement away. One man lost his hold and went into the sea but was pulled back by a lifeline around his waist. He lay on the deck for minutes, coughing and gagging, finally vomiting quantities of salt water into the scupper. His action brought on a wave of seasickness among the men trying to help him, but in a few minutes everyone went back to work, including him. He went over the stern again on a rope, determined to heal the ship.

We seemed a very vulnerable target but apparently we were being monitored by friendly ships. In addition, at least two or three times a day, a large twin-engined Catalina flying boat would thunder by overhead, barely skimming the top of our short radio mast. Twice, British spitfires, low over the water, flashed by wagging their wings as they disappeared quickly into the mist, which seemed always to be present over the Channel. A destroyer circled us cautiously on the first day, semaphore blinking impatiently on our bridge. Someone from our bridge answered and the lean greyhound raced off toward the East. On the second day, there was an aircraft alert. Every crew member, wearing a flak jacket, helmet and life belt, ran to the gun tubs and began cranking the multi-barreled 40 millimeter antiaircraft guns to face the hazy sun. Someone on watch had spotted an unidentified aircraft coming out of the sun in our direction. It turned out to be our friendly Catalina, but I was frankly surprised that the 541 didn't shoot it down. To my astonishment, they hadn't even tried.

During the fading evening light of the third day, the cable was cleared and the diesel engines thrummed the ship back to life. Faint cheers from the crew could be heard on the stern as we made headway. The rudder responded, directing us on a straight course away from the sunset. The heavy rolling of the ship was remarkably diminished as we regained power. Even the towering swells seemed controllable as the 541 traversed up one side and down the other side of the waves. Within minutes everyone on board became brighter and as we moved below decks in the gathering darkness of the blacked out ship, there was again laughter and a good natured spirit emerging. Two men from our compartment went back through the ship to see if they could find something to eat in the mess hall. They returned eating fresh hot coffee rolls, licking the sugary frosting from sticky fingers.

Everyone in our compartment then went to the mess hall to find that the cooks had prepared a late evening snack, knowing that as soon as we were underway, hunger would strike men who had not eaten for days because of seasickness. The cooks on that unlucky tub were the most thoughtful men I ever encountered in the service.

We went to bed full of hot coffee and rolls, knowing that with dawn we would be in France. Shortly before the morning light descended on us, the engines stopped. Groans could be heard from the darkened compartment as we all assumed that we had broken down again. But there was something different about this shutdown. We were not rolling very much and shouts could be heard from the crew on the deck above our heads. Anchor chains rattled as I hurried into my clothes and rushed up the ladder to the outside.

I don't know what I had expected to see, perhaps a harbor, a dock or the city of Cherborg, which we all still regarded as our likely landing place. What I saw in the pearl-like morning were other ships, hundreds of them becoming more visible through the hazy morning light as the sun began to rise in the East. In a few minutes I thought that, through the mist, I could see a coastline emerging a mile or so away. The shore seemed higher than I had expected, almost like cliffs at that distance. Activity on the deck ended as soon as the crew was certain that we had a firm anchorage. Our anchor chain dutifully took its position to the North as we swung in a wide arc with our stern facing Southward. All other ships around us were swinging on their chains in the same direction.

There were several other LST's among the flotilla, but there were freighters, tenders and one or two British destroyers at anchor as well. Nothing seemed to be happening as we spent the morning hanging to the ocean floor. At noon the word spread that we had lost our place in the landing schedule because of the delay caused by our breakdown. It was then that we learned that our landing would not be dockside but would be a runup on Omaha Beach itself. We were told confidentially by a sailor that we had been scheduled to land within 24 hours.

The mess hall was crowded with very hungry soldiers intent on making up for all the meals they had missed. The mood was jovial and excitement was intensified as the coastline, now firmly identified as the Normandy landing beaches, became more visible in the afternoon light. A sailor, no doubt a salesman in civilian life, made a sizable amount of money by renting a pair of 50 power binoculars for two minutes a look, to soldiers eager to see the beach battle area.

However, we were too far away to really see anything. There were too many ships obscuring our immediate view and the mist, supplemented by smoke from the shore, made any clear view difficult. Most of us looked through the binoculars anyway.

That night, after an uneventful afternoon, we were standing on deck watching searchlights far to the South, fingering together a pinpoint in the sky. "Must be a raid on Cherborg," someone ventured.

We listened carefully but we could not hear a sound except the omnipresent noises of a flowing sea and an occasional man-made clatter from our ship. Even in the actual presence of what we believed to be our first real view of the enemy, we felt secure. After our days of floating unescorted in the Channel, there was comfort in being a part of such a large number of other vessels.

The searchlights went out one at a time until there was only one probing finger idly scratching the underside of a cloud bank until it too blinked out. The 541 rolled slightly like a weary old man as we stood gripped in a silence, each with his own thoughts. I remembered my feelings earlier during my time in service that somehow I was going to miss the war itself, that in my endless training and crisscrossing of the United States in trains, the war would end and I would never see a part of it.

On deck in the cold fresh darkness a mile or so from France, I realized that I had made it. Not only was the war not over, but it was reaching an intensity, which could be described as a climax. I could be killed or maimed or blinded. Under the shifting enormity of the sky and the growing murmur of a freshening wind, it was a sobering thought.

I went below to get some sleep. Tomorrow was to be a very big day.

In the morning it was raining, the night clouds over Cherborg had grown into a solid low cloud cover, sending a bone chilling rain down on the fleet of waiting ships. The sea had become choppy and once again men shunned the food, staying below decks engaged in endless card games, which were more boisterous than serious. We waited for the engines to start up to signal our departure over the last few thousand feet of water that separated us from France.

By late afternoon the wind picked up driving the rain more horizontally into faces. Anchors began to drag and break loose from the sandy bottom. Ships, unable to reset them, left their positions among the vessels to steam back out into the Channel in order to ride out the storm with enough room to avoid collisions. The sea began a heaving motion late in the day, pushing the 541 high into the air only to have the water disappear from under the ship and drop her down into the following trough in a sickening roller coaster ride.

Seasickness returned to most and the evening and night were spent in quiet despair. The only human sounds were moaning and men retching while lying on canvas racks, thoughts of war, or for that matter peace, far from their minds.

By morning the sea calmed, the wind dropped and miraculously the sun came out to brighten the spirits and to heal the sick. The dreadful night was soon forgotten as men began to gather gear, pack belongings and make preparations for landing. We were sent into the hold to start up our trucks to make sure that all would be in working order for the debarkation. Except for an enormous cloud of carbon monoxide fumes that sent us back out on deck gasping and dizzy, all trucks started up without trouble. As I was hanging on the rail sucking in clean air, I saw a small object dropped over the side. With a kalunge sound and splash, the object quickly sank before I could see what it was. I turned to see the man next to me stuffing something under his life belt. Sensing that I had seen him, he said in a high falsetto voice, "Oh darn it, I dropped my precious gas mask. Tsk, tsk. I shall save the bag to use for other things!"

With that he turned away from the railing and left. Before the noon meal, I saw three or four other gas masks going to the bottom of the English Channel. The Army was getting ready to steal everything it could from the Navy.

By 1944 we had been issued the new gas masks that were similar to the old issue except that improvements had been made in the filter cannister, face mask and the canvas mousette bag. The new bag was attached to a shoulder strap so that the mask could be carried out of the way at the side or even behind until the need to use it arose. When the signal "Gas!" was raised, the mask could be moved to the chest on a shortened clip on the shoulder strap within usable reach of the face.

However, our focus of attention was on the bag itself, a useful container for personal items. The problem was that the bag was full of gas mask. The solution, incredibly simple, was to get rid of the mask. Mine went over the side on my way to lunch. We were told over the loud speakers that we were scheduled for our beach landing at 2:30 p.m. After an excellent chicken and roast beef lunch, I returned to my compartment with my gas mask bag filled with chicken, beef, rolls, jam and butter. I carefully packed the food in wax paper that I stole from the galley with the help of one of the friendly mess boys. I couldn't figure a workable plan for the ice cream that I had in my coffee mess cup, so I sat on my bunk and ate it all.

Precisely at 2:00 o'clock, the ship's engines began to throb and those of us assigned to drive trucks were ordered into the hold with our belongings to sit impatiently on our vehicles. Soon all others entered the hold to sit in the rear of the trucks ready for the landing. We heard the whining and clattering as the stern anchors let go but were all unprepared for what happened just a few short minutes later. Expecting the slight lurch, which we had been warned would occur when we reached the beach, we were confounded to feel and hear instead a gigantic crash followed by the sound of rending and tearing metal. Our trucks began to wobble as a discernible energy force could be seen moving toward us under the steel deck plates, much like a giant unseen can opener, from bow to stern. The ship came to a solid dead stop. We were no longer floating. A sailor, stationed near the bow ramp broke away and running beside my truck on his way to the stern hold ladder wailed as he went by, "*Now*, what has that dumb ass done?"

Dumb ass turned out to be the young J.G. who was the Captain.

After an exasperating wait in the dark hold with men running and shouting, the bow was, at last, opened and the ramp lowered to admit a flood of afternoon light and our first glimpse of what turned out to be bloody Omaha Beach.

Our attention was not directed to the beach or to the surprisingly high bluffs overlooking the beach but rather to the fact that we seemed to be a long way from where the water met the shore. There were at least 100 yards of water between us and the sand. We saw this as we craned our necks, stood on the hoods of our vehicles, and shouted information back and forth from one end of the hold to the other.

In a half hour or so we were told to return immediately and directly to our compartments with our gear. One more time up the ladders with our duffle bags and weapons brought groans and jeers from everyone. Eventually we were told that we had run across a German underwater obstacle, which had damaged the bottom of poor old 541. It was mortally damaged by every sign we could imagine. In fact, we were sunk.

Further information on the loud speakers provided all on board with the news that we would await the ebb tide before we could land. The tide would ebb the next day in the early morning. At least we would have one or two more good meals. We were instructed to stay in our compartments, to keep the deck clear and be ready to leave at 6:00 a.m. Breakfast was scheduled for 4:30 a.m.

After another good dinner, we gathered in our compartment to play cards, talk and spread rumors. I carefully guarded my gas mask bag filled with food by hiding it in the bottom of my duffle bag, hoping there would be no equipment check before we disembarked.

We awoke early to low racing clouds but no rain. There seemed to be interesting activity near the bow so we drifted in that direction to see why sailors were gathered there leaning over the rail and shouting. There were two bulldozers working toward us from the beach, building a sand ramp out to us as they worked in tandem, moving and shaping a causeway to our dead ship. We could see that the tide had gone out leaving us only 100 feet or so from the freshly exposed beach area. There were one or two German tetrahedron obstacles, similar I imagined to the one that had opened our landing craft, which were now visible off to the starboard bow. Half submerged in the sand, each had a functional quality that made it seem ominous. It was made to rip, to tear, to impale. It was our first view of an actual enemy weapon and we were fascinated by its appearance. I couldn't help thinking about where it had been made, how it had gotten here, who had planted it and what would eventually become of it. I also flinched a little knowing that we had been lucky to run onto one, which apparently had no mines attached to it. I shuddered a little, imagining what a mine might have done to all of us in that crowded hold.

Our thoughts were interrupted by the loud speaker that ordered us to retrieve our gear and report to our trucks. There was some hooting and jeering about the announcement but within minutes we were in our assigned position in the hold waiting impatiently for the ramp to be lowered. After almost a week in the English Channel, we were anxious to get off the water and onto dry land even though it meant entering the war. Sailors moved among the trucks without speaking to us. Distressed over the fatal and final mishap of the 541, each seemed lost in anger, humiliation and deep thought. Finally around noon, amid grinding and squealing, the cables on the bow lowered the landing ramp and we disembarked, our trucks roaring in protest down the steep ramp onto the freshly made causeway to France. It was an exhilerating and manly moment. Metal landing mat sections had been placed on the wet sand to support the heavy weight of the trucks but it took the addition of front wheel drive to move the 6-by to the beach area, wobbling and sliding, to the end of the ramp.

We were not to go far. A beach master, directing traffic on this portion on the beach, waved us to an assembly area marked by red flags stuck in the sand of Omaha Beach. In spite of the warning by the officer to stay in the truck, I jumped out of the cab onto the soil of France as soon as I had shut off the engine. It was a moment I will never forget. Tucked away in my mind along with the other memorable events in my life is the day when I arrived for the first time on the continent of Europe on a wide beach, forever named Omaha. Moving away from the trucks, I had my first opportunity to look around. There are few words in the English language that could be used to describe what I was looking at, because of the enormity of the scene. The Grand Canyon is awesome but its beauty can be translated into words. What I was seeing was ugly and representative only of the destruction capabilities possessed by man alone, or perhaps by God. This was not God's work. As far as I could see in either direction looking East and West along the sandy beach, there was disaster. Twisted, broken and burned landing craft, some in the water, some on the wet sand, marked by the changing tide, dotted the shore line. Several larger LST's were broached sidewise near the steep cliffs that marked the end of "George," the left flank of the U.S. Army V Corps in the original assault. I stood somewhere between the "Dog" and "Easy" portion of the landing beach that was the right flank of the Fifth Corps, encompassing the beach town of Vierville Sur Mer. All of Omaha was about five miles long and had been the original landing site for the 1st Infantry Division. Shattered tanks, trucks, half tracks, and bulldozers were scattered on the sand amidst tangles of barbed wire, beach obstacles, and debris. Piles of cast off equipment punctuated spaces between dead vehicles, helmets, packs, entrenching tools, and even destroyed artillery pieces. The fuselage and tail of a P-47 fighter plane pointed to the clearing sky directly behind me in the water. Looking out to sea, I counted six Liberty ships that had been deliberately sunk bow to stern soon after D-day to form a breakwater for the beach. There were hundreds of ships unloading supplies, most of which were coming ashore in smaller landing craft, churning up on the sand to unload boxes and cans of gasoline in enormous supply dumps. Hundreds of soldiers swarmed and picked their way through the wreckage and confusion on some mission or other. Hundreds more seemed to be just standing around or leaping out of the paths of tanks and other armour, which seemed to be streaming in serpentine columns onto the roads off the beach and into the hills behind us.

The Normandy beach at this point is a wide sandy ledge, perhaps 500 yards from the water's edge to the base of the bluffs overlooking the Channel. The bluffs, in some places, particularly on the edge of the left flank, could only be described as cliffs.

Where I was standing, the bluffs were 200 feet high and were studded with German pillboxes and strong points. Rommel, the commander of the defending German 7th Army, had massed his defense along and among the hills immediately facing the beach, because his planned tactic was to destroy the American forces on the beach and in the water. Infantry, artillery, anti-tank weapons and all of the effective firepower of the German foot soldier, had been deployed to do just that. It had almost succeeded.

Standing on the beach, the fortifications in the hills could be seen clearly. The face of the hills was almost denuded of foliage or anything else that was alive. Large chunks of reinforced concrete lay scattered from the effects of continuous bombardment from naval vessels and the pounding explosions of bombs and artillery. Blackened holes and gaps could be seen in the faces of concrete pillboxes. The long barrels of German artillery pieces canted at crazy angles, testifying to the destruction. Barbed wire and debris lay on the face of the bluffs.

I turned slowly in a complete circle trying to assimilate my first real view of modern war.

When I had completed my 360 degree turn, I found myself looking at the now dead 541. Apparently she had been completely off-loaded because there was no one around her. The trucks, bulldozers and even sailors were not to be seen. However, there was one figure squatting on his haunches near the bow, twisting his head so that he could study the underside of the LST. It was dumb ass. He stood up, placing his hands on his hips and slowly walked up the ramp to be swallowed by the 541.

Whistles began blowing nearby, so I climbed back into my cab to wait for someone to tell me what to do. Within minutes, Lt. Harding could be seen moving from truck to truck shouting something. When he got to us, we couldn't believe what he had to say.

"Everybody out, bring your weapons and packs, stack your barracks bags along side the truck," he shouted.

"Hey, Lieutenant," I asked, "What's going on?"

"We walk up," he growled, stumbling away in the heavy sand, leaving us with unanswered questions.

We assembled at last, after being assured that our remaining gear would be collected by some of our own company supply men and would be returned to us when we got off the beach. It seemed that we had been ordered to deliver the vehicles to the beach depot and that other transportation was waiting for us on the top of the hills to take us toward the fighting.

Struggling into packs, web belts, gas masks, helmets and weapons, we formed up into a column two abreast and on command, moved off toward Vierville to the West. None of us ever expected to see our barracks bags again and considering the stolen property, which had come from the Navy, it was thought to be a major loss by many. I fondled my gas mask carrier, taking pleasure in feeling the many small wrapped packages that were inside. There was very little grumbling as we struggled through patches of deep loose sand. Most of us were deeply impressed by the enormity of what we were walking through. There was no joking.

My hiking companion was Johnny and I could tell from his uncommon silence that he too was caught up in the overwhelming significance of Omaha Beach. We passed piles of wreckage as the beach began to narrow down and flatten out somewhat. Looking ahead, I could see a concrete anti-tank strong point that had been placed on a finger of sloping land coming down from the bluffs. At the point of the pillbox, the beach was only a few hundred feet wide. I spoke to my friend as the sand became wet and hard and the walking became easier, "John, you ever been in a Lit class?"

"Yeah," he said, shifting the load on his back and switching his carbine to his other shoulder.

"You remember when they asked us to describe something like a spring morning, or a goddamed rose?" I questioned. "How the hell would you describe this place?"

"I don't know," he said quietly.

We arrived at the pillbox and stopped. The Captain, looking at a map, told us to take 10 minutes. We shrugged out of our packs, which we left on the sand, but keeping our carbines, John and I walked over to look at the anti-tank gun.

From a distance the pillbox looked fairly intact but once we were to the casement window from which protruded the threatening barrel of a blackened German anti-tank gun, we could see that the strong point had been hit by at least a hundred shells. Peering through the gun port, we could see that the fatal hit had gone through the opening and had exploded inside. The inch thick steel shield on the gun had been sliced away and the cold dark interior of what must have been a tomb for the men inside was pocked and raked by fragments. An iron door on the back of the pillbox hung grotesquely on broken hinges. I could see that the point had been used, probably as a makeshift command post by the Americans who had captured it, because the floor was covered with the debris of men in battle—empty ration boxes, a broken rifle stock, spent 30 calibre cartridges, toilet paper and a torn canvas camp chair. All of the trash said desperate men had been here. A whistle blew on the beach reminding us what lay ahead.

"Quit wandering around like a bunch of tourists!" the Captain yelled. "Stay together." Then he added lamely, "Goddamn it."

After two years in the Army, the Captain was beginning to learn how to swear. We put our packs on and started up a makeshift dirt road, which had been carved out of the ravine formed by the jut of land coming down from the hills. The going was hard because a steady stream of vehicles, some of which were ambulances were coming down the narrow rutted road. We drifted into single file and continued to climb through some bushes and broken trees. The sky was now clear and the summer sun, beating down on our unprotected and overburdened bodies, began to be felt. The ambulances, moving slowly and stopping occasionally to let traffic clear ahead, were churning up clouds of dust. About half way up the ravine, the Captain from the front of the column called a halt. A message to send Lt. Harding up to the head of the column was passed down the line of men as we sprawled alongside the road.

A cursing, red faced Harding loped by on his way up to confer with the Captain, who was probably lost by now. An ambulance jarred to a stop in front of my feet. I could hear muffled moaning coming from inside. I jerked my feet back away from the road as the driver released the brake to follow the disappearing vehicle ahead of him.

When we reached the top of the bluff, we stopped again. I looked back down the ravine to the sea beyond. The water was a deep blue, holding up grey ships that were riding at anchor amid tiny white capped waves. German trenches and gun pits were scattered along the very edge of the bluffs among enormous bomb craters and smaller mortar holes. I could not believe that from such a commanding position they could have been pushed off these hills. The view of the beach was profound. Every foot of the sand and its approaches to the bluffs were clearly visible from the German position.

"Jesus Christ," someone said in a thoughtful way. Casualty figures had never been released but it was common knowledge that we had paid heavily for these French hills. Seeing Omaha Beach confirmed our darkest suspicions that someone had deemphasized the cost.

There was a lot of activity on the relatively flat plateau above the beach. Men and vehicles seemed to be moving in all directions as we

165

stood in loose company formation away from the road and waited. The four company officers were looking at a map and arguing about something. Captain Smart finally raised his arm dramatically and pointed a finger to the East. Harding emphatically pointed a similar finger to the West.

A voice behind me said, "Why don't they send down for dumb ass? He must be looking for a job."

"Hell, let's eat!" someone else shouted.

I looked at my watch, only then realizing that I had not looked at it since that early morning when the tide had changed. It was almost 2 o'clock in the afternoon.

"Was that only *this* morning?" I thought, marveling at how much had happened to me in only one day.

The Captain lowered his arm, also dramatically, and said something to Lt. Bond who blustered over to us with orders to stay put but to break out our K-rations to eat. Out of my gas mask, which I had thoughtfully retrieved from my duffle bag earlier, came two pieces of chicken and a slice of white bread. I felt no remorse at all as I licked my fingers and watched the others eat hard dry K-rations. I just made sure that the gas mask was securely fastened to my body. We were nearly finished eating when I realized that it was cooling off and that we were in shade caused by some black clouds forming up in the South. I swore because my raincoat was in my duffle bag down on the beach. It was supposed to be in my pack but I had stripped the contents down to include only the shelter half and tent pins and a few other personal items. Most of us had learned how to roll a field pack so that it looked like it was full and heavy but was really light and had very little in it. I noticed some others watching the clouds anxiously. Their raincoats were obviously also on the beach or stolen by now.

The Farmer was called over to the officers' circle and he too became involved in the argument. After a few minutes the Farmer and Lt. Harding left the others and began walking down the road to the South apparently looking for someone.

Because of the clouds, I felt an anxiety and a sort of sympathy for the men who were in charge of us. We were certainly not alone. The fields around us were filled with men and vehicles but there seemed to be no direction to the activity. Trucks roared by our relatively small band sitting by the road. Columns of men went by without comment and clouds of dust could be seen behind blasted hedgerows all around us. There were roads and tracks that crisscrossed the landscape, all occupied by units of men and vehicles, intent in the pursuit of their own activity. I could see no buildings anywhere.

"For Christsake, look at that," someone said without surprise.

An American P-38 lightning fighter plane had suddenly appeared out of a field to the East, climbing almost straight up as though some child had shot it out of a slingshot. There was apparently a landing strip nearby. The plane disappeared across the Channel to the North.

There was no doubt in my mind that it was going to rain. I could see rain coming out of the clouds in a grey mist to the South and the clouds seemed to be moving in our direction. My dismal thoughts of having to wrap myself in that cursed shelter half were interrupted by the arrival of a jeep containing Lt. Harding and the Farmer. Both were smiling broadly.

Soon we were back in columns of two's moving easily to the West on a sunken narrow road that none of us had previously seen. Preparing for a long march, we were pleasantly surprised to find that by passing over a slight rise in the next field, we were at a motor pool. There were hundreds of trucks, mostly loaded with crates, boxes and gasoline cans. Suddenly the strange depots on the beach made sense. Vehicles brought ashore were off-loaded there and then moved to this assembly area where the next logistic problem of moving both trucks and supplies to the front could be mastered.

"These first eighty 6-by's are ours to move to Paris," said the Captain to the assembled company. "Two men to a truck," he shouted excitedly.

"Captain," asked Sgt. Hoting from the 1st Platoon, "Where *is* Paris?"

We looked at the horizon in all directions as though we expected to see the spires of the great city. There was an awkward silence that was broken by the arrival of another jeep skidding to a stop in front of the officers.

A grey haired man who appeared to be a civilian got out of the jeep and spoke to Captain Smart. The man, wearing Army fatigue pants and leggins, was covered by a dirty white knee length coat much like the "duster" worn by early automobile enthusiasts. He had a French beret on his head. We were surprised to see our Captain snap to attention and give this bizzare person a formal salute. The driver of the jeep handed out a map case, which was taken by the beret, as he continued to speak quietly to a very attentive Captain Smart. They spread a map out on the hood of the jeep and leaned close to study it. The stranger made a sweeping gesture to the Southeast and shook hands with the Captain who shot him another silent salute as he climbed back into the jeep and drove away in a cloud of dust, wheels spinning. Smart went back to the small group of company officers and apparently told them what had transpired because he too made motions to the South and East. They all seemed satisfied that we knew what we were doing. The Farmer blew his whistle calling us into company formation. We jumped to it feeling the excitement of being in war and the satisfaction of purpose. The Captain addressed the company following his "at ease" order. We were very quiet as a flood of comradeship swept through the group. I had not felt this close to my platoon since the fire in San Dimas Canyon.

Activity continued to flow all around us. Motors raced, tanks clattered, dust hung in the air around the hedgerow roads and units of men passed by in all directions. We were an isolated company of friends in a chaotic and unsupporting world.

The Captain, in his instructions, referred several times to the "Colonel," who apparently was the beret. He told us that we were to leave immediately in convoy and proceed to Vincennes outside of Paris where our battalion six days ahead of us, was bivouaced. He also assured us that the route was posted and that if anyone became lost, he was to look for the battalion direction signs. The battalion headquarters, which had preceded us, had left a trail of bread crumbs for us to follow. In addition we were to stay on N-13, which was the main French route to Caen and the East. After we left Caen, we were to look for N-158, which would take us to Orleans, South of Paris. It sounded simple and exciting. We were proud and thrilled at the prospects of touring the battle area by ourselves, not in the back of a covered truck but in the cab, in command. We were all anxious to start. As we were pairing up, three weapons carriers arrived from the beach with our duffle bags, which we cheerfully claimed with a show of courtesy and an unfamiliar politeness with one another. John and I stuffed our gear in the back of our assigned truck but kept our weapons, helmets, gas masks and web belts in the cab.

As the convoy, headed by our officers in three jeeps, began to snake out of the motor pool, the first large drops of hot rain smattered on the dusty trucks. Bubbling with pleasure, I pounded on the steering wheel and shouted over the engine noise, "God, I'm on my way to Paris!"

John grinned. We were the last truck in the convoy. We went about three hundred feet and stopped. Blocked by a truck ahead of us, we sat for several minutes without being able to see much, but expecting to move momentarily.

After a long wait, our engine began to heat up, so I shut it off. The rain shower had passed over on its way to the Channel but the sky was still a thick heavy grey with no sun showing. I felt a little uneasy because in daylight in unfamiliar surroundings the sun is always a beacon for direction. Without it, you can be going North and think you are happily going South.

Impatiently, I stepped down on the dirt road trying to see what was holding us up. Others were out of their cabs also, some drifting forward to find out what the trouble was. Collecting my carbine and helmet, I yelled for John to stay with the truck while I hurried toward the head of the convoy. I had passed about a dozen trucks before I came to a group of my companions who were watching a column of tanks roll across an intersection that crossed our convoy road. Two MP's with arm bands and slung submachine guns were vigorously waving the roaring Sherman tanks one at a time through the intersection. It was then that I noticed that our jeeps were gone and that this priority column of tanks had simply sliced the tail off our simple supply convoy. Glancing around, I also discovered that as a Staff Sergeant, I was the ranking noncom with my part of the remaining 6-bys. The rain had cut the dust and cooled the air but my watch was telling me that it was close to 5:00 o'clock.

Johnson and Patterson were driving the first truck in our greatly shortened convoy, so I had them collect their gear and sent them back to the end of the column with instructions to send John up with our stuff. We traded trucks, which put me in the front instead of the rear. By the time John came staggering up with two duffle bags and our assorted kits from the cab, the tank column was beginning to thin out with only a few stragglers coming up the road. John was sarcastic and mad at having to carry my bag but as we jumped into the cab, he got over it quickly. I started up the engine, noticing in the rearview mirror that my small company of warriors was climbing back into their own vehicles. As the last tank passed, one of the MP's pointed to me to pass straight ahead. He made the hurry sign, which was to pump his arm straight up and down several times. It was only as we passed through the intersection that I realized that we were crossing a paved road. Mud and debris had disguised the fact as we had watched the tank column roll by. Counting ours, seven trucks got across the paved road before the MP's took up their positions again to run another column through ours. I could see this in the mirror. We were being cut again.

I stopped and ran past my trucks back to the road, but could get no recognition from the MP's who were busy with a flying column of half tracks and weapons carriers. Finally one of them spotted me and the seven trucks. Unslinging his machine gun, he shouted at me, "Get those fucking trucks out of here!"

He wasn't kidding; he was very definite. I turned and went back to my cab. My first command and in less than ten minutes, I had already lost 5 trucks and 10 men.

Putting the 6-by in gear, we rolled slowly ahead along a single dirt road, committed to what I guessed was a Southerly direction, looking for N-13. No one else seemed to be using this track, although we passed several small European burned out automobiles that were overturned and already rusting. One of them was shattered by punched in bullet holes. We could not see much because the sunken road was lined on both sides by ancient hedgerows that were really used as fences by the Normandy farmers. Trees and bushes planted a few feet apart collected debris through the centuries, which became dirt and tangles of wood, branches and rocks plowed from the farmers' fields. After a long time these barriers built into substantially high walls, which then became a type of fence through which cattle and other stock could not go. As our invasion forces had learned, these hedgerows served also as barriers to tanks and made excellent defensive positions for German Infantry and anti-tank weapons. We passed places where the dirt walls had been blasted open to allow tanks to go through. Through these holes, we could see into the field, crisscrossed with tank tracks and pocked with mortar and artillery craters. The fields were silent now, but the debris of furious and costly battle was everywhere. Piles of empty shell casings, sometimes as high as a man's head, marked former artillery positions. Foxholes and slit trenches contained remnants of ration boxes, rifle and machine gun casings, torn paper, abandoned gas masks and broken equipment. Wire and shattered tree branches choked the hedgerows. Nowhere was there a tall tree. It was like driving through a stunted or dwarf-like forest. We ground ahead slowly, passing fields that had been mined and were now marked by strips of white linen, which showed safe passage through the mines. Against the hedgerows were wooden white signboards with the German word, "Minen," and a skull and crossbones painted on them, giving warning to their troops that the fields had been mined.

The road began to widen and to drop away in front of us. I had to shift to a lower gear to keep the truck from slipping on the mud caused by the rain shower.

Since crossing the paved road several miles back, we had not seen another person nor any sign of life. I was grateful when the road flattened out again into a rather wide little valley. John pointed across to a dead rotting cow whose legs were stiffened and pointing into a still grey sunless sky. The cow lay near a mound of stones and broken timber that must have been a barn or a large shed. The hedgerows disappeared as we came to a small river, which had been spanned by an engineer's Bailey bridge. We bounced across and I stopped a short way from the bridge to make sure that my six other trucks were still with us. They were, so we continued. It was after 6:00 o'clock but there was still plenty of summer light to see by. About a mile beyond the bridge, we came to a village, or what had once been a village for there was no building that had not been damaged or destroyed. The destruction was appalling and I was unexpectedly horrified by what I saw.

We drove slowly through the rubble, the truck in low gear, lurching over stones, debris, and personal belongings. There was no one to be seen along the street that extended for three or four blocks. To call it a street, however, is incorrect. It was simply a narrow path that had been compacted into a semi-hard surface by tracked vehicles. The trail picked its way around the larger piles of debris caused by buildings and walls that had collapsed onto what had once been the village street.

The shocking aspect of the scene was the personal nature of it. Mixed with the rubble were symbols and treasures of human beings. There was glass, kitchen utensils, broken chairs, bed springs, clothing, mattresses, a broken mirror, crockery, children's toys and smashed framed photographs. All of it was covered with a coat of dirt that had alternated between dust and mud until the sharpness of everything had succumbed to a grey-like residue, not unlike the finality of cement.

Near the far end of the village, the remains of a single two story wall stood next to the road. A wide window frame hung crazily from the stones and in the glassless window against a darkening grey sky hung a fine white lace curtain. Over all of the village lay the tangles and coils of the omnipresent telephone wires of war.

I had heard of the destructiveness of war. I had seen pictures and paintings of war. I had read about modern war, but until I had passed through this small French country village in the farmlands of Normandy, I had not known of the totality of war. The crunching of French family china beneath the tires of my American made truck was a lesson I could not have learned from books. Books and pictures spoke of battles, generals and soldiers, not of families, nor of generations. Even my readings of World War I had concentrated on the battlefield, the tactics and the slaughter of the soldiers of great armies. I remembered reading an aviator's sighting during the lengthy battle of Verdun. He had reported that the village of Fluery could be identified as a landmark because the color of the whitish clay of the brooding hills of Verdun was a darker brown where once the town had stood. It had been an interesting and remembered report but it was linked with the French counterattacks toward the Forts of Vaux and Douaumont and not with families, nor with generations. I was struck silent knowing that what I was seeing was not just the obliteration of a group of buildings; it was the destruction of the lives of people. Although I saw no clear signs of death, I was sure that the death of people of this unknown little town was a mute companion to the physical end of their collective heritage.

My thoughts were broken by the sight of a person next to the road ahead. I stopped the truck and spoke in halting and unclear French to an old man dressed in a dirty linen smock, digging around in a small tangled vegetable patch with a large square hoe.

"Hey Monsieur!" I called. "Quelle ville ici?"

His back was to me and I had to call twice more before he straightened with some effort and turned slowly to face me. Tufts of white hair stuck out from around his black and greasy beret. His face was grey, almost the color of the village and his eyes, deep sunk and bloodshot looked at me with hatred. He did not speak, but leaning on his hoe, continued to glare, his lips quivering.

I smiled, or tried to in the face of this unexpected hostility. After several seconds of silence I asked again, "Quelle ville?"

171

"Trevieres! Trevieres!" he snarled, turning his back to us to continue working with his hoe.

Trevieres meant nothing to me. I had no map nor had I ever heard the name anyway. With a little more anger than I was prepared for, I jammed the truck into gear and raced the engine as we proceeded out of the smashed town.

"Let's get the hell out of here!" I shouted to John, noting that the other trucks were following.

As soon as we had passed the outskirts of Trevieres, we were once again alone on the narrow road between hedgerows. We drove without speaking through several miles of the same scene that we had been seeing since we left the beach. Once we had to detour through a gap in the hedgerow to skirt around a large burned out German personnel carrier that sat in the center of the roadway. I was surprised at its large size, wide tracks and at the number of large overlapping wheels. I had seen pictures of this type of vehicle but I had not reckoned with its huge bulk. Back on the road we began to ascend slightly out of the shallow valley onto a plateau of rolling hills and shattered trees. It was close to 7:00 o'clock and definitely getting darker, although I was thankful that it had not begun to rain again.

"This is not a very well travelled road," said John, adding, "Do you know where the hell we are going?"

"Of course, I know where we are going," I answered. "We are going to Paris!"

To myself I thought, "I have been in command of this group for only three hours and already have lost five trucks, ten men and now I am hopelessly and absolutely lost."

We continued to grind through the desolation and tragedy around us, pausing once to let two jeeps overtake and sprint by us, each with two men inside who never took their eyes off the road. They carried 29th Division markers on their rear bumpers but were soon lost in the tangle of hedgerows ahead.

About an hour after leaving our friendly Frenchman at Trevieres, we came to a crossroad that had traffic on it. There was quite a bit of traffic flowing in both directions on a two-way, possibly paved road. As we stopped at the intersection, we were confronted by not only long columns but a veritable maze of signs nailed to posts. These markers were division, battalion and company signs. Most were small little arrows that pointed in some direction with the unit number stencilled on—617th, 435th, Division C.P. (command post), etc. We looked in vain for any kind of route marker or for our own battalion markers. There seemed to be hundreds of such markers to choose from, some dislodged and pointing to the ground or to the sky. Many were clearly very old, with faded numbers in either red or black numerals. Field wire was stretched in sagging loops across the intersection in wild disarray. We seemed to have no choice but to join this flow of vehicles. My decision would be whether to turn right or left. After watching for awhile and seeing that most combat traffic seemed to be going right to left, I decided to turn left and join the columns going in what I guessed was a sort of Easterly direction. I would have given anything for just a moment of seeing the sun in the sky.

I opened the door, stepped out on the running board to see if my convoy was all there. They were, neatly lined up, almost bumper to bumper, against all convoy rules.

Knowing that I had to keep the six trucks together or be split into segments, I faced the problem of getting us all out on that road as a convoy at the same time. I reached down on the floor and found in my pack what I would need. It was a black and white Military Police armband that I had stolen from my days as Sgt. of the guard at Warminster. Running back along my trucks, I told each driver to go like hell after our lead truck had breached the stream of traffic going East. I also told them to stop after they cleared the intersection, so that I could get back to my 6-by.

Yelling at John to drive, I slipped on the armband, straightened my helmet, grabbed my carbine and at the first break in traffic, strode out importantly onto what actually was a narrow two-way paved highway. But before I could really get into position to act like a cop, a jeep, followed by three or four half tracks came roaring at me from the imagined West. I had several options, none of which seemed very appealing. I could just keep walking across the roadway. I could pretend that I was crazy, or I could go ahead and act like a military policeman. Maybe it was the growing frustration of the last few hours or the long day, or a delayed reaction to the unhelpful Frenchman, but I opted to act like a cop. I started too late, but once I was committed, there was no turning back.

Throwing up my left hand with flattened palm, I signalled the jeep to stop. I immediately returned my attention to my convoy in a casual way, demonstrated confidence in my complete authority in the matter of directing traffic. The jeep was moving too fast but as I watched it out of the corner of my eye, it skidded to a stop just inches from me. For one horrifying moment, I thought that the first half track behind the jeep was not going to be able to stop, but it too rocked to a halt without incident, as did the remaining vehicles in the column. Continuing to play my part, I sarcastically turned to face the jeep with both hands on my hips.

My blood froze, for there looking out at me with their noses almost touching the windshield from the sudden stop, was a red-faced full Colonel and a Major who was driving the jeep. From their expressions,

I could see that both were very angry. As the Colonel made a move to climb out of the jeep, I spun around and pointing a finger at John, I waved him and his roaring entourage onto the highway. I frantically gave the hurry up arm signal. I could see out of the corner of my eye again that the officers, seeing that the interruption was to be a short one, had settled back in the jeep. The Major raced the engine next to my leg. As soon as Johnson and Patterson, in the last truck churned by me, I leaped out of the way and graciously waved the Colonel through. He and his halftrack thundered by me and skirted around my little convoy, which was pulled over to wait for me to join them. I loped up the road stuffing the MP armband in my jacket pocket, wondering what sort of court-martial offense it was to impersonate a military policeman.

As I climbed in the passenger's side of the cab and told John to pull out, it began to rain. I suddenly felt very tired, almost to the point of exhaustion. It was after 8:00 o'clock and I had been awake since 4 a.m. It was unbelievable to remember that at 4 a.m. we had still been on that sunken LST on Omaha Beach.

"Don't you think we ought to find something to eat?" asked John.

We had been so involved in trying to find our way to N-13 that I had completely forgotten that almost eight hours had gone by since we had eaten beside the road on the bluff above the beach.

"Yeah, let's see where this road takes us and then we can pull over and eat some K-rations."

Each man had packed three meals of rations on the boat to see him through one full day but we had already eaten one of them in the afternoon. *They* had, that is. I found my gas mask and affectionately patted its bulging sides. Because of the drizzling rain and growing darkness, John turned on the headlights. We were far enough back from the front lines that blackout restrictions were not being followed and we observed that traffic around us all had their lights on full. Trucks were also equipped with blackout lights, which were more or less parking lights, useless for serious driving, but did manage a little light, and gave other drivers the clue that a vehicle was approaching. At first we were relieved to be on a paved road but soon discovered that the pavement was broken in many places and gouged with vicious potholes. The rain had increased the muddiness so that any passing vehicle threw a shower of muddy water against our windshield. We took some small satisfaction in knowing that we were doing the same to them. Driving a fairly new and late model 6-by, we were blessed with an electrical windshield wiper on the driver's side. Earlier jeeps, weapons carriers and $2^1/2$ ton trucks had been equipped with simple mechanical wipers, which the driver had to operate by hand by cranking a small handle back and forth as needed. For obvious reasons, the cost effective, trouble free earlier system had proven inadequate and had been replaced with electrical wipers.

We had gone over a mile when, in the darkness, I saw in the pool of finger light from our headlamps, a small cement slab next to the road. At first sight it looked like a small graveyard headstone but as we passed it, I knew that we were no longer lost. It was a kilometer marker and although it was old and weathered, I could make out what was chiseled on its surface. It said RT-172, Bayeux 6 K. Not only were we not lost, but we were actually going in the right direction because I knew that Bayeux was on the Normandy coast between the beaches and Caen. I had read that the Allies, fearing that the famous, priceless Bayeux tapestry was still in the city, had avoided the town as a primary bombing target. Bayeux had suffered damage because it was the hub of several road junctions and had been fought through as the British and Americans forced their way into the city. At the time it seemed unreal that human lives had probably been sacrificed to prevent the destruction of a piece of tapestry but there were numerous incidents during the European war when strategies were designed to preserve important historical buildings, collections, and sites. Ironically the Bayeux tapestry, which is one of the only graphic records of life in the Middle Ages, had been removed from the city by the Germans weeks before the invasion.

Our lights began to pick up numerous wrecked vehicles, all of which seemed to be German. Rusting frames and tireless wheel hubs spoke to the violence of the explosions that had reduced the tangled and twisted metal to unidentifiable junk. We passed a small road coming out of the hedgerow in which sat a burned-out German Mark IV tank, its squat turret, blown from its base, tilted so that its gun barrel rested on the ground in front of it. The dirt road behind the tank was choked with the debris of other vehicles and foliage.

The rain began to let up and finally stopped altogether making visibility easier, even though passing vehicles, especially tracked ones, continued to shower us with thin mud. We were following another truck convoy when we entered the outskirts of Bayeux. There were many stops and starts and traffic became more congested as we spasmotically worked our way into what turned out to be the center of the city. Bayeux was not destroyed as had been Trevieres, although many houses had been hit by shells and some were mere piles of rubble.

There were very few people to be seen and those on the narrow cobblestone sidewalks were old, stooped, and uninterested in the military traffic on their streets. There were no streetlights, only the headlights of the trucks revealed darkened houses and shops. No doors were open, all windows were shuttered and shop windows were covered by sliding corrugated metal panels that protected the glass and provided a seal against possible escaping lights. The doorways to stores and shops were barricaded by locked metal gates. The city was still cautiously alive.

Sitting as a passenger for the first time gave me the opportunity to look closely at the first major French city that I had ever seen. There were, of course, no streetlights, nor for that matter there was no light showing from any building. What I could see of the buildings was an occasional glimpse provided for by the headlights of the flow of traffic. The streets were narrow and in places where buildings had been hit, there was rubble being pounded flat by the passage of thousands of wheels and tank tracks. Wires from collapsed cement telephone and power line poles lay on sidewalks or on the street where they had fallen. Storefronts proclaimed Boulangre or Pattisseire on worn, painted boards and bullet holes and fragment pockmarks around shuttered windows marked places where snipers had hidden during the battle for the town. The noise from the traffic, compressed between the close buildings was often thunderous. Most of the city's buildings seemed to be three and four stories high and looked to be hundreds of years old, which most of them were. Bayeux was an ancient city, having defied even the simplest attempts to modernize it beyond electricity. But then Normandy and the Bocage country had been a quiet agriculture province since the Middle Ages. War had not visited this part of the world within the memory of any of its living inhabitants. The arrival of the Germans in 1940 had marked not only occupation but the preparation of airfields for attack on England and the construction of serious defenses against invasion. The Germans had been most aggressive in their defense of Normandy and the result had been obvious to me over every foot of the way since we had left the beach that morning. I could not help but think of the old French farmer in Trevieres who hated us for what we had done to do his life and to his village.

Traffic began to back up and we realized that we were coming to an important intersection in the center of the city. When the convoy ahead of us turned right in the square, which marks the center of most French towns and cities, we followed. An MP waved us through the square and we began our Easterly exit of the city of Bayeux. I opened the cab door as we rolled along, standing on the running board to see if all my trucks had made it through and were following. I counted five sets of headlights immediately behind us. We were still all together. As I slammed the door shut, John shouted, "Hey, look!"

There on a pole was a route sign. It said N-13. After almost seven hours of driving, we were finally on the right road to Paris. John tapped the gasoline gauge and reported that we should stop soon and add gas from our jerry cans, which we carried in the back with our cargo.

The damage to the Eastern edge of the city was significantly greater than that which we had seen in the Southern and central part of Bayeux. Stone walls near the side of the road were tumbled and broken. Large gaps were evident in many of them and we begin to see more wrecked vehicles and abandoned equipment. German graves, just mounds with handmade wooden crosses, were beginning to appear. These were near the road, some even between the road and the drainage ditch next to it. A few of the single graves had German helmets resting on them.

As we came to the edge of Bayeux, the buildings thinned out and the stone walls between them became longer. We pulled over next to a battered wall, turned out our headlights and stopped the engine. In the comparative silence, I could feel the tiredness seeping through my body. I had to fight falling asleep before we could add some gasoline to our tank.

All twelve of us gathered together in the surprisingly cooling night air and discussed our next move. Everyone was hungry so we sat on remnants of the wall after gassing up and ate. I didn't have the heart to eat real chicken in front of my little command, so I passed up my gas mask and ate K-rations with them.

Listening to them talk, I could tell that everyone had been shocked by what we had seen. Holt, my older and wiser friend, was clearly disturbed by it.

"Isn't there some other way to fight a war besides in people's living rooms?" he asked.

"I knew it was bad, but I didn't expect this." He added, gesturing toward the destroyed house and wall behind us, "Where the hell are these people now?"

In the silence, no one answered the question, but Hollis, who was married with two children, summed up what we were all thinking, "I hope to Christ that this never happens to us back home."

We started to talk about whether we should go on or stay where we were. We were all exhausted but the excitement of the day was still with us and the group was about evenly split over the decision. We finished our rations, throwing the boxes, cans and wrappers into the ditch that was already cluttered with similar trash.

Twelve half tracks chattered on their way East. Patterson, the Cajun from New Orleans, stood up and walked down the line of the wall, soon to be swallowed up in the chilling darkness. I assumed that he had gone to take a leak, but in just a few minutes he reappeared with astonishing news. "Hey," he yelled, "There's a cafe bar down here!"

"God, could I use a drink!" someone moaned.

In seconds all but one of us were standing in front of a dark building that had unexpectedly appeared at the end of the wall. It fronted directly onto the road and from the noise of voices coming through the roll down metal cover over the windows, there were people in there. I had left Baker back with the trucks. He didn't drink and had volunteered to guard our convoy.

Fumbling around in the dark, I found a door latch and by pushing hard against the door, we found ourselves in a little hallway, much like a small boxed off storm doorway. A thick velour drape separated us from a bright light source coming from a room on the other side of the curtain. The voices were laughing and shouting. We pushed our way through the drape into a room about 40 feet square. As we entered, every person in the room turned to look at us. The voices died down as the strangers studied us with curiosity and some amusement. They were all Canadians, the first I had seen in the war.

A Sergeant, leaning heavily on a high oaken bar against the side wall, grinned crookedly and said, "Hey Yanks, come on in and buy us a drink, but leave the guns outside, no guns in here."

We stacked our carbines and helmets in the little anteroom and picked our way to the bar through the Canadians who were seated at small scattered tables. Most of them seemed drunk but all were smiling and friendly. By the time we crowded near the bar, the noise level was back where it had been before we had made our dramatic entrance. I stood next to the Sergeant, blinking heavily against the glare coming from several bare hanging light bulbs over the bar.

"Where does the electricity come from?" I asked innocently.

The Sergeant took a long swig of some lightish brown liquid and said, "We hooked up a generator for Francoise last week. The candles in here were killing us."

Francoise was a very short Frenchman with a Hitler moustache and thick steel rimmed glasses. As he moved down the bar to me, he smiled revealing gaps in his yellowed teeth. He said something to me in French, which I imagined to be a form of "what'll you have?" I fought down the notion of getting out my Madam Mausoly book, instead I casually jerked my thumb at what the Sergeant was drinking and looked around the room. Like all foreign bars full of soldiers, it was also full of smoke. There were five or six naked light bulbs hanging from the ceiling over small circular uncovered wooden tables. There were no windows but there was a padlocked door behind the bar. There were no mirrors, pictures or anything that would identify this grey walled cubicle as a public room. It was just a place to have a drink.

Francoise placed a tumbler glass on the splintered bar in front of me and said something else that I took to mean that I owed him some money. The Sergeant, swirling the remnants of his drink in his glass, chuckled and said, "He wants 50 francs."

Trying to pretend that I knew all along what the barkeep had said, I brought out my package of new invasion currency and peeled off a hundred franc note, which I placed on the bar. The Sergeant and others nearby looked appreciatively at my collection of money. They all moved closer around me as Francoise returned with my change, a few pieces of aluminum coins, which because of their light weight would never be regarded seriously as real money.

178

"What is this stuff?" I asked as I put the tumbler to my lips.

A tall Canadian next to the Sergeant answered, "Oh, it's an apple brandy, a lot like apple cider. It's called Calvados."

I had never heard of Calvados, but I should have been suspicious by the way the circle of my new friends all watched my face as I threw back a mouthful of the glass in one innocent gulp.

My first reaction was apparently anticipated by the circle of faces that began to disappear, one by one, in watery confusion. I was aware of two things: first, tears were filling my eyes and secondly, I was not breathing. I had the incredible sensation that everything from my tongue to my naval was paralyzed. An instant numbness pervaded every organ I could think of. What was really frightening was that it didn't seem to want to go away. Blinking away the tears, I smiled and pretended that my body was functioning and that I was actually able to breathe. By the way the group was grinning at me, I knew that I was fooling no one. Just as I was about to faint, someone began pounding me on the back. The blows started me up again. With a croaking sound coming from somewhere in my neck, I inhaled most of the air and smoke in the little room, keeping it all to myself long enough to regain consciousness. Finally, coughing, gasping and with rapid but rattling inhaling and exhaling, I restored both my vision and the function of my chest cavity.

As the paralysis resided, it was replaced by a stinging heat. It was so hot within my body that when I looked down, I fully expected to see tendrils of smoke coming out of the seams in my field jacket.

I put the glass carefully back on the bar and turned to my laughing and jeering circle of friends. "Jesus," I gasped. Hearing the word made me want to say it again, so I repeated the name "Jesus" over and over. It somehow gave me comfort, although I must admit that between my childhood days of perfect attendance in Sunday School and that night, I had never felt so close to the Man as I had when I drank my first shot of Normandy Calvados. By the time the laughter had died down, I was feeling fine. As a matter of fact, I was really well enough to cautiously sip some more of the firey liquor and to join in the laughter.

The tall Canadian apologized and let me buy him some red wine that he was steadily consuming. As the time wore on I could see that most of my guys were mixing with the Canadians at the tables. However, Holt and Johnny were at the other end of the bar in what appeared to be a heated discussion with two Canadians. I drifted up their way carrying a glass of sour red house wine that I was sipping through numbed lips. When I got to them, they were in the middle of some point or other about which country, Canada or United States, offered its citizens more personal liberty. I listened long enough to tell that it was one of those pointless, uninformed barroom arguments between drunks. I had heard it all before in Tennessee, Maryland, England, and in countless barracks discussions. I was determined not to get involved but as I stood there drinking my wine, I could not restrain myself. Words tumbled across my broken tongue and I could feel myself being swept along by what I heard as glorious eloquence.

Both Holt and John stared at me with what I thought was glowing admiration for my choice of words. The Canadians were sullen but appropriately stunned by my irrefutable logic. I had gotten to the really dramatic part about patriotism as the foundation of American life, when I noticed how loud my words had become. Swinging around to face the room with my sloshing wine glass, I faced a quiet audience. Everyone in the room was listening to me in wide-eyed splendor. Even Francoise had stopped polishing his few glasses with a dirty towel and was looking at me over his glasses. I felt triumphant. I was center stage in a magic moment. At that instant the tall Canadian who had tricked me into the Calvados put his hand to his mouth and shouted, "I'm going to be sick!"

Even with the help of two others who grabbed his arms, he never made it to the velour drape. Vomit began spurting out between his fingers as everyone ducked and crowded together to get away from him. He threw up on the drape, the bar, the floor, one of the hanging light bulbs and on the Sergeant. The light bulb, dripping a glutinous wine laced mess, swung back and forth to create a vivid shadow image across the room. Francoise groaned in despair. Men began to break for the door to get out of there and we Americans joined them. Several men slipped on the now wet and disgusting floor to fall into the steady stream coming from the tall Canadian. Rushing and shoving our way past the wretched creature who was now kneeling on the floor, we gathered our weapons and helmets to burst out into the cold driving rain. The effect was like jumping from a sauna bath into a cold shower. We careened down the ditch, oblivious to the fact that it was now quite full of water. Someone behind me cursed as he fell headlong into the muddy water, his helmet skittering out onto the road. I reached my darkened truck in time to throw up in the ditch next to it. Passing the word from truck to truck, we agreed that we would stay where we were for the night. We were tired and drunk. It was after midnight; we had been awake and active for twenty hours and we needed some sleep.

I fell into a deep coma-like sleep almost immediately, not caring that I was wet from the continuing rain or that it is most uncomfortable to sleep sitting up on a truck seat. During the night I was only vaguely aware of the convoys that passed by in the spattering rain, but from time to time, my closed eyes registered intermittent light patterns as trucks came toward us from the East, vibrating my sleep as they roared by. Sometime during the night, the rain stopped and we awakened to a bright day with a full sun. We gathered on the wall again and ate our 1st K ration meal, some of the men having difficulty forcing hard rations through a mouth tasting of bad red house wine. The sun felt good and we were even cheerful as we mounted the cabs for our dash into Paris. I warned everyone to stay together, to honk horns three times if there was trouble or to let me know if anyone saw our battalion markers. Traffic was beginning to become heavy in the morning light. We started up but had to wait for a dozen or so tank destroyers to hammer by before we could make our break for the road.

We were driving directly into the morning light, which made visibility difficult, but we could see that the fighting had been very heavy in this sector. We began passing Canadian units that were camped in open fields beyond the walk, hedgerows and broken farmhouses. They seemed to be making attempts to dry out their belongings and clean weapons. Vehicles of all descriptions were parked or scattered in the field. We passed a battery of 90 MM antiaircraft guns that were dug into circular sandbagged pits in the ground. I noted that the battery was hooked into a M-4 mechanical fire control system, the same system that I had studied at Santa Anita more than a year ago. I also noted that the guns were covered and there didn't seem to be anyone around. It reminded me that we had not seen or heard an airplane since we had watched the takeoff of the P-38 the day before.

The roads were rural and inadequate, bridges had long before been destroyed by Allied bombing, French Resistance sabotage and by German demolition during their retreat across France. The railroads were in shambles, although feverish efforts were being made to restore them for use by the liberating armies. The logistics involved in supplying fighting units that were, in some cases, 200 miles from the supply depots was one of the worst problems of the European War. The eventual management of the problem will probably be recognized by historians as one of the most brilliant feats in the history of American arms. Most rivers and streams, and France is covered by them, were crossed either by Bailey bridges or by pontoon bridges, erected by the engineers, often under fire. These bridges were tributes to these units and were marked by signs that said, "Cross the XXX River courtesy of the such and such Engineer Battalion." No one ever made fun of these signs, or attempted to deface them; they were respected, and because of the necessary mobility of modern warfare, each was essential. Many thousands of combat engineers had lost their lives for these unsightly marvels of construction.

About ten miles from Bayeux, we passed through a smaller village, which was identified as St. Leger. About all that was left of the town was the city limit sign that displayed the name amid a tangle of broken cement poles and wires. The sign, which turned out to be a standard marking for all French cities, towns and villages, was on a concrete pedestal about five feet high with a cross member naming the village in white letters on a blue background. Above the name, St. Leger, it said N-13, but the curious part was that beneath the name it said, "Non touring Club de France." Apparently the French equivalent of the Automobile Club of America had financed the official posting of the names of cities. This particular sign was leaning at a severe angle and was spattered by shell fragments. I ate some chicken and a stale roll, determined to eat the good food before it spoiled, even though I wasn't hungry. I offered some to John, who was driving and much to my disappointment, he took it. I made a mental note to eat by myself in the future.

After passing through another ten miles or so of indescribable destruction, we came to the bitterly contested city of Caen. It had been the largest city in Normandy on the Orne River. Canals had linked this large hub city with the smaller port town of Riva' Bella about six miles down the river on the English Channel. Caen had been fought over by the Germans and the British and was totally destroyed. Roads had been created by bulldozers indiscriminately slicing through the debris. There was no building, which I could see, that had not been hit, bombed, burned or demolished. Caen had suffered one of the worst poundings of the war and thousands of its inhabitants had been buried in the rubble. We saw a few civilians preoccupied with digging into the heaps, piling stones and usable bricks into neat little squares. Progress through the remains of Caen was understandably slowed to a low gear crawl as we picked our way along a very narrow passage. After an hour or so, we came to what must have been at one time the square in the center of the city. Several roads angled off through the house high piles of broken buildings. In the central intersection stood a frustrated British MP with large white gloves. He was doing his best to keep the traffic moving, but trucks and vehicles were at an absolute stop because all roads leading out of the city were jammed. One truck at a time was being released along the spider web of vehicles but it gave us time to puzzle through the many unit signs that were stuck on poles in the rubble. We could not locate anything that would give us a clue about direction. We just went with the flow and eventually followed a road to the South that turned out to be N-158. Once we were free of the city, we made better time although the wreckage on the road itself made fast driving impossible.

Without knowing it at the time, we were on the road to Falaise that had been the critical road junction over which the German 7th and 5th Panzer Armies had fled trying to escape the trap created by the sweep of the American Third Army coming North out of Argentan to meet the Canadians driving South. We were about to enter the Falaise killing grounds, one of the worst single catastrophes ever endured by

German forces. Eisenhower himself had observed, after touring the Falaise pocket, that it would have been possible to walk for miles on human flesh without ever setting foot on the French soil. Thousands of vehicles and armour had been destroyed by rocket firing British and American airplanes and thousands of Germans had died along that road. Thousands more had escaped the bitterly contested trap, making a dash for their distant second line of defense North of Paris. At the time there was American criticism over the Canadian and British delays in closing the pocket, but there had been no agreement as to the cause, nor was there an explanation as to why so many of the Germans were able to escape to fight again. The wreckage along the road even closer to Caen testified, however, to the fury of the attack and to the disorder of the desperate German retreat. We began to pick our way past entire convoys of twisted and burned enemy vehicles, which were literally bumper-to-bumper alongside the tortured roadway. The remains of hundreds of dead horses could be seen and smelled between and among the destroyed trucks and armour. There were no human remains to be seen beyond an occasional single grave near the roadside. Someone had cleaned up at least part of the mess.

We had travelled about five miles before we approached a small shattered town named Lorguichon. At least that's what the broken sign said. We drove through the rubble and were about to leave the village behind us but were somewhat blocked by a number of American 6-bys, which had pulled off the road shoulder near a large open field. As we worked our way around them, John shouted, "Hey, those are our guys!"

It was. It was our entire company convoy including the two jeeps complete with the C.O. and the platoon officers. We pulled off the road and ran back to join them. There was shouting, laughing, jeering and some welcome back pounding from our lost company. Piecing together the stories from so many voices, we learned that they too had done some wandering around the French countryside looking for a way around Caen. In fact, the entire convoy had, at one time, found itself back at the beach near Arromaches before spending the night as we had near Bayeux. We also learned that somehow the Captain had secured some maps and that the company was now waiting in the field for food to be brought from a depot near Caen.

Everyone began to drift around in small groups, some lighting fires from debris for the cooking of powdered K ration coffee. The field was quite large and strangely empty except for a ring of antiaircraft gun pits near the road where we were standing. Men began to explore and look around to see what could be found in the pits and alongside the road. This rest stop had been the first real opportunity that any of us had had to poke around a battlefield. There soon was shouting and

183

gesturing as items of interest were discovered and brought back to the parked convoy. It soon turned into what could only be described as a pile of junk, some of which was very dangerous. Several land mines had been found and were thrown onto a growing pile of empty 90 MM shell casings. These were German teller mines, large and flat, designed to blow tracks off tanks. Fortunately the fuses had been removed but they were still nothing to throw around. Sections of machine gun belts and ammunition appeared along with a broken 30 calibre machine gun with the barrel missing. A single Canadian hobnailed boot along with a shattered field telephone was retrived from a foxhole and placed on the pile. When two men arrived with a large propeller blade from an aircraft, we all paused to consider that we were really involved in a foolish enterprise. We began to drift away from our task of policing up the Normandy peninsula. Men began to talk about food. My watch read about 2:00 o'clock and the sun was very hot in a fairly cloudless sky. A group of us sat on the ground in the thin strip of shade provided by the trucks. As we waited for the ration truck to arrive, a young man from the 2nd platoon came over to me with a German helmet in his hand.

"Hey," he said, "can you read German? I found a letter stuffed inside this helmet. What does it say?"

He handed me three flimsy pages of thin handwriting that began in German script with the words, "My Dearest Johan." The rest of the letter, most of which I could not really read, spoke of love, privation, and fear. It was a letter from a wife to a soldier. The paper was of such poor quality and had been folded and refolded so many times that it was close to disintegrating in my fingers. The letter went on to tell of the child and of the problems of getting enough food to feed her. It ended with a cry of passion and love and it was signed, your Frieda. Sitting with my back against the hard rubber tire of the truck wheel, listening to the drowsy muted conversations around me, I stared at the letter.

"Where did you get this?" I asked.

Pointing with the helmet, he replied, "Took it off a grave over there."

I carefully folded the three little pages together before I handed them back to him. I then asked him to put them back in the helmet and to return it to the grave, but I don't think that he ever did.

Lt. Harding, coming down the line of trucks, motioned for me to join him as he walked along. "The Captain found out about that little trick with the MP armband," he said.

"He wasn't very happy about it; you could get yourself and him in a lot of trouble pulling a stunt like that—." Then he added, "He wants you in the lead truck in case we need you to do it again."

He was laughing as he walked away from me. The Lt. looked good. Although he was well into his thirties, he was trim and he dressed like a professional soldier. His clothes were always clean and he shaved every day. Having been an enlisted man in the regular Army, he seemed to particularly savour the officer's uniform and his well tailored and expertly cut clothes were of a really fine quality. We had been issued the new combat jacket and boots before leaving Warminster and as he moved down the line away from me, I grudgingly admired his appearance. His helmet was square on his head with the vertical white officer's stripe painted on the back. Carrying a slung carbine on his shoulder, and with his web belt tightly buckled around his waist, canteen and first aid packet in their correct prescribed position, he looked fine. He even still had his gas mask.

I don't know whether it grew out of the invasion planning, but all officers and noncommissioned officers in Europe had stripes painted on the backs of their steel helmets. The vertical stripe, about an inch wide and four inches long, denoted an officer. A horizontal stripe, about the same size, indicated that the wearer was a noncommissioned officer, i.e., a Sergeant or a Corporal. The theory was that the leaders were out in front of the troops and could be identified by their own forces behind them but could not be singled out by the enemy. It was a neat little piece of psychology because it meant never turning your back on the enemy who was anxious to pick off the leaders. Following the invasion, the custom of the stripes was to remain in effect for the rest of World War II. Officers and noncoms never wore any other insignia when in the combat zone. In many cases officers even disdained carrying the telltale pistols and carried instead the standard M-1 infantry rifle like everyone else. In combat, officers also dressed in G.I. issue clothing to lessen the chance of being identified by the enemy.

The afternoon wore on but eventually a truckload of rations appeared and we each loaded up with a full days supply of six K ration boxes or three complete meals. We were ordered to eat our supper meal around five o'clock, which we did. As we ate, the Captain moved among the groups instructing everyone to be ready to move out at six. It seemed that he was prepared to make the final dash to Paris before nightfall.

We rolled out a little after six, leaving behind our pile of junk plus a scattering of debris from our casual bivouac. I was in the lead truck directly behind the Captain's jeep. Lt. Bond and the Farmer were with him, while Lt. Harding and Lt. Hayride followed at the rear of the convoy in their proper place as second in command. Our job was to get through; the task of the following jeep was to herd us along, pick up stragglers and make sure that a proper convoy truck interval was maintained. We were necessarily strung out over several miles since military rules called for 200 feet between vehicles when in areas of combat, air attack, or when there was the probability of being observed by the enemy. None of these conditions prevailed at the time. However, we roared away from the littered field in good order, looking for all the world like we were soldiers who knew what we were doing and where we were going. We made our laborious way down to Falaise, a town just on the other side of extinction. As we approached the remnants of the city in the growing dusk, we encountered more and more wreckage of transport on the road. Vehicles, or what was left of them, lay in the ditches and occasionally sat abandoned in the fields or next to shattered buildings in small villages. I could see no house, barn or structure of any kind, including fences and walls, which were not, at least, partially destroyed. Utter destruction lay everywhere, unattended.

Our convoy, impressive in size and numbers, seemed to command some priority, for in spite of the volume of traffic that we encountered, we were waved through by real military policemen without pause. Even at that, however, it had taken us well over two hours to reach the outskirts of Falaise. It was well along into the fading light of the evening before we arrive at the far side of the shambles. Blackout running lights came on in the convoy as we began the second leg of our trip down to Argentan. There was no letup in the view of catastrophe on the road out of Falaise. Gratefully the dusk settled in a purple haze over the farmlands, softening the brutal edges of the apocalypse. Gradually only those pieces of the residue of killing that could be seen in the hollow light of our masked headlamps were visible. Out of the thick night would appear the flat back of a burned out German tank or the crumpled frame of a truck, sitting next to the road in gaping silence. We began to make numerous stops as we entered the fringes of Argentan and at one of these delays, I persuaded John to drive.

It was close to midnight when we left Argentan, taking the Easterly road toward Duex. Traffic thinned and the roadbed improved somewhat. We picked up speed that made it necessary to turn on our full headlights against the darkness. The bright light blasted our company jeep ahead of us causing the Farmer, who was hunched over in the back seat, to turn around in apparent alarm. His eyes glittered, almost like a cat's, for a brief second but before he could fully react, the driver of the jeep, either the Captain or Lt. Bond, turned on his headlights and we could tell from the sudden illumination around us that the trucks behind us had done the same. If we were going to drive at night, we had to be able to see where we were going, blackout rules or not. In spite of the welcome light, I was suddenly and completely overwhelmed by a numbing weariness. I could not keep my eyes open. The swaying of the truck and the steady noise of the engine, combined with the two days of hyper-energy and tension, were too much for me. I gladly relinquished all sense of responsibility for the convoy to the jeep ahead of us and fell totally and completely asleep.

Although I did not dream at all, there was still a nightmarish quality to the night, for I would awaken occasionally into a Dante's Inferno. I would float between sleep and wakefulness when the cadence of our forward movement changed significantly or when we encountered one of the many halts along the way. When I was able to force my eyes open, they would only register on my consciousness, a brief kaleidoscopic vision of hell.

It must have been the city of L'Aigle on the Risle River that we approached well after midnight. Our truck changed gears as we began to grind slowly downhill. The physical change awakened me and as I shifted my position and blinked my eyes open, I gazed uncomprehending at a panoramic scene that I can never forget. To my knowledge I have never hallucinated, but I am certain that hallucination could not produce a more profound vision than the one I saw. The city lay in ruins between hills through which the Risle River ran. Coming down into L'Aigle from the West bluff, I could see ahead into the shattered town, and beyond the river, I could see the highway out of the rubble and the road leading away to the East.

The only sound was the labored roar of trucks going down and up, into and out of the remains of what once had been a busy river town. The highway was partially blocked here and there throughout L'Aigle. Buildings had collapsed onto the street and the engineers had carved out a twisting truck path through tons of stone, dirt and broken belongings. I stared, open-eyed, for what I saw appeared to be a giant groaning serpent snaking down into the town to cross the river and back up the Eastern bluff to disappear beyond the ridge. Headlights from a hundred trucks or more moved slowly to the right and then to the left as drivers picked their way through the rubble. The illusion of a living motion was caused by seeing these shafts of light from above and behind. We were part of this living snake, twisting and coiling ourselves through the silent and deserted wreckage of humanity. When we reached the Eastern ridge, I looked back to see the serpent's wide-eyed headlights following painfully up the hill behind us. I was reminded of a painting of the French night convoys coming from Bar Le Duc to Verdun during World War I.

"Voie Sacre," I said aloud.

"What?" yelled John.

Transfixed, I had almost forgotten that he was there.

"The sacred way—we are the sacred way," I sighed as I slipped back to sleep, squinting my gummy eyes against the traffic.

I awakened several more times that night, each time noting in my fogged mind that the roadway seemed smoother and that we were

187

passing through more and more towns and villages that were without damage. Even the concrete telephone and power poles were untouched. I saw several gas stations, surprised to see Esso signs near the unused pumps. As I drifted back and forth from sleep to wakefulness, the thought that I should probably offer to drive for awhile never once entered my mind.

Omaha Beach Interlude—1979

My wife and I left Paris early one morning under an overcast sky, losing our way several times as we fought the snarling commuter traffic entering the city on a workday. Finally, after searching for the entrance to the superhighway leading to Rouen, we broke free from the great city and headed North along the meandering Seine River. Stopping every twenty kilometers to pay a slight toll for using the magnificent roadway, we arrived at Caen near midday and drove Northwest on the superhighway, which had been old N-13. Memories of trying to find N-13 on the day our small force had landed on Omaha were fragmented and difficult to piece together. The four lane highway now completely covered or merely bypassed any remnants of the old road as though it had never been there. Caen, of course was unrecognizable, as was Bayeux. Both have grown into sprawling industrial complexes, complete with high rise apartments, which not only disfigure the rolling landscape, but make it difficult to even identify the terrain. We kept to the highway loop around both cities and took the exit ramp that announced a side road to Colleville Sur Mer. Fast travel on the superhighway compressed the distance so severely that I was surprised to discover that within minutes of leaving Bayeux, we had found the turnoff. Considering that it had taken weeks for the Americans and British to clear the area of the enemy, there was something displeasing about traveling through it in only minutes. We drove our Fiat through the gateway to the Normandy American Cemetery, parked in the spacious parking lot and entered the white Visitor's Center. The Center, which serves as an information stop for those seeking grave sites of relatives or friends, is an architecturally understated building expressing a mausoleum quality that inspires visitors to lower their voices in hushed respect. Crossing the marble floor as quietly as possible, we signed the visitor guest book, noting that of the hundred or so visitors on that day, we were the only Americans to have signed. The others had been from the Netherlands, France, England, Belgium, and as far away as Finland. We did not speak to the dozen or so people who were present but rather left the center, and with the help of a mimeographed map, walked the short distance to the Memorial at the eastern edge of the cemetery. The Memorial, with a reflecting pool extending away from a bronzed sculptured heroic figure, contains large stone wall maps in the loggias that are part of a semicircular colonnade. One map describes the battle of the beaches and a similar map of the entire Normandy campaign is depicted on the other. Dates, colored enameled arrows, and unit designations make it possible to follow the struggle for the beaches and the hedgerow country beyond. But we soon tired of the sweeping arrows that marked breakthroughs and major gains, and instead took the gravel path leading from the Memorial to the English Channel and the beaches, now almost hidden in a wet mist. Standing at the concrete viewpoint on the edge of the high bluff, I was once again struck as I had been in 1944, by the courage of the young Americans who had crossed the wide beaches far below to attack and capture the well defended positions where we stood.

We took the zigzag trail that traversed the cliff and arrived on the beach. We walked slowly across the damp sand to the water's edge and stood close together in the chilled air gazing out at the Channel. Before I realized it, I found myself sitting alone on a hillock of sand a distance from the shoreline. Through the mist I could see the bright figure of my wife strolling farther down the beach toward the West. Alone with my thoughts, I sat with my chin on my knees, my back brushing against some beach weeds, which had found their way to daylight through the sand. Intermingled with the taller weeds were a variety of thick leaved plants. Nothing moved in the still air and there was only the sound of the Channel waves breaking on coarse gravel far away. The faint meowing of circling sea gulls could be heard in the mist beyond. Behind me, a hundred yards or so, stood the bluffs, now devoid of concrete fortifications, gun pits, or any of the debris of battle. The beach itself stretched out of sight to the West, but to the East I could see the sand narrow to the point where it almost joined the cliffs, which had marked the left flank of the Omaha invasion beach. I was confused. The landing site, which I had not seen for nearly forty years, seemed so much larger than I had remembered its being. When I had seen it last, it had been covered with the remnants of war and had been busy with the movements of thousands of men, trucks, tanks, and the weapons of battle. Now, deserted, solitary and silent, Omaha Beach was enormous and unknown to me. But as I looked around, trying to measure distances, it came to me that I was sitting very close to the place where our LST had sunk on my day of landing. There was, of course, noting remaining of it or of anything else in the water. Even the line of Liberty ships that had been deliberately sunk off shore to provide the protection of a man-made breakwater were gone. The curling breakers of the English Channel ran their cold course across the unobstructed shelf of sea bottom.

I turned my head slightly, feeling a warm breath of wind from the North. I listened carefully, head cocked away from the moving air, but there was nothing, no man-made sound, only the subtle noises that nature makes in its constant contentions. A small lizzard scampered past my feet and disappeared into the weed bank behind me. A dark winter bird swooped down to the wet sand near the water's edge and danced after each receding wave, stabbing its yellow beak into the sand, which lay under the bursting bubbles of foam. I watched the bird until it flew away to seek a better feeding place.

Finally I rose, turning for one last look at this peaceful beach crowned by innocent cliffs. There were no explosions nor echoes of explosions waffling back from the bluffs, no pitiful cries for help, no machine gun fire, nor any thunder of aircraft ahead. There was only a deep and profound silence.

As I walked slowly down Omaha Beach to join my wife, I felt the inexplicable sorrow that comes with age. Sorrow that life is slipping away, so much of it so mercifully put aside into shadows, leaving the mind with only the distant ripples of questions that are never fully answered. Thousands of humans had died on this sand, and in the hills and fields beyond, but the beach, the sea, and the misty sky above, in nature's process of forgiveness had already forgotten the holocaust that man had delivered here. Omaha Beach is a monument preserved, but it is a staged memory, orchestrated into parklike landscaping on the hills above, but the incredible battle itself can never be imagined by anyone who was not present in the month of June in the long ago year of 1944.

As a last gesture of respect, we returned to the cemetery to walk among the 10,000 marble crosses.

Civilian cemeteries, particularly older ones nestled in churchyards, are often places of curiosity and speculation. Headstones, placed by families, not only reveal love and individuality, but also status. The wide variety of monuments, crypts, vaults and decorative devices set off a city of dead as personalities. Inscriptions tell of the devotion of the living, and the universal practice of recording the date of birth with the time of dying gives one the comfortable feeling that most of the buried had lived long full lives and had died in peace among their loved ones. Places where soldiers are buried are markedly different, for the military cemetery is a statement of a contradiction to the ugliness of war. Their geometric symmetry and quiet beauty belie the noise and jagged confusion of battle. It is irrational that the perfect military cemetery is the end product of indiscriminate fire, blast and flame that preceeds the agony of sudden death. The military cemetery at Omaha Beach, one of America's largest, is the least possible exception to this contradiction. Nearly 10,000 Americans lie in dust in carefully manicured, secluded plots, screened from one group of graves to the next by mathematically placed shrubbery and low trees. There were once 24,000 graves but most were removed, at parental request, to other geometrical burial places in the United States.

To walk through the acres of marble crosses, interspersed with hundreds of Stars of David, is to initially feel peace and satisfaction that the dignity of death has been observed in a fitting way. That is, unless one begins to read the inscriptions on the crosses, each of which states in neatly chiseled letters, a name, a rank, a unit, and a date of death. No date of birth is recorded.

We had entered the tranquil grounds of the cemetery from the West, walking toward the colonade memorial on a wide grass pathway between the rows of crosses. Coming as we were from the far side of the cemetery, we could not at first see the inscriptions that all dutifully faced the memorial. We could see only the magnitude of death, the quiet majesty of the thousands of glittering marble markers, lined in rows, anonymous in their perfection. But we stopped once to look back and with the first reading of an inscription, the marble field transformed into people. I could almost imagine that at the instant of reading the first name, I could hear a roar of voices as though coming from a crowded stadium of spectators. The total shock was real but the heart-break came from beneath the crosses. We began to retrace our steps, this time reading the words and stifling both tears and an incredible urge to shout the names out loud. It was an impulse to break the ano-nymity of the cemetery and return it to the young men buried beneath its parklike beauty. Finally, overcome by a grief as profound as having lost a child to death, we stopped and sat on the damp carpet of freshly cut grass among the crosses. I wept for them, and I wept for a system of nations that could not devise a more creative way to solve differences. These men, now mercifully covered from sight by yards of earth, had been little more than children when life had ended for them. When they had lived, none of them had ever heard of a nuclear missile or of a walk on the moon. The disbelief in such future enterprise would have been shared and ridiculed as being impossible in the Spring of 1944. Nor had they heard of the resignation of a President or of a steaming Asian country called Vietnam. None of them knew that President Roo-sevelt had died, and the most anguishing thought of all was that not one of them knew that their war had ended and that somehow we had won it. But I felt that their personal loss was even more terrible. They had never known the joy of going home, or of the love that had been waiting there for them. None ever knew of the pleasures, the trials, the troubles and successes that would have led them to the maturity of a full life.

None would ever look into the faces of his own children and be comforted by the knowledge that life follows itself in a miraculous design. The shattered bodies, now buried, had all belonged to personal dreams that had ended in the water, on the sand, in the ravines, cliffs, and the field beyond.

I left Omaha Beach with a deep sense of responsibility and gratitude toward the young men buried there. They had helped buy my full life for me and they had been my comrades when I too, had been very young.

CHAPTER IX

PARIS

I awakened cautiously into silence but also into a world lighted by a diffused brightness. It took me moments to discover that the truck was not running. Glancing at John, I saw that he was asleep, leaning far against the cab door, his head resting on a rolled up field jacket. We were in a city, parked along a narrow street in convoy. There was a fog in the air making it difficult to see much beyond the truck ahead of us but I could see a flagstone sidewalk and brick buildings that fronted close to the street. I could not see through the mist up to above the second floor so I assumed that the rows of doorways were openings into apartments. A tree stood next to our right front wheel, the leafy top obscured by the morning fog. The silence was eerie, following as it did hours of grinding convoy noises. I slowly lowered the window so as not to awaken John and breathed the cool air. The smells were city smells, that curious inoffensive combination of odors that comes from animals, people, traffic and the closeness of buildings, which have been occupied for years. However, only persons bred to the city find an excitement in this smell. Country folks gag and sputter in its presence. Sitting quietly in the morning street reminded me of Pittsburgh and of the pleasures of walking for hours among the sights and smells of the city, my thoughts were interrupted by a sound straight from my childhood. It was instantly recognizable to me because there is no other sound like it. It was the clip-clop of an iron shod horse making its way slowly along a cobblestone street. At first the sound was muted through the fog, gradually becoming more insistent until finally there appeared coming toward me out of the bright mist an ice wagon drawn by an old grey horse. The driver who was an old grey man nodded as he passed by, his leather cap pulled low over his eyes, his closed wagon trailing the telltale drops of water from his melting ice. The wagon disappeared into the fog behind us.

Because of the city and its smells, I slipped easily into my childhood, remembering the summer days when I was fortunate enough to ride the ice route with my Uncle John and his mare named Nellie. Uncle John was the black sheep of the family. Married to one of my Mother's sisters, he jovially rejected all family pressures to make him into an office worker or a salesman. He chose instead to drive his ice wagon through early morning mist and to chide barking dogs along his route. He drank; he smoked cigars and he gambled, stopping at secret shops along the route to pay his debts, place his bets and collect his pennies. He had no enemies. He loved his life and he, carrying 25 pounds of ice on his leather shielded shoulder, was my hero. Sometimes laughing, he would take me along on his deliveries during the long summer mornings, which lasted forever. I would sit in the back, skinny legs dangling over the lowered tailgate, as Nellie would make her laborious way over the cobblestones on Brownsville Road, turning down short streets here and there to leave ice in kitchen iceboxes. The real pleasure was the ice. Covered with wet burlap that possesses a smell all of its own, the large block of ice would be uncovered at each stop while my uncle would judge the size of the chunk to be delivered. Yanking his razor sharp ice pick out of the side of the wagon where he kept it, he would, with consummate skill make a line of quick deep jabs in the ice block. Uncle John would then take his ice tongs and lift the gleaming piece to his shoulder to take it on its melting way to some housewife's icebox. So skillful was he that there was seldom any residue from his surgeon like operation. Occasionally, without speaking but sensing my desire, he would deliberately offset a jab of his ice pick so that fairly large splinters of ice would fall to the wet and soggy floorboards of the wagon. I would pounce on these slivers to lick their coldness and to crunch through their brittle shapes with my small teeth. Uncle John would grin and ruffle my hair when he returned to the wagon. I remember the coolness in the darkness of the closed wagon as the summer mornings would move toward noon. When we would return home my bare legs and arms would be cold to the touch and my Mother, who did not understand the mystery of the ice wagon, would dig out the wet wooden splinters from my calves and thighs while delivering a diatribe about her good-for-nothing brother-in-law.

But over the years the ice melted and with the coming of refrigeration, Uncle John drifted into saleswork and odd jobs. Only I, even as a child, understood his sadness and despair at the passing of Nellie and of the time of the marvelous cold wagon.

My thoughts were shattered by the slamming of the cab door from the truck in front of us and soon the street was filled with sleepy eyed and none too jovial soldiers. We were milling around, talking quietly and deciding that we must be in the outskirts of Paris somewhere when the lead jeep came along with instructions to mount up and stay together. We moved ahead into a thinning fog and a bright sun that cascaded down on a city, which gradually appeared out of the mist. Paris was huge. We were apparently in the Southwestern part of the city near Issy and had to cross over to the Eastern side in order to reach Vincennes. John who was now in the passenger's seat was the first to spot the Eiffel Tower. The tower seemed smaller than I had imagined it would be but it was because I had never seen a picture of it in the context of the enormity of the city. We threaded our convoy through empty side streets, empty in a sense of motor traffic, although there were hundreds of bicycles interspersed between a few chuffing wood burning buses and vans. There were very few vehicles except for military traffic. We seemed to be the only convoy in the city, passing slowly by, but being ignored by the many Parisians hurrying to their work or some other destination.

As we crossed the Seine River at the Eiffel Tower heading North, I could not help but be thrilled by being, at last, in Paris. My feelings were magnified as we wheeled by the huge Arch de Triumphe and started down the Champs de Elysee. I noticed the eternal flame that marked the grave of the French unknown soldier from World War I at the base of the Arch. I felt an overwhelming sense of destiny returning to me from my childhood dreams of warfare.

As we entered the gate leading into the sprawling park at the Bois de Vincennes, we saw our first and only battalion marker. A small freshly painted arrow pointed to the direction of the headquarters. The park was a large wooden area with a lake, trails and of course the famous race track. No one was surprised when we arrived at our prepared quarters, stable-like buildings.

Actually we lived in large rambling warehouse structures adjacent to the race course, my entire platoon together in what could have been a jockey dressing area, equipped with several rows of metal lockers fronted by benches bolted to the cement floor. Large overhead floodlights hung from an open beamed ceiling. Our most recent dwelling had been the Quonset huts in Warminster, so by comparison the stable warehouse seemed comfortable and spacious. Rumors had it that we would only be in Paris a few days. But in a few days as military activity increased in the park, it began to look as though the entire battalion was setting up a permanent base. Trucks, tanks, weapons and fire control equipment began to appear for repair and in less than a week a full-scale heavy base operation was underway. Even our squad of optical repairmen set up a small workshop in one of the warehouses and began tedious adjustments and repair on optical range finders, periscopes and binoculars. No antiaircraft gun directors ever appeared so I spent my time watching the optics crew as they replaced lenses and tried to learn something. Our normal working days required some close order drill and calesthentics, but for the most part I stayed out of sight hoping that no one would even think of the need to mount a guard detail. The park itself seemed to be under control of the French Army supplemented by the local police force and we were never required to assume responsibility for guarding the installation. Once or twice I accompanied Lt. Harding as he drove a jeep into the city to handle some paperwork with Army or Corps Headquarters. The city was showing signs of being cleaned up and as the days shortened in the coming Fall, there was clear evidence that Paris was recovering rapidly from its five years of oppressive occupation by the Germans. Sidewalk cafes, although patronized almost exclusively by soldiers, were crowded and increasing daily in numbers. Lt. Harding, never one to miss an opportunity on our trips into the city, always managed to extend our stay by stopping for some refreshments along the way back to Vincennes. Sitting at a sidewalk cafe sipping cognac in the warm sunlight in Paris seemed like a sensible thing to do. The Lieutenant was not an intellectual person but he was pleasant to be with. I suspected that he felt more comfortable with enlisted men than with other officers. In public he was quiet and fairly dignified as he was expected to be but when we were alone he was relaxed and spoke amiably about his past and future plans to stay in the service. He had been married once but his wife had divorced him because he would not leave the Army life and get a real job. He had no interest in the city, no knowledge of French history or even a passing acquaintance with the art collections of Paris. When our conversations revealed that he had never heard of the Bastille, the Louve or even Notre Dame Cathedral, he was unperturbed by the knowledge. He simply wasn't interested, instead choosing to design means to make money out of his overseas experience. Harding was shrewd and calculating when it came to money. Some of his plans to change money into vouchers to be sent home to an obscure bank account sounded highly illegal to me, but finally his concern for the cost of things became somewhat boring and I found them bordering on fanaticism.

One afternoon we were sitting at a cafe next to the curb on Rue de Rivoli watching girls go by, their bare legs moving awkwardly on their worn wooden soled shoes. Leather for shoes had not been available to civilians for many years and it was a very unusual sight to see a real shoe being worn by a woman. It simply meant that she had been wearing that pair for five years or had been saving them for special occasions. I was admiring legs however, having gotten used to the shuffle and clop of homemade footware, when Harding said, "How much do you think it would cost to get someone to make me a hundred pair of those shoes?"

"Why in God's name would you want a hundred pair of those shoes?" I responded.

"I could sell them!" he exclaimed. "If they're wearing them here in Paris, just think how they need shoes closer to the front. Hell, I'll bet people would give anything for them up there."

He was really excited about the prospects and ignored my sarcasm about the probable market for toilet paper, which I suggested was easier to carve out of a block of wood and wouldn't require as many nails.

I was to learn later that Lt. Harding had pursued the manufacturing of shoes and had actually found someone who promised to deliver 100 pairs to him. Fortunately for the Lt. we left Paris before the order could be completed.

Soon after our arrival at Vincennes, we were permitted to obtain passes for the evening. Everyone wanted to go into town and look for the usual things—women and liquor and in that order. Most managed to find both, in that beautiful but enormous city.

We tended to go in groups when we ventured out on pass and Patterson who spoke French fluently was a favored companion even though he did not drink nor was he ever to be seen in the company of a woman. We shunned the Madam Mausoly book because it seemed to us to be degrading to be seen thumbing through pages looking for the really important words, which weren't in there anyway. Our experience proved that there were certain adventures in the human experience, which didn't require verbalization. Without words solid arrangements could be made with smiles, raised eyebrows, hand gestures and the showing of currency.

Vincennes is about four miles from the center of Paris, which is near the Tuilleries Gardens and we walked the distance twice until Patterson directed us to the free subway system. All Allied servicemen were permitted to ride the underground railway without cost and we soon became familiar with the convenient transportation network. We would arrive near the Arch de Triumph for an evening of fun, noisy and jubilant. Heading down one of the side streets we would find a bar, crowd through the French, British, American and French Colonial troops inside and begin drinking. By listening to the bar conversation we would learn where there were women to be picked up. We also learned that French bartenders normally could be induced for a few francs to make some arrangements for those too anxious to waste valuable time looking around. Prostitutes were legal and plentiful in Paris. Generally, for their own protection, they worked in groups on the dark streets, two or three of them together. The main streets such as the Champs de Elysee were always curiously deserted of the little bands of ladies of the night but they could be found on the narrow streets leading away from the broad avenues. Once a solicitation was made, the woman would lead the customer to one of a myriad of small hotels in the area and for some additional francs given to a bored room clerk, use could be made of a shabby room upstairs.

After my experience in Stroud, I determined not to take up with a stranger and particularly not to share a first experience with a prostitute. So I went with my friends to exchange stares with desk clerks who must have thought that I was queer until my companions could reappear stumbling down the stairs, often ashen faced and shaken from the experience. I was amused by the lies about how terrific it had been and by the braggings of how well each had done.

"Boy, she said I was the best ever!" was a common statement from a young man who was as naive as a person should be after his first experience with sex.

The late summer turned to a riot of fall colors on the trees of Paris and the evening winds began to blow with a chilling edge to them. Rumors began to circulate that soon we would be moving.

We learned at 6:30 in the mess hall one gloomy Thursday evening that the battalion would be leaving Vincennes for the front in less than 24 hours. Our stay in Paris had stretched to almost three months and the task of tearing the battalion loose from its almost permanent home was catastrophic. Not only was there the problem of personal friendships and loves to deal with, as we had learned in England, but if an Army unit stayed in one place for any extended period beyond a few weeks, men had a tendency to literally build themselves into their environment. Lumber, paint, better beds, tables, chairs and other conveniences materialized. Shelves were built, lockers assembled, solid bed frames were constructed and generally men molded the surroundings, seeking comfort and some sort of permanent identity. Although there was effort made and pressure exerted to stay within the limits of standard military code, it was also wisdom on the part of officers to be lenient with personnel trying to exist in foreign places. An adage during World War II was, "If it moves, salute it. If it doesn't, paint it."

Anything that was hand built was then carefully painted olive drab, giving it an "Army" look, which mostly went unnoticed during lackluster and only periodic inspections.

With only 24 hours to prepare for a total departure, much thought and argument erupted over what could be saved and moved. The problem was simplified by the announcement the next day that all personnel would travel by train and that only items on the T.E. (table of equipment) would be transported by truck. This meant weapons, personal equipment and duffle bags only. The news was received with groans and a few scattered "48-49's" curses from the amateur carpenters, some of whom, seemingly had rooms full of furniture to abandon. After the announcement, the battalion spent its time crating its heavy equipment needed to operate a base ordnance unit. This was no small task since we had tools and heavy equipment used to do major repair work behind the lines. We had a fully equipped movable machine shop and the shop materials for optical repair alone filled several vehicles. Being a base battalion we were not in the battlefield recovery business but field ordnance units that were unable to effect major repair theoretically transported tanks, trucks, weapons, and artillery pieces to us for renovation and restoration. Mechanical and electronic gun directors were to follow this line of logistics but none ever appeared in my company for our highly trained crews to repair while we were overseas. My squad of gun director experts still had tools, oscilloscopes and other electronic probes that we crated, uncreated and eventually treated with a sort of parental indifference during our subsequent travels. After a while we even lost track of the whole process, disdaining to even claim the equipment from the supply Sergeant when it did arrive at our various locations.

On Saturday morning our large convoy of heavily loaded trucks left the compound for some destination, which was described to us as being somewhere to the East. There was a very decided chill in the air as we found our way back to our buildings to await the call to board the train. We talked about the American troop trains and the British rail system and wondered about the French railroad cars. Speculation about sleeping arrangements, mess cars, toilet facilities and heat dominated the conversations. The general feeling was that the total distance of the move couldn't be more than a hundred miles even if we were to become a base operation for the Germans behind their lines. There was laughing agreement that we could probably shorten the war considerably if the enemy let us work on repairing their equipment. We also agreed that it would be a short trip of only a few hours. We were excited about going to the front because the weeks in Paris had softened our memories of Omaha and Normandy.

An uneasiness fell over some of us when before noon a weapons carrier delivered two days of K-rations per man to the barracks. We were told to eat our noon meal where we were. In the middle of the long afternoon we were ordered out in the street and directed to clean up our area because the Colonel had found some cigarette butts on the ground. We were not to leave the encampment in such a mess. The air was very cold and windy by now with low guttering clouds skipping beneath a heavy cloud overcast. I groaned because I knew that we were once again going to face some bad weather, hopefully however in a warm Pullman car.

At 5:00 p.m. the whistles jerked us awake and into the company street with our gear. We did a right face and started a lurching and painful hike to a railroad siding within the park and about a quarter of a mile away. There were groans, mumbling and curses whenever someone dropped something but with our individual loads of a full duffle bag, helmet, carbine, belt, pack and gas masks it was very difficult to stay together in some semblance of formation as we made our way down the cold and blustery street. I was momentarily amused when I realized that I was carrying everything in the world that belonged to me. I wondered why trucks had not helped us with the duffle bags as they had done on Omaha Beach but I was soon to learn why. In the railroad yard our platoon was guided between two rows of what looked like small boxcars and ordered to halt. Although we were grateful for the chance to put down our gear between the rows of protective cars, there was such a sinister implication about the boxcars that most of the men were silent.

Someone next to me said, "My God, these are 40 and 8 cars from World War I!"

Stenciled neatly on each car, but weathered and barely readable were the words, 40 hommes, 8 cheaveux. The words simply meant that the car could accommodate 40 men or 8 horses. What was not said was that in order for that number to be accommodated, men and animals would have to stand up. I didn't measure the small four wheel car but it looked to be about 30 feet long and about 8 feet wide. There were, of course, no windows, only two sliding doors on either side of each car. We were given a real break, however, because we were counted off in groups of only 20 and climbed into the dark, smelly interior of our assigned 40 and 8. It apparently had been used previously by 8 nervous overfed horses. The doors were left open so that we could see as each man tried to carve out enough space for his belongings. At first I tried to sit on the floor only to discover that it was a very cold piece of sheet iron with no protective covering. Being service troops, we had no blankets. Those marvels of comfort and warmth were only ever issued in camp by the supply Sergeant, so we sat on our duffle bags and as we thrashed around amid curses and accusations, the first flakes of snow began blowing by the open door. Those early flakes in November were to herald the worst winter in 40 years on the continent of Europe. None of us knew it at the time but some of us would lose our lives to the little flakes and most of us would not be completely warm again for five more months.

The desultory cry of "48-49-50 soome shit" rang down the line of boxcars as we sat and sullenly watched the first French snow any of us had ever seen. The flakes looked astonishingly like American snowflakes.

By nightfall we had eaten our dinner rations, broken out our overcoats and gloves, started several fires in the boxcar by burning the wax boxes from our K-rations in our steel helmets. We closed the awkward sliding doors to try to preserve what little heat there was. I had also determined that once again I was the ranking noncom and that future problems, which we would experience on the train., would no doubt fall on my head. I found it irksome to have this responsibility thrust upon me at a time when comfort was all I was looking for. Around midnight I was awakened by someone outside the car who was apparently checking to see that everyone was aboard. A few minutes later our regained sleep was shattered by an enormous crashing jerk that tumbled most of us to one end of the car.

French trains, whether they are made up of passenger compartments or boxcars, were joined together by chain links similar to three gigantic paper clips linked together. Without any hydraulic or air pressure linkage, a poor start by the engineer was simply transmitted down the full length of the train, car by car. Each car had two large nailhead bumpers with an ineffective shock absorber device built inside each one. These stuck out toward the front and rear to keep the cars from banging into one another when the train slowed, went around a corner, or stopped. Since these were metal and often a foot from the bumpers on the car ahead, the effect was seldom anything but a bone breaking crash whenever any of these maneuvers was attempted.

In any event, we were at last underway, being dragged slowly out of the freight yard toward the Eastern edge of the city. In spite of the creaking and squealing noise made by the wheels on the poorly maintained roadbed, everyone went back to sleep, huddled together for warmth among the duffle bags and equipment. While there were no windows, there was an opening about a foot high that traversed each side of the car. This opening was next to the roof and covered by a wide wire mesh. It was too high for us to see out of it but it did provide us with a steady stream of frigid air even though the outside overhang of the curved roof kept most of the snow from blowing in with the cold wind.

I awoke sometime during the night to a silence punctuated only by some soft snores and a whistling wind coming through the wire mesh. We were stopped. I lay there, stiff and cold, until I realized that I was beginning to see shapes jammed together on the floor. Daylight was coming. I could hear a voice outside the car. Someone was coming down the length of the train pounding on the doors, shouting something.

When he reached us he pounded and shouted, "Everybody out!"

As we began to untangle ourselves, we heard him repeating his order to the next cars.

Someone forced the sliding door open and we climbed down painfully into bright daylight, blinking against it. There were about two inches of fresh snow on the ground next to the railroad tracks. Our train seemed to be on a siding since there were two sets of tracks. The rails on the empty set were bright with use. We lined up next to the car looking like refugees or captured prisoners. There were no weapons, or helmets nor any sign that we were anything but a ragged group of very cold silent people. A few swung their arms and one stamped his feet back into life. Wool caps covered our ears and overcoat collars hid blackened faces from the helmet fires of the previous day.

The man who had awakened us was returning, stopping at each car to repeat some instructions. It turned out to be the Farmer. When he got to us he asked, "Who's ranking noncom here?"

After some hesitation, I identified myself from within my muffled covering.

"O.K. Keem, you're in charge of this car. Give the men a piss call and then eat breakfast. Get back in the cars as fast as you can because we don't know when we will pull out."

As he turned to leave he swung around and shouted, "No more burning fires in the cars! The Captain found out about it and wants it stopped. . . . Any more fires, Keem, and it's your ass!"

"Sergeant," I called, "where are we?"

As he walked away his heated response was, "How the hell would I know!"

Fumbling through layers of clothes we all urinated next to the tracks and climbed back into the car. Leaving the door open we ate our cold K-rations. No one lit a fire but we all saved our cardboard.

In less than an hour we heard a rumbling in the distance. It was a train on the main track coming from the direction of the front. It too was a freight made up of 40 and 8's, but this train was packed with German prisoners heading toward Paris. Some of the car doors were open so that we could see inside. It was clear that each car carried 40 men, the maximum number. Some were smiling, a few even waved an arm in greeting, but most were grim looking and stared at us in open hatred. There were American guards, sitting and cradling their rifles against the cold, on top of some of the boxcars.

The long train clattered by at last. Our train soon started with a great crash and we joined the main track as we gained speed. We were passing through huge open farmland covered with the early snow. There was no damage to be seen except of an occasional large farm building, which would reveal a gaping hole in its roof or a shattered wall. Sightseeing soon took second place to the need for warmth. Someone slammed the doors shut and we once again settled in among our belongings in the dim light. There was some joking at first but soon most of us went back to sleep.

The day passed. We ate again in the late afternoon during one of many stops. It seemed to be getting colder and I noticed that everyone's breath was marked by little puffs of steam. There was very little conversation. An attempt to start a card game only resulted in argument and threat. The many stops were curious because we did not seem to be on a siding waiting for another train to pass. We simply came to a jolting stop on the main track and waited, sometimes for hours before we would begin again our slow laborious way to our destination. Just before dark more snow began blowing in through the mesh on one side of the car. It was greeted with groans and quiet curses.

During the stops we would slip out of the car to perform the necessary body functions, which were carried out in an open manner. The only humor present during the entire trip was the discovery that one could spell words urinating in the fresh snow. Competition arose and contests were held to see who could spell out the longest word before running out of the necessary fluid. The warm urine on the cold snow created a tiny steam cloud. It was as though the words were written by a little firey pencil that burned a track as it raced along. We all quit competing when Wasakowski spelled out his whole name. I don't think he had urinated since we had left Paris. He certainly seemed relieved as we climbed back into the car.

Sometime during the cold night we began burning our hoarded cardboard. With at least six fires going, the car began to warm up a little. However, when the train stopped we smothered the fires in case someone came by to check. The alternating cold and comparative warmth created a minor cycle of anticipation but aggravated the impatience experienced during the halts.

We ran out of cardboard around midnight. A search began for something to burn. Duffle bags were rifled for old letters, boxes, anything. A brief experience burning extra wool socks turned out to be unsatisfactory. Perhaps if they had been clean socks it would have made a difference.

It was Roberts who discovered the gas ointment. Each of us carried small canisters of a whitish ointment, which was to be smeared on hands, faces and any other exposed flesh during a mustard gas attack. Mustard gas not only burns the lungs and causes blindness, but it blisters flesh. Many of us still had the ointment canisters, which were in our newly issued gas mask containers. The new gas mask issue had been given to each man in Paris with no comment. No questions were asked about what had become of the old masks.

Roberts, in a frenzy to hold his Zippo lighter to anything to see if it would burn, had discovered that the ointment burned with a hot blue flame. Not only that, but like canned heat, it burned for a long time.

We soon had a number of blue flames in the car. Each eerie blue flame had several men huddled around it. The scene was not unlike a quiet restaurant with tight tables, looking like a blue candlelighted dinner in a swaying, jolting room, with nodding heads and quiet conversation.

We lived through the night. The blue flames gradually died out one by one as we ran out of our defense against mustard gas.

When the faint light of dawn drifted through the mesh, we climbed out of the car to make our second discovery about the ointment. It not only burned but during the night it had given off a black greasy soot that had covered our faces. We looked all the world like a minstrel troop about to enter stage left. We stood and laughed at one another. Some imitated Negro dialects, stomping and shuffling in the snow.

The Farmer appeared and stopped in astonishment.

"What the hell?" he sputtered. "Why do you look like that?"

"Sgt. Keem, have you been burning things?

"Of course not, Sergeant," I replied. "We must have gotten the smoke from that tunnel we went through last night."

"Oh, yeah," he said behind confused eyes. "Well, stay together, we're going to be there soon."

He hurried off, plodding his way down the line of cars. We laughed quietly after Johnson, in his best Negro impersonation asked, "Hey man, what tunnel? I don't see no tunnel."

I don't know whether or not it occurred to the Farmer that it could have been unusual for only one car in the train to have been filled by smoke in a fictitious tunnel.

It never came up in a conversation again. It did remain as a standing joke in the squad for a long time however. Weeks later if we were doing something we had been ordered not to do, someone would grin and say, "Watch out for the Farmer, here comes that tunnel again."

The train had one more short haul to make before we jerked to a stop in a small train station. Craning my head through the doorway, I read the station sign, which announced in faded letters, *Chaumont.*

The sun was breaking through scattered clouds. We were glad to get out of the infernal box cars and into familiar 6-bys, laughing now. The trip from Paris to Chaumont, a distance of less than 200 kilometers had taken us almost 48 hours. Years later I was to drive the route in a rented car on a superhighway in less than two hours.

CHAPTER X

CHAUMONT

In 1944 Chaumont was a medium sized city by the standards of the time. Nestled in a slight valley on the Marne River it had historically been a military base, guarding the Eastern gate to Paris and serving as a major staging area for French conquest. To the West of the city lay an enormous Army encampment. It was actually a small town in itself, built of stone barracks, buildings, parade grounds and storage depots. This little city was situated on the hills that spilled down into the main city of Chaumont. Private houses, shops and commerce snaked up the hills along the road that lead to the Army post connecting to two centers of population, the city and the military garrison. Napoleon had geared his armies here and General Pershing had located his headquarters in the barracks of Chaumont in the preparation for his drive through the Argonne in World War I. We learned all this as our convoy left the train station, roaring through the cold main square of the city, ascending the West hill to the camp.

Our barracks had been prepared, heated and assigned. We dumped our gear on bunk beds, took delight in the heat of the spacious rooms and went to a late breakfast in a real mess hall. Hot food and coffee were plentiful. We were grateful for the simple pleasure of powdered eggs, fried potatoes, toast, and bacon, but most of all a warm room. There was laughter and shouting in the mess hall. Men, warmed and fed, became friendly with one another again.

The mess hall was large, not unlike a college dormitory dining room equipped for cafeteria service. We ate off metal trays and drank coffee from ceramic mugs. None of us mentioned that the fighting was only 30 miles away around Nancy and Epinal. I did wonder what the effect of early snow would be on the war but turned my thoughts back to the immediate surroundings. The Chaumont Army post had been previously occupied by a German garrison. There were signs that the force had been a permanent one and that it had been stationed there for a long time, perhaps during the entire four year occupation of France by the Germans. One wall of the mess hall, an area of 80 feet in length by 10 feet in height was decorated with an excellent mural. The colorful painting was that of an early morning German roll call with each man in a platoon painted in his likeness. Like all soldiers at reveille the men were bleary-eyed, unshaven, pajamas sticking out beneath their overcoats, some shamefully out of the prescribed uniform. A fearsome Sergeant, his mouth open in a soundless shout, harangued a long line of tall, short, thin, fat German soldiers. There was laughter and pointing from the Americans at the tables, as certain characters were discovered to be all too familiar. The artwork was first class, the figures larger than life-size. It was really a good piece of professional artwork and no one had defaced it since that line of honest Germans had left the mess hall for the last time.

Once again I sat in thought, unsmoked cigarette between my fingers, looking from one of the painted faces to the next, all the way down the line. These faces could have been of me and my platoon. If by some chemical magic the color and style of the uniforms could be changed on the wall, I would be looking at the 3rd Platoon Artillery and Fire Control Company. For a moment I was sobered by an unfamiliar fear.

The mess hall mural was not the only artwork in the building. In the fairly modern latrine, above the trough-like urinal, there was some pornographic artwork done by a different German artist. It too was executed with flair and skill, depicting men and women in all sorts of detailed graphic forms of sexual intercourse. It was done as line drawings in cartoon form with the participants saying things in German in little balloons above their heads. They were saying very vulgar and naughty things. On the opposite wall the characters in the orgy were being observed by a painted group of highly agitated German officers shouting advice in more formal balloons over their heads. Even though the drawings were in the latrine, where they were vulnerable, they too had not been defaced.

The artwork represented the private world of soldiers, beyond civilian comprehension, and as such seemed sacrosanct. It did not matter that the artwork was German; it mattered only that it was done by and for soldiers. It was a respected message for young men who carried weapons against other young men who did the same.

We had been at Chaumont barracks for three days when a long convoy of trucks rolled through the main gate, stopped on the large parade ground, and unloaded about 1,000 Black French Moroccan

205

troops. These colonial infantry troops were tall French speaking Africans in French uniforms and red fezzes on their heads. Their French officers were all white. The contingent settled in barracks nearby on the other side of the quadrangle and at first we were curious about them but soon learned to stay away from them for personal safety reasons. They were a tough and violent group, openly hostile toward us. We had to watch our belongings constantly. The Moroccans practiced open squad tactic drills in the spacious quadrangle and it was not uncommon for the squad leader to disappear with his six men into some other unit's barracks where they casually ransacked everything in sight. Anything of value was stolen. We protested to the camp commander, a full Colonel but nothing ever came of it. Instead of seeking official justice we left an armed guard at the door of each barracks at all times. Eventually the thieving stopped. The hostility remained.

Within a week, I along with several other highly trained technicians in our platoon, were assigned to camp guard duty and once again I found myself on an eight hour shift at the main gate. We shared the detail with an engineer battalion and with the French Moroccans.

During the second week I was on my way to the main gate from my barracks, huddled against the cold, and dreading the evening duty ahead. The night shift was difficult because of the Moroccans who were allowed out on the town during the evening and who arrived back on the post drunken and dangerous. None of them spoke English and all of them seemed to enjoy what they considered the charade of checking passes and identifying themselves. One lonely American, at an ill lighted gate surrounded by a dozen or so jeering French colonial giants, was not a cheerful sight. The duty officer, sometimes one of ours, sometimes an engineering officer and occasionally a Frenchman, were seldom available for assistance.

On that particular day, while walking across the parade ground, I tried not to think about it. Instead I mused at the fact that within a day or two I would reach my 21st birthday, a benchmark in growing up. It was hard for me to believe that I was really so young. I was feeling a good deal older than 21.

As I was thinking of home, I heard a clapping shot ring out. It seemed to come from the entrance to the post. With some reluctance I quickened my pace, hurrying toward the gate. As I rounded the building blocking the view of the main gate, I skidded to a stop, fumbling for my pistol with my gloved hand.

There lying on his back in the center of the narrow driveway leading into the post lay a crumpled figure dressed in the sky blue overcoat uniform of a French soldier. His cap, trimmed in red and gold sat upside down on the cobblestones several feet behind his blood covered head. He was, or had been, a French officer. I retreated behind the building sticking my helmeted head around to see what was going to happen. I saw the Sergeant of the guard, a Moroccan, pointing to a building across the street. He was shouting French to the two gate guards who unslung their rifles and together with the Sergeant moved toward the house. They were carefully watching an upstairs open window as they ran to the front of the building. The Sergeant, pistol drawn, kicked open the door and disappeared inside. One of the guards, rifle at the ready, followed him into the dark interior. The other guard, his head held back, aimed his rifle at the window above. In a matter of seconds a muffled pistol shot could be heard. The doorway guard jumped and moved away from the entrance. He did not seem nervous, however, he seemed curiously at ease with his weapon, almost graceful, totally alert.

Suddenly there appeared at the doorway a Moroccan soldier with his hands on his head. He was followed by the Sergeant jabbing his pistol against the captive's neck. They were joined by the two guards, one of whom carried two rifles, his and the prisoner's. They all marched across the road, through the gate, stepped around the fallen figure without a glance and passed me still standing behind the building. The prisoner glared at me with bloodshot eyes, his yellowed teeth clenched together in a lip distorting grimace of defiance. The little detail quickly crossed the parade ground headed for the barbed wire enclosed stockade.

The entire scenario could not have taken more than two minutes but by then a small crowd had begun to gather. Civilians peered through the gate and the officer of the day, an engineering Lieutenant, screeched to a halt in his O.D. jeep just a few feet from the man on the ground. I arrived at the scene in time to hear the O.D. say, "Jesus Christ, look at that!"

I looked and was sorry I had done so. The single bullet had struck the man in the forehead above his right eyebrow. It had shattered his head, collapsing it so that one of his eyeballs hung crazily out of its socket staring at a cobblestone near the head. It was a blue eye. There was a large fan shaped spattering of blood, bone, and shreds of scalp behind what was left of the man's head. My heart pounded and I felt sick.

"You can put that away now Sergeant," said the Lieutenant.

He said it twice before I realized that he was speaking to me. I still had my pistol in my hand. Jerked back to reality, I holstered the pistol and entered the little guardhouse at the gate. Sitting at the Sergeant's desk was a Moroccan soldier talking to someone on the field phone. He startled me and from his slight smile I could see that he sensed that at that moment I was terrified of him. He was calling for an ambulance, which arrived just as the guard was changed. I took over, assuming the responsibility of writing a narrative report of the death at the gate.

With shaking hand I carefully recorded the time of the incident, making sure that it went on the record as having occurred before my shift had begun. After the ambulance had removed the corpse, our job was to wash down the cobblestones. We all pitched in, taking turns filling the single bucket with water and sloshing the human residue toward the street and gutter.

Tiny pieces of that French officer remained in the street for days until the traffic and weather removed all signs that a score had once been settled there. We never knew what had caused the soldier to murder the officer. We heard the next day that the giant was to be executed by a firing squad. We learned soon after that he had been executed.

Events began to move rapidly at Chaumont. There was little time for boredom even though if I worked the night shift I was on my own during the next sixteen hours. There was a subtle urgency in the activity at the camp marked by the comings and goings of staff vehicles and the constant arrival of battle damaged tanks, vehicles, artillery and small arms, set a serious note to the normally slow paced camp life. The stream of weapons, both American and captured German equipment, did give us a firsthand chance to study the weapons of war. We were at first curious about the Sherman tanks. They were the first line medium American tank, armed with a relatively short barrelled 75mm cannon. The Sherman was our major ground weapon, originally thought to be somewhat invincible and feared.

These tanks began to arrive at the post on the backs of enormous tank retrievers, a long and wide bed carrier pulled by a huge armoured hexagonally shaped cab. The rig had a 50 calibre machine gun mount on its roof and it was the largest vehicle that the Army possessed, intended to be used to retrieve disabled tanks at the edge of battle. These awesome carriers were the forerunners of a generation of the trailer trucks of the future that now flood the interstate highways of America. They were so large, however, that it was not uncommon to find traffic blocked for miles because a retriever had become wedged between buildings on narrow twisted streets in small towns and villages.

We were chilled however to see Sherman after Sherman with a neat 5 inch diameter hole drilled entirely through the turret that housed the cannon. This was common although the steel armour plate on the turret was nearly a foot thick. I examined one turret that had been pierced by a shell, which had penetrated one side, cut the breech block off the 75 and had gone through the other side of the armour plate. The white interior was spattered with dark blood. This penetration was the work of the much respected German 88 cannon. There was no artillery piece developed during the war that was as versatile or as deadly as the high velocity 88. The enemy used it for field artillery, antiaircraft and also as a cannon for its heavy tanks. The piece was not only a high velocity weapon but it had a very flat trajectory, sending a shell in almost a straight line for a long distance, destroying what it hit. It was very accurate and we were sobered by what we saw.

Americans, being imaginative, soon developed weapons to counter the superior equipment the Germans used against us. Tank destroyers, TD's we called them, began to appear. They were a simple gun platform, open with no turret, but carried on a Sherman tank chassis. Each mounted a 105 cannon, capable of knocking out heavy German armour. Tactics were refined so that the TD's hunted in teams; keeping on the move to escape return fire, they were highly mobile. They could be used for normal artillery fire also even though they offered little armour protection for the crew. The bazooka, a simple stovepipe-like rocket launcher, which could be carried by an infantryman, became effective against the German tank, bunker and concrete strong point. The Germans, also imaginative, soon improved on our bazooka, developing the Panzerfaust, which shot a much heavier and more effective rocket. It was also easier to aim and to fire.

From a soldier's perspective the Germans were equipped with the all-around best material of the war. Their armour, artillery, machine guns and aircraft seemed far superior to ours. Even some of their small arms became coveted treasures. Pistols, the Luger and the more simple P38, were prized possessions and we had no weapon to equal the Schmeisser 9 mm machine pistol. It had, for the time, the highest cyclic rate of fire of any field weapon in existence. Our only comparable weapon was the Thompson submachine gun. It was a dependable weapon but heavier and slower than the Schmeisser. It threw a larger bullet, 45 calibre as opposed to the 9 mm, which was equivalent to about a 38 calibre, but our Thompson was less accurate. Almost all of our hand weapons were of a large calibre, coming as they had from the historical development of weapons designed to deal with the conquest of the wilderness and with the all important aspect of stopping power against larger wild animals and determined enemies. Even our 30 calibre M-1 rifle was slightly larger in calibre than the German standard infantry weapon, the model 98 Mauser.

The M-1 was a good, although heavy weapon. It was semiautomatic as opposed to the single action bolt operated Mauser, and it held eight bullets in a clip as compared to the five bullet capacity of the German rifle. We all believed that the M-1 was a better piece. Our carbines, also semiautomatic with a clip of fifteen 30 calibre bullets, were better than any smaller rifle that were issued to the enemy. The major problem with our shoulder weapons was that being gas operated and semi-automatic, it was absolutely necessary to keep them clean and carefully oiled or they would not operate. On the other hand one could throw a Mauser in the mud, pick it up, wipe it off with a sleeve and continue to fire it. Trench warfare, dating back to our own Civil War, with its dirt, mud and debris, had promoted the development of single shot, bolt or lever operated military weapons. A piece of dirt, lodged in the gas vent of the barrel of an M-1 or carbine, rendered the weapon useless until it was removed by careful cleaning. As mentioned earlier, the ubiquitous condom, slipped over the barrel end of a rifle kept out dirt until it was to be fired. In action however, an American soldier, throwing himself on the ground, had to be very careful not to poke the end of the rifle into the dirt or he could find himself literally disarmed. In the nature, panic, and confusion of combat, this penchant for a clean rifle often became secondary to protecting one's life. However, most casualties in modern mobile war occur from artillery or mortar fire, only a comparatively small percentage from rifle, pistol or machine gun bullets.

The bayonet, developed as an adjunct to a single load weapon, one that turned a rifle into a pike, became virtually obsolete during World War II. Although all troops were issued one along with the gas mask, there were very few deaths ever documented that had been caused by bayonet wounds in WW II. Automatic and intensive firepower had eliminated the need for a spear. We used the bayonet for opening cans, cooking and for digging. Useful, but no longer classified by soldiers themselves as a weapon. There was a saying about the bayonet, "If you're close enough to stick him, you're close enough to shoot him."

The German bayonet came in a metal case, leather belt attachment and was made of fine blued polished Englenjer steel. Ours were crude by German standards, unpolished steel with a plastic scabbard and a simple bent wire double hook for hanging onto the web belt. The bayonet comparison is a good example of one of the possible reasons for the defeat of the German nation. Germans were, and are well recognized for their careful craftsmanship, and for their meticulous attention to technological detail of all kind. This facet of their national psyche was very evident in their war material. Their weapons were carefully made, often handcrafted. Luger pistols were handmade, each part individually numbered and hand fitted together. There were three different hand weapons that took 9 mm cartridges—the luger, the P38 and the Schmeisser. All of these took different 9 mm cartridges and to attempt to fire a luger bullet in a Schmeisser or a P38 could result in an explosion or a serious jamming of the weapon. The separate cartridges had color markings on them to identify the right bullet for the right weapon. The apparent close attention to the critical design of the weapon itself dictated a certain powder load for the cartridge. In addition to three different bullets for the same calibre weapon, a Luger was manufactured that was identical in size to the 9 mm version but it loaded a 7.65 mm cartridge, close to a 32 calibre bullet. These smaller pistols were hypo-thetically manufactured for the Luftwaffe to carry as sidearms.

We, on the other hand, had only three kinds of cartridges—the 45, which loaded either our standardized pistols or our submachine guns, the standard 30 calibre bullet, which fitted all rifles and machine guns, and a shorter 30 calibre designed only for the carbine. Fifty calibre cartridges were used in our heavier machine guns.

German helmets came in sizes and were personally fitted with a soft leather headpiece that could not be removed. Our helmet, as de-scribed earlier, fitted on a helmet liner with a simple adjustable web strap and came in one size. When adjusted, it fitted all heads from cannonball round to pointed. The steel helmet itself, easily detached from the liner, could be, and was used as a bucket for liquids, a basket, or for cooking and other imaginative uses such as a fireplace.

German hand grenades, called potato mashers because of the long wooden handle attached to the small can sized explosive device, must have been a nightmare to produce. The wooden handle was hollow and screw machined at both ends. One end screwed into the explosive charge while a machined metal cap fitted the other end. To arm a gre-nade one unscrewed the metal cap, pulled on a nylon rope cord that went through the hollow handle to a seven second fuse, which gave one time to throw it before it exploded.

Our grenades had a simple spring release device held in place by a cheap cotter key. Once the safety key was pulled out, the grenade would remain inactive until it was thrown, in which case the spring handle would fly off and a three second fuse would activate. If one did not wish to throw the grenade, he only had to reinsert the safety key and return the explosive device to his pocket or belt. The three second fuse dramatically reduced the chances of anyone picking up the thrown grenade and returning it to the sender and being a fragment grenade, it was very effective if it burst in the air.

The American functional simplicity of standardized production permeated our war effort and the mass production of interchangeable parts was, I believe, a major factor in the defeat of the Axis powers. While they hand fitted carefully engineered material, we outproduced them, crushing them with what must have seemed to them to be an endless flood of material.

While examining a German booby trap triggering device, I discov-ered that the safety pin, which had to be removed in order to arm the trigger, was actually a carefully machined rod. Once removed it was thrown away. A single nail, piece of bent wire or a paper clip would have worked just as well.

The average soldier could not help but notice that while we fought with material that was often inferior in quality, it was superior in quan-tity and in ease of mass production. I'm sure that trained manpower had a lot to do with the German problem. After six years of war the nation had necessarily reduced its labor force to the skeletal limits of only a comparatively small number of highly trained technicians and engineers. This little band, possessed as they were with German standards, managed plants of imported workers, often slave labor, which reduced production output. There was never time to retool for a cheaper and more easily manufactured product. We, on the other hand, had to suddenly gear up from ground zero for an all out effort giving us the advantage in planning production techniques for what we knew would be a long, gigantic and universal war. In the end while we lost three Shermans to their one Tiger, we outlasted them in both manpower and production. Never having American cities or centers of manufacturing bombed or burned helped a lot also.

Around mid November we were walking back from dinner at the mess hall jangling our mess gear to shake off the water when John stopped suddenly and said, "Wait a minute, what's that?"

We stopped our noise and listened. After a short time we heard a faint sort of grumbling sound. It was continuous, not rising or falling like aircraft sounds. It was coming from the Northeast. We hurried through the growing darkness toward our barracks, puzzled but suspicious that what we were hearing was not natural, that it might just be something having to do with the war.

Rounding Company M's barracks building we stopped again, this time in a row. In the sky to the Northeast we could see a flickering of light above the low ridges beyond Chaumont, not unlike sheet lightning but close to the ground. The rumble we were hearing was a great artillery barrage probably 30 miles away. The white light splashed back and forth across the hills in one constant movement. It extended and occupied at least a quarter of the horizon that we were watching. The barrage must have been at least 50 miles from one end to the other. Although we did not know it then, we were watching the major breakout of the American forces on the other side of Nancy.

Later, looking through the windows, from our darkened second floor barracks, we could see the dancing light more clearly. After about two hours there was a discernible surge in both light and rumble and then suddenly the noise stopped and the light over the hills simply went out. We could sense in the blackness and silence that American troops were now moving forward toward what they hoped would be a demoralized enemy.

After going to bed, we talked quietly to one another in our blacked out room about what this offensive would mean to us. We concluded that it would mean a probable move for us whether it succeeded or not. We also agreed that we would be seeing more Sherman tanks with blasted turrets.

On November 25th it snowed, a slow falling big flake snow. It was beautiful. It filled me with memories of ice-skating and long winter walks of my adolescence. I was nostalgic because on this day 21 years before I had been born in a clapboard house on Brownsville Road in the Burrough of Mt. Oliver in Pittsburgh, Pennsylvania.

I had all day to myself because in the morning I was informed that I was to be a substitute Sergeant on the guard shift from 8 at night until 4 in the morning. I was disgruntled because I had intended to go into town with my friends and celebrate. My resolve about a woman was beginning to weaken also. It may have been the artillery light in the sky or the mere fact that now, on this day, I officially had at last become a man, but I felt an urgency that I had not experienced in the past. Would this day be the last birthday of my life?

In spite of the irritation over the unexpected guard assignment, the day went pleasantly. Several days before my birthday, I had received a package from home, which I had not opened, knowing that it was something special to me. It was special. Not too stale cookies, wool knit scarf, a new pipe, tobacco and pouch and something that I could not believe. It was a glass jar of little bay shrimp together with another jar of shrimp cocktail sauce. It was one of my favorite delicacies. I waited until everyone had left the barracks for their duties and then sat on my bunk and very carefully ate each shrimp, covering it completely with the sauce. Spreading it lovingly with my mess knife as a child would spread peanut butter to the far corners of a soft piece of white bread, I ate the whole jar of shrimp. I ate every bit of the shrimp sauce. Never had I savored anything so totally. Then I hid the jars in the bottom of a trash can so that no human would ever know that I would have died rather than share one single piece of that delight. I whispered to myself, "Mother, I love you for giving me one of the best 20 minutes of my life."

The snow had stopped falling by the time I went on guard duty. The clouds cleared off and on my 21st birthday, I was treated to a crystal clear night, a brilliant full moon, and a fresh white covering of snow on the ground. The shaded single bulb light at the main gate created a pool of muted yellow on the snow and miraculously the Morrocans were almost friendly as they passed through the gate on their way into town. Altogether it was turning out to be a rather pleasant evening.

Lt. Harding roared up in the Officer of the Day jeep wearing the O.D. armband. Sliding to a stop on the wet snow he yelled at me, "Sgt. I'll be back in a few minutes!"

With that he wheeled out on the street and drove down the road into town. I had heard the stories about the Lt.'s escapades at one of the hotels in Chaumont. I also knew that he had no business leaving his post as O.D. and that he had no authorized trip ticket from the motor pool to take the jeep outside the grounds. Knowing him, however, I didn't give it much thought. Although when he had not returned after two hours, I did wonder what I was going to say if I were questioned later about his unauthorized leave. As Sergeant of the guard, it was my responsibility to check trip tickets and log all vehicles off and on the post.

The night continued to be quietly beautiful but about 10:00 p.m., I heard a fitful droning aircraft noise to the Northeast. American and British planes made a throbbing steady sound but we had been told that German bombers made an oscillating noise that rose and fell in pitch. This steadily increasing sound that I was hearing could only be heavy enemy aircraft. Standing with my mouth open, staring at the sky, I was suddenly engulfed in darkness as I heard a single siren in the distance and almost simultaneously all of the lights on the post went out. There was a faint barking sound of antiaircraft guns on the far side of Chaumont followed by a quick series of far off crumping explosions, which I took to be a string of bombs.

I had two thoughts race through my mind at the same time—my own safety and Lt. Harding. The Officer of the Day, the man in charge of the post, had never returned from town and here we were with an approaching air raid. I raced into the darkened squad room, shook awake my only supernumerary, told him to guard the gate and jumped into the guard jeep. Without lights, I took the snow covered road down the hill into town at a dangerous speed. The moonlight was bright, however, and I could see well enough to find my way to the hotel where I suspected my O.D. was to be found. The sound of planes was covered by the noise of the jeep but I could hear the guns and continued to feel the thump of bombs in the night air. They seemed to be coming closer. Sliding to a stop right up on the sidewalk in front of the hotel, I barely recorded on my thoughts that Harding's jeep was nowhere to be seen. Crashing through the doors and blackout drape into a small lobby lighted by a single candle on the concierge's counter, I shouted at the old man leaning there, reading a newspaper by the feeble light.

"Oui aye mon officier?"

He blinked. I jabbed my finger at my M.P. armband and yelled, "Mon officier, mon officier,"

I could see that he pretended not to understand but as a thunderous explosion shook some dust down from the ceiling he quickly shouted, "Salle ducentura!" and dropped to the floor behind the lobby desk.

I ran up the stairs, raced along the dark hallway, reading the faded numbers on the doorways until I came to room 203. I didn't bother to knock. I threw open the door and burst into a bedchamber lighted by another single candle in a wall bracket. The windows were covered by drapes but there, sitting stark naked, on the side of the bed, drinking out of a bottle, was Lt. Harding. The woman in the bed, obviously drunk, struggled to sit up. As she did so, her pendulous breasts fell out over the blanket, which she plucked around her waist. Bleary-eyed from sleep and drink, she mumbled, "Quis qiu say?"

Ignoring her, I shouted, "Harding, for Christ's sake get back to the post, we're having an air raid!"

Right on cue, my shout was followed by an enormous series of explosions, close by in the city.

He threw the bottle to the woman and ran for his clothes on the chair. Turning quickly to leave the room, I shouted over the noise, "I'm going back, no one knows I'm gone!"

It wasn't until I got back to the post gate that I realized how foolish I had been to leave to try to cover for Harding. Fortunately, the post was deserted. I couldn't even find the guard on the gate. It seemed that everyone had headed for some imagined place of safety. The bombers were gone by then and only a few antiaircraft guns sputtered away in the direction of Nancy. The lone siren sounded an all clear and just as the post lights were turned on, Lt. Harding drove up in his jeep. He stopped next to me and said solemnly, "Thanks, I'll remember this."

"That's O.K., sir," I replied with an inflection on the sir." I added, "Happy Birthday."

Puzzled, he drove into the compound to join a growing crowd of excited soldiers who had gathered there. Sitting straight in the jeep, Harding actually looked for all the world as though he was dutifully completing his rounds as the efficient and alert Officer of the Day.

There were two more important events that occurred at Chaumont during the week following the air raid. One had to do with life and the other with disturbing death.

The day after my birthday I went into town with Johnny to see what damage had been done by the bombing raid. We walked around the center of the city but could not see signs of recent damage. Our walking, however, took us North of the center square into an area by the river, which I had never visited before. It was an old part of Chaumont, charming in its antiquity. We loitered there sitting in a small cafe overlooking the Marne, sipping brandy and watching the civilians. By late afternoon, warmed by the cognac, we idly watched the proprietor and two waitresses make preparation for an evening meal. Part of the dining room was upstairs and the waitresses passed us as they made many trips up and down the steep wooden stairway to the second floor. Greatly surprised, I caught one of the girls watching me out of the corner of her eyes as she passed by with a tray of French bread. On her return trip she looked directly at me and gave me a small smile. I became interested in her and her subsequent passes back and forth gave me the opportunity to study her very closely. She was mature, perhaps in her 30's. She was not beautiful but there was an elegance about her. She wore her clothes very well. Immaculate black dress and the starched white apron, which seemed to be required of all French waitresses, set off her dark hair and deep brown eyes. Her eyelashes were very long and her rather long face was matched by long slender legs. She had a nice thin hipped figure and I wondered why I had not noticed her before. I was studying her proud bosom, which bounced in a delightful way when she carried a loaded tray on her shoulder, when she astonished and momentarily embarrassed me by stopping and saying in gentle French, "My name is Gabriel. Are you staying for dinner?"

She looked directly into my eyes in a knowing but penetrating way. She smiled as I stammered my way through an explanation that we were not going to stay for dinner and she turned away. John laughed, "You're a jerk," he said. "Don't you really know what she's doing? Hell, she likes you, haven't you been watching the way she looks at you?"

I denied that it was true but was nevertheless pleased by what he had said. The next time she passed she bumped my shoulder with her hip. John saw it and snorted. "You've got to be the dumbest guy I ever knew."

As Gabriel reached the bottom of the stairs, she stopped and looked back at me. With a sudden rush of self-confidence, I knew what I was going to do. On her way back to the kitchen I stopped her with my hand on her arm and asked, "Do you want to go to a party tonight?"

She laughed and walked away. Confused and humiliated, I gulped the last of my brandy, trying to ignore John's advice to try again. I pushed back my chair, anxious to get out of there and I abruptly told John that we were leaving. He remained seated even as I strode to the door struggling into my field jacket. I turned to yell at him but found myself looking into the face of Gabriel. Before I could say anything, she whispered, "Meet me here at 9:00 o'clock."

I had time only to shake my head up and down once or twice before she disappeared into the kitchen. Walking toward the post I felt elated but worried. What was I going to do? What party? What does she expect?"

John, walking fast to keep up with me, said, "You better get a room somewhere!"

I looked at my watch. It was already after 6, so I sent him back to camp with the admonition to cover for me if there was trouble. As Sgt. of the Guard, I had a permanent pass to be gone anytime I was not on duty and I was not on call again until 8 the next morning.

I stopped at a small cafe, had one more unwanted cognac and tried to collect my thoughts. Leaning on the bar, I quickly examined the options open to me. They ranged from trying to actually organize some sort of party down to not showing up to meet her at 9:00 o'clock. Similar to my experience with the bus driver in Stroud, I could feel that something had been set in motion and that I was inexorably being drawn into a situation, which I could well regret. There was a major difference here in Chaumont however. What was occurring was mostly of my own design and I felt a strong urging to see it through. Now I wanted very much to see it through. I left the cafe and found my way to the hotel where I had located Harding during the air raid.

It was a simple matter to pay for a room on the second floor and to receive a key. There were no questions from the disinterested room clerk. He pocketed the money and went back to reading his newspaper. I canvassed the hotel, checked the small room, and discovered that there was a flight of steps behind the lobby entrance, which could not be seen from the desk and which lead to an alleyway beside the hotel.

I arrived at the cafe precisely at 9:00 o'clock with a bottle of wine stuffed inside my field jacket. Gabriel was waiting for me in the doorway in a long black coat against the cold night air. We walked quietly together as I told her we were going to the hotel. Expecting her reaction to be either guarded or negative, I was delighted that instead she took my arm and pressed it against her side. She was almost as tall as I but we walked well together, an electricity flowing between us.

I lead her up the back stairs, being careful not to be seen or heard by the room clerk whom I imagined was still reading behind the unseen counter.

Once in the small room, which I locked carefully, we took off our coats and sat on the bed together. We laughed at the wine, it was very young and not very good even though we shared the single glass in a conspirited way.

I made no pretense that other people were going to arrive or that a party was about to take place. Gabriel made no mention of the fact that I might had mislead her into believing that she had been invited to a gathering. Instead we talked quietly about the weather, the war, and the recent air raid. We drank the wine.

She finally stood up, placed the glass on the dresser, turned out the lights except for a well shaded wall lamp, and turned to me. "Let's go to bed," she said in a small solemn voice.

During the night, I learned many things. I learned that while making love can be primarily physical in nature, it is an emotional experience of sharing as well. I learned that lovemaking is a fulfillment and that it is a private pleasure. Gabriel was the teacher and I the student. She was compassionate and understanding even though I'm sure that her private pleasures were not as great as mine. She made me feel at last that I was truly a man. During quiet moments in whispered closeness, I also learned that she had not heard from her husband since he had been captured by the Germans during the fall of France in 1939.

She had no children but lived with her parents in a close desperation. Once during the night when she fell asleep, I slipped out from under the down quilt, turned out the light, and went to the window. Drawing the blackout drapes, I looked at that part of Chaumont, which I could see. I marveled at the enormous change that had occurred in me in only a few hours. There was no war out there. This was universality that I was looking at and I had finally become part of the fabric that was the human experience. I had completed part of my journey and had reached and passed that elusive milestone that separates the very young from those who are no longer young. It was an exhilerating emotion but it was tempered by the realization that I could no longer anticipate that amazing truth, forever. I knew now what the animal madness of passion was like and how it could temporarily but totally dominate the spirit and the mind.

As I turned back to the bed in the cooling room, I knew that I could never be the same person again. I could be better or I could be worse, but I could never again be what I had been.

We parted in the alleyway in the early morning light in a falling snow, shaking hands in the French manner, in the simple one shake fashion of friends.

Captain Smart called me into the orderly room following roll call to explain to me that, along with Patterson, I would be relieved from guard duty to be assigned to a special detail involving a civilian trial. Patterson had been named because he was the most knowledgeable in the French language and I had been selected because of my experience with the camp guard detail. The Captain explained that there was to be a civilian trial at the City Hall in Chaumont and that the provisional government had asked for American and French military representatives to be present.

Early that afternoon, Frank and I dressed in class A uniforms, were taken to town in the company jeep and with formality were seated with thirty or more people in what must have been the City Council chamber. After a short wait three men wearing long black robes were announced. The audience stood until the judges were seated behind a long table on a raised dais. A podium was placed facing the judges as the one in the middle adjusted his glasses and began reading in a low voice from a long document. I could not follow all of the legal language but between my cursory knowledge of French and an occasionally whispered word from my companion I pieced together that two people were being accused of collaborating with the Germans during the occupation of Chaumont. When he had finished reading from the long page, he asked that the accused stand. To my astonishment a young man and woman who were seated in the front row stood and faced the judges. Neither could have been over the age of eighteen. The young man, with dark hair, was handsome, but the blond girl with him was an outstanding beauty. What surprised me was that her long brushed blond hair hung almost to her waist, an uncommon sight for an accused collaborator. It was the custom of the French during the liberation to shave the heads of females who had shown favors to the Germans during the occupation. It was also the custom to force these females to run naked through the streets after shaving their heads, some of them clutching illegitimate children as they ran. Anytime that we saw a woman with a bandana covering her head we assumed that she had been cavorting with the enemy during the occupation.

This young lady, however, had either been given protective custody or her crime had been more serious than merely sleeping with Germans. The charges, which were serious and included a list of eleven French citizens of Chaumont who had been killed by Germans, were made to the two standing youths and the trial began.

The government, though a succession of local witnesses, presented the case, which seemed to concentrate on the fact that the young man had been able to obtain gasoline for his motorcycle during the later days of the occupation. He and his companion had been seen numerous times driving in and out of Chaumont barracks, then occupied by the German garrison. One witness, an old woman, testified that she had seen them in the company with a German soldier shortly after a neatly laid ambush had killed four local French resistance fighters. Again and again the charges were repeated that gasoline had been somehow made available to the youths. I was surprised when suddenly the prosecutor announced that the case of the government was closed. The afternoon had been so absorbing and had gone so quickly that I could not believe my watch, which said 4:30.

The judge recessed the trial until 10:00 a.m. the following day. Two French soldiers took the prisoners out of the courtroom and the assembled spectators, talking in low tones, left the building.

Riding back to the post, Frank and I agreed that by American standards of law, the government did not have much of a case against the two suspects. To us the evidence was all hearsay and circumstantial.

There were easily twice as many people present in the council chamber for the second day of the trial. Proceedings began almost an hour late because of the need to bring in extra chairs, rearrange the courtroom, and bring the crowd under control. The judges refused to start the trial until everyone was seated and quiet. No one was permitted to stand.

Under way at last, the young man stated his case. His defense was simple, he had been buying gasoline from a German Sergeant in the motor pool. It was a simple black market arrangement. He knew nothing about the ambush of the resistance fighters and the old lady who had seen them in the company of a German soldier had merely witnessed arrangements for a buy with the motor pool Sergeant. The only other witness was the girl's mother who tearfully pleaded that because of their youth the boy and girl should be released.

The judge rapped the audience into silence when it was announced that all witnesses had been heard and that the judges would withdraw to consider the evidence.

We sat in quiet conversation not knowing what to do about lunch, which we had missed. We had received no instructions from anyone nor even an announcement of an adjournment so we simply waited. We did not have long to wait however, for within 20 minutes, the three judges filed in and took their seats behind the table. The chief judge stood, adjusted his glasses, asked the young man and woman to stand and then in a strong voice read the verdict.

Both were guilty of collaborating with the enemy and both would be executed the following morning. The place of execution would be the stone quarry South of the city. Time of execution would be 7:00 a.m. The trial was over.

The two French soldiers shoved through a cheering crowd to remove the sentenced youth from the room. The boy was crying, the beautiful young girl was ashen faced, looking at the floor, ignoring the shrieks from her mother. The room emptied itself of somber and determined citizens of Chaumont. Frank and I stood outside while he discussed the event with an older man who had been present. I tried not to listen. I wanted no more to do with it, but I heard the old man say, "They were guilty, the whole town knew all along that they were friends of the Boche."

We learned that evening from Captain Smart that we were both required to attend the execution. I did not sleep well that night. My dreams dissolved into a dozing sort of reverie in which girls with long golden hair turned into people whom I had known.

Arrangements had been made with the mess hall to feed the two of us at five a.m. but neither of us could eat. We gagged down some coffee and discovered that we were to drive the jeep ourselves to the stone quarry. Apparently no one else was to witness the execution except those assigned in an official capacity. The all night orderly room clerk handed me a map and a trip ticket and at 6:00 we drove out the gate and headed for the South side of Chaumont. We did not talk.

I found the quarry with no difficulty. We identified ourselves to the policeman at the wooden gate blocking the road to the quarry, drove a few hundred feet and were directed by a French soldier to park the jeep.

The quarry was a large but shallow hole in the ground carved out of a limestone deposit close to the earth's surface. Its contents were apparently used for building purposes—there being piles of hand shaped, cinder block sized stones stacked around the lip of the crater.

Peering into the early morning darkness of the quarry hole, I could see that two telegraph sized posts had been erected close to one wall of the man-made pit. I could also see that several police vans and trucks had negotiated the crushed rock road leading down into the hole and were parked in a neat row, significantly on the opposite side from where the poles stood.

Frank and I walked down the road that was still partially covered with a hard crust snow from the recent storm. We saluted a small swarthy French officer who met us at the bottom of the road and were directed to stand with a group of silent officials about 50 feet back from the poles.

It was cold in the quarry with no sunshine on the floor of the pit even though the cloudless sky was beginning to turn a luminescent cerulean blue. I noted that all three judges were present, as was the chief prosecutor and the mayor of the city, along with a few older men whom I took to be government officials. An American officer whom I had never seen before stood with two French officers among the group. No one spoke but rather seemed lost in his own thoughts. Eight French soldiers with rifles stood awkwardly a few feet in front of us, self-consciously facing the poles, busy with their weapons. An officer with them was examining a small automatic pistol that he kept passing from one white gloved hand to the other.

As I glanced secretly at my watch, a door opened at the back of one of the vans and a black robed priest stepped out holding a Bible and rosary beads. He was followed by two policemen, each holding the arm of one of the condemned. As the boy and girl stepped down into the snow and ice, both looked up at the sky. Neither was crying; they seemed almost serene. The boy was dressed in dark blue dungarees with a light blue shirt open at the throat. The girl, who momentarily shivered in the cold, was dressed in a long sleeved white blouse and dark skirt. Her slender legs were covered by thick gray wool stockings. The priest, chanting in Latin, preceded them as they were lead to the stakes. All eyes in the quarry followed the progress of the five people as they picked their way across the uneven surface of the floor of the quarry.

Quickly each captive was lashed to a pole, ropes encircling their waists, holding them tightly in place. As soon as each policeman was satisfied that his charge was tied securely, he moved away behind the firing squad. The priest held his Bible for them to kiss, which they did, made the sign of the cross before the girl, then the boy. Still chanting, he left the youths to join the entourage of assembled witnesses.

A muffled cry escaped from the lips of one of the government officials as the riflemen were called to attention by their officer. The orders were given quickly and obeyed. I had no time for thought beyond wondering why their hands were not tied when a ragged volley crashed and echoed back and forth in the confines of the naked quarry. Both bodies jumped under the impact of the bullets, immediately jerking down against the ropes, which bound them, knees buckling. No one moved as the acrid gunpowder smell drifted into the group of spectators. Blackbirds, alarmed by the gunfire, screamed and whirled in the sky above us. The girl's yellow hair hung like a mask over her face.

Then to the murmured astonishment of everyone present, the boy moved his right arm and groaned. The firing squad gasped; uncertainty held them. Hesitantly, at first, the officer with the pistol stood alone and then quickly stumbled across the narrow space between the riflemen and the boy. He jacked a bullet into his automatic just as he arrived at the figure. He lifted the boy's head by the hair and looked closely into his face. When he released the hair, the boy's head fell to his chest, rolling back and forth slightly. Without hesitation the officer stepped back one step and shot him through the top of the head.

The girl was dead. As observers, we had one last task to perform. The bodies were cut down and placed on their backs to be examined in the growing light. We were instructed to view the remains close-up so that justice could be assured that all spectators to its swift vengence might be satisfied that they were indeed dead. We walked in single file past the bodies. The boy was predictably a mess, the squad bullets having hit him low in the abdomen. The officer's coup de grace had split his skull so that gray cauliflower shaped brain fragments, flecked with blood, were clearly visible, steaming a little in the cold air.

I forced myself to study the girl. She lay straight, with her arms at her side, palms up. Her hair, cloud-like around her head and face, stretched out in the bloody snow for several feet. Its golden color was an orange where blood droplets mingled with the strands. Her mouth and eyes were partially open, one tooth with a tiny drop of blood. The bullets had all hit her in the breast and heart and could have been covered by a small plate. There was much blood on her blouse that was open almost to her waist. A small pink brassiere, punctured by the wounds, held her small young breasts.

A numbness gripped me as I looked at the body. I studied her throat and face, watching carefully for signs of life. I had never actually studied a dead person at close range before. I could not believe that this human being was without life. This was not a game. This person was not going to jump up laughing. She was never going to move again, not even a finger, never. It was not just the cold in the quarry that sent the chill through me; it was the ultimate lesson of finality that I was learning.

I had had somewhat the same feelings on hunting trips when I had picked up broken rabbits in my cold hands and felt the fading warmth of their tiny bodies. However, this day, in a stone quarry South of Chaumont, France, was different. These two dead people were no older than I and the shock of the close-up lesson of mortality was almost overwhelming. The quick efficiency with which it had been carried out and the awful, deliberate act of tying people to poles in order to kill them turned my stomach. I was afraid that I was going to be sick.

No one seemed to mind when one of the city officials knelt beside the girl and with his thumb and forefinger gently closed her eyes. The group broke up, nodding slightly to one another, and in pairs made their way up the rough road out of the pit. As I left the quarry floor alone, I discovered that there was a simple elegance and a growing exhilaration in the act of walking. The muscles in my legs and thighs felt strong and sure, and as the scene behind my back became farther and farther away, I found my pace quickening. I was filled with a bursting sense of release and escape and as I reached the lip of the quarry, I broke into a run with my hands digging into my thighs, grasping the energy that I felt there. I ran, not through fear or anguish, but because of a bubbling sense of physical life.

Frank was not at the jeep when I finally arrived, heart pounding and grasping for breath. I stood there and with head back, I swept the sky with my eyes in a full circle, drinking in the beauty of the clean air and the brightness of being alive.

We drove back to the post in silence. We were alone with our own thoughts, but on our way back to the barracks following the check-in at the orderly room, Frank said slowly, "That was a high price to pay for gasoline. Poor France is going to need young people when this is over."

"That's the war," I said in French and the familiar phrase, often spoken in jest, revealed a new meaning to us both.

CHAPTER XI

MOVING UP

On December first, our Battalion received orders to be prepared to move to the Rhine river city of Strasbourg within 48 hours. We were somewhat apprehensive because the major city had only been captured by the French First Army on November 23rd. Our Company prepared our convoy of twenty trucks for the move after breakfast on December third, but delays in loading and unexplained postponements held us up until well after noon.

Fortunately for us we were able to eat lunch in the garrison mess hall, enjoying a good hot meal before we departed. Finally we rolled through the main gate where I had witnessed the murder of the French officer, a convoy of twenty trucks and three jeeps. On Battalion moves we always were organized and moved as a company as did the other companies of the larger unit. Once again I rode with the Captain and the Farmer, the First Sergeant. The Farmer drove, the Captain sat with his map case on his lap, and I sat in the back fingering my MP armband in my jacket pocket. The second jeep followed with Harding, Hayride, our officer from Louisiana, and my friend John who drove. Lt. Bond brought up the end of the convoy in the third jeep.

Leaving Chaumont with all of its important memories, we headed Northeast toward Nancy with about three hours of daylight remaining in a cold but clear day. Except for an occasionally shouted direction from the Captain to the Farmer we drove in what I savored as a welcome silence. The convoy moved at moderate speed over fairly smooth and clear roads, maintaining air defense interval and generally staying together in an orderly military fashion.

I don't know what I had expected to see in the far countryside North and East of Paris, but I was again reminded from my history lessons that most of France is farmland. It is truly an agrarian culture marked by small villages, which still carry the vestiges of feudal tenant strip farming. Except for an occasional large manor farm, seldom was an isolated farmhouse visible. For hundreds of years, farmers have lived together in villages made up of small clusters of dwellings, often physically joined together into a fortress-like collection of rambling white walled housing. Protected at night in a communal setting the farmers would travel at daybreak to their individual strips of land to work the long hours with plow and hoe. Awkward wagons and carts moved them back and forth from the villages to the well worn land. Highways and commerce, of necessity, eventually joined these clusters of an emerging civilization until cafes and shops began to appear as adjuncts to the villages. Storefronts appeared as side streets branched off to the accompaniment of additional buildings and roadways. Depending upon the extent of commerce or the magnitude of the local agrarian effort, the single village could grow, prosper, and become a significant city with paved streets and treelined avenues. As in every developing civilization, navigable rivers played a major role in the location of significant centers of population. Chaumont, our point of departure on that cold and blustery day, was built on the Marne River. Our destination was Nancy, a large riverport on the Moselle. France is blessed with rivers that flow North and East to the Rhine, South to the Mediterranean, and West to the Atlantic Ocean. The network of water, augmented by a system of connecting canals, spells out the great success of a wealthy and viable nation. During war however these waterways become barriers to cross and each become natural defensive lines for even an enemy who was without determination. As we learned, the German was a determined enemy.

On December 3rd, 1944, there was a bite in the air and although we had the canvas roof in place on the jeep, the wind blowing through the open sides of the little vehicle was uncomfortable and impossible to shut out. Dressed only in field jackets, we huddled forward against the cold and silently cursed the sting on our faces.

Within two hours we arrived at Neufchateau, a sizable city built on the River Meuse. Grateful to be slowed down within the protection of buildings, we stopped to allow the convoy to catch up and reassemble behind us. The Captain called an officer conference at the hood of the jeep and the rest of us gathered in groups to talk quietly and to complain that everything was once again all fouled up, including the prospects of an evening meal or a place to sleep. Daylight was fast fading as we crossed the river and continued our journey across rolling undisturbed farmland. Long shadows from tall rows of trees planted as crop windbreaks fingered ahead of us in the twilight.

In total darkness we arrived in the outskirts of Nancy, stopping to regroup and by flashlight to study the hundreds of unit direction signs.

The silent Captain, apparently knowing what he was looking for, guided us through the military traffic of the city to the Northeast. Nancy was in darkness as we rumbled through the narrow streets with only our blackout lights to mark our progress. There was not a sign of a single civilian. Northeast of the city was a commanding bluff overlooking the river and built there was the principal airport serving this important junction of rail, road, and river traffic. It was our destination.

The Captain asked directions from the sullen guard at the main entrance and the convoy rolled through a massive collection of buildings and depot supplies. Even in the darkness, I could see that many of the hangar type structures had been damaged and were without roofs. In the blackness there were twisted lumps near the roadway that appeared to be damaged or destroyed aircraft. In the darkness we could not tell whether they were American or German.

Coming to a halt in front of a darkened building, the entire convoy was delighted to discover that through some miracle of logistics, our headquarters staff had somehow preceded us and was awaiting the company with a hot meal and beds for the night. We were billeted in a large undamaged hangar, which even had electric lights and a large workers' toilet facility. It was a good place to stay and after a meal of fried Spam, potatoes, green beans and coffee we began to view the Captain with a new, if fleeting, respect.

Canvas cots were set up in long lines; two folded blankets had been placed on each cot along with a newly issued heavy-duty quilt. There were, of course, no pillows. We were never issued pillows overseas, the Army distaining any concession to comfort. Instead I used my laundry bag stuffed with lumpy dirty clothes as a headrest for my sleeping. As the bag became larger and more usable as a pillow, it also brought with it an aroma that argued with sleep and bickered constantly with controlled nausea. We slept fitfully that night amid the clutter of duffle bags and weapons, being awakened twice in the cold and blackness to listen, each in his own way, to the sputtering sounds of antiaircraft fire to the East.

The morning brought low clouds and a cold Arctic wind from the North that rattled the corregated hanger roof but failed to dispel the excitement that we all felt about moving up to Strasbourg. In the daylight we could see that Nancy airfield was in shambles. Hardly any building had been left untouched by either bombs or artillery and many of the shattered aircraft scattered around were German Heikel bombers. One or two twin engine enemy night fighters lay in burnt ruins alongside scavenged American P-47 fighter planes. There seemed to be no other unit on the field except for us plus one or two engineering companies who like us, were preparing to move out in early morning.

Captain Smart called a briefing meeting of officers and noncoms to give us routes and an estimated time of arrival at our destination.

He cautioned us that with predictable heavy traffic, we would find it difficult to maintain convoy discipline. He wanted a noncom in each of the twenty six-bys to guarantee arrival at Molsheim, 9 kilometers west of Strasbourg. His announcement was the first indicator of the exact name of our final destination. With some shuffling of assignments, I found myself in the cab of one of the trucks with a mimeographed map, which only gave route numbers and the names of important checkpoints. Direction and distances between points had not been included so I did not have the faintest notion of how far we were to travel that day. I only knew that we were expected to be in Molsheim by midafternoon. The truck to which I was assigned was being driven by a small round faced T/5 named Elwood and had a 50 calibre machine gun mounted on the cab roof on a scaraff ring mounted within a hole cut in the roof of the cab on the passenger's side. The primary purpose of the machine gun was to serve as an antiaircraft weapon against strafing aircraft. Not all trucks were equipped with the mount but it was not uncommon to see several of these special vehicles in any convoy. The weapon was covered with a canvas cover, which protected the gun and kept wind and weather out of the cab during normal driving. I merely glanced at the weapon as I climbed into the cab and grunted an obscene greeting at Moon-face. He was understandably unhappy since his friend who had lost his seat in the cab had been reassigned to the rear of the truck along with the duffle bags, blankets and 10 other men. I rolled up the window, grateful for the comparative warmth of the closed cab.

We rolled out of Nancy in the early morning, still in convoy behind the Farmer and Captain Smart, who seemed exhuberant over his previous day's experience at finding the airport. His confidence apparently precluded the need for a man in the back seat with an M.P. armband in his pocket. There were some military police in the city but as we passed through the outskirts, it was clear that we were on our own. Within 30 minutes Moon-face had lost all contact with the other vehicles in the convoy and we found ourselves sandwiched between a huge tank retriever and a half track, which seemed intent on deliberately running us down. We were on route N–4 heading East toward Luneville, a major road junction serving both East-West and North-South highways. As we rolled through Dombasie, a small town near Nancy's East gate there was an immediate increase in visible battle damage. Fortunately the half track dropped out of sight behind us and we both prayed that it had run out of gas or better yet had disintegrated in its mad effort to run us down. In any event, we dropped back from the tank retriever, which gave us some driving space and some time to see a little more of the country. We slowed to pass burnt vehicles that partially blocked the road and we found ourselves looking again at

Normandy but without the hedgerows. Our speed and time began to make me a little nervous as we approached Luneville. With the military traffic, constant delays and approaching vehicles that demanded the right-of-way on the narrow road, and stops for unidentified reasons, we had traveled less than 30 kilometers in slightly under three hours.

To our relief the retriever left the road to join another of the ungainly monsters in a field just outside Luneville. We entered the city with an unobstructed view of a population center in abject ruins. The enemy had apparently needed this crossroad junction city, for he had fought hard to stay in it.

As we left the center of the town, an M.P. carrying a submachine gun stepped out in the street and waved us to a stop. Through the open window he cautioned, "Keep your eyes open. There are reports of planes between here and Sarrebourg."

"Better uncover your 50 and keep your interval," he added, moving down past us to warn the vehicles stopped behind us.

I must admit that I was excited as I stood on the seat and removed the canvas gun cover. I had fired a 50 only once at Camp Callan in California during a familiarization exercise in antiaircraft weapons, so I reviewed the loading and firing procedure in my mind as I made sure the gun was ready to fire. I was surprised to discover that a full box of ammunition was attached ready for use. The canvas bag designed to collect expended shell casings and linkage was missing but I had heard that gunners did not like to use them since they filled rapidly, caused jams, and resulted in poor balance when the weapon was being traversed to follow a moving target. Aircraft gunners distained the use of the collecting bag, choosing instead to stumble through the hot shell casings in their mad efforts to traverse against 400 mile an hour fighter planes.

Retrieving my helmet from the floor of the truck cab, I put it on and stood on the seat clutching the sides of the ring mount as we moved forward onto the road, joining a line of six-bys and other traffic. At first the feeling was one of exhilaration and daring—a warrior, secure on his mount, racing, so to speak, into battle along with fearless and invincible companions. I clutched the 50 calibre machine gun, poised, lethal, possessing a masterful sense of purpose, surely the weapon of all weapons, crafted to kill. Designed with a beautiful functional brutality, the weapon, smelling slightly of oil and metal, had a fierce aesthetic quality about it. From its long slender barrel to its wood handled grips and butterfly trigger, which enabled it to be fired by pressing the mechanism with either thumb, it was a strong statement of raw power. As I was musing through thoughts of the sexual implications of modern weapons, I discovered that it was quite cold standing exposed through the roof of the truck. Pretending to be looking for something on the seat, I

228

ducked my head from time to time to get relief from the wind inside the relative warmth of the cab. Moon-face ignored me, concentrating instead on maintaining an interval between us and the truck ahead. After a few kilometers I tired of being a warrior whom no one noticed and instead climbed down from the seat, removed my helmet and enjoyed the comfort of waves of heat coming from the engine. Cold air continued to blast through the open scaraff mount but I found my wool knit cap and pulled the hood of my combat jacket up over my head. I began to doze as the entire line of vehicles picked up speed through the open rolling countryside. Beyond Luneville there was little evidence that the war had stopped for long in the fields and farmlands. The low clouds had broken earlier in the day and although there was still no direct sunlight, the grey cloud cover was high and non threatening.

We passed through several narrow seemingly deserted hamlets where the sound of our truck was magnified by the closeness of the flat white windowless walls that grew straight up from the sides of the roads. The widely spaced intermittent rising and falling of the engine sound compounded my desire to drift off into sleep. Deep sleep came to me.

I was awakened by Elwood who was pushing my shoulder and shouting something that I could not understand. Blinking, struggling against sleep, I became aware that we were stopped and that men were running from their trucks on the flat road ahead of us. Traffic was stopped. There was shouting. "It's a plane, a plane, over there, over there!" yelled Moon-face as he threw open his door and sprinted for the field on the far side of the highway.

I could see nothing as I jumped up on the seat and struggled to the 50. With a pounding heart, I jacked a shell into the chamber almost bending the cocking handle in the process. But by now men were returning to the road from ditches and fields, gathering in little groups, laughing in an embarrassed way. Suddenly two or three of them, far down the road pointed to the left and began scattering away from the trucks that still sat immobilized in the center of the crowned road. Like an unseen ripple tearing toward me, men peeled off and ran, jumping in awkward ways into imagined places of safety. With both thumbs poised on the butterfly trigger, I peered in the direction from which I guessed an airplane would appear. I saw nothing. I shifted my sight down the roadway straining to pick out a speck in the sky.

But without any warning whatever, I was suddenly engulfed by a thunderous clap of noise. Just as it struck me I caught out of the corner of my left eye a glimpse of a shadow of a light blue wing with a Maltese cross as it flashed by directly overhead. "Holy shit!" I screamed into an empty sky.

The plane, probably a Messerschmidt 109, had come and gone within a split second, crossing the convoy at treetop level without firing a single round. The receding sound from the fighter plane blasted back in pulsing waves of echoes as I jumped back from the gun in alarm and confusion. Frightened, I leaped to the side of the ring mount scanning the sky with shielded palm, searching for a sight of the departing German. In moments I saw a tiny speck climbing fast and circling back toward us.

"He's coming back," I shouted to no one, positioning myself behind the gun and keeping my eyes on the speeding aircraft. He flew straight back across the sky before he began a dive, which would bring him back on the identical course he had flown on his first run on the convoy. This time I saw him flatten out to begin his attack from far away. He was a tiny black speck against the horizon but this time I would be ready for him. I tried to swing the 50 around on the scaraff track but it wouldn't move. Alarmed I yelled over and over, "It's jammed, it's jammed!"

Taking the eyes off the speck, I barely had a chance to look at the gun before I heard a deep whining noise coming from the left. I jerked my eyes back to the speck, which suddenly was no longer a speck, but had been transformed into a huge shiny propellor and two short wings. My impulse was to dive to the floor of the truck but the sleeve of my jacket was caught on something on the ring mount. I struggled, yanking my arm back and forth. The plane seemed to be coming straight at me as I jerked myself free in a panic of strength and motion. The gun slid loosely on the ring but the German was almost upon me. Not having time to jump, I began firing just as the plane flashed overhead for the second time. In one motion I threw the 50 to the opposite side of the ring, still firing, trying to follow the plane. Cartridges and metal belt links began to shower into the truck cab as I pressed the trigger as hard as I could. The enormous sound of the plane plus the crushing bang of the big machine gun overwhelmed what little sense remained to me. I was in a world of noise that ruled out all the rest of my senses. I was still firing when the cascading noise of the plane died away. It was only with great effort that I consciously lifted my numbed thumbs from the trigger and felt the echo pressure fade from my pounding ears. Straining again to see the plane, I could not believe the sight that confronted me instead. Somehow I had never noticed that we had been parked on the narrow road next to a two storied farm building. As I had swung around to fire at the departing plane, I had been firing steadily and directly into the roofline of the building.

Standing there in a warm pile of shell casings, smelling the hot oil and burning metal of the gun, I watched with fearful fascination as slate tile began to spill slowly over the side of the roof. It began, at first one by one, until finally gaining speed, large sections of the tile roof gave way and crashed to the ground. I watched gaping at the gradual collapse of the top part of a French farmhouse.

At a punishing close range, I had pumped at least 50 rounds into that roof, stitching a tear-off line that the ancient structure, after years of torment from the elements, could not refuse. While I was kicking the debris from my first victory against Germany out the open door of the truck, Moon-face appeared, crossing the highway and climbing onto the driver's seat.

Looking past me at the still crumbling building, he arched his eyebrows, whistled softly and made no comment.

I was pleased when we took to the road again because the French farmer, dressed in a blue smock, had come around the corner of what was left of his house and had stood next to it, arms folded, looking at me solemnly. He remained, unmoved, when, as we pulled away, I shrugged and shouted, "Ces't La Guerre!"

Later I thought of how pleased he should have been that the tracers had not set fire to his damned building.

During the afternoon great patches of forests began to appear as we made our approach to Sarrebourg. There was also a discernible rise in the slope of the land as we began the climb toward the Western flank of the Vosges mountains.

The dark clouds were low to the ground and visibility began to decline. An oppressive slight mist was collecting in the shallow ravines and a chill was in the air. After I replaced the gun cover on the roof, our breath began to fog the cab as we started the slow climb to the ancient Alsatian city of Sarrebourg. Traffic was very heavy; we looked for trucks from our convoy but were never able to find one of them in the stream of military vehicles that picked its way through the city. Sarrebourg was comparatively untouched by the war since its location on the sloping Western plateau of the Vosges had little strategic value to the Germans who had pulled out of the mountains to the Rhine River when their left flank had been threatened by the advance of the 7th Army from the South.

The Vosges Mountain region of Eastern France is made up of a population of French and Germans who have, through history, been passed back and forth between these two countries for centuries creating a nationalistic pendulum that is unique. Both languages are spoken, French on the Western ranges and German on the plain between the crest of the mountains and the Rhine River known as the Rhine Valley. Some cities have German names, some French depending upon which county ruled the territory at the time in history when the center of population became important enough to commerce to achieve an identity. The mountains themselves slope gradually out of the Western center of France but drop sharply on the Eastern side onto a fairly narrow strip of land, which in most cases, is no more than ten kilometers in width before it edges on the great Rhine River. The topography is very similar to the Sierra Madre Range in central California except that the height of the Vosges is not comparable. While Mt. Whitney in California is over 14,000 feet in height, the tallest peak in the Vosges is less than 3,000 feet—a barrier nevertheless between two nations that had battled for many hundreds of years. The Napoleonic wars secured the Alsace Lorraine region for France in the early 19th century but lost the area to Germany in the Franco-Prussian Wars later in the century. The French victory in World War I regained the territory through the Treaty of Versailles. Germany, contemptuously ignoring the Eastern edge of the Maginot line, had instead swept its panzers through the Vosges in 1941 and had easily reclaimed the Alsatians. Now in late 1944 Alsace and part of Lorraine was once again occupied by the Allies and would soon again be French.

The Vosges Mountains lay like a brooding sleeper from the German city of Kaiserslautern in the North to French Besanson in the South, perhaps 200 kilometers in length and 50 kilometers in width at the widest point. The general shape of the range is that of a large hourglass, bulging to the North and South with the center pinched together at a most militarily strategic city of Saverne. The fairly small city, located in what is accurately described as the Saverne gap, straddles vital North-South and East-West road junctions. An ancient castle looks down on the city from a commanding peak on the flank of the gap. The site of the structure, it is said, was selected by the Romans during their final conquest of Gaul in 50 B.C. But by far, the most important facet of the communication and transportation network of the Saverne gap is the Marne-Rhine River canal, which in its East-West traverse, passes through the gap. The canal, barely 30 yards wide in most places, is a fine example of the construction genius of the Europeans, who, faced with the transport problems of an agrarian economy early in their history, laced a network of canals to give access to and through riverless territory. The Marne-Rhine canal connecting these two important rivers through the Northeastern plateau of France makes it possible to trans-port goods and services from the upper Rhine by way of Paris to the English Channel at Le Havre. Saverne, like so many others, grew into a city, in part because of the barge traffic on the canal. Today, a modern superhighway, crammed with truck transports, bisects the Vosges at Saverne and the roads and canal have become a secondary resource in the fast lane commerce of the late 20th century.

Although the German Army established its line of defense on the Eastern bank of the Rhine, it did so by fighting a carefully planned delaying rear guard action all along the roads leading across the plateau and down the mountain roads that lead to the Rhine Valley. Small villages deep within forests were used by the Germans to deploy anti-tank weapons and blind curves were used as traps and ambushes for

American armor. We began to see many destroyed American tanks alongside the road and several times beyond the gap, we had to negotiate our thrusting way through the clusters of burned-out tanks in villages, which had been the recent scene of the punishment that the German 88 was capable of giving. Saverne itself was the continuing target for far range German artillery as they attempted to close the gap to the steady flow of men and material from the American Seventh Army. The German had also sent his diminishing force of bombers to the gap in an attempt to interdict the road intersection. The canal had sustained several hits from bombs and remained partially inactive. The denial of the use of the waterway to the advancing Americans was of little consequence since our war machine was wheel mounted in nearly every respect, not dependent upon slow moving barge traffic. I have no doubt that there were important uses of canals by the Allies during World War II but I never witnessed it.

The logistic strategy of the invasion of 1944 had been to concentrate all land movement of troops by means of gasoline driven vehicles, the river, canal and rail systems of France having been put in serious jeopardy by the bombardments and air-to-ground attacks, which had preceded the landings. Passable roads and ground hard enough to support heavy equipment was the theme of advancing World War II armies. Defensive strategy dictated denying these routes to the enemy. Roads, highways, and cities that were unfortunate enough to be the location of transportation junctions were ferociously defended and counterattacked, primarily for the control of traffic. Open fields, capable of sustaining armor, were sown with millions of mines to keep the tracked vehicles within reach by forcing them to be targets on roads that were more easily defended.

We cleared the gap with full darkness approaching and by staying on the main road N-4, we followed the traffic flow in a Southeast direction toward our destination, Molsheim. We were exhausted, having eaten only some K-rations that had been given to us in Nancy, a thousand years before. We were growing very cold in spite of the hot roaring truck engine just a few inches beyond the fire wall of the cab. In the slow moving column, we dug out the overcoats from our duffle bags, knowing that the men in the body of the truck behind us must have done the same thing hours ago. We hadn't seen or heard from them since leaving Saverne hours before when we had refueled at a roadside refueling dump. At that time they had been miserable and silently bitter because Moon and I hoarded a spot of comparative comfort on the long journey and would not share any of it with them. The trucks turned on the blackout lights as the evening light disappeared from the threatening sky. We were fully conscious that we were only a few miles from a watchful enemy whom we believed could at any time have us under direct observation.

CHAPTER XII

MOLSHEIM

A long sweeping curve in the highway took us bumper-to-bumper into the medieval city of Molsheim, or at least directly past it since there was no access to the walled town except through a city gate so narrow that it could admit only the smallest of private vehicles. At a roadblock near the city gate, after an interminable wait, we were directed to some buildings on the road to Strasbourg. We found the low barracks type buildings on a side street off the main road and were pleased to see that two or three of our convoy had already arrived along with the two lead jeeps. I reported to the Captain, who was sitting behind a battered desk, much like a schoolmaster, in a small orderly room at the end of the first barracks building. A makeshift orderly room sign on the door proclaimed that this was indeed our unit. The Captain was now morose, clearly concerned that less than a third of the convoy had arrived, and at least six hours beyond the estimated time of arrival at that. We were assigned to one of the barracks nearest the orderly room and informed that hot food was ready in a nearby mess hall. After a good meal we settled into the barracks, selecting from a large number of bunk beds, those that we favored because of location near or away from overhead lights or for their proximity to the two large effective heaters on either end of the spacious room.

These barracks, we soon learned, had been used by the laborers who worked in a nearby German torpedo plant. The buildings were undamaged, warm and comfortable. It had been a long weary day of driving but I was excited in the knowledge that I had had a victory; I had shot down my first farmhouse. We slept soundly, interrupted once during the night by the arrival of two more truckloads of cold, noisy and complaining men.

In the morning we assembled for roll call to discover that two trucks were still missing. The third trailing jeep had arrived shortly after midnight after a fruitless search for the stragglers from the convoy. During breakfast one of the prodigal trucks arrived. Their story to the Captain was straightforward. Separated from the convoy near Luneville, they had gotten lost and had found themselves down below St. Die in the French First Army sector. The Captain did not suspect the story nor did he ever learn that at Luneville the group decision was to return to Chaumont to visit some terribly missed girlfriends. It was fortunate for them that in the long cold drive they had time to sober up before arriving at Molsheim. The company commander sent Lt. Harding and a driver back to seek some trace of the last lost six-by as the company, now assembled, marched in formation to the torpedo plant located several blocks away. Our task, as he explained before we marched, was to clear the plant and prepare it as a base operation for artillery and fire control repair.

The plant itself was in shambles, for not only had it taken a bomb hit during the last few days of German occupation but the German labor force had systematically sabotaged all machinery and had destroyed all records. Large overhead cranes, capable of traversing the entire length of factory buildings, had been deliberately run off the ends of their rails and all equipment to make machine parts had been pounded with sledge hammers to make them useless. But the most perplexing problem was not the destroyed factory, for we had no use for torpedo making facilities. The real problem was the explosive used in the torpedoes, which was discovered in the plant. One sealed room contained hundreds of packages of a grey clay-like substance that was identified by Lt. Harding as a type of plastic high explosive.

In order to clear the plant, regain electrical service, reweld the damaged roof and install our own repair equipment, we had to first remove the dangerous explosives. A conference of officers and noncoms was held in the factory main office, which was built in the center of the main building and had been encased with glass windows looking out into the plant. All of the many windows had been shattered in the bombing however. The Captain's voice rose above the crunching of glass as 24 booted feet shuffled in the ankle deep debris made up of glass, broken wood, bent steel and aluminum, and the thousands of wet paper records from the plundered office file cabinets. After explaining the problem to us, the Captain asked, "Does anyone have a suggestion?"

After a period of quiet murmuring, he went to ask another question, "Has anyone had any experience with explosives?"

The glass stopped crunching and there was a long unbroken period of absolute silence as eleven men realized the direction the commanding

235

officer was taking. He tried to catch the eyes of the assembled men as they, in turn, tried desperately to become invisible, or at least inconspicuous. Everyone seemed to be intently studying either the floor or the ceiling. Finally, breaking the silence the Captain sighed and said in a low voice, "O.K., I'll make the decision. . . .Dismissed."

There was a small rush for the single doorway as we all began a disappearing act. We scattered like quail into the far reaches of the factory, each with a fear of his own that somehow he was going to have something to do very soon with a very large explosion. My own fatalistic feelings were soon confirmed when Sgt. Fletcher, our overweight and bespectacled orderly clerk, found me behind a packing crate and with a wide grin informed me that the Captain wanted to see me at once. Back in the shattered office, my commanding officer was very direct. "Didn't you take that explosives course at Santa Anita?" he asked.

"Yes sir," I replied, "but so did every man in the company."

He shuffled some papers from behind his desk.

"So did all the officers," I added lamely.

He flushed a little and then announced, "Sergeant, I want *you* to dispose of these explosives. Do it anyway that you wish but I want them out of these buildings no later than tomorrow afternoon. Battalion has ordered that we do this job ourselves. Bomb disposal is busy in Strasbourg."

He closed my service record file and by way of telling me that I was dismissed, he added, "If you need some men, let Sergeant Fletcher know."

Looking away from me to the top of the desk, he said louder than he had intended, "But don't ask for many men though. We're going to be real busy around here trying to clean up this mess."

Outside the factory in the cold clean air, I tried to think my way through what I remembered about plastic explosives. Our one day explosives orientation course, taken more than a year before had been concerned only with the handling of dynamite and had been conducted in a remote area of the San Bernardino mountains next to a dry river bed in the hot California sun. Each man had had to handle stick dynamite, crimp and affix a detonator, wire the plunger and after shouting "Fire in the hole" three times, set off the charge. At the time it had seemed like a dangerous and altogether worthless piece of knowledge to have in wartime. I could never believe that an enemy tank crew would watch an idiot crimping fuses and shouting "Fire in the hole" three times in succession before he tried to direct the tank to be blown up by driving over a planted charge. Plastic explosives were a fairly new invention, having been developed to affix to difficult structures such as bridges, railroad tracks, and electrical towers. They were also used in booby traps and anti-personnel devices. The civilian instructors whom we had had in 1943 had never mentioned the handling or uses of plastic as an explosive. However, I finally did remember that an English officer in Warminster had lectured to us about new uses of plastic explosives. He had given us a frightening demonstration of its plasticity by bending, molding and actually bouncing a handful of the claylike substance. I also vaguely remembered, at last, that he had mentioned that it could only be fired by a detonator and that it could be burned without exploding. At least that's what I thought that he had said. I couldn't be sure but under the circumstances of a possible sudden death, I decided to seek out my good friend Holt. He, among his other talents, had a penchant for remembering odd bits of information.

"Yes, the Limey said it could be burned," he said, "but remember," he added, "he had a piece of English plastic . . . could be a lot different than this German stuff."

We talked about the possibility that the Germans had developed a newer type of plastic, one that was pressure activated but, in the end, we agreed that in the rubble of the factory, we had both seen torpedo detonators. In addition, neither of us had ever seen a Hollywood movie that had not shown a torpedo without a detonator on the front of it. The authenticity of Hollywood seemed like pretty thin evidence to go on but we had little else upon which to base a judgment.

"I have one more thought," said Holt. "How do we really know that this stuff will explode? All we have is Harding saying it will."

We then discussed the possible alternative uses of the substance, perhaps it was used in another part of the production of torpedoes. We couldn't explain, however, why the stuff was kept in a carefully sealed and bolted room. We each listened to what the other knew about the manufacture of torpedoes, but it did not take long to recognize that even with pooling our knowledge that we actually knew precious little about the subject. About all that we knew was they were carried in submarines, shot out of a tube, and through some mysterious guidance system, found their way to a floating target. With this great storehouse of information about the design and manufacture of the torpedo, we had no means to speculate as to the uses of the plastic beyond the gut feeling that the damned stuff was either a primer exploder or the main charge itself. The conclusion was that it was *probably* an explosive and that it just *might* burn without blowing us to hell. Early that afternoon, after returning from the compound mess hall with both of us feeling as though we had attended the Last Supper, I carved off a two inch block of the plastic with a bayonet and we walked to the center of an open field behind the factory. With more than simple hesitation I placed the small cube on the ground and with squinting eyes, I forced my Zippo cigarette lighter against the edge of the plastic. The flame sputtered for a moment and then starting with a small dazzling magnesium sort of light, the little block began to burn with a crisp blue-green flame. A thin acrid smoke escaped into the air as Holt said quietly, "We'll never know if this stuff is supposed to go bang, but at least we know that it burns."

With the help of a weapons carrier, we moved the entire cache of plastic from the factory, transported it to the field, where we fed it piece by piece into a spectacular blue-green fire. By dinner time the factory was cleared and all that remained was a large black spot in the center of some farmer's field. Compared to the men working inside the frigid unheated factory, we had had a fairly comfortable afternoon, warming ourselves next to a conflagration created by an unlikely, never to be identified, fuel.

The Captain beamed at me that evening in the mess hall. Although he didn't speak, I had the sinking feeling again that he had just made a brilliant personnel decision. In the factory the next morning, while I was pretending to be busily moving junk around, the grinning Fletcher came by with the order that the Captain wanted to see me at once. I knew that I was in deep trouble when he laughingly called after me, "Try not to blow yourself up this time!"

Captain Smart had a plan. It was simple. In combat zone every commanding officer needed a demolitions man. He no longer needed an electronics fire control expert or even a Sergeant of the guard who owned an MP armband. What he really needed was a noncom who was an expert in the handling of explosives. With ill concealed pride in his own judgment of needs, he announced that I was to be that man.

When I seemed not to respond with delight at this unexpected promotion, he became a little petulant, then finally angry. Aware that I did not share his open enthusiasm for this change in my duty, he informed me that I would be assigned the weapons carrier so that I could begin to gather all unexploded or discarded shells, bombs, mines and other ammunition in order to dispose of them.

As I started to leave the now clean office, I could not help but wonder if the man really had grown to hate me over some real or imagined infraction of some kind. Turning in the open doorway, I asked on impulse, "Sir, can I have Corporal Holt assigned to my detail?"

Without looking up from his paperwork, he told me to see Fletcher and have the change made on the duty roster. As I left, I wondered why he also hated Holt whom I had asked for because of his intelligence and sense of logic. If I were to be plunged into something that I knew nothing about, at least I could get some respectable and careful advice.

Holt and I assumed a daily patrol of the area weapons carrier, stopping at each building to see if anyone had found anything lethal for us to play with. As the factory was cleaned up, an astonishing amount of explosives began to appear—stacks of unused German artillery shells, several land mines, piles of grenades, both German and

238

American, unused partial belts of machine gun ammunitions and several boxes of German bazooka shells.

With the help of a can of gasoline and several wooden packing crates, we built a large warm bonfire in the field and burned what we could. The belts of ammunition were throw into the fire to sizzle and pop without danger to us. Without the breach of a gun to contain the gas that gives a bullet its velocity, the cartridge merely explodes fairly harmlessly, popping the bullet loose in the process. Sometimes the spent bullet would travel some yards, so we stood back some distance until the firecracker-like noise ceased. The powder from the artillery shells, resembling rabbit pellets, was likewise burned, accompanied by a disagreeable smoke and odor. Before the powder could be removed from the casing to be burned, the separately armed shell itself had to be carefully removed and this was done in the factory using tools, patience, and cowardly caution. We saved the shells for a later disposal but had some revengeful fun with the casings once the powder had been removed. In each casing there was a long metal tube that extended from the primer into the powder chamber. This device was the primer that exploded when the primer cap was struck with the sharp blow of the cannon's firing pin. This smaller explosion in turn exploded the larger charge in the casing, which sent the shell containing its own explosive charge on its way to do harm.

Working in a corner of one of the buildings, we would place the empty casing on the floor and by watching for the precise unexpected moment, one of us would strike the primer pin with a hammer sending a crashing sound of explosion reverberating within the confines of the building. Men would jump in the air, fall to the floor or scream obscenities. This little game of surprise event went on for a few days until we accidentally fired a casing just as Lt. Bond entered the building. He jumped very far in the air and I believe that he wet his pants. In any event we were ordered never to do that again and were sent back out to the fields to do our noisy work.

For what we planned to do in order to dispose of the German artillery shells, we found a small town about two miles South. Having a $^3/_4$ ton weapons carrier at our disposal, we made many unauthorized excursions into the countryside to look around and in our travels, we found the village of Barr and a dirt road that snaked away from the town into the mountains. Ignoring advice not to travel the road, which we received from a German speaking farmer, we proceeded to make a lurching four-wheel drive progress to the edge of the woods. There we found what we had been looking for. Just beyond the entrance to the forest, parked on the rutted road, was a German 20 ton Mark IV tank and behind it a large armored personnel carrier. The tank had taken a hit and was without a complete track on its left side. The personnel carrier, designed to hold about 20 soldiers, seemed to be in working condition but apparently had been prevented from coming out of the woods on the narrow road because of the disabled tank.

We examined both vehicles carefully, watchful for booby traps and trip wires. The tank, built for a crew of five, had been stripped of both machine guns but the 75 mm cannon in the turret seemed to be operable. There was no ammunition for either the cannon or for the missing MGS but we did find a heroic magazine picture of Adolph Hitler taped on the inside of the turret. The crew had either used all of their cannon shells in their fight against the French or they had taken the ammunition with them as they had abandoned their tank. We speculated that because of the weight of the shells, the gun crew had used their ammunition in the final flight. On the floor of the open personnel carrier we found some personal items—letters, wet Strasbourg newspapers and some surrender leaflets dropped by the French to the retreating Germans. The leaflets acknowledged the courageous fight that the Germans had put up, the treachery of German leadership, an offer to return home to their loved ones and a chance to put an end to the useless and wasteful war, which had, of course, been caused by Hitler and his henchmen. Our real discovery however, was a brand new German bazooka that we found under the carrier in a wooden crate. The rocket launcher was assembled but from its condition it appeared to have never been fired. We examined it with interest because we had never seen one, not even at Chaumont where captured weapons were displayed regularly. Loading the launcher in our own carrier, we navigated back down the road past the farmer who merely made an obscene gesture at us before returning to the task of spreading some hay with a large wooden fork. An unconcerned emaciated cow chewed laconically on the meager pile of moldy substance.

On our short cold drive back to Molsheim, we discussed our plan to get rid of the half dozen mines and the 30 or so artillery shells that we had on hand. No longer interested in just making noise, we decided to destroy the tank and the personnel carrier with our supply of explosives.

Our first task was to learn how to operate the rocket launcher so that we could blast through the armor on the tank. We had heard that the German bazooka was far superior to the American original for penetrating armor plate.

We went to our field behind the factory, taking a few rockets and our prized launcher. An American bazooka operated by using dry cell batteries and two loose wires, which were connected to terminals by the loader at the time of firing. This process completed the circuit through the rocket itself and armed the launcher only when it was loaded, aimed, and ready to fire. The German model operated on a different principle. It fired a black powder charge and the circuit operated internally, thus freeing the loader from the chore of connecting and disconnecting loose wires. Unfortunately this fine point went unnoticed to us as we handled the launcher and somehow in the process of clicking and pushing things, we unknowingly armed the launcher. Undaunted, with only a few days experience with explosives, Holt, balancing the launcher on his shoulder, said, "Put a rocket in it and let's see what happens."

Taking a projectile from the wooden box, I slipped it in the back end of the tube-like launcher and stood off to one side. Holt swung the weapon as though he were going to aim at a tree about 100 yards away. However, his fingers were on the pistol grip trigger and with an enormous jet of flame shooting from the end of the tube, the projectile hit the ground only a few feet in front of him. It exploded with a convincing crash, tearing a long rut in the winter sod almost 12 feet long and deep enough for a man to hide in. Visibly moved by the accidental discharge of the weapon, Holt handed me the tube and announced that he was not going to fire the contraption again. Feeling somewhat the same way, I nevertheless accepted because I was anxious to put a few rounds into that German tank. Gingerly, I balanced the tube so that if it would fire again it would fire in a higher trajectory rather than at the ground. Peering through the sight, which had a confusing number of meter settings, I yelled at Holt to load a rocket. I had the tree trunk dead in my sights expecting to see it shatter when I sent the armor piercing rocket on its way. There was no recoil when I pressed the trigger, only a wave of heat from the rocket as it lunged out of the front of the tube. A deflector shield, built near the front end of the launcher prevented me from being roasted alive but the flame and blast from the rocket created a quick hot wind that I felt on my face, hands and legs.

It was clear from the beginning that I had missed the tree completely. As soon as I saw the departing bright flame, I knew that I had miscalculated the trajectory and that my missile would pass over the tree and find a target near a farm three hundred yards in the distance. I dropped the launcher, ran a few steps in order to see around the tree, and with great fascination watched the arch on the tiny flame in the sky. Both Holt and I saw it at the same time. The little speck was going to hit next to a cow shed. It was going to hit a cow standing next to the shed. With a flash of explosive flame and black smoke, the rocket designed to penetrate armour plate, hit the cow in the center of its back. When the smoke cleared, there was nothing to be seen on the ground, only small pieces of black cow coming down from a great distance in the sky.

"Oh, shit," said Holt slowly.

We packed the launcher and the remaining rockets into the weapons carrier and headed back to the compound in time for dinner. That evening I was called into the orderly room to face an ashen faced Captain and a very angry Alsatian farmer who was holding a wicker basket filled with butcher sized chunks of what must have been, a recent cow. The old farmer was shouting German at the Captain while reaching into the basket from time to time to hold up to Captain Smart's face dripping and ragged pieces of skin and lacerated meat. When the farmer noticed me, he guessed that I was the one to shout at, so he quickly turned to me and through a quivering ungroomed handlebar moustache, he continued his shouting with no apparent need to breathe.

His face was wrinkled and there were only three yellowed teeth that I could see through the hair, which all but covered his mouth. His eyes, terribly bloodshot, blazed at me as he began showing me pieces of cow. Every once in awhile I could make out a word such as dumbhead, idiot, etc. The scene was so bizarre that I stiffled the irreverent desire to order from him some of the choice cuts of meat that he held near my nose. However, I could see that the Captain, who had controlled his nausea, was talking on the field phone in an agitated manner and soon Lt. Hayride came into the small room to lead the farmer out the door into the cold night. The Captain and I stared at one another, while we listened to the fading shouts of the Alsatian farmer as he was taken down the main road into Molsheim.

"Sergeant, I want that bazooka in this office right now," said the Captain finally. "You just cost the U.S. Army $150 for that cow," he added in a flat voice. "Now get out of here and don't do that again."

I left with mixed emotions. On one hand I had thought that maybe the incident would have provoked the Captain enough to take me off the demolition detail but on the other hand I didn't want him angry at me when it came time to reassign me to something that could be worse.

"How could any other assignment be worse?" I said aloud as I hurried to the weapons carrier to get the German bazooka.

When I leaned it in the corner of the orderly room, I saw that the commanding officer was anxious for me to leave so that he could examine and handle the captured weapon. I momentarily thought about warning him about the trigger arrangement but dismissed the thought in hopes that he might wind up accidentally blowing a hole in Lt. Bond.

Holt stopped me when I returned to the barracks and said, "You know, I wonder what that cow thought just as the rocket hit it?"

The next day it turned a bitter cold. The sky was clear but everything had frozen during the night. Even the sod in the fields was like cement and a killing frost covered tufts of vegetation that had managed to survive the long winter snows. At the company motor pool we had trouble starting the weapons carrier because of the cold but we both grinned when we saw that some smart ass in the company had painted on the side of the small truck a white silhouette of a farm house and that of a cow. I had extended my score of victories.

Perplexed over the loss of the destructive bazooka, Holt and I decided that we would still like to use up our supply of explosives in an attempt to smash the two hidden German vehicles. We drove to one of the smaller factory buildings that was in the final stages of preparation for installing our repair equipment, and examined our stock of shells and mines. We discovered that a detonator on German teller mines was so made that it could be unscrewed and that the wooden handle on a German potato masher grenade could be threaded into the body of the mine to serve as a detonating device. First it meant removing the explosive head of the grenade from its handle and it also meant that any fool wishing to explode the mine in this manner had only seven seconds to get as far away as possible before it went off. We decided to try it.

The drive up the rutted road to the vehicles was not as difficult as it had been, due to the solidly frozen mud, but the shells, mines and grenades rolling and banging around in the back of the truck was not a reassuring sound. We passed the farmer with the rake who again gave us the obscene sign and went back to nurturing his cow.

The tank and personnel carrier were still there so we set about planting our charges. We took the Mark IV first, mostly because it was in the front blocking the road but also because in the back of our minds was the notion that if we could get the personnel carrier started we would create a stir driving it into the Company compound back at Molsheim.

It was hard work moving and stacking the shells in the cold, and even with gloves and heavy hooded field jackets, we were shivering. As we completed the job on the tank, I noticed that the sky was beginning to darken as low clouds began to appear from the West spilling down over the crest of the mountains. By setting off a few carefully placed grenades, we had been able to clear a small space in the frozen ground under the big front of the low slung tank. Into this depression in the ground, we stacked as many of the 88 shells on top of one another as we could get in. From the ground to the tank we were able to wedge nearly all of the highly explosive projectiles. In front of and against this deadly pile, we wedged a teller mine. Not even sure that a small grenade detonator would explode the mine, we gingerly screwed the long wooden handle into the center of the ominous device. We stood back, looked at our handiwork and discussed what we would do if it didn't work.

"Who's going to come back here and disarm the mine?" asked Holt.

"We could train a cow to do it," I suggested.

It was decided that since Holt, thirty-two, was so old and didn't move very quickly that I would make the run from the seven second fuse to the weapons carrier, which would be running, ready to drive at great speed away from the explosion. Holt backed the truck up to a few feet from the tank and we rehearsed the maneuver. It worked fine. I pretended to pull the grenade lanyard, began counting, jumped on the open tailgate of the truck and yelled for Holt to *go*. We rocketed down the slope of the hill, bouncing over the ruts, while I finished counting off the seven seconds. Holt stopped the truck when I yelled again and we looked back up the hill measuring the distance that we had traveled. The tank certainly didn't seem very far away but we concluded that if we were still going fast at the time of the blast, we could probably add many more yards to our escape route before we felt any effects of the explosion.

Remembering the cow, we carefully looked around the fields and even scouted the woods to make sure that no people or animals were close enough to be injured by what we intended to do.

We were ready. Refusing to shout, "Fire in the hole," I readied myself, calculating the running steps I would have to take to reach the tank. With my foot firmly planted on the mine, I took a deep breath, yanked the nylon grenade lanyard and made a leaping dive for the engine racing weapons carrier shouting, "Go!" over the unexpectedly loud engine noise. Holt couldn't hear me over the engine noise. For what seemed like an eternity nothing happened until I frantically screamed, "Go!" at the top of my lungs. The truck leaped ahead, nearly throwing me out of the open back as we assaulted the frozen ruts in a mad roaring engine dash down the hill. Thrown from side to side in the empty bed on the truck, I could barely see the tank with my watering eyes as it gyrated in all directions.

Then suddenly a long flash of fire appeared under the tank. Simultaneously an eruption of the earth occurred followed immediately by a concussion so strong that it lifted our little truck off the road and pushed it at greater speed down the slope. Stunned by the force of the blast, I managed to stay inside the truck, watching in fascination as the 20 ton tank seemed to disappear in smoke, dirt, and a towering column of thick red flame.

It was only when a rock struck the open tailgate that I recognized the real danger to us. We had passed the test of the concussion and blast and were still racing away from the inferno but we were not going to be able to outrun the debris, which began to crash down around us. With genuine horror, I watched a great piece of metal plate tumble end over end through the air to slam down on the road just yards behind us. It was instantly buried in the frozen earth with only a smoking fragment of it showing above the ground. Rocks, metal, tree branches and large pieces of sod began to hit in the fields and on the road in front of us. We were under a gigantic umbrella of falling debris and not anywhere near the margin of safety necessary to be out from under it. The truck was struck several times and the windshield shattered in a hall of bouncing pieces of stone.

Because of the proximity of the mountains and ravines, a thunder-clap of noise crashed back and forth from the instant of the explosion until, in succeeding but dimishing waves it faded away to a low grumble in the distant ranges. Holt stopped and turned off the truck engine, leaning his head on his arms on the steering wheel. We sat in silence until a small stone made a clunking sound on the hood. To be coming down that long after the explosion, it must have fallen from an incredible height.

Holt said softly, "I have a great idea. . . . Let's don't ever do that again."

Looking back to the wreckage at the edge of the woods, I could not help but agree with him.

As we climbed out of the weapons carrier to look at the damage that had been done to it, we saw the farmer with the rake running up the hill after his badly frightened cow. Seeing us, he stopped and with a show of a slow but accurate movement of his arm and hand, made the obscene gesture.

We walked back to the woods to see what we had done to the tank, taking care to step around a gigantic scattering of chunks and pieces of metal. Smoke and small fires in the woods obscured our vision until we arrived at the site of the explosion. We looked in awe at a large crater in the road. The 20 ton tank was on its side among shattered stumps of trees. Its bottom and tracks completely blown away it lay awkwardly, smoke coming from the gaping wound in its underside. The upper armored body of the tank was relatively intact, as was the squat turret, although it had been blown off its ring and was canted sidewise, its long barrelled 75 mm cannon pointing to the sky. To our surprise the personnel carrier was now sitting at a right angle to the roadway, its front wheels and engine completely destroyed. We stayed long enough to make sure that all fires caused by burning oil and the heat of the explosives were out in the mangled forest before we walked back down to the truck.

I was sobered by what had occurred. The savage nature of war with its destructive violence somehow seemed very clear and depressing in my mind. Just for fun of it we had made scrap out of two carefully crafted vehicles. They were the enemy of course . . . but were they? There could have been five humans in that tank.

We came to the farmer who had succeeded in leading his lonely cow back to the hay pile but with his back to us, he would not turn to face us. But as we drove by, I studied the stooped man, dressed in stiff dirty dungarees with large cow shit covered knee length boots. He appeared very old. Suddenly I understood him; I understood his previous gestures to us and I felt for his frustrations and despair at being

245

caught between two waring armies. Here he was, trying to eke out, what must have always been, a terribly meager life in the rocky soil of the Vosges foothills. Into this personal struggle had appeared armed, uncaring, insolent strangers who burned and destroyed with absolutely no regard for him. I was sure that it did not matter to this farmer whether his far away government was German or French or for that matter Ethiopian. His life was, and always had been, that sick cow, the few acres of field to tend and the struggle for bread for himself and his family.

I looked back to see him one more time but a depression in the road blocked him from my sight and I could not forget him and I was sorry for what we had done to his field and woods without ever having spoken to him. I was also aware of a new sorrow that I felt for the machine gunned farmhouse and for the bazooked black cow. I was learning about the casual loss of humanity that goes with war. War is not just death or destroyed buildings, burned out tanks or shot down airplanes; war can be a terribly impersonal episode in lives and can cause lasting scars, because, like a never healed wound, its effects fester in our quiet knowledge, that deep within each of us, a non human can dwell.

CHAPTER XIII

THE COMING BATTLE

That night after chow, I was reading on my bunk in the warm barracks, as a slow deep snow began to fall.

The following night there was a German air raid on Strasbourg. We blacked out the compound, watching the probing search lights to the East from 10 kilometers away and listening to the crump of explosives. Military traffic began to increase, much of it headed North toward the 7th Army front beyond Hagenau. We were informed that we were now a unit of the 14th Armoured Division. The cold and snow were relentless, giving us only a few breaks in the weather between snowfalls, blowing winds and zero temperatures. We were grateful for our warm barracks and for the electric heaters that came from the restored power in the factory. I continued with my duties as demolition noncom but once the explosives had been disposed of I was often called upon to help move damaged trucks and other vehicles from a temporary parking depot to the shops for repair. There were definite signs around us that our enemy across the river was becoming more active. Our own defenses were being strengthened; when the weather permitted, reconnaissance planes appeared more often and truckloads of troops began moving into the Molsheim area. Our damaged vehicle depot began to attract more tanks with holes in the turrets and we were busy during daylight hours making repairs on the less damaged equipment.

On December 17th we received word through Battalion that the Germans had started an offensive drive through the Ardennes forest on the First and Ninth Army front. The news was taken in stride. We were confident and sure that if a battle did develop in the North, it could be nothing but a weak last ditch effort on the part of the Germans.

No one at that time was aware of the collosal movement of German armies, which had taken place in order for them to mount the attack. Our thoughts were of the coming Christmas. We had been promised turkey by our cooks. But the traffic continued to increase, MPs appeared at the main road junction leading to Strasbourg and troops began to dig foxholes and machine-gun pits in the hard frozen ground along the roads. We were ordered to wear our helmets and to carry our weapons at all times. We went about our work in an unconcerned, almost uninvolved manner, marching in formation through the snow from our comfortable barracks to the warm factory, trying not to notice the strangely noncommunicative infantry soldiers around us.

The news from the North was not good. On December 21 we heard that the 101st Division was trapped at Bastogne and that the Germans were breaking through our lines. Our casualties were reported as being very, very heavy. Rumor was that our neighbor to the West, the 3rd Army, might be pulled out of their position to help keep the Germans from making a big breakthrough on the entire front. Courier jeeps began to race back and forth along the main roads, sliding in the rutted snow in spite of their four wheel drives. We began to read bulletin board reports of the far-off battle, and pass on rumors, which we heard from troops traveling through the area. Our nightly sessions in the barracks were subdued and morose, no one wanting to talk about the women in Molsheim or the availability of local Schnapps. Our officers were suspiciously absent for long hours at a time, summoned to attend meetings at Battalion headquarters in the old walled city. They would return to secret themselves in the orderly room for long animated discussions. Try as we would, we could not get Sgt. Fletcher to tell us what they were talking about so we did the next best thing, we speculated and spread implausible rumors about moving back to Chaumont.

On Christmas morning we were called to formation on the company street to hear the Captain make a solemn announcement. Effective immediately our entire Battalion was to be broken up and each of us was to be used as a replacement in 7th Army units, which had suffered, as he put it "unusual and unexpected losses." Some men would be sent to infantry replacement depots, called Repodepos, for a quick familiarization course in infantry weapons. Others would be sent to field units without receiving any additional training. Some of the officers would be reassigned but our company would continue to exist, maintaining a skeleton headquarters in order to keep communication lines open to each of us. We were to keep our rank until further notice. When the present emergency was over, we would attempt to reassemble the Battalion and company.

The effect on the company of the remarkable and totally unexpected news was immediate. There was an electrifying tension that gripped every man in the platoons. We looked at one another in shock and disbelief. We had come so far together in the war and now, with our training and mission, we were to be used instead as replacements in companies made up of strangers. Men shifted their feet in a light drizzling snow suddenly overcome by the chill of the morning.

The Captain, in a tight, strangely emotional voice, ordered us to pack our personal equipment and be prepared to fall out at 2:00 p.m. for assignments to our new units. Transport would be waiting for us. It was only after reaching my bunk that I realized that for the first time in years, no one had yelled "48-49-50." The news had been too staggering and the implications too serious for each of us that the orders were beyond simple dissatisfaction.

We packed quietly. There were no jokes, no shouting, no horseplay, only a few questions among us that went unanswered. Most questions were concerned with who would make the assignments and who would be the unlucky bastards sent to the Repodepo. Strangely the murmured questions died away and a stoic silence fell over the barracks. Only the occasional noise of metal hitting metal, as helmets, mess equipment, weapons and canteens kept an unrhythmic cadence to our consternation. Not knowing what to expect, I took care to pack my personal belongings—paperback books, pipe, tobacco, cigarettes, precious foods, notebooks, maps, photographs of my loved ones—all in my empty gas mask mussette bag. I dressed in my cotton long underwear, slipped into two pair of both socks and pants, put on my wool knit sweater over a wool shirt, laid out my overcoat and field jacket and stuffed the remainder of my spare clothes into my duffle bag. I took care that my blankets and quilt were on top within easy reach and that my wool knit cap and muffler were within easy reach. Then I turned to my equipment—checked my pack and webbing, made sure that my canteen was full of water and cleaned and oiled my carbine for the first time in weeks. Sitting on the bed with the small weapon in my hands gave me a new and different feeling. I wasn't preparing this suddenly tiny and ineffective looking piece for target practice or even for an inspection. I was cleaning it with care because it might soon make the difference between living and dying. With great seriousness of purpose, I checked each bullet in all three of my clips, clicking them out, one by one on the stripped bed, carefully wiping each with my handkerchief. Studying each one as I placed them back into the clips, I felt unnerved. Finally I checked my first aid packet to make sure that the large pressure bandage was intact in its small metal case. There was nothing else to do but wait for orders.

Around one o'clock, numbers of trucks and weapon carriers began to arrive at our compound. Nearly all of them were marked with the 14th Armour stencil and all were driven by unsmiling strangers.

Sharply at 2:00, the Farmer blew his shrill whistle and we formed up for the last time in our familiar company formation. There was no talking as the company commander gave the "at ease" order. We were rigid and attentive as he began reading names from his clipboard. He would first read a unit number and then a list of names assigned to that unit. Most groups were of squad size, although 25 men were assigned to a tank retriever company. About halfway through the list, he called my name along with 12 others. We were to join a light weapons company of the 14th Armoured Division. I knew all the men in the group personally, but was dismayed that my friend, Holt, was not among them. However, for an instant I felt relieved to hear that Sergeant Fletcher was also assigned with my group and I had a fleeting belief that with his orderly room connections, he would have found a way out of a dangerous assignment. Ten men, most of them unskilled, were sent to a nearby Repodepo. They were cooks, assistants, and company laborers, but two of them were renowned troublemakers and goof-offs. We were sent back to the barracks to pick up our gear and to receive our freshly cut orders. Once again, being a staff Sergeant, I discovered that I was the ranking noncom in my group of 12 men and that I was responsible to see that we arrived together at our destination. Pushing my way through the now noisy and cursing crowd in the barracks, I found Holt and we compared notes. He, along with two others, was on his way to a light vehicle repair company. Because the whistle was shrilling again, we had little time to say anything to one another but for the first time since we had met on a night troop train in Pasadena almost two years before, we shook hands.

"Take care of yourself," he said.

"Yeah, you too," I replied.

We found our trucks and as we drove out of the compound, I had the feeling that I was never to see some of these people again.

The low sky continued to spit a light snow.

The next ten weeks of my life were to become a most confused period of time, and even today with notes, old maps and faded photographs, it is impossible to put it all into proper sequential order. Events moved so rapidly, sometimes even overlapping, that it is hard to recollect which events occurred during one 24 hour period. I am puzzled that on a single date, four or five important events could all take place. Those ten weeks were not at all like a carefully edited film when one scene leads logically into the next, and the story line spins inexorably into conclusion. Instead the period of time sometimes seems like a series of unrelated vignettes, with no thin thread of logic tying them together. The German January offensive against the 7th Army broke units into scattered fragments and the stages of piecing Dever's VI Corps back together was a difficult and exhausting time for simple soldiers. The severe weather, of course, with its numbing effect on battle, reduced us often to creatures whose primary purpose was to survive the elements. These periods of concentrated effort, directed toward a cocoon existence, leave spaces and nights of blank memories except for the cold and what one did to keep from dying in it. Keeping notes or diaries was forbidden by the Army, but when it was possible I made marks on maps and jotted down dates and events on the backs of precious letters from home. But the story is incomplete, sometimes suspiciously inaccurate because I often not only did not know the date but seldom knew exactly what day it was.

I remember the five days in the woods living in a Napoleonic bunker full of 18th century sword blades but I cannot in all honesty state when the experience took place. Was it before Hagenau? After? In addition, there was the terror and the constant despair. The fear of death or mutilation is not a companion to clear thinking nor is it related to the desire to keep careful notes on one's behavior.

The events of December 1944 and January of 1945 did occur. Some of these single events are dug into the folds of my memory so deeply that they will remain there until my mind ceases to function. Others are bits and pieces surrounded in a fog that does not disperse but rather thickens with time. The temporary retreat of the 7th Army in the face of the enemy attack was no doubt orchestrated in warm headquarters war rooms by quiet men who knew the secrets of logistics and the methods of retreat and eventual recovery. But to the soldier in the field, without information, it translated into confusion, rumor, fear and to an existence near the edge of panic. Orders were issued, countermanded, and carried out under the extreme conditions of weather and in the presence of a skillful and determined enemy who, with his back to his homeland, fought with a persistent ferocity that left no time for anyone to rest.

We knew that the Battle of the Bulge raged to the Northwest of our position and we harbored a deep fear that the Germans would launch desperate new weapons against us, which could actually swing the war to victory for them. German strategists were at the time admired throughout the world for their imaginative and often dramatic victories against impossible odds, and as the battles before the Rhine shifted in their favor, it created apprehension in the field. We carried our gas masks with us during this time and there was a tight sick fear when the popping of small arms fire could be heard between the thud of artillery and mortar explosions. We seldom spoke of it, but there were occasionally muted conversations about the enemy's treatment of prisoners.

It was the time when we actually believed that we could, even then, lose the war.

Not wanting to talk to a sullen driver, I sat in the back of the 6-by with my charges. We sat quietly on the facing wooden benches, piled our duffle bags, packs and weapons on boxes of C and K rations between us in the center of the truck bed, and took our leave of the ancient city of Molsheim.

As we turned left in a Northerly direction toward the front, someone said bitterly, "I thought we were going to have turkey today. . . . Fucking belly robbers!"

Several helmeted heads nodded in agreement but no other voice was raised in either agreement or in further protest. Somehow it seemed not to matter now.

Even before we cleared the city area, Cross, who was sitting near the tailgate stood up and rolled down the tarp that covered the back end of the truck. It flapped constantly in the wind and offered very little refuge from the stinging cold that worked through the canvas tarpaulin on the sides of the truck bed behind our backs. We huddled in the semidarkness looking for warmth, not much caring.

CHAPTER XIV

HAGENAU

Dressed as I was, now with field jacket and overcoat, I was not so cold that I could not speculate as to where we were headed. Traveling North out of Molsheim, we were only about 40 kilometers from the city of Hagenau, which we had learned was the front lines. I sincerely hoped that the truck would stop long before we reached that point but as we ground away mile after mile in the snow, my hopes began to fade. There were endless sudden stops, some of them so forceful that we were thrown together like so many brown bundles of carelessly wrapped cold flesh. On two occasions, the truck slid off the road into the deep ditch next to the asphalt and the driver had difficulty, even with 6-wheel drive, in dragging us free from the snow. We could see nothing of course; we only knew that the muffled conversations that we could hear from time to time probably came from guards at roadblocks.

Finally after one long wait, the driver shut off the engine. We were apparently either at our destination or we were to experience a longer than normal stop. Expectantly the helmets rose more or less in unison but nothing was happening outside the truck. In the comparative quiet, marred only by a slight winter wind that lifted the tied down tarpaulin so that it slapped back and forth, we heard the sounds of artillery fire. It was not the muffled continuous sounds that we had heard in Chaumont. These were thumps and separated, so that each explosion was identifiable as a single round. In spite of ourselves, we glanced at one another; Dunbar showed a tight nervous grin. Once between two well spaced rounds, we heard the faint popping of a machine gun. Several of us, pretending to be looking for something else in the pile of equipment, secured our carbines and casually held them between our knees, gun butts on the floor.

Soon after, the truck engine roared into life and we lurched and skidded into the city of Hagenau.

We were ordered out of the truck by the driver who merely pounded on the tailgate and shouted, "This is it," and disappeared. We climbed down painfully to find ourselves standing in a large courtyard surrounded by three story stone buildings. The courtyard, although covered with snow, showed some flagstone through the many tire marks that crisscrossed it in many places. It was almost dark and there did not seem to be anyone around. I shouldered my duffle bag on its long handled strap, picked up my webbing and carbine intending to ask for some directions when a door in the closed building opened and a bare head appeared.

"You the replacements?" asked the head.

I answered "yes" by holding my carbine in the air over my head. The head made a quick gesture, which I interpreted to mean, "Come over here."

As I started my stumbling walk with my load of equipment, the head disappeared and the door banged shut.

As I walked, I noticed several parked vehicles, ambulances, half tracks and six-bys that were scattered around near the buildings. Two jeeps stood near the door where I was headed. The artillery rounds were now making a crisp banging noise. Struggling with the door, I finally entered a very small dark room occupied by three people and one chair placed next to a battered square table that had a single guttering candle stuck to it in its own wax. Two bareheaded men sat on the floor working on a smoking oil burning heater and the chair was filled by a large middle-aged redheaded man. No one spoke to me. Finally the redhead snapped, "Who the hell are you?"

I told him, dug out my papers and handed them to him.

He took them from me, studying them briefly and then glared at me with such hatred that I became nervous. "Jesus, fucking Christ," he hissed slowly. "I need men and they send snotty nosed kids up here."

"*You* are a staff Sergeant?" he snorted.

One of the men on the floor stopped working with a butterfly valve and looked at me maliciously.

Red roared, "I don't suppose you have anyone with you who knows a fucking thing about weapons?"

I tried to explain where we had come from and what we had been doing in Molsheim before we were reassigned, but it was clear that he was dissatisfied with everything I said.

In the small room and in the flickering candlelight, the man looked enormous. He literally bristled with anger and I presumed that he was the 1st Sergeant. He turned to speak to the men on the floor just as the door opened behind me and a voice said, "Captain, the Colonel wants you."

I was startled to discover that the redheaded man was the company commander, but he made an open palmed gesture of exasperation, stood up and shrugged into a large fur lined parka. As he brushed by me, he snarled out of the corner of his mouth, "Lester, find some place for these assholes and keep them out of my sight."

As he slammed the door he shouted something about the "God-damned brass." A single shell banged nearby.

Lester, with a flashlight, took us through the courtyard to an adjoining unheated building, which in the darkness, looked like it had been a school or a university classroom building. We struggled up to the third floor where Lester casually assigned us to space by flicking his light into two adjoining rooms. Then in a spasm of conscience told us where the company mess was located off the courtyard. Fishing out our mess gear from our packs, we dumped everything else on the floor and groped our way back down the wide stairs, looking for the mess hall. Finding it at last behind two steaming garbage cans of hot water sitting in the snow, we entered a fairly large overheated, lighted room on the ground floor. There were many men there who watched us curiously as we crowded through the doorway.

One of them seated at one of the many picnic-like tables yelled, "Close the goddamed door . . . blackout!"

The last man in the rear hurriedly closed the door that lead directly outside to the courtyard. Many of the occupants at the tables sneered openly while others appeared genuinely angry over our intrusion.

The meal was at least hot, if not good, considering the circumstances. We sat together alone, trying to extend our stay as long as possible by smoking and drinking overcooked coffee.

Men drifted in and out until we were practically the only ones left in the room. The artillery fire had died away and our depression and fears were beginning to die away with it. At last a cook came out of an adjoining room and told us to get out if we wanted to clean our mess gear. He was closing down the chow line.

During dinner I had described my meeting with the redheaded Captain to my companions, but aside from someone's hopeful suggestion that if he couldn't use us, we might be sent back. There was little comment. In low whispers we talked about how we were going to get through the night without heat or light. All of us had noticed that Lester's flashlight had shone on glass all over the floors of both rooms so we assumed that our quarters were windowless. We had four candle stubs and one flashlight among us but decided that to show any light at all would be dangerous. We decided that we could handle it in the dark. We dipped our gear in the scalding water on our way back to the two rooms but before we got across the compound, George, a tall thin optometrist from Covina, showed me that ice had already formed on his canteen cup. Fully dressed as we were in our overcoats, we lay on the floor, covered ourselves with our blankets and quilts in the glass and plaster to await the coming of the next day.

By putting my head down under the blankets, I warmed my face and hands with my breath, somehow feeling removed from my surroundings and secure from harm. There was no sound. I felt only the pentrating cold. From the far side of the room, near the broken doorway, someone finally said, "Merry Christmas, folks," but not one of us laughed on that Christmas Day in 1944.

Exhausted, I awakened only once during the night. I was terribly cold and took a long time falling back to sleep. My thoughts were of home and of the Christmas that my family must have had that day. The unimaginably delicious turkey dinner, the warm kitchen smells, friends dropping by to visit, laughter and humor from my father. No one knowing where I was or what I was doing half a world away.

I wondered what my mother would have thought if she could have seen me lying on broken glass in a shattered building on the edge of France, cold, hungry and honestly frightened. The thought almost made me cry in my loneliness but I took some solace in knowing that my mother could not possibly conceive of such a thing. I wanted to believe that it would have been beyond her experience or imagination. Thinking of her, I was once again thankful that war had not been visited upon America for almost one hundred years. That night I wanted desperately for my family, home and friends to remain exactly as I had last seen them. "Be there," I said to myself. "Please, be there."

We awoke in the early morning light having learned an important lesson about such freezing temperatures; to protect oneself from the cold, it is just as important to have blankets under you as it is to be covered by them. Cold comes from all directions. Stiff and hurting, we looked out our broken windows to the East to gaze at a rose colored sunrise. The sky, except for a light battle smoke was, at least temporarily, going to be clear. We watched the activity in the courtyard as men began to work at starting the assortment of vehicles. Each man was made clearly visible to us by watching the jets of air stream coming from warm lungs. Our own breath clouds hung in the morning air. Hoods were opened so that men could tinker with frozen engines, and the grinding of complaining starters filled the compound. Some of the vehicles started but most of them were abandoned by stoop shouldered soldiers who kicked their way through the snow toward the warmth of the mess hall.

We gathered our mess gear and joined the lines moving toward the steaming water in front of the dining hall. Not so much interested in powdered eggs or burnt toast, we instead savored the heat in the room, feeling our faces and fingers tingle as the circulation was restored.

The hot coffee was as welcome as was the silence, which we endured from the men of the weapons company. We could tell from their glances and whispered words that we were recognized as the replacements, but the open contempt that they showed us was disturbing.

During the morning we tried to stay warm in our two rooms but the effort was not very successful, so we occupied our time by clearing out the glass, plaster, and debris from the rooms. We threw it all out in the wide hallway, which was already so filled with rubble that one had to walk across mounds of it to get to the cluttered stairwell.

Three of us decided that sitting in the freezing windowless room was not a very interesting thing to do, so we took our weapons, helmets and as bundled up as we could become, we went out to look at the city. The rest of the group sat huddled on the floor, trying to play cards with fingers fumbled by heavy gloves.

Hagenau, yet another ancient city, sits astride the Moder River. On the edge of the Lorraine plateau, it was not a large city in 1944. Edged on the North by the dark Hagenau forest and having a population of less than 20,000 people, it was nevertheless an important traffic junction for trade from all directions. Five important highways converged on the city, and while the Moder River, flowing to the Rhine, was not in itself an important river artery to the commerce and travel of Lorraine, it was part of the network of riverways that dominated the choice of location for cities and towns. The Moder flowed directly through Hagenau, crossed by several bridges, serving the highways from the South and North.

The early morning smoke, fed by the fires and battle of the day before, hung over the shattered city making visibility somewhat difficult, but we did manage to identify the building where we were billeted as a walled college or university complex.

The old grey stone oblong buildings, many of which were now without roofs or windows, had been built many years before and were ugly and utilitarian in design. Leaving the interior courtyard, we passed through a broken iron gate onto the main road leading to the center of the town to the North. Two blocks to the South was the frozen Moder River, crossed by a broken stone bridge, which had been temporarily repaired for use by Army engineers. Traffic on the road was very heavy. A stream of trucks and armour ground their way into the center of town, competing on the narrow rubble filled streets with ambulances, jeeps, and weapons carriers moving back toward the South. The snow, now frozen, was being churned into chunks of ice and inexplicably sticky mud by the hundreds of tracks and wheels. Walking on the main highway was both dangerous and difficult. The sliding tanks and trucks were a serious danger to anyone trying to navigate what had once been sidewalk area and the loose bricks and cobblestones below the ice made simple steps a treacherous exercise. Past the university we left the main road and took a short side street into the city. While moving traffic was almost eliminated, we did encounter parked vehicles on the minor street and passed damaged houses filled with glum but enterprising combat troops. There were small fires burning in empty fuel drums on sidewalks and in houses. Some houses had their broken windows boarded over with ingenious smokestacks leading from interior rooms inside. Many soldiers crowded around the outside fires and we were welcome to share the heat. Dressed as we were, we were unidentifiable as anyone but just another dogfaced soldier. No rank or unit insignia appeared on anyone's jackets or overcoats, ours or theirs, and except for our carbines, which identified us as either service troops or officers, we received nothing but some half interested curious glances.

The talk around the fires was of women, liquor, and the stupidity of the division command. There was also joking and ribold tales told about the amorous adventures of friends who were present around the fires.

We drifted from fire to fire towards the city, vaguely aware that as we moved, there were fewer and fewer men, fires, or vehicles on the narrow street. We came at last to a blockage of the road. Buildings on both sides had tumbled onto the pavement making passage impossible. Curious, I climbed up over the snow covered pile and looked out over the remaining ruins of Hagenau. It was virtually a no man's land of a broken and still smoldering city. As I watched, a wall collapsed two blocks away sending a cloud of dust and ashes into the air. I could see no vehicles except a burned out Sherman tank, its turret piled high with snow, sitting at a brick strewn intersection. There was an eerie silence over the entire scene, the only noise being that of wind and some far-off muffled shouting.

Looking for some sign of life, I caught some movement in a doorway beyond the barricade to my right. It was a helmeted American soldier watching the streets ahead, his rifle stock resting on his right hip. The fresh wind was blowing his overcoat away from his legs but he was intently studying the gutted landscape of the city.

Perhaps I moved or he simply caught sight of me out of the corner of his eye, but he slowly raised his free arm and made signs for me to go back over the pile of rubble. He went back to his vigil, looking all the world like a solitary hunter waiting to flush an unsuspecting pheasant or a covey of quail.

My companions and I made our way back to our billets, noting that by then there was a noticeable decrease in traffic making its way into the city. The ambulances, jeeps, empty trucks and weapons carriers were returning in a steady stream to cross the bridge to the South and out of the city.

After another welcome meal, I went over to the orderly room, hoping to find out what I could from Lester. His was the only name I knew in the entire company. I entered after knocking properly, only to discover that the sole occupant of the room was my redheaded Captain. He was sitting in the chair behind the candled table, bundled in his parka. He had been drinking from a bottle that stood on the table in front of him. The oil heater was not working; the room was cold, and the Captain was blowing puffs of steam from his slack lips. Fixing me with bloodshot unfocusing eyes, he asked me what I wanted. Trying not to upset him, I took off my helmet and scratched my head through my wool knit cap.

"I was wondering if you had any orders for us . . . sir?"

Not meaning to, I had added a touch of sarcasm to sir, but in his condition, he seemed not to notice. Although his words were slurred, he answered after some thought, "Yeah, fix my fucking heater."

He grinned, pleased with himself.

Back in the rooms, I found Jones who had once been a cook's assistant and who had a good reputation with stoves and heaters. I explained the Captain's request and Jones reluctantly dug out a screwdriver and a pair of pliers from his mussette bag. Grumbling, he fought his way through the hallway trash. He returned in about an hour, flushed and a little drunk. He had not only fixed the heater so that it was now working but had been invited by an impressed Captain to share a drink or two. The two of them, it turned out, had just finished the bottle. Jones reported that when he had left, "Frank" was asleep on the floor. The two of them had gotten very friendly in only a few minutes. During the afternoon we covered the high windows in our rooms with patches of boards, cardboard, and some tarpaulin from a truck in the compound. The rooms were now pitch black but within minutes, considerably warmer. We looked for an old oil drum so that we could make a fire but couldn't find one small enough to carry up three flights of steps. We lighted a candle and the room, no larger than 10 feet square was transformed into more homey quarters. Driving some nails in the walls with our carbine butts, we hung up our gear, sat on our blankets and talked about what was going to happen. It was clear that no effort was being made to send us back to Molsheim, so we decided that our safest course was to scrounge for ourselves and stay out of sight. We agreed that we should not draw attention to ourselves by going to the mess hall together but would go there only at crowded mealtimes three or four at a time in shifts.

That night there was no sound of war, and we slept well and warmly in our dark but private chambers. There was a large but waterless bathroom down the hall that we used even without water. At odd times during the evening and night we simply used the hallway. We were the only group on the third floor and it was surprisingly scary to be groping around in the rubble of the old building trying to find a very black room in which to urinate. The combination of the stillness, the darkness, the enormity of the ancient building, and the thinly suppressed tension that I felt in the combat area, caused a skin-stretching fright that I had never experienced before in my life. I was to dream of that brooding dark building for years to come.

In the next few days, trucks loaded with dead began to appear in our compound around mealtime, the drivers taking advantage of what was probably the only operating mess hall in the entire city. They would park, eat, drink coffee and then leave for some unknown graves registration unit to the South.

Near the end of the month, during a break in the weather, several of us were outside scrounging the compound area looking for boxes that we could use to make some furniture, when we were startled by a new and curious whistling sound. I froze as the sound escalated into an earsplitting shriek unlike any sound I had ever heard. But before I could move, a shape flashed by overhead, so close and fast that I could only quickly distinguish that it had been an airplane. It had two large pod like engines under its wings but beyond immediate comprehension was the fact that it had no propellers. I had just seen for the first time in my life, a jet airplane. Later I was to know that it was a ME 262, one of the first German jet operational fighter bombers, but on that clear morning I had never even *heard* of an airplane that could fly without propellers. The idea was as preposterous as the notion of a plane without wings.

A shattering crash of sound followed the jet into the compound and like an aircraft, it was gone in an instant. Slack jawed, we stood where we were, disoriented and dismayed. I saw a very high tiny speck zip across the sky and begin a dive back toward Hagenau. This time four distinct red flashes came out of its nose as I watched. His pass was undoubtedly aimed down the Moder and his target was probably the bridges only two blocks away. Fascinated by its speed, I watched from where I was standing in the courtyard, temporarily incapable of thinking about seeking a shelter. Rapid explosions along the river preceeded the jet but in seconds the screaming sound and the awful enemy weapon had come and gone. I had never seen anything move so quickly. The now familiar booming crash followed the plane as it disappeared beyond the town headed for the Rhine River. Before the sound died completely, there was an explosion near the bridge beyond the roofs and a column of black oil smoke and flame shot into the air.

There was much confusion now, men running into and out of buildings, trucks being started and more men rushing to the main road outside the college gate. I followed to the gate, grateful to see that the bridge was still there but unable to see the river or to see what had been hit and was burning. When I arrived at the bridge, there was a crowd looking to the West, up the river. The jet had strafed the viaduct road next to the river and there were at least six vehicles on fire, one of them, a 6-by, on its side on the road. Many men were running amongst the wreckage but some of the brown bundles on the road were motionless. A medic, followed by several others, ran out to the victims and began working on them. An ambulance appeared from a side street, silouetted against the flame and black smoke from a truck that had been loaded with five gallon gasoline jerry cans. The medics and ambulance driver were in great danger because every few seconds one of the gas cans would explode, sending the container a hundred feet or so in the air to tumble a blazing trail of burning gasoline as it crashed back among the houses and vehicles. And even from the bridge a hundred yards away, we could feel the heat from the voracious fire. However, we were all soon ordered off the bridge and instructed to return to our units by an angry MP officer who slid to a stop in a jeep on the center of the bridge. I hurried back to the compound with Sgt. Fletcher who lived in the other room and whom I had not seen for two days. He seemed very withdrawn and did not speak to me.

I met Lester in the courtyard and asked him if he had ever seen an aircraft like that one before. He said he had not but that we had better stay close to the company area. Lester was the company clerk and had spoken to us once or twice since we had joined the company five days before. He was not friendly but he was helpful and would answer questions. Cross, Jones and Dunbar had made friends with some of the men, which at least gave us some rumors to talk about and to report.

We learned that Hagenau had been fought over for several weeks, changing hands many times due to heavy German counterattacks that were sprung from the heavily forested areas to the North. With the Moder to our backs, the U.S. Army had been stepping up its fight to clear the city and to establish a stable line to the North beyond the many road junctions. Casualties had been heavy, ambulance traffic steady and reinforcements were due soon. There had been no real pressure from the Germans for over a week, but the appearance of the German jet seemed to create a nervous watchfulness among the troops in the area. The air attack, although slight by World War II standards, was made by a German first line plane and apparently was made to cut the bridges behind us. There was quiet speculation that we could expect a German attack soon.

What little news we heard from the Northwest was not encouraging. Patton's Third Army was involved in an attempt to relieve the beleaguered city of Bastogne and German panzers were still on their way to the Scheldt River and the important supply city of Antwerpt. We were to learn much later that by the 30th of December, Bastogne and the 101st had been partially relieved through a corridor punched by the 4th Division armour and that the German drive had been stalled near Deviant, a full 100 miles from Antwerpt. Our news was days late, sometimes twisted in the telling, out of fear of the enemy.

As the new year approached, the 7th Army front, although stretched to its limits by being forced to take over territory caused by the westward movement of the 3rd Army, seemed stable, the brief air attack notwithstanding. We believed openly that the Battle of the Bulge, on such an enormous scale, had used every German soldier available and that the enemy facing us was subsequently weakened.

That evening after chow, we were happily surprised when Jones appeared in our warm candlelighted room with a new bottle of Scotch, which his friend Captain Frank had given him. It was not a very good Scotch but it was liquor and we prepared eagerly for New Year's eve in Hagenau. We had decided that each of us could have two good swallows if the bottle was to go around when Cross made the sound suggestion that we could each have a lot more if we didn't share with the six men in the other room. With our fingers to our lips, we silently passed the bottle for the 1st drink. New Year's had begun. Our party was interrupted at about 10:00 p.m. however by a high oscillating droning sound followed immediately by the sounds of many antiaircraft batteries in and around the city. The banging of the 90 mm's and the chunking of the 40's were very loud and continuous. We could see the flashes through and around our makeshift window corners, so in the fashion of men well on their way to drunkeness, we reasoned that the windows should be uncovered so that we could witness the fireworks, which we pretended was part of the New Year's celebration staged for our benefit. With great glee and much horseplay, we tore off the wood, cardboard and tarpaulin to look out at an incredible night sky. Many searchlights, bouncing scattered light back from a high cloud cover, were probing for a small window in the sky, attracting shell bursts and tracers into the small targeted area. The little spot moved slowly across the sky from West to East but when the lights went out two or three at a time, the firing stopped as suddenly as it had begun, and our open windows became rectangular holes of blackness.

''Shit, that wasn't much of a party,'' someone said drunkenly.

''Probably reconnaissance,'' Dunbar said. ''Probably trying to use up our ammunition—damned Communist plot.'' I laughed at the incongruity for even then I knew that politically, there was no wider spectrum than the one between the Nazi and the Communist doctrines. In my drunken condition, I reflected briefly over his comment and the fact that as soldiers, we had seldom if ever discussed the politics of World

War II. I was sure that some of my companions had absolutely no idea about the causes of the war or for that matter, few had a very thin grasp of which countries were involved, why these countries were fighting, or whether they were Axis or Allies. Most, I'm afraid, had never heard of the Treaty of Versailles or the Sudetenland. Most assumed that the Germans had simply started the war because they wanted to finish World War I. The bottom line for Americans was to fight to win. The Germans were the enemy, so our job was to beat them as quickly as possible and get on with our lives back home.

In the darkness we couldn't see to recover our windows, so we sat on the floor on our blankets, passing the bottle around until it was sadly empty. Someone, it was too dark to see who, threw the empty bottle out through the window. We all cheered when it smashed on the courtyard below. Hugely funny to all of us was the comment, "I hope it didn't hit any one of our swell friends in this company."

We had no friends in the company, so we rolled in laughter, becoming weak and incoherent in the hysterical process. Although I hardly knew two of the men in the room, we all agreed in a show of drunken companionship that no better group of close friends had ever shared a bottle so well. One by one the young men fell asleep in the freezing room, this time warmed from the inside.

As I lay with my head turned looking at the window space, my eyesight became adjusted to the night light and fascinated, I watched the two window rectangles become grey and then almost bright. I had just glanced at my luminous watch, the one given to me by my loving parents on the day I left for Ft. McArthur, when I heard a cannon bang once toward the Northern part of the city. It was 11:00 p.m. and the German surprise attack on the American 7th Army had begun. The attack would be named Nordwind by the Germans and would engulf our entire front in ferocious fighting for the next six weeks.

The single cannon shot was soon followed by many more until there was a continuous thudding and banging. The grey rectangles became a kaleidoscope of flashing light, some so bright that momentarily I could see my companions in their blankets on the floor. Soon, I sensed that everyone was awake in the room, lying quietly in awed silence. The exchange of fire went on all night, becoming louder at times, until towards dawn the windows became rose-colored and then red. We could smell smoke and knew that fires had been started in the town. So far no shells had hit in our area, and the morning light somehow made me feel a little more optimistic or at least a little less frightened.

I was startled when a voice from the dark doorway shouted above the noise, "Sergeant, get down to the orderly room, the Captain wants you!"

Struggling out of my cocoon of blankets, I clamped my helmet on my head, grabbed my carbine and jumped down the three flights of steps two or three at a time. The courtyard was deserted but the small candlelighted office was crowded with serious faces. My little unit on the third floor must have been an afterthought by the Captain, because as soon as I packed myself into the room, Big Red, in a voice loud enough to be heard over the shelling said, "We may have to pull out of here. I want every noncom to keep his men together. I don't want to have to break my ass trying to find people. . . . When we leave we may not have much time. I want everyone of you to touch base here on the hour."

He pulled up his parka sleeve and holding it near the candle, looked at his watch on his hairy red arm. "It's now 0730 hours. Starting at 0900 I want to see each of you in this office. You platoon Sergeants start loading equipment in the 6-bys. We won't leave any weapons around here this time for the Krauts to use. O.K., now get your asses out of here." "Oh," he added, "have every man load up with ammo and C rations. Rations are in the mess hall, ammo in the weapons carrier."

The morning was a madhouse. One of our buildings took a hit, blowing a hole in the roof and showering slate tile into the courtyard. We loaded up on plenty of C rations—there were torn open boxes all over the mess tables with no one counting the number of cans taken by any one man. I had dumped some of my now useless articles of clothing—clean underwear that I was astonished to find, summer shirts, towels, handkerchiefs and dirty laundry into the hallway, to make room for cans of C rations. Although the duffle was now very heavy, I reasoned that I could manage it. I knew how important it was to have food on hand.

The ammo truck was worthless to me and my unit, there being no carbine ammunition available, only 30 calibre M-1 clips and some 45 shells. We scrounged the buildings and in a back room found a pile of M-1's, which probably had been recovered from the dead. Selecting one that was operational, I threw my carbine on the pile and went back to the ammo truck picking up two bandoliers of M-1 clips. The heavier 12 pound M-1 and ammunition slings were going to be a small problem but in the constant bombardment around us I hardly gave it a thought. I threw the two cloth bandoliers containing about 100 rounds over my shoulder, slung my M-1 and hurried back to our room.

Every hour I reported to the orderly room only to be told to stay ready. We ate some of our C rations, ducking involuntarily every time an explosion occurred nearby. A truck near the bridge exploded for some reason causing pandemonium on the street until it burned out and was rolled over the bank into the icy Moder. The traffic lane across the bridge had to be kept clear. From our windows we could see that vehicles kept coming and going in the courtyard. Several 6-bys, parked near the far end of the compound were being hastily loaded with crates, weapons and boxes. Other 6-bys came in empty and were parked near the loaded trucks. A weapons carrier arrived loaded with dead, their unmoving feet and legs sticking out of the back above the tailgate. The driver, when he discovered that there was no longer a free mess hall at this location, backed his little carrier around and headed out the gate toward the bridge. An ambulance, driven by an Italian volunteer came in for fuel. Although he was wearing a Red Cross armband, we could tell from his shapeless uniform that he was Italian. He also wore the tell-tale cap with flaps that buttoned over the top but could also be buttoned under the chin to warm the ears. He was sent away.

During the overcast afternoon several empty jeeps arrived and were parked with the loaded trucks. A single courier jeep arrived periodically with messages that were taken to and out of the orderly room. The concussion caused by the constant thumping of large guns, the bark of howitzers and the bang of tank artillery caused a steady pulsating painful ear pressure and the fires in the city grew larger, some ominously closer. An occasional ricocheting tracer bullet could be seen arching across the sky to fall among the houses.

During my five o'clock visit to the orderly room, the Captain looking haggard and drawn, handed us each a simple map with a circle drawn around a small town. He explained that when we were ordered to pull out we could do so in small groups. We were to reassemble at Hockfelden, a small town to the South and West, about 25 kilometers distance from Hagenau. The railroad station at Hockfelden would be our assembly point.

It was almost dark by then in spite of the flashes and the flickering red sky. On my way back to the rooms, I stood for a moment in the courtyard and suddenly there came to my mind a line from a poem that I had read in high school English in another life long ago. It was called "I Have a Rendezvous With Death" and had been written by Alan Seeger, a soldier who died in WW I. I could only remember part of a line that went "at midnight in some flaming town." When I had first read the poem at the age of 15, I had been fascinated by the heroics and fatalism of it, but now as I looked at the red sky and felt the crash of shells, I found a cold fear envelop me. Had I wished too hard for heroism? Was there some fatalistic power ready to punish me for my youthful wish that somehow I too might make such a great sacrifice? Was some incalculable debt to be paid, collected by a super fiendish accountant who lived off the adolescent wishfulness of youth?

Another shell hit one of our buildings close to the gate, sending a shower of stone and tile into the street beyond. I ran into our building, my M-1, heavy and awkward as I negotiated the steps to the third floor.

Through the windows the burning city gave us the light that we needed to make sure that we had all of our gear ready to move. We sat and waited. Suddenly I was very tired, my hands and head felt heavy with a numbing fatigue. But I had no time to consider as the noise outside simply faded away and I fell into a deep sleep, hands folded on my lap and my back against the wall.

Someone, from a far distance away was calling my name in some swirling dream. I felt a shaking on my shoulder and as I jerked awake the noise outside quickly returned, louder than it had been before. It took moments to recognize Fletcher who, in an agitated state, was telling me something important. "The Captain says that when we're ready we should take three jeeps and go!" he shouted between explosions.

"I just came back—we're to get out of here right now!" he yelled.

It took me awhile to digest what he was saying but the orders from Big Red were explicit so we gathered everything we had and dragged it down the steps. Once in the courtyard it was clear that the battle was coming closer. Very distinct rifle shots could be heard and the hammering bursts of a machine gun seemed very close by.

The courtyard was deserted except for all of the vehicles. For a moment the thought crossed my mind that at least some of the trucks should have departed long ago but another shell hit the building that we had just vacated so we threw our belongings and ourselves into the closest three jeeps and wheeled out of the compound toward the gate.

Dunbar was driving our lead jeep with me in the passenger seat and Cross and George jammed in the back among the duffle bags. As we approached the only gate out of the courtyard, we saw immediately that we had a real problem facing us. A disabled halftrack, sitting on the main road to the bridge, was all but blocking our way out. We skidded to a stop in the snow looking for a way through. It looked hopeless. Jumping out of the jeep with my rifle, I ran through the gate to the halftrack to see if it could be moved. It would never move. It had taken a shell in the engine and had been abandoned. I looked around for something, anything . . . because a panic was beginning deep inside me and I was glad that no one noticed in the noise and confusion that a gutteral sob had broken from my throat. This last minute obstacle was cutting off our escape. It was unfair, it was not right! Running around the back of the halftrack with a pounding heart, I nearly smashed into George who was staring and pointing up the street into the burning town. I looked at what he was pointing at, conscious at the same time that except for the occasional bang of what sounded like an anti-tank gun, the shelling had stopped. The angry popping of machine guns sliced through the darkness. An incongruous high pitched whistle was sounding far down the street and as I watched, I saw running stooped over figures several blocks away, darting from doorway to debris piles. With their helmets and white snow capes silhouetted against the glow from the many fires, they could only be Germans. A machine gun hammered a burst and one of the figures fell on its face next to a building.

Partially hidden behind the halftrack, George and I began to fire our rifles at the running shapes. My heart was pounding so hard that it was making a rapid physical noise in my ears. I was not aware of anything around me except for my pounding heart and a quick sinking feeling in the pit of my stomach. Leaning against the halftrack, I tore off my right glove that was jamming in the trigger housing of the rifle, threw it away, inserted a fresh clip and began pumping bullets down the street—as fast as I could, aiming at the moving figures. A white caped figure fell in the snow. The clip bounced into the air with a chinging sound after my last shot and I was fumbling in my bandolier for another clip when I became aware that Dunbar behind me was shouting something at me. George was still firing and because of the bang of his rifle I could not understand what was happening behind me. My hands were shaking as I glanced back to try to make out what Dunbar was telling me. A surge of relief swept through me. Two of our jeeps were already on the road speeding toward the bridge. Dunbar, yelling from the driver's seat of our jeep, had the engine racing and was ready to roll. For the first time I could hear shouting and engines starting in the courtyard. I grabbed George by the arm, swinging him around, and we vaulted into the jeep as it was moving onto the main road. Not looking back, we hunched forward as Dunbar hurtled the little vehicle at the bridge ahead. There was no traffic on the bridge, but we crossed it at a speed so great that our wheels left the surface of the roadway as we hit the crown bump in the center of the span. We crashed back down on the far side of the bridge in the glow from the flaming town and sped down the curiously deserted road. A mile out of Hagenau we stopped to look back.

A cherry red glow, punctuated by several columns of flame, stood out on the near snow covered horizon. The barrel of my M-1 was still warm in my bare right hand.

"Jesus, that was close," said George. "I hope the others made it out," he added.

Trailing behind the other jeeps, we drove without lights across a beautiful peaceful landscape. The contrast between what we had just been through and that of the untouched beauty of the countryside was unbelievable and when a bright moon broke through the clouds, the scene was almost dazzling. The deep snow seemed to be covered with diamond dust as the ice particles on its surface reflected the moonlight. The sheer emotional relief, compounded by the spectacular vista, was so intense that when I heard someone crying, I didn't comment. I felt like crying myself. On our way to Hockfelden we passed very few vehicles, only twice going around armored columns on the roadway. We saw no troops either on the road or in the fields and villages. After Hagenau only a few miles away, it was almost as though we were driving on a different planet that had no knowledge of war. The cold clear air was almost refreshing as it whipped through the open jeep, biting into our cheeks and noses.

We were the first to arrive at the deserted railroad station in Hockfelden so we forced open the lock on the station door and made a fire in the potbellied iron stove by breaking up some old furniture that we found in an office adjoining the waiting room. We heated our C-rations on the top of the stove and as always, burned our fingers trying to open the cans with our tin snapover can openers. Candles were lighted in the rapidly warming room, but exhaustion soon replaced any conversation as we fell asleep.

I had learned that we had made our escape around the halftrack because Fletcher, driving the second jeep, had smashed his vehicle, time after time, into the rubble next to the gate, forcing a narrow opening wide enough to allow the jeep to leave the courtyard. Before falling asleep next to the stove, I made a mental note to thank him again for his quick thinking.

I was awakened by someone actually kicking me in the side, not just once but several times. Angrily, I jumped to my feet, but I was stopped cold by the face of Lester, the orderly room clerk. He looked like an old man, but it wasn't his haggard appearance that made me hesitate; it was the cold hatred showing on his face.

"Come with me," he ordered with no evidence in his voice or manner that he expected me to do anything but exactly that.

I started to pick up my rifle and helmet but he told me in an even voice to leave everything where it was. I was told that I wouldn't need anything. I followed him outside into a morning mist that swirled around the station platform. We walked in silence for a short distance on the wood planks and then entered an office that had in it an ancient telegraph key, bolted to a small wooden table. On the other side of the room sat three officers on straight backed wooden chairs, leaning forward. Elbows on their knees, they studied me closely. Two of the men were dressed in GI issue olive drab combat jackets open at the throat, showing single silver bars. The other man was dressed in an officer's dress shirt, much darker, sporting Captain's bars. He too wore an open field jacket. All three were armed with 45's hanging from their hips. The two 1st Lieutenants' boots were muddy and dirt was caked on their pants below the knees.

I had never seen any of them before but as there was an evident seriousness about the three, I found myself straightening my shoulders and pulling my own combat jacket into place. I shuffled my feet into a position of attention and stood before them, arms at my sides. Lester moved over to sit casually on a low window sill.

I began to feel very apprehensive and I'm sure that my nervousness began to show. The Captain, clearing his throat slightly, said in a hard voice, "Sergeant, we are holding you for court-martial for desertion in the face of the enemy."

I must have blinked because his statement was the most serious single thing that anyone had ever said to me in my life. As I felt the blood rushing to my face and my heart beginning to pound, he went on to say, "You stole three jeeps and left an area of combat without orders to do so. You may have cost the lives of several men in this company and we are not going to let you get away with it."

I struggled with my throat; it wouldn't swallow; a strange white light began to appear around the edges of my vision and I had trouble standing straight. I began to sway with dizziness. I could not make out the words, but the Captain was saying something to Lester who produced a folding chair from behind the telegraph table and not too gently shoved me into it. I could barely hear what words were being spoken but I soon knew that at least I was not going to pass out. I felt sick. The officers all leaned back in their chairs apparently trying to give me a chance to compose myself.

I concentrated very hard, looking at the backs of my hands in my lap. They were both trembling. I took several deep breaths and the room stood still and the Captain slowly came back into both focus and full color.

Satisfied that I was going to be all right, the Captain went on, "Sergeant, as you know you could get a death penalty for these charges. They are very, very serious."

He gave me a few moments to think it over and then asked, "In your own words, will you tell us what happened last night in Hagenau?"

I studied the faces, looking for either the joke line or some measure of sympathy. There was neither. Three stony stares were all I received for my effort.

Finally gaining some control over myself, I related as simply as I could the sequence of events that lead up to the little squad leaving the courtyard. My voice was unsteady and once I had the awful feeling that I might cry. When I was finished one of the Lieutenants asked, "Who is this Fletcher?"

I explained that he was a buck Sergeant in my squad of replacements, really second to me in rank.

The three, with heads together, said a few low words to one another, the Captain nodded, straightened up and asked Lester to bring

Sgt. Fletcher in. The four of us sat facing one another in absolute silence after Lester had left the office. I had no idea what to expect next. I only knew that our bespectacled orderly clerk was a loner and that he was also smart. Smart enough to place any blame on me at any time, I thought.

In a few moments Lester brought in the Sergeant who stood beside my chair. At that moment I hated him, not only for what he was about to do to me but because he was immaculately dressed in comparison to the rest of us. His pants, neatly pressed, were regulation, fitted into his clean combat boots and his G.I. knit pullover sweater was without holes or dirt anywhere. He even had a cap on his head. But when I looked at his face, I was totally surprised. Even before anyone in the room could speak, tears began to roll down his cheeks, his lips worked to control himself but he could not. Cupping his face in his hands, he began a racking cry. He could not stop, his shoulders shook, his cap fell unnoticed to the floor and his overweight frame wobbled where he stood.

I glanced at the officers who were clearly surprised and I guessed embarrassed by this unexpected loss of control.

The Captain motioned for Lester to take me out of the room. As we closed the door I could hear one of the officers speaking softly to Fletcher, trying to calm him down. Although surprised by his action, I was not puzzled by his outburst. It was an act, put on to demonstrate that although he was contrite, he had only followed my orders. He would explain how sorry he was for my deceit and they would forgive him.

I was taken to a small separate windowless room, which appeared to have been a place for railroad baggage storage. More properly it could have been called a closet because it was so small. There was no furniture, only a few empty wide shelves for the storage of suitcases or boxes. Lester motioned for me to go in, which I did, but before I could turn around he had closed the door. I heard a key turn in the lock.

Enough light came in from around the old loosely fitting door that I soon could see well enough to sit on the wooden planked floor with my back resting against the far wall facing the oppressive door. It was the first time in my life that I had ever been locked in a room. I tried to think but a deep dread dominated and held me in a solitary grip. In the darkest part of my depression was the question, "What will my family think when they hear this?" and the answer, "I have shamed my parents."

In my auguish I knew that they would find out that I had been court-martialed for cowardice—perhaps *shot* for cowardice. I no longer could help it. I sat with my face in my hands in a railroad station in Hockfelden, France, barely 21 years of age, and cried bitterly to myself. After some time, exhausted, I stopped.

Waiting in the semi-darkness of the little cell seemed like an eternity to me. Once, after hearing trucks outside, I feared that the company had left, forgetting that I was locked inside. Strangely enough I did not wonder what would happen to me, I simply assured that my life was over, that it had ended in a disgrace so final that it could only result in my complete withdrawal from the human race. I was no longer a person, I was only a stump of silent numbness.

The key turned in the lock and blinking against the sudden light, I followed a non speaking Lester back to the telegraph room. He held the door for me to enter and as I passed him I searched his face for some clue, but there was only impassive avoidance. The folding chair was gone. Fletcher was gone. I stood at attention before the three officers, biting my lip to keep my composure.

"At ease Sergeant," said the Captain.

Did I hear correctly? Wasn't there just hint of forgiveness or at least sympathy in his voice as he spoke those three words?

The Captain leaned forward on his elbows. He started to speak to me in a low voice. "First, I want to explain to you that your company commander is not here because he is looking out for the casualties from last night." He continued, "I am from battalion and was sent here to help conduct his investigation. These men, he gestured to the Lieutenants, are company officers whom you have never met."

He then asked one of the officers to explain to me what had happened to the company at the Moder bridge the night before.

The Lieutenant, a young articulate man with blond close-cropped hair, described the events that had taken place. He was precise, but I thought, without showing any hatred toward me.

That part of the town had been overrun by the German night attack. The company was late in leaving because of some misunderstanding or a foul-up in communications. At this point the Battalion Captain flushed a little and studied the seam in his trousers.

The half track blocking the gate had delayed them further until it could be hammered out of the way by heavy trucks. Apparently the column itself became tangled inside the courtyard because lead vehicles intending to pass through the gate were jeeps and *had to be* moved out of the way to make room for the truck, which was to be used to clear the disabled half track. By the time the column could pass through the gate the Germans had a tank in the street and the last two trucks in the column were destroyed on the bridge by cannon fire. There had been a number of casualties, although the blond Lieutenant was uncertain of the exact number.

When he stopped speaking, he looked expectantly at the Captain who cleared his throat and told me some astonishing news.

Sergeant Fletcher had admitted openly to them that because he had been so terrified, he had lied to me about orders to leave. He had never seen the company commander, had never received orders.

After telling me this, the Captain sat up straight, looked briefly at both Lieutenants, nodded as he said to me in a kind voice, "Sergeant, we have concluded that this event was not your fault. True, you might have double-checked with the orderly room, but with the battle and confusion we feel that you were justified in believing Sgt. Fletcher. He has admitted that he lied. We do not want an incident involving replacements at this time."

He glanced at the blond Lieutenant for an instant, and returning to me added, "Perhaps if you and your men had been absorbed better into the company roster, you would not have felt so isolated and independent."

This time it was the Lieutenant's turn to turn red and to study his creases. "One more thing, Sergeant," the Captain said in a low fatherly voice, "you have no responsibility for the casualties last night. Your leaving when you did in no way delayed the departure of the company. In fact if you had stayed to leave with the column, you too might have been caught on the bridge."

My eyes were watering and I could feel a tightness in my throat. I blinked back the tears and studied these men. In a sudden flood of feeling, I knew that they were friends, they had been fair and just to me, they were beautiful.

"You are free to go Sergeant," the Captain said.

I snapped to attention and with an unpracticed sincerity, I gave them the most military salute I could manage under emotional circumstances. I even tried to keep my broken finger as straight as I could.

"Thank you, Sir," I burbled.

Doing a careful about-face, I marched through the door, which Lester opened for me. Outside alone on the station platform in the clean bright air, I leaned my head on a wooden post of the station and sobbed with an uncontrolled relief exploding in my chest.

"What happened to Fletcher?" asked George when I finally returned to the waiting room. "He came in here, picked up his stuff and left with someone in a jeep, seemed to be in a hurry."

We learned later that day from a now friendlier Lester that Sgt. Fletcher had been transferred. We were never to hear of him again.

CHAPTER XV

WINTER WAR

For three days we waited for orders in the railroad station. Hockfelden had become a center of furious military activity and alarming rumors. To our surprise, trains began chuffing into the station to unload armor from long strings of flatcars. Traffic on the road going in all directions was continuous, even during darkness, and columns of truck loaded infantry and artillery kept constant movement. With so much activity it was difficult to tell whether we were retreating or advancing since movement seemed to be in all directions but mostly on the main East and West highway. The rumors, sometimes merely words shouted from the rear of a passing truck, were sometimes encouraging, sometimes not.

We were aware that a major German attack had been launched on New Year's eve with the probable intention of cutting off the 7th Army on the Rhine Valley plain. The enemy drive had penetrated deep along the crest of the Vosges with the objective of retaking the Saverne Gap and closing the Western escape route. They were perilously close to doing so. We heard that a full battalion of the 13th Armoured Division had surrendered without a fight. We heard that Strasbourg had been abandoned but that Hagenau had been retaken by the Americans with help from the French and had done so in spite of its untenable position. Hagenau was in serious threat of becoming another Bastogne if the Germans succeeded in outflanking and cutting the roads. Stories were told that the roads out of Strasbourg were jammed by civilians fleeing the undefended city for fear of German retaliation. The population flight was being called, "The night of the great fear" by the inhabitants of the important city. There were rumors of American counterattacks, Germans surrendering in division strength and of giant enemy air attacks on France, even on Paris.

273

However on January 5th, the most alarming news was confirmed by our company officers. A crack German SS Division, under the command of Reichsfuhrer Heinrick Himmler himself, had recrossed the Rhine between Hagenau and Strasbourg and had captured the small city of Offendorf and two other towns South of Hagenau. The German ring was closing from both the East and the West and our front was in real danger of imminent collapse. There was open talk among the men of having to fall back behind the Vosges in order to save the American 7th Army.

We kept our gear handy, our equipment ready to roll. Big Red began to speak to me on my occasional visits to the orderly room that had been established in a hotel across from the station. Once on the station platform in the bitter cold, the blond Lieutenant from the telegraph room shot me a tight smile as he hurried past. People were quiet as they moved around, some even grim, and there was no laughter in Hockfelden. With our company's help, small supply depots of stacks of fuel, ammunition and food began to appear in the snowy fields along the main East-West highway and MP's worked hard to keep traffic flowing as smoothly as possible through the narrow streets of the town. We kept a watch on the hotel from the station, waiting for a battalion jeep to bring the orders for a pull-out.

In a forest somewhere North of Saverne, we entered a windowless concrete bunker, one of three or four, which had no heat or light. With groans and curses, we threw our gear on the cold slab floor, trying to see by the light coming through the doorway into the dark refrigerator like interior. Peering into the gloom, I could make out rows and rows of storage racks that all but filled the long narrow room. Several flashlight beams struck through the darkness revealing bundles of something stacked neatly on the metal shelves of the storage racks. Finding my own flashlight, I approached the closest rack hoping to find either something valuable or at least useful, such as food or fuel to burn. Instead I found sword blades. Tightly wrapped in heavy cord and Cosmolined with grease were literally hundreds of thousands of wide blades without handles or even hilts. The blades were dated 1763, carried a Toledo marking and the seal of Louix XV. They were in excellent mint condition. Most were wide with thick grooves along the length of the blade but there were also thinner blades with only slight grooves.

We discovered that the bunker had a doorway at each end so we began carrying the bundles, two men to a load, to the open ends, pitching blades and finally the racks themselves far out into the snow.

Even though there was a light snow falling, we commented that it was at least 10% colder in the bunker than it was outside in the snow. While most of us worked to clear some space inside, several men started the necessary scrounging for oil drums and for something that would serve as stovepipe.

Even though the frigid building was less than we had hoped for, it did represent the first real shelter that we had seen for many days. Except for an occasional shelled or burned farmhouse or barn, we had been outside in the winter and snow for almost two weeks. By now I was wearing over my own long johns and trousers, a pair of German fur lined coverall pants, German fur lined Luftwaffe boots, and had found an Italian cap with ear flaps. I could be recognized as an American only because of my G.I. combat field jacket. In addition I had stolen from a Sherman tank crew a pair of long gloves that fitted by adjustable straps almost to my elbows. The work of moving the blades was warming but even then I could feel the cold deep within me. My face was numb, my clouded breath forming ice on my wool knit scarf, wrapped across my chin and mouth. More than anything that I could wish for, I wanted, even for just a short period of time, to be warm.

We walked back and forth, quietly, not speaking much, a line of moving, almost desperate men.

By early winter nightfall, we had space, candlelight, and an oil fire burning in a drum next to one of the doors. Miraculously some stovepipe had been found, probably stolen, and we had an exhaust system trailing smoke and fumes out through an opening that we punched in the wooden space above the doorway. Within hours the concrete interior warmed enough so that our complaining could be switched from the cold to the lack of proper food. Grumbling loudly, we ate our familiar C rations. Soon afterward I received word from the C.O. that I was to mount a 24 hour two man guard on the bunker, beginning at once. I cursed to myself because assigning men to this miserable detail was not going to be an easy task because a steely bitterness was beginning to envelop the platoon. It was deeply felt by everyone, including me I'm afraid, and only found its release in a growing defiance for our officers and noncoms. The bitterness came because of the weather, the seeming fruitless moving around in the endless forests, the unnecessary suffering and the apparent lack of understanding from our leaders. The inability to supply us with hot food and proper winter clothing was also paramount to this deep resentment.

I sat on my duffle bag and with my flashlight prepared a list of guards to cover the next 24 hours. Because of the cold, I planned for only two hour watches. No man could survive unprotected outside for more than two hours. I included myself and the other platoon noncoms on the duty roster. When I called out the names there was, at first, an ominous silence but I was relieved when after finally reading the long list, to hear the almost forgotten cry of "48!"

The bunker fairly rang with the full chant, then with muttering and cursing, men moved to identify their relief guards and the potentially dangerous crisis was, at least, temporarily past. I honestly don't know what I would have done if they had refused to be assigned to the guard duty. In an hour we had exterior guards watching both ends of our shelter and had been informed that a latrine was being dug beyond the last bunker. This later announcement was received with laughter. The thoughts of the luxury of a latrine, to men who had been living like frozen animals in the woods, was preposterous.

I calculated that I had not defecated for at least four days, not since the floor of a farmhouse somewhere North of Thionville. With full nightfall the bunker became comfortable. In fact for the first time in over three weeks, I was able to take off my field jacket, two pairs of pants and even my boots before wrapping myself in my blankets to lie on the concrete floor.

I did not sleep at first because I wanted to watch the rear door to make sure that the guards remained outside and that they were notifying their relief properly. After the first two hours the guard came awkwardly through the door, stiff with cold, rifle slung on his shoulder, trailing a blast of cold air, snowflakes swirling in a frenzy behind him before he could close the door. We huddled in our blankets, waiting for the warmth to return.

It was near the beginning of the second shift when I must have dozed, consciously savoring the body warm blankets. I was awakened by the familiar blast of air that entered the now dark room, which was lighted only by the flickering red light from the oil heater. I lay on my side watching a figure close the door softly and move to the heater. My first reaction was one of anger over the guard leaving his post to come inside for some heat. My second reaction was one of puzzlement. The figure warming his hands over the oil drum was not the guard. This tall man was dressed in a long cape with a large wing-like collar pulled up around his face. He wore a flat hat of some kind on his head and had no rifle. I watched him carefully as I slid my hand outside my blankets to reach for my pistol, which was next to me on the floor.

All at once there was a loud clattering noise opposite from where I lay and before I could react a voice near the clatter shouted the single word, "Hey!"

At the sounds the figure turned quickly and slipped out through the door. By now I was sitting up, a dark fear that this was not the dream I had begun believing it to be. The man opposite me was also in a sitting position fumbling with a weapon.

"Did you see that?" he asked loudly enough to begin to disturb sleeping figures on the floor.

I cautioned him to be quiet as I struggled out of my wrapped blankets. Free at last I went to the doorway and opened it a few inches, my loaded pistol in my hand. The snow had stopped falling and the sky had cleared off enough for starlight to brighten the ground over the freshly fallen snow. I looked in all directions but could see no one, not even the guard. As I was about to close the door against the biting cold, I saw what was to remain a haunting mystery to me for the rest of my life. There were *no footprints* anywhere in the snow outside that bunker door. A different chill ran up the back of my head, caused not by the temperature, but because in that instant I was afraid for my sanity and for my mortality.

I waved off my awakened companion, who was named Sands, and went back to bed to lie sleepless for hours, watching the comings and goings of cold guards as they went in and out. If it had been a dream, how could anyone else have seen it? If I had been hallucinating, how could Sands have been any part of it?

I cautiously talked to Sands the next morning, assuring him that it was probably just a French woodcutter or farmer who stopped by to get warm. He explained the clatter. Armed with a carbine, he had pressed the clip release catch instead of the safety. The carbine designer, in his wisdom, had placed both releases next to one another on the weapon and the world will never know how many men died attempting to release the safety but instead found themselves disarming the little rifle. The clatter was caused by a full clip of bullets falling to the concrete floor.

I never told Sands about the clear cover of snow outside the door.

The next day we witnessed several miracles—a mess hall was opened with hot food, the latrine became useful, and out of the late afternoon gloom appeared my old friend, Lt. Harding.

I was sitting on my blankets cleaning my pistol when through the doorway next to the heater stepped Harding. He saw me immediately and smiling, came over to me. It was the first time in a month that I had seen anyone from my old company. I had almost forgotten most of them.

We exchanged greetings and I learned that he had been assigned as courier officer to keep contact with company personnel during this reassignment period. He drove around, delivering mail and checking on performance. He had some welcome mail for me and for the others from the old company, but the best news that he could bring me was in his question, "Hey, would you like to be my driver? I'm supposed to have one and I've been looking for you. I'll get you reassigned out of this outfit if you want to go with me."

It took only a few minutes for me to have everything I owned packed in the back of Harding's jeep. It took him a little longer to arrange with Big Red for me to leave.

As we left the bunkers in the deep snow, we drove past an American supply depot that had been deliberately burned by our troops during the recent pull-out. As we skidded past, I noticed stacks of charred typewriters and mimeograph machines near one end of a large collapsed warehouse. Destroying office equipment seemed wasteful, but at the same time there was a gleeful satisfaction in seeing the justice in it.

In spite of the fact that I was assigned officially as the driver, Lt. Harding always drove. He liked to drive; it gave him time to think of ways to make money. Our task was both easy and difficult, easy because we were virtually without any direct supervision or time frame, and difficult because we were often in danger, both from the driving conditions caused by the weather and from the Germans. Our duty was to run a continuous loop of contact with the 200 men of our original company who had been assigned to some 30 different units scattered along the 7th Army front from Strasbourg in the Rhine Valley to units deep in the Northern Vosges near the mountain town of Wingen. Our travels took us westward through the Saverne Gap to Sarrebourg and as far North as Sarreguemines. Toward the end of January the furious battle of the Moder River had petered out in mountain snowstorms and the 7th Army front was beginning to stabilize. There was still enemy action but there was evidence that German units were being withdrawn from our front to be sent to other more threatening fronts to the North and West. The Rhine River and Strasbourg were once again secure. Only the Colmar pocket to the South remained, but American units were being sent there to assist the French in its destruction. There was an air of optimism once again as we refitted and tried to gain our breath following weeks of desperate fighting. The bitter winter continued to send men to their deaths and we began, at last, to receive some heavy winter clothing. Shoe packs were issued, a heavy rubberized well lined type of goolash, which was to be worn only with heavy socks. They were warm and dry, a great improvement over the standard combat boots that were comfortable but never completely waterproof even with heavy coats of dubbin smeared on the reverse leather surface. Frostbite, frozen feet and trenchfoot, the soldiers' constant companion in wet cold weather, took an enormous toll on the men of the 7th Army. Heavier jackets and long fur-lined hooded parkas were also issued on a limited scale, presumably to the men in the lines who needed them most. It was not uncommon however to see these treasured garments being worn by the troops in support areas, well behind the lines.

The two of us, ranging across the entire front in our jeep, had no trouble in securing food, equipment and clothing. There was great personal value to me in traveling with an officer who had been an enlisted man. Harding would disappear only to return from a supply depot with new jackets, parkas, boots or anything else that we needed. As an officer, he merely signed receipts for these items and we drove away.

At first I distained the new clothes, preferring to keep my German pants and boots and my coveted warm wool Italian cap. But I changed to G.I. issue clothing after we were detained at a roadblock one after-noon near a mountain village. We not only did not know the password and countersign, which is changed constantly to confuse the enemy, but the suspicious rifleman guarding the road actually believed that I was an enemy infiltrator. The suspicion was heightened when he discovered that neither of us knew who had pitched for the Brooklyn Dodgers in 1940 and that we had a schmiesser machine pistol in the jeep. Roadblocks were a constant problem for the both of us because we were always asked questions designed for "red-blooded American men," such as queries about baseball and who was currently married to Betty Grable. We seldom knew any of the answers and reverted instead to smiling and joking. Passwords were answered by Harding who simply said, "Beats the shit out of me!"

On this occasion we were asked to leave the jeep, disarmed, and taken into town at gunpoint to be questioned by a wild-eyed Captain sitting in the hotel lobby. It took only a few minutes to identify us from our dog tags and Harding's officer I.D. card but the incident reversed my feelings for the German clothes and their weapons. At the next supply depot I redressed as a G.I., but I kept my Italian cap, wearing it under my helmet instead of the basic wool knit. We also made a stronger effort to learn what the daily password and countersign was to be, but moving continually along the front presented an almost insur-mountable problem to us. On one occasion a rifleman next to a half track blocking the road gave me the password. Not knowing the coun-tersign, I said, "I don't know it, but I do know the names of all the Presidents of the United States. *Do you?*"

He waved us on but I could see that he was greatly perplexed by my response. I, of course, didn't know the names of all the Presidents but I was fairly sure that if I had begun with George Washington, I could have just recited the names of the men in my company and the roadblock guard would never have known the difference.

Sometimes it would take us several days to complete our run, de-pending upon weather, traffic, and whether or not Harding could dis-cover a worthwhile card game along the way. Somehow we always seemed to be in the immediate vicinity of a good battalion or regimental mess hall around mealtime and with proper introductions and a reason-able explanation, the Lieutenant managed to gain our admittance to the best food in the area. The food, prepared by cooks and served hot, was a welcome change for me. A highlight was an engineering battalion mess that served fresh meat. No one asked where they had gotten it or what sort of animal it had once been.

We stayed overnight in houses, hotels and other buildings—some-times with the units that we were looking for, sometimes on our own. Every town had a billeting officer who would direct us to available shelter. Usually he crowded us in with other men, but it was shelter and it was always warm.

Because of the fluid nature of the war, units shifted around, making it sometimes difficult for us to locate our men from one visit to the next. It was time-consuming and occasionally our wanderings led us into danger.

One of our first loops nearly ended in disaster for me in an unexpected way. Returning from Sarrebourg through the now safe Saverne Gap, we decided to spend the night there after the Lieutenant learned at a fuel stop that there was a game with pretty good stakes taking place in a quartermaster unit in town. Harding arranged for a place for me, dropped me off there, and departed for the game. My billet was a private home, adjoining others alongside the winding main road on the Eastern side of the city. I was given a bed in the cellar, sharing the space with two other amiable transients who knew one another. The rest of the house, although furnished, seemed to be empty of inhabitants. After chow, which we ate with a nearby medical unit, we settled in our cellar, playing a little card game of our own by candlelight. Poker with three people is not much of a challenge, however, and we were just about to give it up about 11:00 p.m. when a thunderous explosion rocked the house.

Although I jumped in the air cursing, my companions seemed not to have noticed the blast. I asked, "What was that?"

They explained that it was "Alsace Alice," a 16 inch railway gun that the Germans had been using for the past few nights in an effort to disrupt traffic in the gap. The Air Corps had been trying to locate the gun that was firing from 35 miles away on the other side of the Rhine. Apparently it was kept in a tunnel during the day and run out at night to be fired when it couldn't be spotted by our aircraft.

"Don't worry," said Tom, one of my new friends. "It takes 18 minutes for them to load and fire the damn thing and we only get three or four shells a night."

"Not only that," said the other man named Eldon, "But they really don't seem to have the right range."

"Yet," Tom added with a grin.

Their remarks did very little to console me. I had seen what much smaller shells could do to buildings and to people and I knew that a 16 inch shell was fired by as large a piece of artillery as you could get.

About 18 minutes later, right on cue, another thunderclap shook the valley, this time further up in the gap.

I had known nothing about Saverne being shelled, so I practiced some words to say when I returned to our headquarters at Molsheim, and blowing out my candle went to bed. In the darkness the cellar was warm and the folding cot a welcome relief from sleeping on the ground or on cement. I was soon asleep being cheered by the fact that 30 minutes had gone by without a communication from the other side of the Rhine River. I assumed that they were finished with their work for the night.

I don't know when it was or how it happened but the next thing I was conscious of was a noise so loud and a simultaneous impact so great that every cell in my body jumped from the shock. Instantly the world above me collapsed, covering me with debris. I gagged in a choking cloud of dust.

The entire incident was so instantaneous that I had no time whatever to do anything but shut my eyes. Fortunately when it happened I was lying on my side and took the full force of the falling house on my right side. Dazed, I had no control over my thoughts, I struggled weakly trying to understand where I was and what I was doing. I drifted somewhere else, vaguely conscious. Breathing the dust was difficult but the panicky need for air brought me around. My next immediate reaction was sheer terror. I was pinned. My head was being held down by some giant hand, I could not move my legs. I tried to shout but the mud from the dust in my mouth only produced a gurgling whimper. I freed an arm, immediately reaching for whatever it was that held my head pinned in place. My free hand grasped something covered with rough fabric. With a strength born of absolute desperation, I struggled, finally wresting my head from under the heavy object. Free from resting on my head, it bumped on the cellar floor, dislodging another shower of dust from above.

I rested, sobbing with relief that my head and upper body were free to move. I tried to look around in the absolute darkness but except for some scattered stars showing through a matrix of crazy timbers above me I could see nothing. Still coughing in the dust, I managed to clear some dirt out of my mouth with my fingers. I felt my head, it did not seem to be bleeding and except for a tender bump that I could feel in my hair, I was O.K.

My overwhelming impulse was to get out of there as quickly as I could but I found that I could not move my legs, they were pinned under something heavy and unyielding. Reaching down with my arm from my sidewise position, I felt a large piece of timber or floor joist from the floor above. My cot had been smashed and I was lying on the floor. By shifting my hips and squirming my legs slowly, I was able to roll over on my back, free from under the weight of my body. I slid out from under the weight and stood up, unsure as to what I should do. Dizzy and suddenly sick, I leaned on a shattered beam trying not to faint. It was only then that, for the first time, I thought of the other two men in the cellar.

"Tom," I croaked, "Eldon, are you all right?"

There was a faint noise from the dark corner of the cellar where I had last seen them sleeping. Climbing over the debris, I struggled through the darkness toward the noise and was glad to hear their voices coming from behind a large obstruction. Among the three of us, we managed to move beams, broken floor and stone that was imprisoning the two of them against the cellar wall. They were both unhurt and amid racking coughs caused by dirt and dust, we managed to agree that we were all alive with no broken bones. Helping one another, we stumbled over the fallen objects until we found a way up out of the cellar. Luckily we were more or less fully clothed. I was without my field jacket but had had sense enough to keep my shoes on when I had gone to bed. The others had done the same. Otherwise we would have had a difficult, if not impossible, climb over the rubble.

Even before we reached ground level, I could hear shouting voices and vehicles moving on the road above us. We finally cleared the rubble, to be witness to a scene from the Inferno. Flashlight and headlight beams were crisscrossing from all directions on what once had been a group of buildings. Men were shouting from the main highway and it seemed as though there were a hundred people running to and from the ruined buildings. Figures holding flashlights scrambled over the ruined houses looking for survivors. I noticed that there were no fires as we joined people running toward the center of the destruction.

By morning light we were able to see that the shell had hit in a fairly open space behind the row of houses next to the highway that snaked through the gap. A large crater marked the point of impact. The old stone buildings, reinforced only with pegged timber, had simply collapsed upon themselves from the concussion from the nearby explosion. Luckily no fires had resulted making rescue work less difficult.

I worked all night in flashlight and headlight beams next to strangers, both military and civilians, as we clawed our way through tons of wreckage listening and looking for injured people. We found many who were simply in shock, some with crushed and bleeding bodies, and several who were beyond our mortal help. They were all taken to a nearby school building where Army medics and French civilian doctors had quickly set up an emergency first aid facility in the gymnasium.

Throughout the long night we carried moaning and screaming French people into the school, laying them in rows on the floor to await their turn for medical attention. They were all mostly women, children and a few older men. The dead were placed against a far wall in a row all of their own.

From the beginning the rescue effort itself was directed by officers from our Army as we combed through the remains of the buildings. Everyone worked feverishly together, bound in a determined spirit of compassion and mercy. I never once thought of the cold or of the fact that I had no gloves and that my fingers and hands were torn and bleeding from lifting stone and timber. Other men next to me were in the same condition but with the need to hurry our task, our own discomfort went unnoticed.

By dawn we had recovered all of the wounded and the dead. Exhausted, we stood around the school in small quiet groups covered with dust, dirt and spattered with dried blood from the victims. Unexpectedly, a Red Cross truck appeared and clean American girls gave us hot coffee and stale doughnuts. I spoke a few words to a bright blond girl from Akron, Ohio, holding the paper cup in my dirty hands and wondering what we were all doing in this place so far from home. Sitting on a stoop in the trampled snow, I was sipping the coffee and eating the donut with a huge appetite when Harding drove by slowly in the jeep. Spotting me, he stopped and asked, "Is that you?"

I was so covered with dirt, hair matted with dust across my forehead, that he almost didn't recognize me.

"Yeah, I guess it's me," I answered, then added, "This was a swell place you found for me to spend the night, Lieutenant."

I climbed in the jeep to learn that his all-night card game had been played on the West end of the town and although he had heard the explosion and commotion, he had actually not known what had happened until he had driven up looking for me. I returned briefly to the cellar to salvage my belongings, finding them covered with rubble. Digging out my helmet, weapon and duffle bag, I was able to see that a large square floor joist had probably saved my life. It had fallen at such an angle that it created a protective roof above my cot, blocking out most of what could have crushed me. Even at this, however, the cot was smashed to the floor and I could see that the weight that had held my head had been the arm of the sofa from the living room above. We left the remains of the house before Tom and Eldon came to find their gear and I never saw them again. I slept all the way back to Molsheim where I cleaned up as well as I could without a shower. Harris got me some new clothes from a quartermaster depot as I heated some water in my helmet and washed the dirt and grime from my face and hands. Putting on new pants, I was surprised to discover a large angry bruise and a small puncture wound on my right leg. I sprinkled some sulfa powder on the deep but almost bloodless mark, put on a Band-Aid and promptly forgot about it. In the late afternoon we started out again on our loop with some mail and some orders for some minor transfers of personnel. I had very little to say, my thoughts were of bleeding children and dying women.

* * * * *

Passing through a plateau, we discovered that a new fighter airstrip had been built since we had been along that route before, so we pulled off the road to watch a plane that was preparing for takeoff. The runway was really only a rolling field that had been cleared of tree stumps, boulders and other obstructions. Trees lined both sides of the mountain meadow, closing in on a packed muddy pathway used as a landing strip. Frozen now with patches of snow showing, the surface was rough with ruts and potholes. Several large tents were pitched on the other side of the runway and four or five fighter planes were parked at all angles among the trees near the tents. Smoke from tent stovepipes served as a makeshift windsock for the pilot of the plane who was about to taxi to the far end of the runway for takeoff.

It was a big fighter bomber plane, a P-47, used for low level bombing and strafing support. A mechanic was leaning into the open canopy of the plane in animated discussion with the pilot who was warming the huge Pratt and Whitney 2000 horsepower engine. Even from our far distance away, the thunderous noise made conversation difficult for us but there was a comforting sense of American power coming from the big radial engine, one of the largest ever made for a single seater fighter plane. Harding and I grinned at one another. Finally the mechanic gave a thumbs up sign, jumped down from the wing root and ran away from the plane, holding his hands over his ears as he scampered backwards to watch the big bird taxi away. Loose snow blew against him from the propeller blast, which also caused the tents to buckle and to flap frantically. The P-47, painted in olive drab camouflage with its white stars on blue circles, filled me with pride as it bumped and lurched down the runway to the engine run up area near the far edge of the evergreen trees. Airplanes, civilian or military, were in my mind, heroic symbols of man's sense of adventure and of his ingenuity in the everlasting struggle with technical challenges. I loved to watch them. Fighter aircraft of World War II still had the aesthetic qualities of flight, soon to be lost in the clumsiness and bulk of the future unheard of power of the jet engine. The British Spitfire, perhaps the most beautiful airplane ever built, the American 51 and the German ME 109 stand out in memory as functional masterpieces of grace and purpose.

Over 15,000 P-47's were built during the war and were appropriately called "Thunderbolts" because they were armed with eight 50 calibre wing machine guns and could carry a ton of bombs. The pilot, with his canopy still open, reached the run up area at the far end of the runway and was increasing power to check his magnetos, his source of electrical power. We could see the plane lunging against the wheel brakes, tail bouncing in its urge to take to the air as the pilot checked both magneto systems separately and then together. Satisfied, the pilot rolled out to the runway, closing his canopy and swinging the plane in a small arc to line up with the rutted pathway. The blue sky dotted with small cumulus clouds gave promise to a clear flight. With a powerful roar, the Thunderbolt started its takeoff roll, tail coming quickly off the ground, the huge four bladed propeller slicing through the cold air.

We were sitting on the warm hood of the jeep watching the spectacle when Harding, grabbing my arm, jumped to the ground and pointed to the sky behind the P-47, which was just clearing the ground. Coming fast over the tree tops directly behind the Thunderbolt was a German ME 109, flashes of flame coming from the 30 millimeter cannon in its nose. A crisp barking sound could be heard over the thunder of the plane taking off as the German quickly closed the distance between the two planes. Before the American pilot could retract his landing gear, the shells struck his aircraft. He was no more than 100 feet in the air as his plane shuddered and pieces of it began falling to the runway. The German had stopped firing even before his sleek fighter passed directly over the stricken American at an incredible speed. The Messerschmidt, its wings a sky blue on the bottom, came within 20 feet of the crippled P-47, its black helmeted pilot in his greenhouse cockpit clearly visible from our view on the ground. Waggling its wings, the German quickly disappeared over the treetops, skimming away to the East. The Thunderbolt engine, smoking, began a stall, then immediately fell off on one wing and with a furious explosion of flame, it went into the ground upside down behind the line of trees. The ground shook from the impact as the ball of flame turned immediately to black smoke. The entire action could not have taken more than four or five seconds.

Men rushed from the tents, piled into several jeeps and went racing away down the frozen runway toward the crash. I could feel on my face, a warmer rush of air coming from the burning plane. There was nothing that we could do to help, clearly there was no survivor in the downed plane, so we climbed quietly into the jeep and drove away.

Sitting next to Harding, I felt somewhat stunned by the horror that we had just witnessed. My thoughts were conflicting. How could such a brutal death come so quickly out of a beautiful blue sky and to one who was totally unaware of catastrophe and who was virtually unable to defend himself? Surely the German had been simply on his way back to a field on the other side of the Rhine when he just happened to see the American taking off. A few unplanned cannon bursts in a few unanticipated seconds gave him a white star to paint on the fuselage of his fighter that night. He was no doubt happy, laughing as he told his squadron of his great luck. And the young man in the Thunderbolt passed through the concentration necessary to lift his heavy fighter from the runway to an instant death, now lost to his family, friends, and to himself. The months of training, of preparing for war, and the quiet secret dreams of what it would be like when it was over were now gone. I was learning that war is not only brutality, it is also a constant inner horror of uncertainty, and that it brings with it especially to youth, a numbing sense that time could be running out.

*   *   *   *   *

Coming out of Sarrebourg toward the gap one late afternoon, we crested a small hill in a blowing snow. Although there was little traffic at the time, visibility was low and driving was treacherous. We were both bundled in our parkas intent on reaching Savern or even Molsheim in time for some evening chow. As we passed the crest, we could see that something ahead was blocking the road, so Harding, cursing at the delay, slowed down to a very low speed, our four-wheel drive whining in protest. As we approached the obstacle, we saw several running figures disappearing into the nearby forest. They looked like French civilians. As we got closer, we could see that there had been an accident. A jeep had hit the back end of a civilian truck with such force that the little vehicle was wedged fast under the bed on the truck. The jeep had a 14th Armour stencil on its rear bumper, its windshield and canvas top had been sheared off by the flat metal bed of the larger truck.

As we slid to a complete stop, we could see no one around. Jumping out into the snow, we discovered two soldiers, both officers, lying side by side on the road. There was no one in the truck and except for fast fading footprints in the snow leading away from the accident into the forest, there was no sign that anyone had ever been there. We bent over the men on the ground. One was clearly dead—his skull broken horizontally above his eyebrows, his hair blackened with blood. The other man, Lieutenant's bars shining brightly on his open collar, was still alive but in dreadful condition. His face had been literally torn off when the jeep had slammed under the truck. His nose was ripped back and lay on his forehead among splintered fragments of bone. Bright red bubbles of blood, coming from a gaping hole where his mouth and nose had been, would form and then burst, spattering the new snow next to his head with little droplets of red. We could not apply a pressure bandage because it would suffocate him so we knelt helplessly beside him doing nothing. Harding flagged down a truck going toward Sarrebourg, telling the driver to send help for the dying man. Returning to kneel again, he helped me to cover the man with my parka. As we were doing this, we noticed a terrible thing. The man had been robbed. He, and the dead man, had been dragged from the wreck and robbed. Their pockets were all turned inside out and both of their shoulder holsters were empty. The dead man's belt and boots had also been taken. The civilians whom we had seen running from the wreck had systematically stripped the dead and dying Americans of everything they had.

I cursed.

By the time an ambulance and an MP jeep had arrived from Sarre-bourg, it was growing dark and mercifully the red bubbles had stopped. We left the scene as the two bodies were being loaded in the ambulance and driving carefully, we entered Saverne. We looked for a place to eat but finally agreed to drive on to Molsheim. Neither one of us was very hungry.

*   *   *   *   *

We stopped the jeep next to a modest stone house on the outskirts of the city, Harding announcing that he had to see someone for a mi-nute. I was mildly curious as he rapped politely on the front door but I was not surprised when the door was opened by a small young woman in a black knitted sweater. She was a pretty woman with an oval face framed by dark hair. Her dark eyes opened wide and she smiled broadly when she saw us standing there. Ushering the two of us into a warm kitchen, she made us sit at a small wooden table while she departed. I said nothing to Harding but I noticed him watching her figure as she left the room. I certainly had watched her figure, which was very good, especially her breasts, which were covered only by the sweater and which swung in a tantalizing manner when she walked. She reentered the room followed by an older woman who greeted Har-ding with obvious affection. After introductions, Harding and the young woman left the kitchen and I heard them going upstairs. The old woman and I sat at the kitchen table without speaking. I drummed my fingers on the table, tried smiling, but gave it up when her reaction was to stare at me stoically. She had thin grey hair, dark button eyes and a very respectable moustache, which curled up a bit at the ends. After a few moments of an uneasy silence, she sighed, rose to her trou-bled feet and waddled across the small kitchen to bang around in a cupboard full of pots and pans. Producing a huge blackened iron skillet, she placed it on the wood-burning stove next to the table. Satisfied that there was a sufficient fire in the stove, she proceeded to break fresh eggs in the skillet. As the half dozen eggs popped and crackled, she found a loaf of French bread in another cupboard and cut it in half with what could have passed as an oversized machette. With a large wooden spoon, the old woman began digging out the soft white bread from inside the crust until she had made a crust-only container out of the half loaf of bread. I watched her with deep curiosity but my real senses were occupied with the sweet smells of frying eggs. The small kitchen, warm from the stove, was filled with the distinctive aroma of fresh eggs popping in real butter. Inhaling in long deep breaths, I savored a marvelous odor that I had not smelled since childhood when my mother

287

would make a special Sunday morning breakfast for me and my sister. As I sat, trying not to exhale, holding the delicious smell in my nose, the woman scooped the eggs from the skillet and filled the crust container with them. Then without a word she surprised me by handing the half loaf to me. With a reverence proper only for the deeply religious, I held the warm crust container in my hands and thanked Him in a solemn voice. I bit slowly through the crackling crust and tasted the steaming hot eggs. I had not eaten a fresh egg since leaving the United States. The flavor of sweet butter and bursting yellow yolks, combined with a bread that only the French can devise, was sublime. I ate slowly, filling my mouth, chewing each separate bite carefully and completely, before filling my mouth again. All too soon the miracle was gone, leaving me only to check between my teeth with my tongue, searching and finding particles of bread crust. Wetting my fingertip, I salvaged the crumbs that had fallen on my lap and on the table. There was no question about it, the fresh egg and breadcrust combination was the best thing I had ever eaten.

I walked over to the woman who was now scrubbing the skillet in a pan of soapy water, her back to me. She jumped when I put my arms almost around her plump body and hugged her with a genuine warmth. Turning, she smiled and kissed me on the cheek, her moustache brushing the corner of my nose. As I was thanking her again, we both heard a rhythmic bumping noise coming from the room above us. Making a clucking sound, the woman rolled her eyes in mock disapproval as we both sat again at the kitchen table, this time to talk quietly about the war and fresh food. Harding and the young woman eventually entered the kitchen looking a little flushed, arms around one another's waists.

Later we drove away, not speaking, each with his own secret thoughts of true pleasures in the world. I found another piece of bread crust between two of my teeth and smiled.

*   *   *   *   *

A mile or so beyond the deserted village, we discovered a tank destroyer unit of six vehicles parked off the road among the scattered pine trees. Harding thought that he recognized the group, so we parked the jeep and went over to talk to the men who seemed to be resting, working on the T.D.'s in a relaxed manner. It turned out that he knew some of the officers, so while he was sitting under a tree talking to them, I tried to barter for some 10 in 1 rations with a TD crew. The snow under the trees was very light and there was a pleasant feeling of the softness of pine needles under foot. When I told them what I was doing, the crew was friendly, badgering me about the soft life I was leading driving around the countryside. I learned that they were preparing to move out soon to secure a road junction held by the Germans about a mile up the road. No one seemed concerned about it because late reports indicated that the Krauts had already pulled out. The TD unit was waiting for some air cover however, the plan being that the suspected German positions around the road junction were to be softened up by fighter bombers before the column moved up. One of the officers with Harding was speaking into a walkie-talkie unit, stopping occasionally to bang it on its side with the palm of his hand. He finally threw it on the ground.

Mild laughter erupted from the group around him. The casual picnic-like mood of the men in the trees changed when we heard the approach of low flying planes from the South. Two P-47's each carrying two bombs roared over the treetops, the wing man for the lead fighter bomber tucked neatly behind his leader's wing. As soon as the thunder of their passing had faded, orders were given—men climbed into their TD's, engines burst into life, and the tracked vehicles moved toward the nearby treeline. Harding and I walked behind the blue smoke monsters curious to see how they would deploy for an attack. Before we reached the edge of the trees, we could already hear the crump of bombs a short distance away, a sign that the attack had begun on the road junction. The TD's moved out in the woods in a line onto a stubble cornfield and stopped, big engines popping at idle speed. In the open we could see the planes in the clear sky, diving one at a time to drop their second bombs. Black smoke was rising beyond a second stand of trees on the other side of the field and seeing the smoke, several men in their open tank chassis cheered and shook their fists in the air. After the bombs were dropped, the two planes, big radial engines booming, came back straight toward us at low level, leaping over the far treeline before turning over the cornfield, slamming into a sharp banked turn, bounding away to the East.

In a few moments the commander, a Captain, standing in the TD on the end of the line, gave the forward signal, engines roared as the beasts began to lurch forward. At that instant the ground around the vehicles exploded in the cornfield and the P-47s, wingtip to wingtip, flashed by overhead. Harding and I, standing back in the trees to watch the destroyers depart, pressed ourselves against the tree trunks as branches began to rain down through the edge of the forest. We had just been strafed by our planes, firing a combined number of sixteen 50 calibre machine guns. There was great confusion among the tankers. Those who were able to move quickly scattered into the cornfield, sending up great chunks of black earth from their racing tracks. Some men jumped from the TD's and ran back into the woods, many without weapons or helmets. People were scattering but in the two stalled or disabled tanks, crewmen were swinging machine guns around to face the direction in which the planes had departed. The Captain, holding a pressure bandage to his face, began running over to the stationary tanks as the planes reappeared, this time higher and beyond the woods. They were apparently either uncertain about what they had just done or they were surveying the damage. It was quickly obvious that the respite was temporary as both fighters banked and drove back at the cornfield on their second run. In the short time between attacks some of the men had retrieved their weapons and the maneuvering TD's were manning their own 50 calibres ready to answer back. As soon as the 47's flattened out in a shallow dive, the tank destroyers opened fire with every available weapon. The noise was enormous as a tracer curtain of bullets was sent into the air at the oncoming planes. The tremendous ground fire must have put both fighters off target because one "jinked" and fired into the forest again and the other tore eight rows of bouncing dirt and snow through the empty section of the cornfield. The machine guns swung quickly to follow the planes, cascades of empty shells and linkage tumbling to the ground. Trees cracked and crashed behind us and we could hear large branches and chunks of bark and debris thumping on the ground as the firing stopped.

"Watch it," someone shouted, "Here they come again!"

But they did not return, instead we could see them climbing together to the West, I thought that I could see a thin trail of blue smoke trailing back from the wing man.

Miraculously, no one had been killed, but several men, the Captain included, had been wounded in the attack. One of the TD's could not be restarted so a messenger was sent back to battalion to protest the attack and to request a postponement on securing the road junction. We took our leave of the unlucky company, walking back to our unhit jeep in the woods through piles of freshly cut tree branches. The effect of the American's strafing power was very impressive.

Several days later, on a bulletin board in our headquarters in Molsheim, I read an ungrammatical directive from division. It stated that "effective immediately ground troops would not fire at aircraft irregardless of their nationality." Our TD friends must have hit that son of a bitch.

* * * * *

We had picked up Dugan from a vehicle repair company North of Sarrebourg in the mountains. He was being transferred back to Molsheim to rejoin our company headquarters and although it was snowing when we picked him up, Harding decided we could make it all the way back to Molsheim before dark. The jeep was open at the time. We had left the framework for the canvas top at a repair shop for some necessary welding. We had snapped it in two, sliding into a railing on an ice covered bridge one dark night, and the canvas cover would not stay put without being stretched in place by the folding frame.

Harding and I sat in the front, leaning forward for as much protection as we could get from the windshield, but Dugan perched in the rear was completely exposed to the snow and freezing air. We were well back in the mountains on a road so narrow that it made driving difficult and at times hazardous as we bumped and slid down long passages through the forest in a snow that had become thicker by the minute. Visibility was very poor and because of the cold, we did not attempt to speak to one another as we drove.

Although Harding and I had our parka hoods pulled up over our helmets, Dugan was still wearing his issue overcoat and short Army gloves, which left his wrists exposed.

Dugan had always been a very quiet person. He was a small man from a ravine in West Virginia and had been a coal miner all of his life in a family of coal miners. Uneducated, he had few skills beyond an uncanny flair with growing things. He grew flowers and vegetables around the post in Warminster and was a favorite odd jobs man with the company officers. Married, he had two children, both boys destined for the mines. He never mixed much with the men in the company, not for unfriendly reasons, but rather because he had nothing in common with anyone. He did not drink, smoke, or womanize. Neither did he read; we suspected that it was probably because he did not know how, for he never received any mail nor was he ever seen writing a letter home. However, he was cheerful, as though he was away from home at summer camp or on a vacation trip of some kind. I always believed that after 10 years in the coal mines, he was taking simple pleasure from walking around on the surface of the earth, tending to green and growing plants.

On this day in the Vosges, there was precious little that was green and growing except for the endless forest now being buried in huge white snowflakes. Alone on the back road we pushed our four-wheel drive jeep slowly through drifts, which were building and making progress difficult on the narrow pavement.

Grinding up a slight hill, we came to a small farmhouse and a partially collapsed shed at a crossroads. I nodded as Harding pulled off the highway and parked by two 6-bys that were standing next to the house. As he turned off the engine, I turned for the first time since we had left to look back at Dugan.

My first thought was that he must have fallen out of the jeep, for there was nothing in the back but a pile of snow. I was about to speak to Harding when a small short gloved hand punched its way out of the center of the snow pile. It reached up and proceeded carefully to dig a hole near the top of the mound.

Harding and I watched, fascinated, as the hand, making little circular motions, continued to enlarge the hole until we could see a face. At least we could see two wide unblinking eyes peering out at us. Harding, at last, shouted, "Dugan, are you all right?"

The hand stopped moving and after a few moments, a small voice from inside the mound of snow said, "The only way I could be colder would be to be bigger."

We dug him out, surprised that so much snow had fallen on him in such a short time. Except for chattering teeth and red wrists, he seemed to be none the worse for his temporary burial, so we three struggled to the door of the farmhouse, which we found bolted shut. Shutters covered the few windows and there was no smoke coming from the single stone chimney. The house was locked and empty.

We were about to climb back in the jeep when I noticed some oily smoke coming through the shattered roof of the shed that had been built behind a high stone wall, probably as a shelter for stock.

Climbing through the drifts in the still falling snow, we discovered four men sitting on the ground around a gasoline fed fire.

They greeted us with measured indifference, inviting us unenthusiastically to join them around their fire. There was some shelter from the snow but the battered roof did not keep out all of the large flakes. The value of the shed was in the stone wall, which gave protection from the wind and permitted an open fire to be built.

We sat in a circle around the fire, feet perilously close to the flame, which was fed periodically by one of the men who splashed gasoline from a C ration can on a few pieces of damp wood. At first we sat in silence, grateful for the heat on our feet and faces. Dugan seemed particularly grateful. In time we learned that the four men were driving the trucks to Bouxwiller on the other side of the mountain range and had also stopped at the house for some shelter from the storm. They were waiting for the snow to stop.

Conversation occurred in bursts, centered around the same old questions, "Where are you from? What outfit are you with? How long have you been here, etc?"

Once Dugan unintentionally called Harding, "Sir" and that ended most talk when the four fire builders discovered that there was an officer among them. They need not have worried, since the Lieutenant was completely at home with enlisted men.

For almost an hour we sat in the snow looking like a group of very cold Indians attending an unproductive powwow. At one point one of the four said to one of his companions, "Jim, I think your shoe is on fire."

Jim, without moving, looking blandly at his shoe and after a few moments, replied, "Naw, I think it's my pants." He continued to sit there without moving.

The rest of us studied the smouldering edge of his trouser leg for a long time and watched as finally the tiny flame lost interest and went out.

The snow began to taper off so Harding, Dugan and I pushed ahead to Molsheim, arriving there well after midnight.

*   *   *   *   *

Crouched over, helmet bobbing and carrying a rifle, a man ran toward us on the sunken road. He was taking great care to keep his head down below the level of a snowy embankment, which shielded the twisting roadway leading into the valley floor far ahead. Our jeep slid to a stop, still in the trees, which opened in a few yards onto a large snow covered field. The narrow rutted road left the forest just ahead to cross the open field on its way to the valley. The man straightened as he entered the heavy treeline and approached the jeep, breathing heavily, puffs of steam coming from his open mouth. He wore only a tanker's field jacket with a bandoleer across his chest. As he cradled his M-1, he leaned close to Harding to tell us that the road ahead was under fire from a machine gun placed in the trees on the far side of the open field. A flanking patrol had been sent down the road to come in behind the trees to flush the Germans. Still gasping as he turned to leave, he told us that we would be better off to leave the jeep where it was and get down. I grabbed my rifle and a bandoleer as Harding searched through our gear for his carbine. Taking off our bulky parkas and throwing them in the jeep, we both ran for the trees alongside the road. When we reached the trees and were standing next to a large pine, we heard the flat cracking of a machine gun firing several short bursts. From where I was standing I could see the sunken road ahead and ten or so American figures crouching behind the embankment. There were two bodies lying far down on the roadway. As I watched, another burst sent a shower of snow from the top of the embankment to drift down on the men behind it. One of the crouching figures, an officer or noncom, was pointing down the road urging the men to spread out. They began to move carefully until they were 20 or so yards apart. Suddenly a very short burst down the line must have caught one of them as he was moving, because he was thrown backwards onto the road. As he lay spread-eagle in the snow, his helmet bounced crazily several yards down the sloping road. The leader, on his knees behind the bank, gave a hand signal and simultaneously the men threw themselves on the low embankment and began firing rapidly at the treeline across the meadow. The machine gun answered in a long burst, sweeping the entire length of the sunken embankment. As the gun fired, all but two of the men ducked down under the protective edge. Two of them, those closest to us had been hit when the gun had begun firing and lay where they were, one sliding slowly backwards down into the roadway ditch, his rifle staying perched in the ledge where it had been. The remaining men then sat with their backs to the embankment, facing the roadway. One scuttled sidewise over to his dead or wounded buddy and carefully pulled him down from his exposed position on the top of the bank. He bent over him and then shook his head in the direction of the still kneeling leader, before returning to his position.

Harding and I, without a word, left the protection of the pines and began running toward the embankment. As I approached the edge of the treeline, I bent as close to the ground as I could in order to stay lower than the natural parapet. As I did so, the heavy cloth bandoleer across my chest swung down in front of me and caught my running feet, tripping me forward. I cleared the trees in a long dive, pitching clumsily behind the bank, my rifle and helmet torn from me in the heavy fall. The bandoleer, now free, crashed its heavy load of clips across my face. I had fallen only a few feet from the dead man who slid off the hillside, my helmet coming to rest against his smashed and bloody head. As I dug in the snow for my rifle, I caught a glimpse of Harding sliding by me to the next open position in the line. I clamped my helmet on my head, noticing that the top of it was smeared with the blood from the man whose place I was taking. I leaned back against the hill, panting and checking myself for injuries. Except for a cut on my lip from the bandoleer and some snow that had gone up the sleeves of my jacket all the way to my elbows when I pitched to the ground, I was unhurt.

Catching my breath, I looked down the length of the embankment, seeing at once that it was much lower in height than it had appeared to be from behind the trees. It was really not much protection at all. Several men down the line were curiously craning their necks in our direction. The leader, uncertain about who we were or what we were doing, rose slightly from his knees and began a duck walk toward us. Harding, crawling on his knees, met him halfway. The two began a discussion, helmets nodding from time to time. They separated, Harding returned in my direction as the leader stopped at one of his closest men and spoke to him, pointed toward our jeep, which was still sitting in the center of the road behind the treeline.

The man immediately came toward us in a crouch, not looking at me as we went by. When he reached the trees, he straightened, hurried to the jeep, and began backing it up until he and the vehicle disappeared from our view. I looked at Harding who was 20 yards away beyond the dead man next to me. Jerking my thumb in the direction of the Germans, I made a sign of wondering what was going on by shrugging my shoulders and making a palms up gesture with my hands. We had heard no firing since the last two men had been hit. The Lieutenant grinned and with hand gestures informed me that the squad's walkie-talkie radio was not working, that the jeep had been sent to get help and that we were going to keep up a distracting fire until the flanking patrol could be in position. By pointing to his watch and holding up five fingers three times, I assumed that the patrol was to be there in 15 minutes. Then holding up a finger telling me to wait, he turned in the direction to the squad leader waiting for his signal to fire. I took off my gloves, unlocked my safety, stuck several clips in the snow near the top of the parapet where I could see them, brushed snow from my rifle and lay on the embarkment, watching for the leader's signal, ready to push myself up to fire. Kneeling, he looked carefully at his wrist, looked both ways to make sure that we were ready and then lunged forward up on the embankment to begin a rapid fire with his rifle. I jumped to the edge, my own rifle firing a shot before I was even in place. I don't know what I had expected to see, but I was temporarily confused by seeing nothing but a peaceful edge of forest, black green against the bright snow of the wide field. I fired at the bottom of the trees, all seven remaining rounds went into the forest at nothing in particular. The bang of my M-1, the kicking jerk of the recoil against my shoulder and the need to resight after each round, occupied me totally. I could hear the banging of other rapidly firing rifles and the pop of Harding's carbine and when my clip spring ejected, I quickly reloaded, hearing my heart pound in my ears. I was ready to fire again when the machine gun, which I imagined was aimed at a spot between my eyes, began to answer. It swept the line again, this time in short bursts, mercifully beginning at the far end this time. I was well down by the time chunks of frozen snow rattled down on my helmet. The firing stopped, leaving only flat echoes among the trees. I lay on my back, head pressed against my helmet webbing, gasping for air, heart exploding rapidly in my chest. I could hear nothing. I could only stare at a spot in the clear sky above me, but in a few moments I could hear a voice from a great distance away calling, "Medic—medic."

I moved my heard to the right far enough to see that one more man lay on his back in the roadway and that someone down there was calling for help. After a time my heart stopped its pounding and except for my hands that kept trembling, I began to calm down. I busied myself pulling on my gloves over my now purple hands.

As Harding yelled something to me that I could not understand, I looked up to see the jeep arrive near the edge of the trees. Two men with musette bags and large red crosses on a white circle painted on their helmets, jumped out and began working their way down behind the embankment. Staying low they went from body to body finally finding the one on the road that was still alive. Together they pulled him by his legs under the bank and began treating him for what looked like a neck wound.

Still on my back, I was horrified to see the squad leader getting ready to give us the signal to fire again.

"Jesus, no! Leave them alone, they'll go away!" I whispered.

However, the machine gun was ready for us this time. It began firing before we could give the signal and I thought that I could hear the crack of rifles also coming from across the field. The leader waved us off and we went back to crouching against the bank.

As I sat waiting, rifle cradled across my lap, a gradual feeling of personal withdrawal crept over me and I began to watch carefully that spot in the sky again. I was numb and disoriented and I began to convince myself that I was not part of all of this. As soon as the spot told me to go, I was going to get up and go home. I knew that my mother would be worried that I had stayed out so long to play. She always worried about me. I drifted as I listened to someone singing a line from a song over and over. I realized that it was me.

Someone was calling my name. I jerked back to the cold, the embankment, the rifle, the spent cartridges lying in the snow, and to the dead men. It was the Lieutenant asking, "You O.K.? I thought you'd been hit."

I waved a feeble hand in his direction and yelled, "I'm O.K., let's get the hell out of here."

At that moment there was movement on the road behind the jeep and I almost shouted with happiness to see a group of reinforcements coming in long spaced lines down through the trees.

I looked expectantly at our leader to see what he was going to do, but he was studying his watch and signaling the newly arrived men to stay where they were in the shelter of the trees. I had completely forgotten about the flanking patrol, which must by now be near their position.

We waited for a long minute before we heard the crump of grenades and the popping of distant rifle fire filtering across the field. I could even hear some faint shouting as the firing died away with one or two shots coming at the very end. The squad leader stood up cautiously on the road, shielding his eyes from the glare coming from the snow and waved his hand in the air. He held it there until he apparently received an answering signal, for he called to us that we could get up. I struggled to my feet, along with everyone else, surprised at the pains in my body and the sudden dizziness that caught me.

Coming toward us across the field was a small group of men. At that distance and in the bright light, I could not tell who they were until the group had pushed its way awkwardly halfway across the clearing. Walking in front was a German in a long grey snow streaked overcoat, his hands on the top of his helmet. He fell twice in the snow, but was jerked to his feet by an American holding a rifle walking behind him. There were five others, Americans, one carrying a long shoulder stock German machine gun on his shoulder, the others pushing slowly through the snow, rifles slung.

Harding and I walked slowly down the now incredibly exposed road to the squad leader, joining him just as the patrol jumped and slid over the edge of the embankment.

The Americans looked weary, two of them were angry, proding the German from behind with their rifle butts. He was sullen but when he saw the dead on the road and the medics giving plasma to the wounded man, he became agitated and began a dry whimpering noise in his throat. He was a very tall man, well over six feet, giving the Americans around him with their bulky equipment, the appearance of being dwarfs. The flanking patrol leader said in a flat heavy voice, "There were six of them . . . they got Jenkins and Charlie."

We all looked at the prisoner who was now staring at the ground, fingers still laced together across the top of his helmet. He was wearing grey wristlets that covered his hands but not his reddish fingers. He was clearly the oldest man on the road, with an unshaven face showing patches of grey against his dark sunken averted eyes. I studied the man as the squad leader began questioning him in broken German. Over his tightly buttoned overcoat, he wore regulation equipment, black straps across his shoulders connected to a wide black leather belt that held his flat canteen, bayonet and gas mask cannister. A rain poncho, folded neatly, hung from the back of his belt. But what caught my eye was his grey, aluminum belt buckle. Stamped on it in a circular design with the words, "Gott mit uns"—"God is with us."

I looked carefully at the dead Americans on the road and I suddenly felt a heavy sickness. God is not with them—God is not even with us—He couldn't be. God has nothing to do with this. Twelve lives had just been spent in some unfathomable argument over this little plot of earth. This slaughter is the work of man and if there is a God, He is greatly saddened this day to see again what animals we really are.

As the squad leader continued talking to the prisoner in German, I slung my rifle, turned, and began walking slowly in the center of the road back up toward the jeep. I was completely weary, walking with my head down, watching my feet take steps ahead of me without any directions from my brain. Before reaching the trees, I made myself stop at the feet of the man who had been killed before I took his place on the firing line. I did not look at the top of his head but rather studied his face and body. I swore to myself that I never wanted to forget what I was seeing. He was not a man. He was, like me, a boy. His young smooth face had never seen a razor blade and his half open hazel eyes were meant to be looking at girls in the corner drug store of some

Midwestern town. The tips of his teeth were young and white. His hands, crossed at his waist, were dirty, his fingernails clogged with dark dirt. I knelt down and touched his cold hand and hot tears came to my eyes, followed immediately by a volcanic rage. Jumping to my feet, I shook my fist at the field and sky, screaming in a broken voice, "Who needs this fucking place!!"

*   *   *   *   *

Harding had a scheme and as usual it had to do with money, large sums of money. For reasons that I never discovered, the Lieutenant had a bundle of new large denomination German Mark notes, which he intended to convert into cashier's checks to be sent to his bank account in the states. The practice of men sending money home was common, permitted and even encouraged, if the sums were not suspiciously large.

During our occupation of Alsace and Lorraine we encountered the widespread use of German money among the inhabitants who were often reluctant to accept our invasion currency, preferring instead to barter with the more familiar Mark. This practice lead to some interesting temptations on the part of the Americans who, loaded with explosives, found access to caches of money. It was strictly forbidden to loot but the odd house safe or strong box was terribly vulnerable to plastic explosives or a well placed bazooka shell, and it was not uncommon to find next to shattered homes these items that had been opened forcibly. There were also banks and business vaults for the enterprising soldier and there were endless stories of untold wealth being buried for later recovery when the war was well over.

Most of what we heard was nonsense, of course, and I'm sure that most of the safes were found to have been emptied well in advance of the errant bazooka shell. But the money stories persisted, probably because of the shaky economy of war torn countries and the outrageous nature of the "get rich quick" mentality of many Americans. Cigarettes, preferably American, became the currency of the land and the buying and selling of cigarettes was the main business transaction occupying both soldiers and civilians. In Chaumont, I had bought a sterling silver cigarette case and had had it engraved with my name for five packs of cigarettes. And even though cigarettes sold for 20 cents a pack in the states, the small shop jeweler was overjoyed with the deal. For many yeas after the war, American cigarettes were still being used as stable currency in bankrupt and rebuilding countries. Packs and cartons of cigarettes were major items in any black market operation.

But Harding had been recently unnerved by a directive from the division finance officer, stating that no large denomination currency would be accepted for conversion to cashiers checks. The order apparently originated to discourage theft, black market sales and large scale gambling. The directive also had an immediate effect on the local economy, as civilians refused to deal with large denomination notes believing that their banks might soon either discount or disclaim the money. Big bucks were hard to get rid of.

The indomitable Harding was not to be discouraged by this turn of events, however. He formed a plan. He and I, along with his bundle of notes, would take the jeep into the mountains where villagers had not heard of the directive and there in the back country we would transform the large notes into smaller usable pieces of money.

Early the next morning we drove North on a clear untroubled day to perform a financial miracle for the Lieutenant's bank account.

We left the main road, striking out for the North range of the Voges, looking for smaller roads and taking them whenever we could find one. We found many small roads that were not on our maps and unlike country roads in America, they did not necessarily lead to isolated farms. They instead, invariably led to a village or another road junction. We crisscrossed back and forth going deeper and deeper into the small mountain valleys. Soon we were alone, having not seen other vehicles for some time, grinding and bumping along over rutted roads covered by virgin snow. Stopping on the crest of a hill, we saw below us what we had been looking for. It was a sizable village complete with a church spire attracting 50 or so buildings to it. The road down to the village was little more than a cow path but with a determination that I had seldom seen in Harding, he navigated us down the precipice and onto an unpaved street leading directly into the town. Curiously enough, there was no sign of life anywhere. No carts, dogs, or even cows could be seen and there seemed to be a tense silence behind shuttered windows and closed doors. I had an apprehensive feeling that we were being watched but I dismissed it as Harding stropped the jeep in front of a small cafe. The bar restaurant looked open. At least the large glass window looking out on the street was not covered as so many of the others had been. I suggested that it might be wise to put the jeep behind the building in case we were spotted by an overzealous M.P. After searching for a while, we found a tiny alleyway and parked the jeep away from the main street.

We took our weapons and made sure that nothing else that could be stolen was left in the vehicle and with a convincing show of nonchalance, we opened the door to the cafe and entered smiling. It was a small room with an ancient carved back bar against one wall and two or three tables near the window. It was warm and smelled of potato soup and onions. I was taking deep breaths of the soup as a plump older woman entered the room through a door behind the bar. We were by then seated at a table next to the window when she saw us.

Her reaction was one of startled surprise and total confusion. She stood against the high bar, both pudgy hands on her mouth, breathing heavily. We sat looking at her and smiling while she stared at us until finally she blurted, "Amy, Amy," calling the word over and over.

"I hope this Amy person likes us better than this old woman does," I said to Harding.

Before we could speak further, an old man appeared behind the woman. He had patches of bristles on his head and face and was wearing heavy black suspenders over a faded shirt that had no collar. He put his arm around the woman's shaking shoulders and together, facing us, they did a duet stare number. She whispered to no one, "Amy."

"Amy's a funny name for an old man wearing suspenders," I thought as Harding, ignoring the tableau, smiled and shouted, "How about some beer?"

There must have been something magic in the way he spoke for the old man broke into a wide completely toothless smile and dove under the bar, reappearing with two glasses and a large brown bottle with a rubber stopper in the top. He scampered over to our table pouring as he came. Harding waited for him to put down the glasses and then handed him one of his big bills. The man looked at the bill, looked at Harding, turned to the old lady who was still leaning on the bar, and spoke a torrent of German in her direction. They exchanged several sentences before Amy pointed his face back to us and announced, "Nein."

He gestured to the beer and then pointed to himself and to the old lady. He didn't want us to pay for the drinks, they were on the house. As I glanced at the Lieutenant, I knew that we could have a serious problem here. This old man *must* take the money. We didn't come here for free drinks, we came to change money.

I need not have worried, however, for Harding was up to the challenge, with a warm smile he stood and put his arm around the innkeeper. Shaking his head and saying, "No, no," he cajoled and soothed the old man who finally took the proffered bank note and backed away bowing and smiling. Both of the old people left the room as we sipped our warm and terrible tasting brew.

The woman returned as we heroically drank our beer. She had with her two handfuls of small notes and coins. It looked as though she was clutching her life savings to her wide bosom. Tears were beginning to glisten in the corners of her rheumy eyes as she stacked the bills and coins on the table, the process taking her several minutes to count in German before she left the room. We could hear the two of them talking heatedly behind the closed door. The woman was crying.

A little puzzled, we were about to call out and order another bottle of beer in order to exchange another note, when we heard an unmistakable sound outside. Down the street beyond our field of vision, we could hear the roar of an engine and the rumble of a large vehicle. Curious to see what it could be we waited at our window seat, elbows on the table sipping the last of our beer. We didn't have long to wait as the noise became louder and the front end of a box-like vehicle edged into our view. We sat like curious tourists looking out the window at the side of a German armored car, which had come to stop in front of the cafe.

There have been moments in my life when I have reacted quickly and well. Then there have been many other moments when I have not reacted at all. I have been frozen into immobility, dependent upon someone else telling me what to do. This was such a moment but the problem was that no one was telling me anything.

Harding was just as astonished as I, as we sat frozen in position, beer glasses in our hands, heads turned looking at the German cross stenciled on the side of the green grey armor plating just a few feet away. As we both began to slowly lower our glasses, a turret on the top of the armored car crashed open and the head of a German soldier appeared. He was hatless with long stringy black hair hanging around his ears and as he hoisted himself up in the open turret, we could see that he was wearing a pair of binoculars around his neck. We were transfixed by the sight of the enemy who was almost within reaching distance of our table, but he did not look in our direction, instead, steadying his elbows on the rim of the turret, he studied the street ahead through his field glasses.

So as not to attract his attention, we carefully slid out of our chairs and tried to back out of sight. But the window was so large and the room so small that it was impossible for him not to have seen us if he turned his head and looked into the cafe. We edged back into the room watching him as he laughingly shouted something down into the interior of the car. He was still laughing as he resumed looking down the street through the binoculars. Harding and I drew and loaded our pistols quietly, although the noise and vibration from the powerful engine of the armored car could be felt in the wooden floor of the cafe. I didn't know about the Lieutenant but I felt very exposed and naked at that moment, aiming a weapon at an armored car full of Germans, with bullets that probably would not even have chipped the paint on that monstrous vehicle. My heart was pounding and I felt a little sick at my stomach.

Soon, however, the German with the glasses, without turning his head in our direction, busied himself with his climb back down into the car, pulled the turret shut over his head and to our great relief, the vehicle proceeded to back itself out of the view. As the rumble died away, I looked at a very pale and visibly shaken Harding. His small dark eyes were darting back and forth and he swallowed several times as he holstered his 45.

Within minutes we had retrieved the jeep and with great caution surveyed the street before speeding back out of the village to the cow trail. Churning up the hill at high speed, past the crest without looking back at the view of the village, we plunged into the protection of the deep forest. Returning the way we had come, we followed our tire tracks, which were the only ones to be seen on the frozen road.

Within a mile of the village we were stopped by an American patrol backed by two tank destroyers.

We were ordered out of the jeep, again at gunpoint, and because we, of course, did not know the password or countersign, were taken to a savage looking Captain in the first T.D. He was both angry and incredulous that we had somehow passed through his lines into a German occupied town. His anger was prompted by the fact that our action might have alerted the enemy to his approach and could have cost him casualties. Harding's weak response about a reconnaissance mission was dismissed as "bullshit" and resulted in a torrent of abuse, ridicule and threats from the red faced Captain to report the incident to Division. Our names and unit designation were carefully recorded by the angry man and we were sent on our way back to Molsheim.

We drove in silence, for it was the only time I ever saw the Lieutenant worried and crestfallen. He drove with full concentration, only occasionally shaking his head and talking to himself.

We had gone only a few miles when I sat up straight and exclaimed, "Now I know who Amy was!"

Harding didn't take his eyes off the narrow road but I knew he was curious for after a time he asked, "Who?"

"The old woman wasn't saying Amy," I said. "She was saying *Amis*, the German word for Americans."

The discovery explained the couple's surprise, and their overt generosity in trying to buy us a round of drinks. It even explained their fear of offending us if they had refused to take the large bank note. Living as they did in the remote mountain village, it was probably that we were the first Americans either had ever seen in their entire lives. For the sake of all Americans, I hoped that we had made a good impression.

The money incident did not stop with the chewing out that we had received at the tank destroyer. Within two days Harding was summoned to Division headquarters, transferred out of our company and I was summarily sent back to the light weapons company and the now rusting sword blades.

At the time I did not know that I was never to see Lieutenant Harding again, but the knowledge would have made little difference to either of us, parting as we did with a handshake and a friendly clap on the shoulder.

We had been friends, although never really close because we had almost nothing in common. But we had been through a lot together.

He had come to trust and respect me and I had come to enjoy his protection and his weird obsession with money. Even though in the end, his devotion to accumulating a fortune had spelled professional trouble for him. In any event the days of freedom and adventure as a courier driver had come to an end.

CHAPTER XVI

REGROUPING

When I returned to Big Red's company, the bunkers were the same, but the men were happier. They had settled in, remodeled the latrine, opened a light weapons repair shop, acquired sleeping cots, and had installed refrigeration in a newly built mess hall. I was also surprised and pleased to discover that several other men from my original company had been transferred in, including my friend Holt whom I had not seen for many weeks. My only displeasure were the words from a bleary-eyed Big Red that he was so glad to have me back that he was going to make me permanent Sergeant of the guard. The duty was not difficult since we maintained only four perimeter posts and a single roadblock for traffic entering and leaving on the one dirt road leading into the bunker area. My job was to supervise the roster, which was punitively prepared by the orderly room each day, and to spot-check the guard posts at irregular intervals. In effect, I had very little to do since most of the men drawing guard detail were the original Hagenau replacements and the new men who had been recently transferred to the company. We all knew one another, they trusted me to run a fairly lax guard detail and to keep our little band out of trouble with the orderly room. I made sure that the most visible guards at the roadblock were always alert, courteous, and efficient so that when company officers passed to and from the encampment they would be properly impressed. The perimeter guards, invisible in the surrounding forests, gave me their word that each would more or less be on guard duty. Occasionally, dropping by the mess hall for coffee in the afternoon, I would find one of my posted guards doing the same. A simple frown from me would send the man scurrying back into the trees with his rifle.

The great German winter offensive, begun in 1944, had ended. The enemy, seriously crippled from losses on both the Eastern and Western fronts, still fought ferocious defensive actions as he fell back to better positions. But the Allies, unrelenting and smarting from their own losses during the winter, pursued after regrouping, with a renewed determination to end the war. Important German strongpoints and towns fell to the British, French and Americans. On March 7th the Rhine River railway bridge at Remagen was captured intact by men of the 9th division and the German Rhine defenses were pierced in an important way. The battle along the entire front from the English Channel to the Swiss border had been carried to Germany's doorstep, but it had not been without enormous cost, not only in human lives but also in material. Toward the end of February, the most severe winter in over 40 years was followed by a meteorological phenomenon, an unseasonable period of rain and warm temperatures. Deep accumulations of snow melted away in only days, resulting in serious flooding in all areas, disrupted communications, and caused the breakup of major highways. Bridges were washed away by record rains while roadblocks disappeared under the pounding of the thousands of vehicles necessary to keep the attack pressed to the enemy. Logistics became a nightmare as trucks disappeared to their axles in cloying mud and heavy tracked vehicles were all but immobilized, relegated only to hard surfaces that were difficult to find. Twice our bunker company was called to assist engineers in their desperate attempt to keep N-4 open through the Saverne Gap. Men were strung out along the highway with shovels and piles of hastily acquired gravel and larger rocks. As trucks and armor passed over the broken roadway, each man would immediately fill with gravel the reawakened potholes and ditches that appeared in the roadway as the traffic passed. This detail was a 24 hour task but was accomplished by determination of purpose. The German was off balance and we would not release our hold on him.

Living in the bunkers became not only a constant problem of mud but one of moisture. The concrete walls ran with water and the warm moist interior of the bunker filled with a humidity so high that a thin fog covered us and our belongings. A dampness, which even affected our mail, making it limp and water spotted, caused an unfamiliar discomfort after the harshness of the cold and snow. Again we struggled to be comfortable, cheered finally by a rumor from the new courier officer, that our fire control company, even our entire battalion, might soon reassemble in Molsheim. Jones brought in several bottles of Schnapps that night and we had a fine time drinking and laughing together, telling the old stories about our training days in California. I pretended not to notice that all four of the perimeter guards had come in from the rain and were drinking with us, but late in the evening several of us took turns being violently sick in the latrine, throwing up through freshly painted toilet seats. It was a rare treat to be sick in a real toilet again.

Two days later the orders arrived stating officially that our little band of fire control men would leave the company of light weapons warriors and report back to the old torpedo factory in Molsheim. We left the new friends we had made with little reluctance, even though Big Red himself came to our bunker as we prepared to board the two 6-bys and thanked us for our help, wishing us good luck in the process.

As we rolled out past the now unguarded roadblock, I noticed that some wag had made a little picket fence flanking the entrance with sword blades. With points stuck in the ground, rusted, some even bent in places, they were a reminder of the thin thread that ties together young men who fight in wars. The men who forged those blades were gone, as were the dreams of conquest that the weapons had intended to perform, but we had weapons of our own almost 200 years later and ours were also our path to conquest. The blades jiggled from the vibration of the trucks as we passed. Thought to be modern and invincible in their time, they were now made fools of because of their uselessness. Would a bank of soldiers, someday in the future, make a mock fence out of our rifles?

It took the better part of three days for our old company to reassemble in the torpedo factory barracks, but when we stood in formation at morning roll call on the third day, there were many who were not present. The company itself was only at sixty percent strength, Captain Smart visibly moved by the losses we had suffered. By piecing our information together, we were able to determine that some had been killed, others wounds, some permanently transferred, a few in hospitals with injuries and disease. The men who had been sent to repodepots were simply unaccounted for. No one knew what had become of them. In spite of the sobering knowledge of losses, the reunion was a happy one as friends were reunited and stories told. Each truckload of arrivals was greeted with the howls and jeers of the backslapping survivors of the winter war, and on the warming air of the coming spring there was an unmistakeable confidence and optimism present because of being back together again. The optimism was intensified when we discovered that the Farmer was no longer our first Sergeant. We heard that the company commander, frustrated at last by the Farmer's incompetence in trying to keep the records of the disembodied company, had transferred him to a job at battalion.

We had a new first Sergeant, a well-liked and witty man who had many friends in the company. His name was Lou and his jovial give-and-take with everyone got the job done and was much appreciated by both men and officers. Lt. Harding had been replaced by a small heavy-set man from Oklahoma who wore a troubled look and was never seen to smile. He was completely G.I., even down to always wearing a regulation necktie. His name was Fox and although not well-liked he was accepted in a good-natured way by the remnants of the old company.

Within a few days we were alerted that we would move North immediately, but by this time we were all so accustomed to constant moves that the news was not disturbing and we knew that we could be ready to leave with everything we owned in a few minutes. We left Molsheim early the next day, heading Northeast through the Saverne Gap for the last time, toward the walled city of Metz. I sat in the back of a 6-by with George and Holt, talking quietly and enjoying their companionship as we bumped over the still stricken roadbeds caused by the recent rains and floods. My last sight of Saverne was that of the old castle on the hill, still being watchful after the many centuries of guarding the pass. Five years later I was to have a delightful lunch in the castle with my parents, marveling then at the spectacular view of the peaceful green and crop filled valley below.

The convoy came to an unexpected halt near the city of Metz at noon. We were parked next to a moderately sized stream that fed into the Moselle River and there we were told by a joking Lou that we were going to be given a hot shower in a mobile shower unit set up next to the small tributary. At first there were groans and complaints but once we unloaded in the warm sunlight we saw the humor and the pleasure in the event. Herded ten at a time into a small dressing trailer next to the shower unit, we undressed amid catcalls, jokes and ribald remarks. Sitting on a wooden bench, peeling off my trousers, I was aware for the first time that I had not had all of my clothes off for over 10 weeks. I had not seen my own body for more than two months and as I got closer to my skin I was uncertain as to what I would discover. What all ten of us discovered about ourselves was that we were a sickly white color. I had never seen bodies so white. Amazingly, except for my face and hands I did not seem to be at all dirty. Examining my feet I found that even between the toes there was no evidence of dirt. However I had grown very long toenails. Completely disrobed we sat like so many alabaster figurines until a shouting Sergeant instructed us about the mobile shower unit. When we were to be in place under the ten individual shower heads, the hot water would be turned on for exactly one minute so that we could get thoroughly wet. Then there would be two minutes for soaping hair and body followed by a two minute rinse. The shower would take five minutes and anyone not completely rinsed would likely spend the rest of his life covered with soap.

A whistle blew and the ten of us, naked and laughing, trooped into the shower. There are no doubt words in the English language that could adequately describe the beauty of those 300 seconds in that trailer, but I honestly don't know what those words would be. The experience of clean hot water was so satisfying, so personally rewarding that it was sensuous in its fulfillment. I lathered, I washed, I scrubbed, I washed my hair, I covered every inch of myself with a thick coat of soap and in the final rinsing away of those delightful suds I felt an almost delirious pleasure.

Returning to the dressing trailer, we found another miracle waiting for us. Our old clothes, ripe with continuous use, had been set aside during the time it took for the shower and waiting for us were brand new clothes, new underwear, socks, and winter uniform pants and shirts. To add one final touch of purity to our joy, we had a fine hot meal in a nearby building across the roadway.

When we loaded back into the trucks, we were happy, contented, and somewhat nostalgic. The hot shower, clothes and food may not have been much, but after 10 weeks of fear, sorrow, and freezing cold, it had seemed to be an ample and completely satisfying reward. Lurching along in the afternoon sunshine, someone in our truck produced a harmonica and we sang some quiet songs, not the brave war songs of basic training days but rather the sentimental bittersweet songs of home, such as "Home on the Range" and "Danny Boy."

We passed around the city of Metz and heading Northeast, we continued our journey into third Army territory. Our destination, we learned at a fuel stop, was Longwy, France. We did not make it to Longwy on our first day but instead at nightfall, billeted in an old chateau North of Longuyon. The estate was so large that our entire understrength company was easily accommodated in the spacious palace-like main building. Although slightly damaged by artillery fire, the centuries old chateau still retained its Louis XV elegant and charm. Partially furnished with antiques, which included inlaid furniture, tapestries, and a sizeable collection of huge hanging portraits, the building was truly a mansion. Two servant housekeepers nervously guarded the artifacts against theft and damage and in addition we were ordered by the Captain to touch nothing that belonged to the unoccupied estate. We were told that the owners had been taken away by the Germans when France had fallen in 1939.

A company mess was set up in the spacious kitchen and we ate like kings in the great candlelighted mirrored ballroom, sitting crosslegged on the beautiful handcrafted inlaid floor. Conversation, influenced by the impressive historical atmosphere of the chateau, was hushed and everyone was careful not to burn the vast expanse of floor with carelessly handled cigarettes. The respect shown for the wealthy beauty of the past was a sharp and a somewhat puzzling contradiction to the savage and often unwarranted destruction of the present. Some of us sitting in the ballroom had a long and serious discussion about middle-class values and virtues, coming to some conclusions about societal class structures and the desires of people to move respectfully from lower to higher circles.

After dinner we discovered by candlelight, the empty wine cellars beneath the chateau. They were huge connecting vaulted rooms with curved stone ceilings blackened by years of torchlight and candlesmoke. Stone flagstone floors were swept clean and there was a tomb-like atmosphere as we explored the seemingly endless rooms in the flickering light of handheld candles. In one of the far rooms we found a long mahogany back bar, which must have been over a hundred years old. Hand carved with human and animal figures, it was a marvelous piece of craftsmanship.

The company slept well that night, feeling comfortable and far from the war. We were delighted at breakfast, this time in the ballroom struck with morning sunlight to hear that we would be staying for several days of rest in the chateau. Having nothing to do, we walked through the meticulously cared for gardens, threw stones in the creek and pond, enjoyed the luxury of the spring air and the warm sun on our backs. Men wandered around in small groups to sit under the willow trees in quiet conversation.

In the early afternoon, Sgt. Striker, platoon leader from the 1st platoon and an entrepreneur from Michigan, approached the first three grade noncoms in the company with an idea. The nine of us would put in $20 apiece and he would buy liquor to be sold to the rest of the company while we were at the chateau. We could make money for an obscure first three graders fund, which he had difficulty describing in any detail. We hastily agreed to the plan and with the Captain's permission, he disappeared with our money and one of the company's jeeps in the direction of Longuyon about five miles away.

That evening we lighted a passageway through the wine cellar and opened the mahogany bar for rush business. We had located tables, chairs and enough candlelight to throw a warm glow against the curved ceiling. Business was slow at first but by midnight the cellar rang with the shouts and laughter of almost everyone in the company. No one seemed to care about the overpriced drinks and before the night was over we had drunk all of the schnapps and cognac and were reduced to drinking a poor grade of unlabeled red wine. Several of the younger men passed out during the evening and were gently carried by drunken but solicitous friends to the corners of the room where they would be in no danger of being stepped on. An uncommon camaraderie permeated the entire group and when our smiling officers appeared for a brief visit, they were greeted with roaring cheers from all of us. Pledges of everlasting friendship were heard and specific promises were made to meet in hometowns when the war was over.

It was an unique moment for the company, one created by the relief over the passing of winter battles, the curious warmth of the ancient cellar, and the remembered comfort that we had been given in the past few days.

Just before we staggered upstairs to our rooms, the First Sergeant, in a rare display of seriousness, proposed a toast. Banging repeatedly on the bar for attention, he managed finally to quiet down the room, even the group singing at one of the tables. In the absolute stillness of the room he raised his glass to undivided attention and said, "Here's to those of us who are not here . . . here's to the rest of us . . . may we never forget this night."

Suddenly sober, we drank with him, lifting our glasses, canteen cups and bottles in a precious moment, which to all was sacred. We helped each other up the steep flight of wooden steps to the floor above. Some of us, in our drunkenness, no doubt were crying.

Longwy, astride the Chiers River in Northern France, is a mining town and had a population of 20,000 people in 1945. It lies next to the border between Belgium and Luxenbourg and was the Western anchor point of the Maginot line, that curious anachronism, which grew out of the fortress mentality of World War I. The Maginot line, the dream of Sgt. Henri Maginot, a French soldier wounded at Verdun and who rose to important political power in France, was built as a series of deep concrete interconnecting fortresses reaching from the edge of Belgium all the way to the Swiss border. Considered impenetrable, they faced toward Germany as had the forts of Verdun in the Great War—Douaumont and Vaux. The terrible lessons of the open trenches of Verdun had been sealed deep in the French national psyche, leaving behind them a philosophy of watchfulness and defense. The determination of the phrase carved in the hills above Verdun, "They shall not pass," dominated the military ventures of France following War War I. Either by national lethargy or by ignoring the development of air power and armor, the French had been caught sitting in these colossal forts by the aggressive German Blitzskrieg in 1939. The French, reluctant to extend the line of forts across the Belgian frontier, relied instead on the forts within Belgium itself. The mistake was to cost them the war. Germany, as it had in World War I, struck again through Belgium, outflanked the Maginot forts and rendered them useless. As the German panzers rolled behind the forts to attack them from the rear, they were faced only with collecting French prisoners. The guns of the great steel reinforced forts could not be turned to point back to the heart of France.

Throughout my travels in the Vosges and particularly in the Longwy area, the empty and abandoned casements of the network of forts could be seen, their blind empty sockets of gun ports staring mindlessly in the direction of Germany.

The western edge of the Maginot line was dug deeply into the brooding treeless hills above the ancient city of Longwy. Locked and abandoned, the entire two hundred miles of forts had no use beyond having been considered briefly during the great German winter offensive of 1944 as a possible fall back defense line for the hard pressed Americans in Alsace Lorraine.

Longwy itself was not only a mining town on the edge of vast iron and coal fields, it served also as a railway and river shipping center for that part of France. Nestled on the river between impressive bluffs, the city is barely visible until it is almost entered either from the hills surrounding it or from the narrow valley through which the river flows, wandering across the country, eventually joining the Meuse.

As a transportation center, the city had been the target for Allied bombers over the years and the center of the city, near the river, had sustained considerable damage. On one particular night raid by British bombers, a German ammunition train, passing through the town, had been hit by bombs and exploded, killing many civilians and destroying several blocks of houses. Most of the people of Longwy however, while deploring the loss of lives, were not overly bitter about the raids, choosing instead to regard them as the consequences of a necessary war. There had been no extensive ground battles fought near or in the city so that except for the bomb damage, there was no evidence anywhere that a war was in progress. Away from the center of town, there were treelined streets, shops, manufacturing plants and a large railroad switching yard.

The company was billeted in a concrete German built apartment building on the North edge of the city. Functional but ugly, the building was originally intended to house workers and their families during the German occupation of France. The rooms were small but by using bunk beds we were able to sleep six men in a room and with the kitchen and large dining hall, we were comfortable and well fed. Several children from the neighborhood, including a midget with a squeaky voice, visited our mess hall after each meal to salvage scraps of food. Each child carried a galvanized bucket, taking home the precious food that we thought of as our garbage. Their on-schedule visits were a disturbing reminder of the serious shortages suffered by people during the war years.

Spring came with a rush to Northern France, bringing with it warm air and sunshine. Tulips and daffodils appeared in houseplanters and blooming dogwood dotted the hillsides around the valley city. Early evening walks to town invariably led to a graceful stonewall bordering the Chiers where one could rest under yellow green willow trees and smile at the many young girls who strolled in pairs in the long evening shadows. It was a time of serenity and of new friendships. The city bustled with both passing military traffic and civilians on bicycles, and bars and cafes did a sparkling spring business catering mostly to our company, which was the only unit quartered within the city at the time. Because we were the only semipermanent band of soldiers, we received the direct attention of the people of Longwy, who treated us as friends and took us into their homes. I dined with several families who in the best French manner, extended their hospitality to me. Dinner was often extravagant in the face of shortages and there was always a marriageable daughter on display, often combed, brushed, embarrassed and in her Sunday clothes. By this time my French was almost fluent and I enjoyed the conversations around the dinner table, taking great delight in flattering the Mother for her culinary skills, the daughter for her beauty and the Father for his good fortune in his choice of wives. The families were very curious about me, particularly about my family life in California. I am afraid, that on occasion, I shamefully exaggerated living conditions in America and bragged openly about my fictitious exploits in the land of movie stars. Families would listen wide-eyed to tales of Hollywood parties, gasping over the importance of my friends among the movie greats. I did not mean to deceive them, but caught up in the excitement of new friendships, I spun out what I chose to think of as harmless stories to entertain them. When invited into a home I always took, in addition to cigarettes, small gifts to members of the family, processed canned food for the Mother, a more personal trinket or scarf for the daughter, an Army souvenir for a younger brother, and when I could get it, pipe tobacco for the Father. These presents were gratefully accepted, especially the food and the tobacco. On one occasion a father had to leave the table to cry over a treasured gift of American pipe tobacco. He had not seen real pipe tobacco for over three years and was overwhelmed. Following the meal, after six or seven courses, probably saved from a week's worth of rations, I would take the daughter for a short stroll along the river road, returning within a respectable length of time to deliver her back to her family with politeness and respect. I was learning the formality and customs of the French family and found them rewarding and satisfying.

Before leaving Longwy in April our company arranged to have a party for the many friends we had made during our month long stay in the city. A public invitation was posted at the city hall and we all pitched in to show our appreciation and gratitude for the many kindnesses that had been shown to us. Our cooks baked large sheet cakes covered with sugary white frosting and through some miracle of supply, had obtained two crates of fresh oranges. Someone arranged for the use of a large hall in a school and even a small string orchestra was recruited. Wine for the adults and powdered milk for the children were to be provided along with festive balloons and paper bunting. The mayor of Longwy would speak. On the day of the party we worked hard to have everything ready for an expected crowd of one hundred, but when the time came for the happy time to begin, we were a little worried because many more than that expected number were crowding into the hall. We were not concerned that the growing crowd would become a problem, we were only worried that we had not made enough cake for everyone to share. As the party progressed, following a nice welcome speech from both the Captain and mayor, there was some crowded dancing to the waltzes played by the ancients on the band platform. The crowd was orderly but clearly anxious for the food to appear. Some scattered shouts for the food to be brought out could be heard, so the cooks and their helpers brought from an adjoining pantry, large trays of cakes and the crates of oranges. By the immediate surge in the crowd, I could tell that there was going to be trouble. The six men carrying the trays of cake and oranges over their heads moved into the hall, attempting to cross the floor to place their burdens on tables against the far wall. None of them made it. Pandemonium exploded in the room as shouting and screaming people grabbed for the food.

A swirling mass of maddened humanity assaulted the men with the trays, knocking several of them to their knees and trampling over them to tear the cake into pieces. Men and women stuffed handfuls of cake into their open mouths and reached for more. Oranges bounced beyond straining fingertips as people went down in the struggling hysterical mob. I pulled a whimpering little girl out from the stamping feet of the crowd, protecting her with my body. There was enormous noise and screaming everywhere. In minutes the food was gone and the crowd began slowly to untangle itself from the melee. Several women and children lay crying on the floor but in a short time everyone stood and we could tell that except for torn clothing and bruises, there had been no serious injuries.

The mayor, hands raised, was attempting to quiet the remaining cries and accusations of those who had not gotten to the food in time. Finally the crowd, now looking embarrassed, became quiet and faced the mayor who was about to speak.

In very precise formal French, he reprimanded the group of silent civilians, calling upon them to feel shame for their behavior. Turning then to the Captain, he offered sincere apologies and begged his forgiveness on behalf of the people of Longwy. I stood to one side, still holding the little girl in my arms, feeling her warm thin arms around my neck, feeling an anger toward a war that turned people into a mob fighting each other for oranges and a taste of white sugar frosting. I felt a sickness for a time when the mayor had to humble himself and his people for being hungry. And I felt a shame for the Americans who had caused the embarrassment through a thoughtless vulgar display of fancy food that the citizens of Longwy had probably not seen for years.

CHAPTER XVII

GERMANY

Word came back to us that one of the men of our advance team had been shot in a small town in Germany. It was the first news we had received from a special detail that had been sent beyond the Rhine River to make preparations for the arrival of the company. Information on the shooting was sketchy but from what we could learn he had been hit in the legs by a sniper during the night. The news itself was sobering because our time in Longwy had lulled us into a sense of detachment from the war, and the thought that we were going to soon reenter danger again seemed unfair and unnecessary. Allied armies were on the move, slicing through Germany from the West. Russia, capturing city after important city, was preparing to launch its final attack toward Berlin and we had a hard time believing that anyone needed a fire control company during what we all believed were the last few hours or days of the war in Europe. On April 1st we learned that Okinawa in the Pacific, just a few hundred miles from Japan itself, had been invaded by the 10th Army. It appeared to me that World War II was coming to a quick close and that with a little luck, I would survive it. As I busied myself for our departure by sorting through my belongings, I felt a familiar fear that at the last moment of the war something would happen to me. We were told that our destination was Butzbach, a small manufacturing town North of Frankfort.

On a warm cloudless day in early April we left in open trucks, waving to people on the sidewalks who returned our farewell with smiles and small cheers. Crossing the Maginot line above the bluffs, we traveled into the Dutchy of Luxembourg on dusty crowded roads, becoming strung out and separated immediately. After passing three knocked out German panther tanks near the entrance to the undamaged city of Luxembourg, we stopped to regroup. We were parked on one of the wide boulevards of the beautiful ancient city, built on hills above a small river, dominating the skyline with church spires and palaces. Sitting in tree shade in the open trucks as we waited for the convoy to close up, we were pleasantly surprised to be served coffee and doughnuts from Red Cross girls who handed the items up to us from the wide sidewalks. They were American girls and soon, shouting questions about hometowns were in progress. American girls are different, not only because they look clean and well-groomed but because they are healthy looking with clear skin, bright straight teeth and happy smiles. Slips of paper with names and addresses were passed back and forth along with promises to call or to write to relatives and girlfriends. When the rest of the convoy arrived, we left, waving and cheering, to a tiny corner of America, which we had discovered on the streets of a foreign capitol.

Because of the heavy traffic on the main highways, we made it to Saarbrucken by late afternoon. The city was in ruins, with at least half of the buildings in this industrial complex damaged or destroyed. The contrast between the condition of the German city and Luxembourg was very evident. Saarbrucken was flat, horizontal, barely visible on the skyline, while Luxembourg stood proudly in a vertical way, seen for miles away. We ate K rations and stretched out on the rubble of a smashed building, hoping that it would not rain through the shredded remnants of roof. Before I finally fell asleep in the darkness I mulled over in my mind that it had been only 85 short years since my great grandfather had left Germany for the mountains of Pennsylvania. I was the first of his offspring to ever return his footstep to the soil of his fatherland. The thought was disturbing to me and raised several questions in my mind. What if he had never left Germany, would I be wearing a field grey uniform instead of olive drab? No, I reasoned, probably I never would have been born at all, given the chance linkage of my own parents and grandparents in America. Should I feel some reluctance about fighting against the land of my forebearers, all of whom had roots in German soil? I had no such feelings, I was an American, deeply proud of the democratic process and of American values. Even though I might actually encounter distant relatives in the days ahead, I could feel no sorrow for the German people who, through overt and capricious action, had brought me to this place to lie in broken glass on a cement floor in Saarbrucken. I drifted into an uneasy sleep, dreaming of castles and burning villages.

The following day on our torturous passage of Kaiserslautern and during a mid morning stop to regroup the convoy, we heard a low grumbling noise coming from the sky to the Southwest. It built steadily into a continuous roll of thunder before we spotted in the clear blue sky vapor trails from an enormous bomber force. Tiny specks, eight miles above the ground, were on their way to the heartland of Germany.

The sight and sound of hundreds of bombers scratching their white signatures of vapor across the bowl of sky was totally awesome. We began to try to count as squadron after squadron passed overhead but after several hundred had gone by we gave it up. The entire majestic armada took well over thirty minutes to pass. After seeing Saarbrucken and witnessing the destruction on the narrow choked road into Hamburg and Kaiserslautern, few of us could imagine what more damage could possibly be inflicted on ground targets. The sides of the road, often nearly impassable, were littered with battered and burned remnants of German armor and equipment. Dust hung over the road made by the churning American track vehicles and scattered by the long lines of convoy trucks. The sunlight breaking through the motes of dust shone balefully on the remains of a broken and fleeing Army. Kaiserslautern, on the Northern edge of the Vosges, here called the Pfalzerwald, was in shambles. Hardly a building was untouched and telephone cables lay in tumbles across the dust caked residue of what once had been a fairly large and important city. A few knocked out American tanks lay in roadside fields and ditches but for the most part the damage to the cities and roads seemed to have been caused by U.S. bombing and strafing. Burned German staff cars and civilian vehicles were pockmarked with large calibre bullet holes, some rusted ones were already giving way to the vines and weeds of spring. Wooden boxes of German artillery shells and Panzerfausts were scattered along the ditches along with the inevitable makeshift crosses with helmets perched on them. In an open hilly area east of Kaiserslautern we stopped near a hastily assembled German supply depot next to the road. Hundreds of boxes of unopened Panzerfausts lay unstacked in the field along with thousands of teller mines. There was no artillery or small arms ammunition, nor was there a drop of gasoline in any of the large quantity of jerry cans scattered in the field. We descended on a twisting battle-scarred road down onto the Rhine plain and entered the city of Ludwgshafen built on the West bank of the Rhine across from Mannheim. Both cities had been severely punished by battle and bombs. We rolled through Ludwgshafen and onto a long pontoon Bailey bridge, which was guarded at both ends by dusty MP's with submachine guns. At the center of the bridge, engineers down in the pontoon boats were making repairs and splicing additional cables to keep the boats in place against the sluggish current. Both sides of the narrow one-way crossing held hundreds of telephone cables, stretched across the pontoons to keep them dry. The former concrete and steel bridges lay in twisted ruins in the river. Mannheim was almost unrecognizable as a city. It had been flattened so that the only remaining walls of large buildings were gaping fragments of solitary columns. An occasional shell of a building punctured the horizon line here and there but as we lurched off the rampway at the end of the bridge, we entered a totally devastated area. Thick dust covered everything within blowing distance of a roadway that had been bulldozed through the rubble to clear the way for East bound traffic. MP's, armed, waved traffic with vigorous arm signals trying to keep everything moving in and out of the city as fast as possible. There were a few civilians moving and poking through the remains of buildings and all were either children, old women or very old men. None of them looked in our direction as we passed, not even to acknowledge the derisive shouts and curses coming from one or two of the more revenge minded men in our convoy. It was as though we were not even there in the minds of the Germans. Our route through the city took us past a gutted opera house, its elegantly gold leaf decorated balconies hanging in twisted and broken angles.

We passed close by an old shawl-covered woman, bent over and walking with the help of a very short cane. She carried on her back a small, carefully tied bundle of tiny sticks. To my surprise, we passed several bombed homes on the far edge of the city where women and small children were sitting in the rubble chipping away at bricks and stones, stacking them neatly in piles. The sight of the methodical Germans, already rebuilding before the war had crossed the near horizon, angered me and I shouted at them. "How soon before you're ready for us again?"

The other men in the open bouncing truck nodded their approval.

North of Mannheim we found ourselves on a stretch of autobahn highway. It was a magnificently engineered four-lane divided highway that skated across the rolling hills to the North. None of us had ever been on a roadbed so smooth or so beautiful. We gained speed, overtaking and passing columns of American Shermans, also heading North. The Shermans were charging along near maximum speed for them; we must have reached a speed of 45 or 50 miles an hour. I had not traveled this fast in a vehicle since leaving the United States. In the open truck in the clean air away from the dust, it was an exhilerating sensation.

Several times we slowed to leave the autobahn, detouring through forests and ravines in order to find a way around bombed out bridges. Curious about some painted markings on the highway that flashed by under our wheels, we saw a dozen ME109's parked in the trees next to the highway. The inventive Germans had used portions of the highway as landing strips for their fighters, having no doubt planned the roadbed around prevailing winds when the autobahn had been built in the 30's.

Not far from the aircraft we passed a long column of German prisoners marching in the grassy center divider between the lanes of traffic. They were being herded along by a Sherman tank that followed them from the rear, a man with a cradled rifle standing in the open turret. The prisoners, while not marching in step, were in a military formation, eyes straight ahead, heads up, defiant. They too did not even glance in our direction.

We arrived near the outskirts of Frankfort to discover that if anything the large industrial city had seen more destruction than Mannheim. More than half of the city lay in dusty ruins but people were working at digging in the shattered buildings, stacking bricks and sorting through debris. It took a long time for us to pick our way through the city, stopping every few yards because of traffic and obstructions. Many streets were unsafe to travel on because of the imminent danger of collapsing walls. The vibrations caused by heavy traffic were a continuous threat to portions of buildings that still stood. Bomb squads worked in the rubble, digging out and disarming unexploded bombs.

Finally we left the city to strike off to the North on a secondary but well engineered road. As soon as we left Frankfurt we were in rolling farm country, fields bordered by clumps of well cared for forests. There was a distinctive visible difference between the French farmland and German fields. These fields of spring wheat and hay seemed somehow more orderly and more neatly maintained. While we could see villages and towns, there were also more individual farmhouses, all painted and well cared for. Suddenly I knew why Pennsylvania had been heavily settled by German immigrants. The farmlands in the low hills beyond Mannheim could have been the central valleys of the Allegheny Mountains where I had lived. Immigrant farmers settled in land, which was familiar to them, because of the makeup of the soil but perhaps also because of a deep spiritual urge to find a place that reminded them of home. I am sure that serious genealogy researchers consider this theory in their tracings of family moves from one country to another. North of Frankfurt we began passing through small towns and villages that were displaying white flags of surrender. Open windows of undamaged houses had white bed sheets and curtains hanging from the openings in the universal symbol of surrender. Thirty miles out of Frankfurt we arrived at our destination, the small town of Butzbach.

Europe Interlude—1983

In the fall of 1983 we found ourselves on a business and vacation trip on the continent of Europe. We anticipated the journey with great enthusiasm. However, what I had not anticipated was the simple fact that the Europe of 1944 was no longer there. Just as America had changed in forty years, so had France, Belgium, Luxembourg, and a little frightenly so, Germany.

Cities, which were once moderate in size, have become enormous, many of them built of high rise glass and concrete complete with apartment complexes and sprawling suburbs. Some cities have made the effort to retain ancient stature, many of these resorting to traffic-free walking malls in the old historical inner portion, but they have only created an incongrous marriage of walkways, gurgling fountains and modern lighting that compete with sculptured blackened stone and leaded windows.

Even the wartime open city of Heidelberg, having created a pedestrian mall out of Haupstrasse in a feeble attempt to preserve its heritage, has been in turn swallowed by a gigantic industrial complex so great that it extends from the Rhine River miles away to disappear along the steep bluffs that face the Neckar River to the east—bluffs that were, only a few years ago, covered with trees and marked only by the occasional crumbled castle tower built in the Middle Ages. To the south of Heidelberg, large sky-threatening apartments, cities in themselves, have been constructed on the once forested hills to house the thousands who serve the plants and factories.

Munich, bombed 83 times during the war, rebuilt its inner city in a spasm of Teutonic defiance, duplicating its original cathedral, museums, public buildings and famous city hall. But the replaced carvings and intricate towers are now made of new white stone, and the pristine quality of the reconstruction does not even serve as a counterpoint to the new, red tile pedestrian mall and stainless steel posts topped by orange, high intensity lamps. At night the efficient lights reflect from the sides of these, somehow saddened, old new buildings. The rebuilding of Munich as it used to be is farciful in nature and in concept and standing in front of the impressive, but nevertheless unoriginal city hall, we could not help but wish that the city fathers had visited the city of Coventry in England before making the curious decision to recreate the unrecreatable.

By contrast, the Coventry planners, in their unique British wisdom, had rejected the idea of rebuilding the 16th century cathedral, which German bombers had left in ruins on the night of November 14, 1940. Instead of reconstruction, which would have been regarded as a form of blasphemy, the remaining structure was cleared but allowed to stand as a symbol of the alienation of man to his God. The insanity of war and of man's incapacity to deal sensibly with differences is commemorated in two words on a large stone sheltered in the shattered wall of the apse behind the place where a glorious altar once stood. The words, chiseled neatly into the granite, are simple and completely moving. They state, *Father Forgive*. No one who has ever experienced any aspects of war could be unaffected by these words implanted in the ruins of this once great cathedral. But the people of Coventry, not satisfied with merely asking for a universal forgiveness, compounded the impact of their statement by building another larger cathedral adjoining the ruins. Gothic in concept and style as was the ancient building, the new cathedral is constructed of modern materials, and its interior arches, soaring above the floor, are made of unstained polished wood. Extensive use of stainless steel and aluminum set off immense stained glass windows behind the altar. The entrance wall that faces the remains of the old cathedral are made entirely of full paneled and beautifully etched clear glass. The effect is openness. In itself, the cathedral is breathtaking in size and beauty, but an unexpected additional emotional impact is instilled by its symbolic roofline. A slightly curved portico roof extends from the very top of the new building and reaches in the direction of the old destroyed cathedral. Functional, it covers people who walk the short distance from the ruins of the old into the sanctuary and safety of the new. The roof reaches into the past, touching, with promise and understanding, times of madness. There is a constant flow of visitors who mingle with church members and a hushed silence, shared among those who sit in quiet wonder, is broken only by the sounds of those who weep openly in the presence of man's uncommon and contradictory capacity for greatness.

The cities have changed, but a more dramatic break with the past is evident in the extensive network of superhighways. Travel on these high speed, beautifully engineered ribbons of concrete, not only makes travel easier but also reduces the amount of time to drive from one point to another. A journey across Europe, which used to take days, has now been reduced to hours and minutes. And like the superhighways of America, the European roadways are designed to be one continuous nonstop experience. In order to make fast travel possible, the highways snake around cities, bypass smaller towns, ignore villages, zoom through freshly cut mountain passes, and all but make it impossible to see anything but fast moving cars, trucks, and roadway signs that announce, almost apologetically, the exits to the other world. Unless one drives the secondary roads, there is no opportunity to sit in small cafes, eat and drink local foods and wines, and talk to people. Trying to find the way by using back roads in Europe is no easier than attempting to retrace Route 66 across America. The real tragedy is the loss of contact with the people and the inexplicable feeling that once on the freeway and outside the cities, the country is deserted.

By taking the time, however, side trips along still existing sections of N-7 or N-4 in France, can stir memories and reveal to those who know where to look, the faint marks of a war that seemingly is all but forgotten in the vigor of the present time. There are still signs of fading house repairs that mark old shrapnel wounds on roof lines and near edges of windowsills. Some old familiar buildings still stand, silently guarding now unimportant road junctions and forest edges for which men died. Once, Northeast of Verdun, we saw, in the distance, an abandoned cluster of destroyed farm buildings, which overgrown with brush and trees of a respectable size, had never been reclaimed from the artillery and mortars that had set them in ruins.

CHAPTER XVIII

BUTZBACH

Butzbach, a small village of less than 4,000 people, was nestled in a farming valley next to rolling wooded hills. The town itself was adjacent to a small railway station. There were shops, restaurants and public buildings on the square. The clean, well kept town had not been bombed and except for U.S. military vehicles, the city was isolated from the main stream of traffic from Frankfort to the large cities in the North.

As our convoy rolled through Butzbach, there were very few older people to be seen on the streets, those we saw stopped to watch us with a mixture of curiosity and a prideful defiance. We found our company markers to the entrance of an industrial complex and as we climbed down out of the trucks, we were whistled into company formation. The Captain introduced an officer who identified himself as the military governor of the region. He spoke to us at length in an informative but serious manner, warning us of the dangers that we might encounter. We were told that the Butzbach area was a major training and staging area for the German Army and that while it had been technically secured, there were probably isolated pockets of bypassed Germans still in the area. We were to go armed at all times, to observe the 6:00 p.m. to 7:00 a.m. curfew and never to speak or fraternize with the civilian population. He explained that G-2 had uncovered a last ditch plan to arm a civilian guerrilla movement of young men to be called "Werewolves." According to our military intelligence, they were being instructed to fight to the death. The officer cautioned us that we were never to leave the compound alone for any reason and that we were to remain absolutely alert for signs of sabotage or direct attack. We were sobered by his instructions, filing into our crowded office building billets with a seriousness that I had not seen since the winter battles.

The Captain called for me to take some men and do a careful reconnaissance sweep around the wooded hills to the East.

The industrial plant had been used as a stamping mill, part of the huge diversified military production plan of the Germans who spread the war industry to small towns and villages in order to escape the destruction that Allied bombers had been delivering to the large industrial cities of the Ruhr Valley. The entire plant of six or seven buildings was self-contained, having its own heat and power plant in a separate coal fueled building. Everything in the complex had been systemically sabotaged, as had been the case in Molsheim. This time however, the destruction was diabolical, for not only had the machinery been destroyed but the Germans had made every effort to damage the facility itself. Wires had been cut into small segments, windows broken, plumbing dug up, and the power plant made virtually useless. The Captain, through the local military governor, located and sent for the former civilian plant manager and his staff of supervisors. They arrived, having been removed from their homes in Butzbach and herded into the back of a 6-by. All eight of them were older men, dressed in shabby suits and worn shoes and it was clear from their defiant stares that they had no intentions of being cooperative. The plant manager, a small fat man wearing a homburg, was openly hostile, shouting in German about the outrage at being forced from his home.

Our officers listened to him for awhile, finally anger showing on their faces as they formed a tight circle around the bitter man. To my surprise, the Captain, who was normally a calm person, in an impatient and threatening manner drew and cocked his pistol against the plant manager's face. The man immediately turned pale and became silent. The entire group then marched into the main factory building, all of our officers and some of us with drawn weapons, herding the civilians through the doorway. Inside, the Captain, still holding his pistol against the manager's neck, explained through an interpreter in a few words that he wanted the plant operational within two days. He was adamant about the need to restore power and about the overhead cranes that had been run off their tracks. The manager and his staff, although remaining sullen, were clearly frightened, perhaps remembering their treatment of their own labor force and not knowing what we might do to them. We put our weapons away as the Germans talked together in subdued argument for a time, some of them agitated, pointing at the dangling severed power lines and shaking their heads. Finally the manager approached the Captain and in a subdued way asked if he could round up some other men from the town who were familiar with the plant's power and who might be able to help. The Captain agreed and by noon the plant was being repaired, under our watchful eyes, by civilians in shop coats and coveralls. Within hours we had the power restored and the cranes were operational. A general cleanup of the plant was undertaken with the help of some of the civilians who had agreed to work for C-rations. A full day's work could earn three cans of rations, which each man collected late in the afternoon before leaving on the long walk back to Butzbach. There was something degrading about a skilled technician waiting in a line behind a truck for three small cans of meat and vegetable hash. But it was also satisfying to see the German humbled in this manner.

In one of the offices we found two large drawers containing hundreds of Nazi party membership books, which had belonged to the plant's faithful German work force. The civilians were clearly apprehensive about the discovery and staged a clumsy accident in an attempt to destroy or damage the incriminating books as they were being shipped off to the military provost. Both boxes were dropped awkwardly in the compound by the Germans who tried to scatter them into the piles of debris from the factory. However, all of the records were recovered and the four Germans involved were sent home without their C-rations, ordered never to return.

Across the narrow street in front of the compound was a separate barracks building behind a chain linked fence topped by many strands of barbed wire. We learned that every morning through the single locked gate had come 50 or 60 Polish slave laborers who worked under guard in the plant. There was no evidence of these prisoners and the German civilians refused to answer questions about their whereabouts. As near as we could tell the Poles had simply been "sent away." The interior of the nearly windowless barracks building was starkly bare of furniture except for rows of tall bunks against each wall. The bunks were four high, made of slats of wood, with no bedding or belongings anywhere in the room. At the entrance to the barracks near the gate was a single small guardroom built with a window looking into the long barrack's interior. On the far end of the dark room was a single uncovered toilet. The ominous silence of the room was not only depressing but filled me with a slow anger and a growing fear for the fate of the men who had been forced to spend the years of their lives making parts for an enemy war machine.

We soon found their disguised common grave in the field behind the barracks. Civilians from the town were ordered, while we watched, to uncover the shallow grave site, doing so slowly with shovels and rakes. There were gasps from everyone as the first dirt caked arm was uncovered, soon followed by other arms, legs, heads and torsos. The stench from the bloated bodies carried in the clear air for a mile around the grave site, gagging the workers who covered their mouths and noses with handkerchiefs and begged to be allowed to leave. The shallow hole was finally emptied of some 60 murdered men who were then laid out

324

side by side in the fresh long grass in the field. Weeping and disclaiming townspeople were brought to the field and, under guard, were forced to walk along the entire length of the dirt encrusted bodies of the recipients of the glories of the Third Reich.

The bodies, partially decomposed, with dirt caked in their mouths and eye sockets were indistinguishable from one another. Some were clothed, some were not and we could not tell whether the men had been shot, strangled, or simply suffocated in their common grave. There was a dirt grey similarity about the row of corpses making the sight, if anything, more terrible to view. Most of the townspeople, along with us, vomited not only from the sickly sweet odor of decay, but from the lonely anonymity of the dead.

Under a clear blue sky I forced myself to walk the line, slowly moving from one still figure after another lying in the soft blowing fallow grass. Dry-eyed, I was determined that it was also a sight, which I never wanted to forget.

Security at the plant was taken seriously and we mounted a full 24 hour guard on the buildings and brick wall that enclosed the entire complex. Guards carried loaded weapons, at night occupying concealed positions both inside and outside the buildings, within shouting distance of one another. As Sergeant of the guard my post was at the main entrance but I made rounds to the guard positions at least once on every four hour shift. I shared the duty with two other assistant platoon leaders and we carried submachine guns as we stepped carefully from one guard post to the next making sure at night that we were identified by a password well in advance of our being seen as a dark moving target. The plant was blacked out at night making it difficult to negotiate a pathway through and around the scattered buildings. Several civilians, who had ignored the curfew, were fired on by guards at the main gate. One German, riding a bicycle late at night, was killed on the road to town. We were cautiously aware that one of our greatest dangers lay in shooting at one another as we moved or made unnecessary noise in the darkness. Occasionally an animal, a cat, dog or opossum, foraging near the walls at night, would be shot by an alert although nervous guard.

During our first week at Butzbach, I was relieved of guard duty and informed that once again I was company demolition noncom. We were beginning to accumulate shells, mines, grenades and panzerfausts faster than we could safely handle them, so Holt and I, taking short drives into the woods, began a rampage of explosions that shook the valley and rattled the windows of the homes in Butzbach. The woods were deep with some narrow dirt roads choked with abandoned German armor and artillery. Some of the armored columns had been destroyed, presumably by the retreating Germans, but most had been simply left standing mutely in the forests. We managed to start one or two of the tanks but they stopped almost immediately when they ran out of fuel. Most of the vehicles were without a drop of gasoline. Remembering Molsheim, we made no attempt to blow them up or did we experiment with short fuses. Instead, with ease, we located deep training bunkers that had been dug into the ground and covered with logs, branches and dirt. There were entire encampments of these bunkers in partial clearings among the trees. They had been used as training sites for Germans on bivouac exercises, a number of them containing abandoned German uniforms and weapons. Apparently many of the young recruits had slipped quietly out of their uniforms and into civilian clothes to fade back to their homes in order to escape capture, imprisonment, or imagined punishment for having served in the German Army. We found a complete officer's uniform scattered on a bunker floor. The first Lieutenant, by his ribbons and iron cross decorations, had seen a lot of service and had served his country well. Making sure that a bunker was unoccupied and not booby trapped, we would climb in and out of it, stacking our shells, mines and rockets on the floor to be exploded by delayed fuses, sending logs spinning through the tree tops in teeth jarring explosions.

We began to see an occasional German civilian poking around in the forest. One unafraid old man scolded us like children for endangering people and, more importantly, for scaring the birds away. Dressed in suspendered short leather pants and wearing a tailored tweed jacket and tweed hat, he bristled at us, shouting in German about our poor attitude. Striding away from us with his heavy walking stick prodding the dirt road, he continued his harangue until he was out of sight. We thought about firing a shot near his feet but happily concluded that he probably also yelled at the German Army when it occupied the woods. He was his own person, without fear.

During our demolition detail an order was posted in the city that all weapons were to be collected from German homes. The official announcement, made by the provost, was that any weapon capable of use or not and owned by a German, was to be turned over to the military authority at once. Failure to do so would be punishable by imprisonment or death. The precautionary action was taken to control any armed threat to the occupying Army and if the Werewolves were to become active they would be handicapped by the lack of weapons to be used against us. The populace took the order seriously and a huge stack of weapons poured into the provost office in the city hall in Butzbach where they were unceremoniously transferred to a concrete bunker against the hill near our compound. We were ordered by the provost to destroy them. I am not a great lover of weapons but I do admire craftsmanship and treat history with thoughtful reverence. In the random pile I found historical treasures, pikes and broad swords from the

Middle Ages, several ancient firelocks, many flintlock long barreled rifles in excellent condition, antique pistols of all descriptions and commemorative swords from wars and events long forgotten. But the greatest agony that I felt was seeing the number of family shotguns and fowling pieces mounted on hand carved wooden stocks, some carved so intricately that they were of pure museum quality.

While we were deciding how to destroy the collection, a jeep load of officers from Frankfort arrived to examine the stock. One bespectacled Major, who obviously knew what he was doing, retrieved an inlaid box of 18th century silver dueling pistols and four or five gold and silver braced flintlock pistols. He carefully placed them in his musette bag as the other officers, rumaging through the pile took the pistols and swords that pleased them. They knew something, which none of us in the field knew, that when the war would be over they could claim the pieces as legitimate souvenirs and crate them home. If I had known that such a directive would be coming down to us, I would have salvaged some of the treasures.

When they had left, we carried the remaining pieces to the open field, throwing them into a gasoline fire, not watching the barrels twist in the heat or the wood carvings dissolve into blackened soot. We worked hard and the fire burned all afternoon leaving a glowing yellow light that could be seen from our compound even late in the night. The senseless burning of history and family was another kind of sadness that I wanted to remember.

The next day we began collecting and smashing all radios owned by the civilians. They were not to listen to the voice of Germany still coming from the propaganda ministry in the hard-pressed city of Berlin. There was fear that Hitler might rally the population to a last death defense in a national redoubt in Southern Germany and that instructions to the people would come from him in radio broadcasts. Owning or listening to a radio was punishable by death. We destroyed many radios, until some wisdom prevailed at a higher level and we were instructed to tag and keep the radios in a safe place. Someone had finally figured out that if we had no means to communicate with the population when the war ended, we would have great difficulty issuing general orders and instructions to scattered populations. The radios would be reclaimed in due time so that official broadcasts could be made and properly received.

Slightly before noon on April 12, we fired several mines in an empty bunker and were bored with watching the dirt and debris crash back down through the trees to raise a cloud of forest dust. As we reluctantly struggled back into our scratchy wool shirts preparing to return to the factory for chow, the jarring explosion, like the others before it, sent its thunder back to us from across the valley. We checked, making sure that we had not started any fires in the dry timber, before climbing into our weapons carrier. As we did so, we heard a jeep, coming up the forest road from the direction of Butzbach. Trailing a cloud of dust and blowing its horn, it squealed to a stop in front of us in our sunlit clearing. Since this was the first time that anyone from the company had ventured into the woods to find us in our demolitions work, my first reaction was that, by some miracle, the war had ended.

But I could see immediately that this was not the case. Sands, the driver and new company clerk, was not smiling as we walked over to the jeep, coughing in the dust that rolled in behind him in a sun struck cloud.

"President Roosevelt is dead," he said in a tight voice. "You better get back, we don't know what's going to happen."

The company gathered quietly in the mess hall as Captain Smart read a message from Eisenhower, the supreme commander. President Roosevelt had died that morning in Warm Springs, Georgia, of a massive cerebral hemorrhage and Vice President Harry Truman had been sworn in as President of the United States. There was a stunned silence in the room, men looked at their hands, at the floor, and some at one another in disbelief. The news could not have been more unbelievable than if the Captain had just read that the Allies had surrendered to Germany. Roosevelt was not just the President, he was the commander of all U.S. military forces, and more than that, to young men he was a tradition. He had been the President for over half of my life and he had brought hope to my family during the Depression. I had been a child when he had become President, so that during all of my formative thinking years I had looked to him with reverence and admiration. Most of us in that room had grown up with the unstated conviction that the word, President, was synonymous with the name Roosevelt and now he was dead, gone.

The announcement, coming as it did with no advance warnings about his health, created an instant vacuum of clear thought and an immediate sense of instability. Captain Smart tried to reassure us that the war would go on, with to us an unknown man named Harry Truman at the helm and, that the death of Roosevelt would make no difference to the outcome of the certain defeat of Germany and Japan. But we were unconvinced. Our one and only powerful leader had just died, leading to the hurried questions founded on fear and collective paranoia. Here, deep in Germany, surrounded by a hostile population, fighting an unpredictable Germany Army, we asked, "Who was Harry Truman? What would Hitler do? What would our Allies do? And more importantly what would the Russians do?" For days we had been hearing of Russia's intention of fighting us when it reached our lines. And to us, in a state of shock, we saw enormous advantages to Stalin now that President Roosevelt was out of the way.

That evening, sitting on our bunks, we discussed the possibilities, and as uninformed as we were, concluded that the only option open to our Armies, was to keep going as we had been doing. The death of the President affected us all so deeply that it had resulted in the only truly serious discussion among a large group of men that I had ever encountered in my two years in the Army. Some of the men succeeded in getting very drunk that night but as I lay on my bunk in the dark noisy room I thought emotionally of home and of my father who had had great faith in President Roosevelt.

Once we had cleared our immediate area of explosives, the demolition work tapered off, although I was sure that there were still hundreds of tons of ammunition scattered throughout the wooded German training camps. Mercifully the decision was made at a higher level to leave the forests to the Germans to clear when the war would finally end. We were hearing stories of a linkup of U.S. and Russian armies, which was imminent somewhere in the center of Germany. During the last week of April, the weather turned hot and blue cloudless skies brought a heat shimmer to the golden fields of grain in the Butzbach valley. We had begun to operate as a repair and maintenance station as soon as our complex had been cleared, but the task often involved trips to field units to bring needed equipment back to the plant for the work to be done. We formed teams, often only two or three men, to travel by jeep to units to pick up the vehicles, artillery, optics and instruments that needed work. In the warm early summer days it was a pleasant detail, involving short unauthorized sightseeing excursions into the countryside that was mostly unmarked by the war. The farmland was dotted with small isolated villages, which could be reached over dusty dirt roads, and these small crossroad clusters, of often not more than a dozen buildings crowded around a church spire, were interesting and fun to visit. The arrival of two American soldiers in a jeep would bring curious but solemn children who accepted our chocolate only after receiving a nod from a nearby adult. The population of farmers, convinced finally that the Americans were not going to burn their houses or destroy their crops had become more open in their relationships with us. While remaining withdrawn and sullen, the civilians had succumbed to their curiosity about us and some were even hesitantly friendly, offering a small smile when not being observed by other Germans. We, on the other hand, bending the fraternization order slightly, enjoyed being inspected on our jaunts and playing the role of the benevolent, but firm, conqueror. But we kept our weapons handy and seldom stepped out of the jeep in any of the villages.

Late one morning as the heat was beginning to be felt, John and I drove our jeep North toward the city of Wetzlar to pick up on the other side of the city an American ambulance that had been slightly damaged in a strafing attack. From other trips we had learned that Wetzlar, a city built in a rather steep valley on a river bearing its name, was difficult to drive through. Twisting streets, sharp inclines and broken bridges turned the town into a traffic jam nightmare. On our first journey North, we had gone there deliberately because we had heard that the Leica camera factory was located in Wetzlar and that the excellent German cameras could be had for the taking. When we arrived, we were surprised to see that the large factory had been completely undamaged, either by bombs or by sabotage and was closely guarded by American M.P.'s. We were turned away by the contemptuous guard at the main gate. Consequently, we were not interested in returning to the city and instead sought a way to bypass the main part of Wetzlar on our way North. About halfway to Wetzlar, five miles or so, we spotted to our left a likely looking narrow dirt track, which lead up a gentle slope into a road in the forests beyond wheat fields. Spinning off the asphalt highway, we bumped along the path, our wheels cutting swaths through the jeep high wheat on either side of us. The tall grain lashed us through the open sides of the jeep and the lurching and jumping ride soon had us both laughing and with me hanging on to my passenger's seat. To avoid a large boulder in the path, John swung the jeep crazily into the wheat field where we were immediately cut off from forward visibility. The tall grain was transformed into a fascinating golden curtain, which never completely parted, as we hammered across the ruts and holes of the field. John tried to swing the bucking jeep back to the path but suddenly we came to a jarring stop in a hidden irrigation ditch. The jeep was pitched forward at an awkward angle, rear wheels spinning in the air. Shaken but unhurt, we tried to back out of the ditch with our frontwheel drive but there was not enough power there to move us either forward or backward. We climbed out, standing in head high wheat deciding that we were going to need help digging the jeep out of the ditch. We walked on our own tracks back through the crushed and broken wheat, coming at last to the path. We were several hundred yards from the highway and fairly close to the forest edge but knowing that any help that we could get would come from the highway, we started back up the trail, which had been made wider by our jeep. It was hot and we were dusty from the wheat; irritating chaff was beginning to itch inside the collar of my wool shirt.

We had not traveled far on the path however, before we heard a shout coming from the forest behind us. Turning, we saw a strange and unexpected sight. Over the bright yellow brown fields and against the dark green edge of the pine forest, a small white flag on the end of a long stick was being waved back and forth. Three figures could be seen standing with the flag. One of them raised an arm, motioning us to come back in this direction. Puzzled, John and I walked slowly up the path toward the trees, finally leaving the planted wheat as we came to a fairly wide strip of pasture between the field and the narrow road leading into the forest.

I was not at all prepared for what we found beyond the wheat field, for there standing at attention was a German officer, next to him were two German Sergeants, one of whom held the pole with the white flag attached to it. We stopped on the grass strip uncertain as to what we should do. The uncertainty was compounded when I saw, in the trees behind the officer, a two file column of German soldiers, also standing at attention. The column was so long that I could not see the end of it as it disappeared back in the trees.

John whispered to me out of the side of his mouth, "I hope to God they want to surrender."

In the silence of the moment I took a few steps forward until I was in the shade of the tree line. The officer left his two Sergeants and took several marching steps toward me until we were only a few feet apart. He was dressed in an immaculate Weirmach Captain's tunic with brightly polished boots and belt and was wearing a dress uniform cap placed squarely on his head. He was a man in his late forties, grey stubble of close-cropped hair showing at both sides of his cap. Almost exactly my height, he looked at me expectantly out of hard sunken blue grey eyes.

He was thin, almost gaunt and I could see from the four ribbons on his chest and the Iron Cross first class at his throat that the man was a veteran of many battles. I saluted him awkwardly, conscious that I was dressed only in dusty torn trousers and sweat streaked open necked shirt. I not only did not have a helmet on but my head was uncovered by any military cap. My boots were dirt caked from the wheat field and although I was wearing a pistol on my hip, I really didn't know whether it even had a clip in it, let alone a bullet in the chamber. I had an impulse to apologize for my appearance when the Captain returned my salute smartly and swiftly went for his own pistol. I felt a frozen fear as, taking his Luger from his holster, he pointed it in our direction and took a precise step toward me. As he did so he flipped the pistol in his hand, presenting it to me butt first. The men behind him remained rigidly at attention, eyes forward looking at their Captain. I tried to appear military as I stepped to him to receive the pistol but I knew that to him I could only be a dirt covered unmilitary amateur soldier who didn't even know enough to wear his helmet. As I touched the butt of the Luger, our eyes met and I saw a deep hurt in the strong face. There was no shame, no defiance, only a tiredness and an acceptance of truth in the deep set eyes. He nodded briefly to me as I took the heavy weapon from his fingers. He then unhooked his ceremonial dagger from his belt and handed the scabbard and hanging belt to me. It was not an S.S. dagger, it was a standard Wermach piece. This man was a regular Army officer, not a Nazi.

"I am Captain Heinrich," he said in a quiet voice in German, waiting politely for me to speak.

"And I am Sergeant Keim, Army of the United States," I replied, noting with a tiny satisfaction that his eyes had flickered slightly when he heard me speak my German name. I had given the pronunciation the full Teutonic inflection.

From that moment on I had no further ideas. I had just accepted surrender from an undetermined number of armed Germans. I was at least a quarter of a mile from anyone except John, whom I knew to be unarmed, and my only transportation was unseen and jammed into a ditch in a farmer's wheat field behind me. To make matters worse I had very little command of the German language, knowing only a few words that I had picked up during the few weeks since we had been in the country. The words, which I had learned, were all meant to be yelled from the back of trucks at women and phrases such as "You have a pretty ass," seemed inappropriate in this situation. Not having been permitted to speak or fraternize with the local population had meant, among other things, not learning the language.

The Army had taught me many valuable things: how to jump in burning water, how to tell which poison gas was killing me, how to guard empty buildings, how to avoid passwords, how to fall down in a parade, how to get a marksman medal and how to put on a condom. But not one word had ever been spoken to me about how to accept a surrender.

While I had been racking my brain for a solution, the Captain had turned and was shouting orders to his men who immediately began marching straight out of the woods toward the wheat field, When the last of the column had cleared the trees, the Captain called to it to halt. I saw that the head of the two file column was well into the wheat field astride the path leading back to the highway. There were over sixty of them, helmeted, wearing full equipment and each carrying a slung Mauser rifle.

Many of the rifles were unfinished, the wood stocks were raw wood, unstained. The platoon was apparently from one of the training camps, probably from deep in the woods, not having been found by the American patrols. Most of the soldiers were very young, probably 16 or 17. Some of the youngest were crying, tears streaking their dusty faces. One or two older men were actually smiling, glad to be out of it at last. The platoon, although disciplined and military, was a ragtag group coming from the very end of Germany's manpower pool. Compared to them, I felt old and wise in the ways of war.

But as I studied them, I wondered if I was related to any of them through some common ancestor from 200 years ago. Would one of them suddenly recognize me and cry, "Vilhelm, where have you been?"

However, few of them even looked at me and those who did gave only a defiant sign of a bitter contempt.

The Captain, looking somewhat puzzled by my inactivity, motioned for me to join him at the head of the column. Relieved that someone knew what to do, I pushed the Luger and dagger under my web belt and, trampling through the wheat, joined the Captain and his two silent Sergeants at the head of the column. I shouted to John to bring up the rear as we began a deliberate march to the main road, the Captain beside me and the white flag overhead immediately behind us. Suddenly in an emotion filled voice, a soldier in the column began to sing the opening words to a German marching song, but the Captain, furious, ordered him to be silent. We passed the track to the disabled jeep and reached the highway soon after. Shouting orders, the German Sergeants lined up the men on the shoulder of the road while the Captain held the white flag and I frantically looked for help from passing vehicles. Many trucks, halftracks and several tanks rolled by in both directions, some coming very close to running me down as I waved my arms and pointed to the fully armed platoon of German soldiers standing patiently behind me. No one would stop. It was a scene from a bad movie or a poor joke book, a hatless dirty American soldier, jumping up and down on a highway all the time being viewed from behind by a stoic but fully equipped enemy platoon. I was about to ask the Germans if they would mind stopping someone for me, when an MP jeep skidded to a halt in a cloud of dust just beyond the platoon. Backing up to me, an incredulous MP officer demanded to know what I was doing.

I explained everything except the jeep in the ditch as he stopped the next empty three trucks on their way in to Wetzlar. While the German and the American officer exchanged words, I carefully slipped the Luger and dagger out of sight under my shirt. The American was concerned about the Mauser rifles and other weapons, and the platoon was quickly disarmed, piling their equipment, including helmets into the back of the first 6-by. John and I waited, as inconspicuously as possible, until the captured platoon had boarded the remaining 6-bys and sped away toward the North. The trucks were followed by the two officers in the MP jeep and as it passed, we both came to attention and saluted. The German returned our salute.

We hurried back to the jeep and with its shovel and tools we dug the damned thing out of the ground by ourselves. Then retracing our trail through the wheat to the highway, we drove the normal way into Wetzlar almost three hours late. I hid my treasures under the jeep seat.

The Luger Interlude—1962

Alone, in the darkened split-level room in Los Angeles, I held the heavy weapon in my hand, palming it to feel its weight and balance. It was a beautifully made Luger, a 7.65 Luftwaffe model with the engraving of a first quality piece marked on its jackknife action. It had remained until then wrapped carefully in an oily cloth in its holster and placed in a tight box, behind worn shoes in my bedroom closet. Since I had returned from the war, I had never fired it nor had I even taken it out of its box. It was a souvenir of a time to be forgotten. The pistol had been given to me by a German officer somewhere North of Butzbach just days before the war had ended and except for a pit mark on one side, the gun was in perfect condition. I had had a difficult time getting it home, guarding it against theft and an unscrupulous supply Sergeant who attempted to collect all company war souvenirs for his own purposes. I had buried the pistol in the dirt floor of my tent on the bluffs above Marseille rather than surrender it to him. The disfiguring pit had come from the moisture in the ground. I removed the clip from the handle and examined it along with the spare clip in the black leather holster; both were full. I had sixteen cartridges, their copper jacketed bullets green with a fine mold. Clipping each cartridge out of its holder, I carefully cleaned and lightly oiled each one, placing them upright in a tight row on the low coffee table in front of me. I looked at the bullets, a helpless weariness growing with me.

"Not again," I thought, "not now, not when it's finally beginning to fall together." But deep inside, even beyond the dread and the fear, I knew that it *could* happen again, that the desire for peace had never been a counterbalance to the senseless determination of the leaders of nations. I had seen the destroyed cities, the refugees, the brutality and cruelty of concentration camps and I had seen the marks of death.

It was October in Los Angeles, the rainy season was about to begin, announced by sunless days and darkening cloud banks. There were clouds in the world also, this time over Cuba, and what was occurring was being called the missile crisis. During that day a blockade of Russian ships had been announced and the world was holding its breath on the edge of a nuclear war, waiting to see what the Russians would do. The incident was no war game to view with indifference, it was reality and it was underway at the moment.

After quietly opening and closing bedroom doors to make sure that my wife and three infant children were still sleeping. I slipped the loaded Luger in my windbreaker pocket, found a working flashlight and went out into the midnight darkness to the garage. There I found a crowbar and the box of well hidden supplies of bottled water, canned milk and other nonperishable food. Also gathering up some blankets and a rain tarpaulin, I left the garage with my arms loaded and headed for a new storm drain that had just been completed a block away. I had watched the multimillion dollar construction project for the months that it had blocked off the end of our residential area. Built under a street, it was a deep reinforced concrete square tunnel that was very large and ran for miles, connecting with other tunnels and eventually reaching the ocean 20 miles away. I had been particularly interested in a raised manhole entrance shaft that had been placed in an orange grove several yards from the storm drain itself. Making sure that I was not observed on the deserted street, I stumbled through the dirt clods among the orange trees, dumped my load behind the entrance shaft where it could not be seen from the street, and as quietly as possible, pried open the manhole cover with the crowbar. Sliding it sidewise made a metal-on-metal grinding sound, bearly audible among the fruit trees. With my flashlight I descended an iron rung ladder into a deep black hole that ended at the entrance to a small horizontal tunnel leading to the main drain. On hands and knees I crawled through to the deeply buried storm drain, which was larger than I expected it to be. Easily 15 feet in height and width it was exactly what I was looking for. The entrance tunnel was connected to the storm drain so that it entered about 10 feet above the floor of the drain itself, leading directly onto a wide concrete shelf low enough to permit a person to stand. Throwing the beam of my flashlight in both directions in the chilly drain, I could see that the tunnel was very long, the shaft of light fading away before it encountered any object in either direction.

By making several trips I moved my supplies to the wide shelf, covering the cache of food, water and blankets with the rain tarpaulin. I made sure of two things; that my pile of goods was far enough away from the tunnel entrance that it could not readily be seen, and that I could, with my flashlight see clearly anyone entering the drain through the entrance hole. Finished, I sat on the edge of the concrete shelf, smelling the pervasive odor of fresh cement and holding the butt of the Luger pistol in my jacket pocket. An automobile rumbled by overhead, its noise barely heard through the thickness of street, dirt and the reinforced concrete of the storm drain. I shined my light on the gaping tunnel entrance, pointed my Luger at it to calculate the range. I was sobered to the point of depression, but I also had a strong resolve that when the bombs came I could and would protect my little family from anyone who threatened them. I would shoot my neighbors. I would shoot anyone who came through the tunnel. We would try our best to survive. Walking back to my home in the darkness, my hand found the pistol in my jacket pocket and my mind went to the officer who had handed it to me at the edge of the woods above Butzbach seventeen years before. What had become of him? Was he still alive? A bank executive perhaps, or the owner of a small Gasthouse in Bavaria, maybe lying dead in a shallow grave in Indochina having died for France as a professional soldier in the French foreign legion.

I knew that if he were alive he would remember the young dirty American Sergeant with the German name. His surrender had been his last official act as a German officer and he would have remembered it for the rest of his life. I felt the smooth warm metal of the Luger barrel against my abdomen and wondered what Captain Heinrick would have thought if he had known that his pistol would one day be 8,000 miles away, being carried by the same hatless Sergeant in a determined defense of his little children.

The next day Mr. Nikita Kruschev announced that Russia would comply with the U.S. demand for the removal of nuclear missiles from Cuba and several days later, during a drizzling late night rain, I removed my cache of supplies from the storm drain.

I placed the unloaded Luger back in its box where it remains to this day behind the shoes in a bedroom closet, waiting futilely, I hope, never to be used.

CHAPTER XIX

GERMANY SURRENDERS

On April 30 during the evening meal in our mess hall, we heard some astonishing news from a courier driver who had stopped over for chow. The Russians were in Berlin and Hitler had committed suicide. Not only that but the U.S. First Army had linked up with the Russians on the Elbe River and whole German armies were surrendering en masse. Enemy resistance in Italy was collapsing and the 7th Army had reached Munich. It looked as though, at last, the war in Europe was about to end. But then for several days there was no news at all, only rumors that at any moment we would receive word that the final surrender had been signed. We stayed close to the post, leaving the compound only for supplies, anxious to be around if word came down that the war was over. We gathered in groups whenever possible, doing our repair work on trucks and artillery in a perfunctory manner and going to the main gain whenever a jeep arrived. When the news came, it did not come by jeep however, instead on May 6 a telephone call from Battalion informed the orderly room that an announcement of the surrender had been heard on the British Radio network. There was much confusion over the announcement. It seemed that Supreme Headquarters was denying the radio report and was instead announcing that an agreement had been reached with the Germans to cease all hostility on May 9. The conflicting reports made it difficult to understand what was actually happening and the rumors about Russia began to surface again. We heard that our Armies were being redeployed so as to be in position to fight the massive Russian armies advancing from the East. The pervasive fear that we were going to have to fight Russia was very real and alarming. I remembered the prophecy of my Germany POW friend, Franz, in Camp Forrest and felt a hollow fear that he might have been

337

right. I was surprised that there were so many men among us who felt that we should fight the Communists.

"We might just as well, we're going to have to fight the bastards some day. Let's get it over with while we're here," was a common statement heard in the mess hall and in the barracks.

The cynic's response was simplicity, "Against whom are we going to fight World War IV?"

The hours and days dragged on amid rumors and more contradictory announcements until early afternoon on May 8 when we received an officially confirmed report from Battalion that the war was definitely over. Not only that, but the Russians were celebrating the victory with our forces on the front.

Our reaction was explosive. We fired our weapons into the air, making the plant compound rock with the confined echoing noise. We laughed, cheered and pounded each other on the back. I ran into the guardhouse at the gate, took a submachine gun and fired it at the tall brick chimney, which stood at the power plant. Starting at its base I fired full clips, running the bullets up the entire length of the structure. Chips of brick and mortar showered down into the compound as everyone began firing at the chimney. The German civilians who were still working for us came out of the buildings to watch the frenzy of released emotions but some of them became agitated over what was rapidly becoming the destruction of their chimney. Good naturedly, we stopped the firing and turned our attention to the more important problem, getting our hands on a lot of liquor. We ran to find Sgt. Striker, who it turned out, had been working on the problem for several days, anticipating the terrible thirst that would overcome the company when the war finally did end. He had already sent three trucks to nearby Bad Nauheim to pick up champagne from a bottling plant. By six o'clock we had 3,000 bottles of very new champagne sitting in cracked ice in the plant washroom. There were several large stone circular waist high sinks made for general worker washup purposes and into these had been poured cracked ice, obtained from God knows where, and into the ice had been stacked enough champagne to give each man at least 20 bottles. That evening was, without question, the scene of one of the wildest, most drunken parties ever held. Almost everyone took part in the celebration, even some of those men who never drank. There was something very special about champagne toasts being drunk to mark the end of the war. Contests were held to see how many bottles could be consumed by one individual, and slurred speeches were made to no one in particular. The results of the alcoholic orgy were predictable but we didn't care. The war was over, we were certain that we were going to be sent home.

I had been intoxicated before, sometimes really drunk but never had I even achieved such a pinnacle of outright drunkenness as I did on May 8, 1945. The following day was a living nightmare of pain and persistent nausea. Two hundred men stumbled around over hundreds of empty bottles and groaned in a collective agony. Nothing helped, not even the coffee, which the cooks swore would cure anything. Everything tasted like aluminum, and intestinal stress only helped to accent the bloodshot eyes blinking in pain against the unmerciful daylight. Several men were unable to leave their bunks, choosing instead to merely moan and beg for help.

Somehow we managed to live through the day and by evening some few of those with iron stomachs went back to the washroom for more champagne. Most of us however declined the temptation.

That evening we received word that within 48 hours we would board a train in Butzbach and head South to Marseille to board a ship for home. The welcome news had a miraculous effect on the hangovers. We stopped whimpering and began packing, talking all at once about plans after our discharge from the service. The most often repeated joke was, "The *second* thing I'm going to do when I get home is take off my pack."

Two days later another company came to replace us at the plant and we loaded once again in boxcars in the small railroad station in Butzbach. This time, however, the weather was warm and the cars had been cleaned for us beforehand, so as we trundled out of the station we were comfortable and happy.

Germany Interlude—1985

The drive from Salzburg, Austria, had been very tiring, even though the autobahn had provided an excellent straight shot out of the southern mountains across the plains of central Germany. There had been alternate periods of heavy rain and much traffic, including several military convoys, some German and some American. But a truck had overturned about 40 miles from Munich, causing a long delay before we could reach the haven of our old hotel near the center of the city. A German police helicopter had flown low over the stalled line of traffic giving loudspeaker instructions to the frustrated motorists who had stood on the highway next to their cars.

When we finally did arrive, we encountered the same downtown parking problems enjoyed by every city on the face of the earth. The hotel staff was helpful in securing a place to park on a side street but they were not overly friendly toward us. We appeared to be an unwelcome intrusion. After unpacking, we went to dinner in the hotel dining room, too tired to seek out one of the more famous restaurants of the city. The food was good however, and we washed down braised wild stag on noodles with an excellent local beer. Relaxing over coffee and brandy, we noticed that directly across from where we were seated was a small private dining room. The door to the room was open and we could see and hear six or seven men and their wives. The group had just finished its meal and were busy with loud conversation and wine. Out of curiosity I studied the group because the men appeared to be my age. The women sat together at one table and the men were grouped at another.

Suddenly one of the men stood up and rapped on the tabletop for attention. The small room fell silent and the women turned their faces in a respectful way to the man who was about to speak. He was a short heavy man dressed in a gray suit, and it became clear at once that, as he began to speak in a low voice, he was emotionally involved in what he had to say. Although the general restaurant noise made it impossible to hear everything that he was saying, I occasionally caught enough of the speech to know that he was reciting the history and record of his Germany army unit. At one point he named, with pride, the battles in which his unit had been engaged. Included in the long list of Russian campaigns were the names of French cities such as Strasbourg, and toward the end of his recitation, the word, Hagenau. As the speaker continued in a choked voice, the women did not look at one another and the men murmured, sometimes shaking their heads in remembrance. One man, head bowed and eyes closed, wept openly. Following the speech, each man stood at his place at the table with a raised glass and, one by one, said a few words. The names of comrades were solemnly announced, sometimes provoking gentle laughter over the telling of an incident. Toast after toast was made.

When my wife and I left the dining room, the group was still there, but by now the men were laughing and singing, the women still sitting quietly alone, playing no part in the good and bad memories or of the camaraderie of Germany's last great war. As we entered the tiny heavy elevator that would take us to our room above, I wondered to myself, "Should I have gone into that meeting and announced to them that I had also been a soldier and that even though we had fought one another, we were all comrades together from long ago?"

The question went unanswered. I slept poorly that night in Munich. Perhaps I was still tired from the long drive from the city of Salzburg.

We stayed two nights in an old historical hotel in Neustadt, a small town in the Black Forest country. During the days, we drove without plan, expressing astonishment over huge industrial centers carved out of clearings and located on plateaus within the once heavily forested region. Nuclear power plants were constructed along slow moving rivers nestled next to their gigantic cooling towers and spewed clouds of steam into the bright blue sky. Smaller villages, never touched by the war, still persisted and gave some semblance to tradition as each one coveted a narrow ravine or a landlocked valley. Cowbells and lumbering operations broke the wooded silence but for the most part, the power lines, cement blocks and hard steel have bitten deeply into the once fabled Black Forests of Germany. What has not been destroyed by the energies of expansion is slowly dying from the acid rains of France. Farmers and dairymen fight without much success, to hold on to what they have in the face of an industrial nation seeking space for its enterprises. Only in the poster area of Garmisch and the German Alps, where scenery itself drives the commerce, is there a feeling of the old Germany of lederhosen. In this preserve, even the roads are moderate in size, although innumerable commercial ski slopes have torn the mountainside forests into vertical strips to accommodate an escalating year-round tourist industry. The mountains remain, but the forests are giving way to a vigorous and expanding nation.

On our second day of exploring the country around Neustadt, we found ourselves to the East on a high treeless plateau. Having driven in an undirected manner, stopping occasionally to view villages and rich farms, we discovered that we were lost. Although roads and highways are well marked in Deutschland, we had become involved in a superhighway cloverleaf construction project and had mistakenly taken the wrong turn. We decided to follow the secondary road anyway, as it seemed to lead to a fair sized city built along a treeline on the opposite side of the plateau. The city turned out to be Huflingen, so we drove around the town observing parking decks and pedestrian malls intermingled with old churches and ancient buildings. Even well off the beaten path, Huflingen was also suffering from progress. But as we left the center of the city by a different route, we passed a row of well spaced barracks buildings behind an old long brick wall. It was a German military compound and young soldiers in disturbingly familiar grey-green uniforms were everywhere. Groups of twos and threes were strolling along the roadway and as we passed an iron bar gate, we could see squads at drill, brandishing American M-16 rifles in mock attack. Try as I would, I could not help but feel the tightening in my stomach as we drove slowly by the main post gate. An armed sentry looked up with some curiosity and watched us carefully as he continued to check the papers of two soldiers who were leaving the post. From the short distance, I could see his black leather belt from which hung his holstered pistol. His belt buckle was the familiar grey aluminum and I said aloud, "I wonder if God is finally with them?"

Dinner that evening at the old hotel at Neustadt turned out to be an event. The hotel was a local favorite gathering place for eating and drinking and on this evening a surprise birthday party was given for the conductor of the town's symphony orchestra. He was in his 70's and was greatly moved by the occasion. The highlight of the celebration in the crowded low ceiling dining room was an impromptu performance, in his honor, from the entire orchestra. Several selections were played, as toasts were drunk amid the cheers and short congratulatory speeches. We joined in on the celebration, accepted by the people of the town, even though we were recognized as strangers. Small town hospitality is universal and is practiced with great dedication in Europe. When the orchestra had concluded its numbers, its members joined the many groups at tables and before long the singing of childhood hiking songs exploded from sections of the room as the entire assemblage became a boisterous community gathering. Through the shouting and laughter, glasses clinked and toasts were exchanged between neighboring tables. We drank large quantities of the excellent local beer, served by laughing waitresses who moved easily among the many tables carrying pitchers of the brew.

As the evening progressed, I noticed that I was being watched by a man seated several tables away from where we sat. He was with a rather subdued party, two men and two women who looked to be husbands and wives. They were all well dressed, he in a dark blue fashionably cut suit and deep maroon necktie. The man was strikingly handsome with blue eyes and a full head of straight silver hair carefully combed back from a well tanned forehead. He was my age. When he caught me returning his gaze, he slowly averted his eyes and began talking quietly to the woman seated next to him. I continued to study him as I sipped my beer.

As often happens in a large group of noisy people, there comes a moment or two when the volume of noise drops almost to nothing and a peculiar hush interrupts all sound. These moments are often infrequent and always brief, but as I watched the man with the silver hair, the room unexpectedly grew quiet and almost as though I had willed him to do so, he turned his head and looked directly at me. At that instant we communicated with one another, and we both knew, that for a few seconds we had exchanged the present for the past.

He too had been a boy, and had been behind the hedgerow, standing back in the shadows of the sniper's window, narrowing his eyes along the sights of the rifle barrel, running, bent over, carrying the box of ammunition, trailing behind the Tiger tank over the crust of snow, coughing in the smoke and flame, snaking through the trees in his white winter cape and cloth covered helmet, and he had held the grenade in his freezing fingers.

He had been there, and as we two older men looked deeply at one another, *he* knew that I also had been there. As the noise in the dining room cascaded once again to the level of shouting, we gave to one another an imperceptible nod of agreement and then looked away.

CHAPTER XX

MARSEILLE

Our first task in the boxcar was to get organized and we did so in a light-hearted fashion. There was no need to close the sliding side doors, the weather was good, the sunshine continuous and the breeze soft and clear. There were 12 of us to a car allowing us plenty of room to place our weapons, helmets, packs, gas masks and all of the now unnecessary accouterments of war against one of the end walls of the car. We were dressed in our green cotton fatigues, most of us in just pants and T-shirts, and there was a prevailing atmosphere of a leisurely summer camp outing. Once free of the things that we did not need, we settled in the remaining part of the car with our personal belongings and our mess kits. We sat in the doorways, legs dangling outside the slow moving train and cheerfully watched the beautiful German farmland moving majestically past us. We talked quietly, laughing often in the manner of excited young men who were going home after a long absence.

The joviality began to be restrained by the time we arrived in the railyard at Frankfurt because the journey of less than 30 miles had taken us more than six hours to complete. More than once we sat immobile for over an hour waiting for repairs to be made on the roadbed or waiting for trains ahead of us to be cleared to move on. The railyards at Frankfurt were almost totally destroyed with only one or two tracks operational. From the size of the yard it would have appeared that the facility could have, at one time, handled 100 trains or more. It had been reduced to a single main track leading in and out of the city. The station itself lay in tangled ruins and everywhere there were workers filling bomb craters, laying track, and removing wrecked locomotives and smashed boxcars. The sight was sobering and we began to realize that it might take us quite some time to reach Marseille by train.

Our cooks had transformed one of the boxcars into a kitchen so that during our stops we had been able to walk along the train with our mess kits, be served hot meals, and return to our own car to eat. We spent the night sleeping in our cars in the yard at Frankfurt.

During the next 48 hours we worked our way down the East bank of the Rhine through Manheim, Karlsrue, and Freiburg, arriving at Mulhouse, France, late in the second day, crossing the upper part of the river over a railroad bridge swarming with engineers trying desperately to keep the bridge open to creeping traffic. The trip to Mulhouse had been revealing and depressing. Anyone who has ever traveled by train knows that railroad tracks are not laid through the better sections of a city, that instead they follow the path of industry and low income housing. That fact, together with catastrophic bombings, presented us with a picture of destruction that we had not seen even from highways and roads.

Monumental effort to restore service was being made all along the line but the terminals presented bottlenecks of twisted track, shattered trains, and tons of rubble, sometimes higher than our train passing cautiously among the wreckage. Railyards and their surrounding industrial centers had been prime targets for the bombers, which had methodically transformed many of them into surrealistic lunar landscapes. The covering snow was gone, leaving mounds of dirt encrusted and dust covered rubble, under which there was bound to be hundreds or thousands of human bodies. Men, civilians and U.S. engineers, paused in their work on the tracks, leaning on shovels and picks to stare as we silently passed by. At no time during the war had I felt such a deep sense of the destruction as viewed from an open boxcar door. Perhaps it was because the attention to the battle was no longer the prime motivator and that what remained was to crawl animal-like from cellars to rebuild what was left.

I crossed the Rhine into France with no regrets at leaving the soil of my ancestors. Germany was in ruins, far beyond what I had imagined it would be, but it was over and the task at hand would occupy those who had survived the inferno.

We traveled through Burgundy, the Northern part of which had been the scene of the First French Army's fall battle with the retreating Germans. Much of it was destroyed. But when we arrived in Dijon, it and the small towns and villages, appeared to have escaped all but the bombings and aerial attacks on the rail centers. We lay in the railyard in Dijon for hours waiting for clearance to proceed South to Lyons. And it was here that we encountered, on a large scale, a phenomena of the backwaters of war, refugees. As we made our laborious way down the Rhone Valley to Marseille, we were to see these pathetic people in ever increasing numbers. There were hundreds of thousands of displaced

344

people on the move, many of them young men recently released from prison camps, but many more were families of solemn ragged adults and gaunt unsmiling children. Dirty, hungry and dazed, they clung to the sides and tops of train cars, watching ahead, counting the miles of slow journey. Occasionally we would glide so slowly by one of these refugee trains that we could hold brief conversations with the people sitting on the floor of the crowded boxcars. Someone from our boxcar would shout a language, trying to determine nationality and invariably one of us could say a few hurried words of encouragement in their native tongue. There were Poles, Hungarians, French, Germans, Belgians, Russians, but most were Jewish, returning home to search for loved ones and friends. When possible we would throw candy, cigarettes, rations—anything that we had to the wildly outstretched hands, trying to ignore the screaming and the fighting for the food as we passed by their doorway in which dwelled a world of indescribable suffering.

*   *   *   *   *

We arrived late in the afternoon heat at an encampment of hundreds of tents built on the hilly bluffs overlooking Marseille and the Mediterranean Sea beyond. It had taken us five full days and nights to travel the 700 miles from Butzbach.

Assigned to squad tents of 12 men each, we soon discovered that we were to wait for the rest of the battalion to join us for the trip home. Although at first there was something ominous about our need to travel as a battalion back to the States, I discounted it as natural suspicion and joined with the others rejoicing that we would be together as a complete unit again. Some even suggested that perhaps a parade was being planned for our homecoming, maybe even in Los Angeles with its street car obstacles.

We settled into an unhurried camp life with movies at night on an outdoor screen and no one seemed at all concerned that we were issued summer uniforms along with new web equipment and combat boots. The cotton summer uniforms, which made us look like gas station attendants, were welcome in the fierce heat of Southern France in May. This part of France is much like the American Southwest with few trees on open craggy hills. Cactus grew throughout our treeless camp and we savored the rare breeze blowing through the sides of the rolled up flaps of our tents. We had no duties to perform and after morning roll call, we were free to roam the vast expanse of the camp, to lie in our tents waiting for the next meal, or to accept an afternoon pass into Marseille. Buses left for town each afternoon with loads of soldiers eager to walk the streets of the ancient seaport, seeking the shade of its many sidewalk cafes and its beautiful tree lined boulevards. Marseille, as a major French seaport on the Mediterranean, had had its port facilities destroyed by the Germans before their retreat to the North. Half sunken ships lay in the wide harbor and dockside facilities had been systematically dynamited to prevent their use by the invasion forces of the 7th Army. Like most European ports, buildings had been built fronting directly onto docks and many of these had been seriously damaged by the demolition work. It is probable that Allied bombers had also pounded the harbor prior to the invasion but within a block or two of the harbor, there was little or no damage to the beautiful white city that sprawled up the slopes to the hills above.

Walking the streets in small groups was a curious mixture of anticlimax and boredom. The savage early summer heat of the Mediterranean sun made escape into dark little bars mandatory. The bars were usually crowded with Americans and aggressive prostitutes, who were part of an army of such ladies plying their trade in the port city. These adventurous encounters in cool dark cafes revealed that many of my comrades, now concerned about going home, were not interested in a risky few minutes of love with a stranger. These were not the same young men who had found London and Paris such an amorous challenge, these were men who listened carefully to the camp warnings that Marseille had the highest venereal disease rate in Europe. It was not time to take a dose home to a prospective wife in spite of the often shouted offers from prostitutes across the room.

We all enjoyed the aggressive behavior however and often visited one particular bar noted for the young ladies who exposed their breasts in an energetic sales campaign. We had been warned also about the huge black-market operation, which was in business in town. Stories of murder and torture appeared in the local newspapers and arrests were common, although it appeared that the local police, working with the military, were hapless in the face of the massive black market. A little grateful that Harding was no longer around, I accompanied my friend, Holt, into town one afternoon to meet with, as he described him, a friendly contact. Telling the bartender who he was, Holt and I sat at a table in the far corner of a long dim bar to wait for the arrival of a summoned friendly contact. Soon, standing in the doorway against the blinding light from the sun baked street, was an enormous man, weighing at least 300 pounds. Waddling over to our table, he dragged two straight backed chairs together to support his size and weight. In spite of the heat of the day, he wore a shiny black suit, his fat fingers covered with expensive stones, and his dark face so evil that he looked Mongoloid. He nodded to Holt and turned to stare at me, making it clear that he had no intention of speaking as long as I was there. So I sauntered over to the bar with my drink to scowl amiably at the three ladies sitting there.

In time, we left, my friend wordless but worried. He had been losing heavily in high stake card games in the camp, and word was that he owed three or four thousand dollars to two men in the company. Perhaps he spoke to me because he needed someone to know what he was doing but I finally got him to reveal his dangerous plan. He was planning to move a truckload of canned food, which he had stolen from the poorly guarded camp depot over a short period of time. He had the stack of supplies hidden in a ravine near the depot and only needed a truck for transporting the goods to the black-market contact near the edge of the city. His plan was to drive the 6-by through the unfenced hills to the East, avoiding the guarded section of the post. He was my friend but I did not offer to help him, nor did he ask for my help. To cover himself he secured a pass the next afternoon and disappeared. I watched the silly Broadway extravaganza movie that evening, glancing at my watch every few moments in a growing panic for the safety of my friend. At lights out, he had not returned to the tent. His empty accusing bunk was next to mine, filling me with guilt that I did not go with him. Dozing through the night, I was awakened at first light by Holt stumbling through the tent to sit heavily on his bed, his head in his hands. In the faint light I could see that his trousers were torn at both knees and that there was a streak of blood on his forehead. I whispered, "Are you O.K.?" but he held up his hand to tell me that he did not want to talk and stretched out on his blankets, groaning to himself. Following roll call he took towels to the shower and I did not see him until after I had eaten breakfast. He was sitting on his bunk when I returned, swinging my mess kit free of water. It took several hours of questions because he did not want to talk about it, but I finally pieced the story together. He had stolen a truck from the motor pool, loaded his food, and had driven down the unmarked and dangerous hillsides until he came to a road that took him toward Marseille. He had kept the appointment on a dark side street waiting impatiently for his contact who arrived late accompanied by four other men. The encounter was brief. Two of the Frenchmen held him while the other two beat him up. The large Mongoloid had merely stood aside as an amused witness. Leaving Holt lying in the road, they had taken the food and the truck. He had received no money from them.

*   *   *   *   *

Late in May the final element of our battalion arrived in camp and there was a stir of excitement as rumors flew that we would be leaving soon. Passes were cancelled and we were confined to the post. No one minded because we were going to board a ship for the last voyage that would take us home. On May 25th the entire battalion was taken by a long truck convoy to the shattered docks in Marseille. There we loaded onto small lighters and, under a sunlit sky, crossed the harbor to a large grey ship anchored beyond the sunken wreckage. It was a large ship, 630 feet in length, easily four times as large as the Liberty ship in which we had crossed the Atlantic over a year before. It was a troopship, named the "General H.W. Butner," not designed to carry cargo except for the supplies needed to house and feed over 5,000 men. The large holds were packed with racks of canvas bunks, four high, with narrow walkways between them. But in spite of the size, there was an all too familiar fear about once again being sent below a water line into a windowless and comparatively airless room. Assigned to our compartments, we stacked our weapons and gear on the canvas bunks, and crowded onto the decks to watch the comings and goings of the lighters bringing more troops to the ship. That evening, with the help of several Navy tugboats, we moved out into the ebbing tide and sailed slowly away from the coast of France. The lights from the city created a dome-like glow in the darkening sky, ending six years of blackout. It was the first lighted foreign seaport I had ever seen in my life and I chose to think that it was a symbol of gratitude from a Europe freed at last from Nazi oppression.

CHAPTER XXI

JOURNEY TO WAR

In the early morning light we sailed past the majesty of the Rock of Gibralter. Morning sunlight bathed the huge white rock monolith rising at the edge of the blue Mediterranean. As two British destroyers escorted us through the surprisingly narrow passage into the Atlantic Ocean, we could see to the South the low dark brown shore of Africa. Both ships set their sirens howling a farewell as they swung about in racing circles back to Gibraltar. We waved an appreciative and fond goodbye to the British Navy, and returned to our bunks to settle in on a routine for our short voyage across the Atlantic.

We learned from an officer on the first day at sea that because of the speed of the ship it would not be necessary to cross in convoy but that we would still observe evening blackout precautions. We were told that the Butner could outrun any submarine in the Japanese Navy, even it if had some in this hemisphere, and that the ship itself was adequately armed to deal with any emergency.

Someone with a bunk deep in the hold asked whether the ship could outrun a torpedo but the question was brushed aside as being frivolous. However, we couldn't help but wonder what chance we actually would have if we just happened to sail past a submarine lying in wait for a lone target.

We also observed on the first day that the Navy sailors working the ship were reticent and glum about something. They moved about the decks without speaking or smiling as they readied the ship for the open sea. In spite of all of our efforts to discover which of the East coast ports was our destination, we were unable to get anyone from the ship's company to open up to us. They simply said that they didn't know where we were bound for.

Once well clear of the coast, the ship increased speed and we, who were familiar only with convoy traffic, were astonished at how fast we moved through the water. Watching the trailing white wake far out behind the ship was a favorite occupation for those of us who preferred the open windy deck to the closeness of the holds below. We ate our two meals a day in a large dining hall, standing at high tables to gulp down plenty of good but plain food. Atmosphere throughout the ship was genial and relaxed as we soon forgot about errant submarines in our excitement about going home. Although the night blackout precautions were observed, we were permitted on deck during the dark hours of the night. These were favorite times because with the clear skies that we were enjoying, one could see thousands of stars in the heavens and by polling information, we began to identify numerous constellations. On our fourth night out, while we were trying to find the individual planets in our solar system someone said, "Why is the North Star over there?"

After several minutes of argument, we agreed that it was indeed the North Star and that it was almost directly behind us. We were headed almost due South. We watched for almost two hours speculating that perhaps we were following a zigzag course to avoid possible submarines. It was not the case; the ship held the course for the two hours as well as during the entire night. First on deck in the morning I noted, with a curious feeling of having been betrayed, that the sun broke the horizon on our port side. We were definitely not crossing the North Atlantic on our way to New York.

After two days of pressure questions, we learned from one of the sullen Marine guards on board that we were headed for the Panama Canal, and much to my delight he speculated that we were probably headed for Los Angeles. The men from California greeted the news with smiles and cheers and rumors of early discharge filled the hold. Even when San Francisco entered the rumor mill as the possible port, we from Southern California were not discouraged, after all it was only a day's train ride between the two great cities. Men from the Eastern seaboard were glum at first but they soon succumbed to the general jovial atmosphere and accepted the West Coast as our destination with reluctant approval. Most of them had girl friends around Los Angeles anyway.

Within a few days we were riding at anchor on a glassy sea East of the entrance to the canal, waiting for our scheduled entrance to the Gatun Locks. The equatorial heat was unlike anything that I had ever experienced. It was not merely oppressive; it was a stifling sensation, filling the lungs with preheated air and making every single breath a gasping effort. Our ship was not air-conditioned in the holds, it relied on air vents, and in the open Atlantic there had been a steady steam of cool air circulating. At anchor however, with nothing more than an occasional hot breeze entering the vents, the holds became a nightmarish sweatbox. The great iron sides of the ship itself radiated waves of heat throughout its interior and even the bright hanging light bulbs seemed to add to the agony. Men packed the open decks like animals, searching for a cooling wind. The night brought rain, not a cool rain but a torrent of warm water, which at first hissed and then evaporated almost immediately on the hot steel deck plating. Shoes had to be worn, even at night, against the scorching decks. We all, of course, were ordered to carry our life jackets with us at all times and the hot kapok added to the frustration and misery.

After 36 hours we weighed anchor and began our entrance to the locks. To our surprise we received orders over the loud speaker to clear the decks. Everyone was sent below, the justification being that we were not to be identified as a troopship by possible spies.

The order angered me personally, not so much because it was foolish and that it would have been clearly obvious to any spy that we were a troopship whether there were soldiers on deck or not, but more importantly because it had been a dream of mine to someday see the great Panama Canal. Now, below decks, in the dizzying heat, I would pass through the Canal without seeing one bit of it. I presumed that during the next twelve hours we passed through the Eastern locks, navigated the Gatun Lake and the great Gaillard Cut and were lifted gently down the Miguel and Miraflores Locks on the Western side of Panama. Neither I, nor any of my sweltering friends saw a single moment of it.

Late the next day we docked in Balboa on the Western side of the Canal and were herded off the ship 200 at a time to spend an hour in a barbed wire enclosure on the dock. There, by standing in line for most of the precious hour off the ship, we each received a warm bottle of Coca-Cola and a hard donut served to us by bored Panamanians who were totally indifferent to our discomfort. As we boarded the ship across the deck level gangplank, I noticed that another contingent of fully armed Marines was slowly boarding through a doorway in the hold.

Back on the ship, I vowed that I would not go down into that oven to sweat through another night, so I hid under a stack of cork life rafts during the routine clearing of the decks. There was very little space under the rafts, which were held in place on a slightly raised metal angle rack next to the scupper line of the ship. But by lying flat and turning my head to one side, I had room enough to breath and soon fell asleep. The next thing I knew I was gagging in a fountain of water. As I was awakened from my drugged sleep, I was confused as to my whereabouts. I struggled to get up but was held fast by the life rafts over my head and by the surging water that engulfed me. Knowing that I was drowning gave me the superhuman strength to kick myself backwards out from under the rafts and to stand upright in the heaviest rainfall I had ever experienced. The tropical downpour was so heavy that water on the sloping deck could not run off fast enough and was inches deep on the surface of the ship. I had been trapped under the rafts next to the scuppers, which had been unable to drain the deck fast enough. Staggering through the stinging rain across the barely visible deck, I found the entrance to the hold and greeted the rush of heat with a feeling of frightened relief.

Six days out of the Canal we were still headed West. There was growing concern about what this meant since some of us knew that California now lay to the North of us.

The next morning we awoke to discover that during the night we had been joined by two cargo ships on our flanks, that we had reduced speed to accommodate them, and that we were all steaming directly West. In low angry voices we discussed the turn of events in the hold and on the deck, trying to guess the significance of both the deliberate Westward direction and the fact that we were now sailing in a convoy. Although we argued all around the hard facts, realistically we could come to only one conclusion: we were not going home, we were headed into the Pacific theater of war. Anger, over what we believed to be a deception, was replaced by bitterness and an ugly mood made worse shortly after by a laconic announcement made over the P.A. system that we were now on our way to Ulithi Atoll in the Caroline Islands and that we would be told our final destination when we arrived there.

There was instant shouting and cursing throughout the many holds of the entire ship at the announcement, and the Marine guards on the ladderways moved nervously back and forth. There was no one who could tell us where Ulithi was, none of us in the hold had ever heard of it and the lack of information did nothing to temper our collective mood. Since leaving Marseille, we had already been at sea for 18 days and I knew enough about the planet Earth to calculate that the Pacific Ocean was very large, that tiny islands and atolls were mostly scattered in groups on the Western and Southern edges of the great ocean. If we were going to Ulithi, we had a long trip ahead of us. I tried to remember my geography and felt chagrined that while in Europe I had paid no attention to details of the Pacific battles. The thought had never entered my mind that being committed to the European theater was no guarantee that I would not also be used in the war against Japan. Lying quietly on my narrow canvas rack, I guessed that there could be at least 10,000 miles between the Panama Canal and the Caroline Islands.

Estimating the ship's speed at roughly 12 miles an hour, I concluded that the ship made a little under 300 miles every 24 hours. We had been gone from Panama for six days, or 1,800 miles. The conclusion was staggering. Even if we did not join a larger convoy that might reduce our speed further, we still had 27 days of sailing before we arrived at some unheard of atoll named Ulithi. That fact, coupled with the knowledge that it would not be over even then, and that our "final destination" would be announced only when we arrived at Ulithi was very depressing and I gave myself over to a deep bitterness bordering on plans for revenge against the injustice of it all.

When the Ulithi announcement had been made, there had been at first anger and open hostility but both of these emotions had been replaced in time by a sense of almost silent hopelessness. Most men moved around the ship in a somnambulistic state, sleeping sometimes 12 hours a day, in the grip of denial and protective withdrawal. Only occasionally would there be brief flashes of broken emotions. Fist fights would occur between friends, often as the result of a very minor difference of opinion or unintentional slurs, but always the incidents were followed by apologies and forgiveness. There was an unspoken concensus that each man, in order to survive the dreadful reality of the ship, needed to be left alone as much as possible.

We wore trousers, T-shirts and boots, shuffling in long lines to the mess hall twice a day, dragging our life jackets. We were given salt tablets against the heat and officers supervised the taking of atabrine, a drug against malaria. Everyone took a small yellow atabrine tablet twice a day at the entrance to the mess hall. The only way to avoid the bitter pill was to miss meals; few ever did that even though stories were whispered that the drug was ineffective, would color a man yellow and would absolutely make him permanently impotent. When asked how a malaria carrying mosquito could possibly get to the middle of the Pacific Oean, we were told that we were being given atabrine in order to get used to taking it. The explanation went unchallenged since the question was moot anyway. The simple truth was that if you wanted to eat, you took atabrine.

It was a constant problem trying to stay clean in the heat and the salty grease that covered and finally permeated the interiors of ships during long sea voyages. A few saltwater showers were available in each hold, but they were worse than nothing, even when taken with a special green soap that had the consistency of volcanic pumice. The ship's laundry tried to provide some service by washing our clothes but with over 5,000 men on board, the service was, at best, sporatic. We washed our own socks, underwear and T-shirts in the saltwater sinks in the head and tried to dry the salt streaked garments on our canvas bunks. The crowded ship itself was a problem just to keep clean. Once a day everything that was stacked on the floor had to be placed on the bunks in order for someone to sweep the ever present litter out of the hold. The process made for arguments over whose fault it was that torn paper was found under a lower bunk or who owned the dirty socks found in the narrow aisleway.

Announcements over the ship's public address system were made constantly, everyone feeling a surge of anger as the frying sound heralded yet another order of some kind. Abusive shouts and obscenities rattled the holds each time we heard, "Now hear this, now hear this . . . sweepers, man your brooms for a clean sweepdown, fore and aft."

But the anger mounted to a ship wide roar each time we heard the announcement that officers could pick up their clean sheets in the wardroom. Jammed like dirty animals in the sweating holds, our frustrations boiled over at the announcement. None of us below the water line had seen a sheet for well over a year and at no time in my years in the service had the differences between the treatment of officers and enlisted men seemed so contentious and deliberately callous.

*   *   *   *   *

As I had done for many weeks in the afternoon light, I stood next to the loose chain guardrail behind the life rafts and stared dumbly ahead at the hard blue horizon line trying to will a landfall to appear. But nothing had ever appeared out there but scattered little white clouds and tiny whitecap waves chopping away at one another. Although I was not permitted to stand behind the rafts, I did so anyway, moving out from behind them only when a passing sailor or angry Marine guard caught me standing or sitting there. I had discovered the tiny secluded spot and it was my private hiding place away from the crowded holds and decks. Tiring of looking at the horizon, I let my eyes drop to the white slurring wake and watched it break away from the sides of the ship, making an insignificant energy mark in the mindlessness of deep blue water. I stared at the wake for a long time until guardedly, as I had learned to do, I let my mind slip away from me to wander into the repetitious and consuming water. Learning days ago that I could do this, was a secret from anyone on the ship. I absolutely knew that I could actually transfer my mind into the water itself. Fascinated again, I watched as the familiar little crystal like specks flashed on and off at the edges of my eyes, giving way slowly to a soft grey curtain of overall diffused light, and I could feel myself falling into a state of being free. With a slight surge of secret delight, I slipped away, transformed into a free-floating feather.

But before I could fully complete the transfer, there appeared directly in the center of my clouded sight a remarkable and singularly beautiful thing. A flying fish, disturbed and bursting from the side of the ship, shimmered in a bright silver light and leaped across my vision.

Skipping across the water like a flat stone, it raced away in the long afternoon light away from the great grey monster that had disturbed its watery audit. It was soon followed by hundreds of bright flying fish, skimming away in an anguish of fish fear to splash back into imagined safety. The sight of the flashing silver cloud was so beautiful and so spontaneous that as I gripped the chain guard, I could feel tears welling in my eyes. Suspiciously, I looked around me, to make sure that only I had seen the miracle. Satisfied that it was mine, I had it all to myself, and I would never share it, never. After weeks of not ever being out of arms reach of another human being, I had finally secured for myself, a moment of my own. I slid down behind the rafts, sitting on my life jacket with my knees under my chin, smiling wickedly to myself.

Later at night, lying in my solitary bunk in the hot darkened hold, I became frightened when it finally came to me that I was living on the thin edge of madness.

*   *   *   *   *

During our fifth week on the ship, we heard that a man in the Engineer Battalion had committed suicide. There were also rumors of mental breakdowns throughout the ship.

While dozing in my bunk early one afternoon, I was disturbed by voices that drifted in and out of my dreamless sleep. Angry at being awakened, I looked to see three men talking to someone in the bottom bunk across the aisle from me. All three were hunkered down, talking quietly to a man who was crying. Lying on my side and feeling perspiration roll off my back between my shoulder blades, I watched the scene with detached indifference. They continued talking to the man in a soothing manner but they could not stop his crying, his sobs breaking and becoming a continuous howling noise. One of the men stood up and walked away, to return in a short time with a bespectacled Naval officer in a clean white uniform. Together they helped the man out of the tight space and led him away, his wailing whimper gradually fading away as they left the hold. He was the same man from Arkansas who had been so terribly seasick on the Liberty ship voyage to England, a quiet, friendly man, taken now to the hospital ward deep in the ship. His personal battle with ships and the sea was now over at last. Later that day I awakened again to look at his claustrophobic space, only to see that someone had removed his gear and personal belongings, leaving only an empty sweat stained canvas rack to mark the place where a good man had been robbed of himself.

We received war bulletin news over the P.A. system also. Perhaps the reports were intended to inspire us and keep our fighting spirits at an imagined fever pitch, but often the overstated reports were greeted by jeers and curses. We did not care how many tons of bombs had just been dropped on Tokyo. An eager Marine guard, trying to clear a ladderway, was attacked by a furious, out of control mob and thrown into a companionway. He immediately returned with a combat team complete with helmets, rifles, bayonets and an officer. The man, who had been attacked, attempted to identify those who had attacked him, but identification was impossible, although two suspects were led away as symbols to be imprisoned for the remainder of the voyage. Tension continued to mount, often intensified by an eerie dead silence that would momentarily grip the entire hold full of staring men.

Early on the morning of the 31st day out of Panama, our small convoy was joined by several other ships. Destroyers whooped along on either side of us and a larger armed ship flying a British flag took position in the lead of the group. We crowded the decks, savoring the excitement of seeing something different. The surging release of emotions was magical, as men, unused to even talking to one another, began animated discussions. There was even some laughter on the deck as the constraints of the weeks at sea were broken.

In this atmosphere of release we sailed slowly into the protected harbor of Ulithi Atoll in the Caroline Islands. A giant flotilla lay there. Hundreds of ships of every description swung at anchor, separated from one another by patches of calm, blue-green water under a clear bright sky. Smaller ships and boats scampered back and forth among the vessels sending sheets of white foam from their sterns as they performed their military duties. We anchored near a monstrous U.S aircraft carrier, its sides so high that even from our distance away, it looked like a large floating unnamed grey building with a large black edged white number on its control island. The excitement of the sight of this colossal assembly of ships was soon dissipated however, as we completed our anchorage. As soon as we came to a full stop, the full heat of the tropics returned, and the holds again transformed into ovens. The fierce sun made it almost impossible to remain on deck but the stale unmoving air of the holds was worse. We sweltered, suffering, beaten down once again into an enervated silence. We lay at anchor, uninformed, blacked out at night, for two hot days and nights.

*　　*　　*　　*　　*

Early in the morning of the 3rd day we were loaded, two or three hundred at a time, in landing crafts for a short compassionate recreation visit to a nearby island named Mogmog. The logistics of moving everyone on board back and forth to the island was accomplished with efficiency and when our turn came, we formed a quiet line that snaked through the mess hall and down through parts of the ship that we had

356

never seen before. Arriving at a large open supply door at the waterline, we jumped into a throbbing LCI that bucked and roared to hold its position next to the troopship. Once loaded with 50 men, the seaman, running the craft from the rear, deftly moved away from the mother ship and we began a bouncing ride across the wide lagoon to a long wooden jetty that ran out from a very flat piece of land. Climbing out of the landing craft onto the jetty to meet our sailor guide, we joined hundreds of other disembarking soldiers and sailors. Our guide took us to a designated place on the beach where he reviewed the rules of being ashore. The slips of numbered paper, which each of us had been given on the troopship, could be exchanged for two cans of beer or for two bottles of Coca-Cola, one choice. We were to observe restricted areas, swim only where the area was posted, do no damage to the island, not collect seashells or fish, and finally to reassemble at this spot posted by a large numbered sign in exactly four hours. We were free to go.

Without hesitation I separated myself from the group and made a dash for the beverage distribution palm thatched shack. There after a long wait, I turned in my slip, received my two warm bottles of Coke and walked through milling tanned bodies in the direction of the beach. My walk took me around numerous softball games in progress (What redblooded American boy could resist playing ball in the sun if given the chance?), but I arrived at the edge of the water alone, where I immediately took off my sweaty clothes and sat in the shade of a small grove of palm trees at the edge of a dazzling white sand beach. Mogmog Island was an undetectable tiny speck in the vastness of the Pacific Ocean, flat with its highest point measured in feet, on the fringe of a glassy bright green lagoon. I sat motionless for several minutes, breathing deeply and collecting my thoughts, calming myself. When I finally believed that it was all real, I took a final deep breath and looked cautiously around me. The first thing I looked at was the palm tree. Standing up slowly, I put my fingers on the rough surface of its curved trunk, realizing that it was the first growing object I had seen in six weeks. I had almost forgotten the rich colors in a tree trunk, the deep iron greys and the titian browns, mingled together, all growing. My eyes followed the trunk up to the rattling palm fronds, which were catching the soft trade winds high in the sky. After weeks of only grey, the brisk green of the newer fronds against the ultramarine sky seemed almost too brash and unfamiliar. I studied the tree carefully, seeing its beauty, savoring the knowledge that it was actually a living thing, that it was a testimony to the recurrence of life. It was another moment I did not want to forget.

I spent my four hours alone, walking to the far end of the near deserted beach to swim a little in the warm but refreshing water. A barechested sailor sat on a large coral boulder nearby, rifle cradled, watching for sharks as I swam. When I walked down the curved beach toward the assembly point in wet sand, I did so carefully, enjoying the jarring sensations in my legs when my bare feet struck the sand.

I stopped once for a few moments to sit again and to gaze out across the flotilla, locating the General Butner among the scattered greyness of war. Barechested, I closed my eyes and shoulder high, stretched my arms out at full length. I swung them in slow arcs from side to side, finger tips encountering nothing in the empty space. Glowing a yellow orange beyond my eyelids was the hot noon sun and the slight sea breeze moved the long hair next to my ear. After awhile I stood, knowing that I was going to be all right. Never again would I let myself drift close to madness, never again would I give outside human forces the chance to break my spirit.

In friendship I joined the sunburned group for the trip back across the lagoon and when we arrived, I entered the loading door into the troopship without hatred, fear or bitterness. This great grey ship had taught me a valuable lesson about myself. It had taught me that if I were going to survive, I would need to be constantly aware of the dangers around me. Dangers there, which if I were not on guard, could take my mind.

CHAPTER XXII

OKINAWA

Fifteen days later, in late afternoon sunlight, we anchored off the brooding coast of the island of Okinawa. We had traveled over 20,000 miles since leaving Marseille, France, and had spent 62 days at sea aboard the troopship. There was never an official announcement made of the number of mental breakdowns or suicides, but several months later we were to read a newspaper clipping sent from home to one of the men in the Company, that a request had been made for a Congressional investigation into the voyage. We had nearly circumnavigated the globe, going from East to West and no one had the answer to the question, "Why didn't we come the other way? It would have been a lot closer?" I only knew that it was with an enormous feeling of release that we loaded into bobbing landing craft to be put ashore and away from that ship forever. Landing in LCI's on a narrow sandy shoreline on the west side of the island below the capital city of Naha, we loaded into waiting trucks to be taken to a prepared encampment. As we passed through the city, I was saddened to see once again the effects of modern war. It had been over two months since I had seen a city that had been wrecked by warfare and this time the devastation was virtually complete. Except for one or two reinforced concrete buildings, which stood upright on the shallow plain leading to the shattered harbor, there was nothing to be seen except piles of burned rubble, the remains of mud walls, and broken tile. European cities, constructed of stone and concrete, remained as ruins, but Okinawan cities and villages were built mostly of wood, mud, and thatch, unable to withstand the effects of artillery, heavy weapons, and fire. Small mud and stone foundations and broken red tile marked the places where prosperous homes had once stood; burned and blackened ground was all that remained of lesser dwellings, built without tile roofs. Tangles of phone and electric wires, covered with the dust and ashes from the wheels and tracks of hundreds of vehicles, snaked through the destruction. We noticed immediately that there were no civilians to be seen anywhere on the road or working in the rubble. We had returned to the war, away at last, from the freshness of the sea air and now breathed the smells of death and of the land scorched by fire and blast.

Our company position was located next to a never-to-be-identified river in a narrow treeless ravine about two miles east of Naha. Squad pyramidal tents had been pitched by an advance party and a mess tent prepared for immediate use. As soon as we had dumped our gear on bare cots, we were assembled into company formation and given instructions by an officer from a nearly infantry unit. He was very specific in his warnings to us. Pointing out that although the entire island had been officially declared captured late in June, there were still perhaps 20,000 armed Japanese soldiers holding out and fighting. We were to regard our position and the island as a dangerous battlefield until all of the remaining enemy soldiers could be accounted for. He particularly warned us about Japanese night raids. He concluded his remarks with the ominous fact that while close to 100,000 Japanese had been killed on the island, less than 5,000 had been taken prisoner, most of them wounded. This enemy was not the German who surrendered with honor. This antagonist was a fanatic who fought to die for his emperor. The officer explained that every Japanese soldier believed that to surrender was to disgrace one's ancestors.

That evening we heard artillery fire coming from the Southern part of the island. It was a strange sound, thumping away in the distance, sending a chill through me and reminding me of my naivete in thinking that after Europe I would never hear that sound again. Looking up at the darkening hills surrounding our camp, I felt, once again, the cold fear of being secretly watched by someone surely more cunning and stronger than I.

I had been afraid at night in Europe, the dark forests of France in the snow, searching and straining ahead for movement, holding my breath and listening for sounds coming from the trees. I had heard the faint screech of German tank tracks in the distance, the shrill signal whistles of German patrols but never had I felt fear that was so pervasive, so surrounding in nature as I did now. It was a feeling not measured by distance ahead. It was around and directly behind my head, breathing in my ear. The fear of night was to last, to some degree or other, until I was to leave that accursed island months later.

The morning light brought with it a release from the thick fear, the surrounding hills in the bright light became only scarred and broken terrain, and breakfast away from the sea was tasteless but somehow reassuring.

As we busied ourselves settling into our camp, the Captain asked me to take some papers into Army headquarters in Naha. Pleased at the prospect of having a jeep to drive, I left the camp alone and drove out of the ravine in the direction of the city. There was very little traffic on the road and I had no trouble locating headquarters. It was one of the only concrete structures that still stood near the Eastern edge of the city. A bored Corporal took my papers from behind a battered desk and I returned to my jeep in the courtyard, determined that I would deliberately lose myself on my way back to camp.

Instead of heading East, I struck out for some ridge-like hills to the Northeast, picking my way through the rubble, choking in the dust from the suddenly busy traffic on the roadway. After two months on the troopship, there was an exhilaration in the physical act of driving the spirited little vehicle. Dodging oncoming trucks, weaving through a column of churning amtracks, and careening around sharp curves, was not only a physical but was also an emotional release for me.

I had driven about two miles on the unpaved dirt road, which had been cut by bulldozers across the rising ridge ahead of me, when I came to the remains of what must have been a small city. Near the top of the ridge was all that remained of Shuri, the once ancient 16th century capitol of the Ryukyus. I pulled off the narrow road to better view the massive pile of rubble. The castle itself was only tumbled rock and dirt. All that remained within the two or three acre walled city compound were the sagging and broken concrete walls of the Methodist church, which had been built in 1937 when Christianity had visited Okinawa to stay. Because of its commanding view, Shuri Castle had been used as a strong point in the defensive strategy of the Japanese 32nd Army in its reluctant and bloody retreat to the South. In addition to air strikes, mortar and small arms fire, the old city had taken 200,000 rounds of artillery fire during the course of its capture, some large calibre shells coming from the battleships and cruisers, which I could see clearly lying on the Western edge of the island below the ridge. Stripped and shattered oriental tree trunks stood at crazy angles on the horizon, jutting from the mounds of earth that might have been garden forests for ancient nobility. Two or three burned-out American tanks, half buried and covered with a thick dust rested mutely next to the compound. Part of a windowless, burned concrete structure leaned almost to the ground at the far edge of the ridge. It had been a Latter Day School for the teaching of teachers. Traffic continued to rumble by my jeep as I looked at the end of what was once the nerve center of a vigorous, despotic, oriental empire.

Below me to the North, I could easily see the flatland area of the narrow Ishikawa Isthmus, barely three miles across from sea to sea. Beyond the isthmus, near the horizon, I could make out the giant Kadena and Yontan airfields, the first day objectives of the three division landing force that made up the XXIV Corps of the American 10th Army under General Buckner. To my left I could see Machinato Airstrip, a single fighter runway built on the West coast. Behind me, also on the West coast, lay the huge Naha Naval Base Airfield but from where I stood, even on one of the highest points of land on the island, I could not see Yonabau Airfield on the East coast. These five military airfields were one of the important reasons for the invasion, to provide the Americans with a strong airbase capability only 300 miles from Japan itself.

On April 1st the invasion of Okinawa was made by elements of the 96th, 27th and 7th Infantry Divisions, accompanied by the 6th Marine Division and supported by several battalions of the 1st Marines. Simultaneously, the 77th Infantry invaded neighboring IE Shima and occupied all other important outer islands to the West of Okinawa. Once ashore on the West coast, the major landing force encountered very light resistance and within 24 hours had not only cut across the entire Ishikawa Isthmus but had firmly secured both Kadena and Yontan Airfields for the Americans. After sending the 6th Marines to secure the Northern part of the then divided Okinawa, General Buckner positioned the 7th Division on the Eastern half of the island and the 96th on the Western side to begin the sweep to the South against undetermined Japanese resistance. The 27th remained in reserve. Unknown to the Americans at the time was the fact that Allied intelligence had underestimated the numbers of defenders and had terribly underestimated the ingenuity of the Japanese commander, General Ushijima.

From where I stood I could see below me the battered remains of Kakazu Ridge on the left, the first major obstacle encountered by the 96th as it moved South off the flat plateau of the Ishtmus. Kakazu was the Japanese left flank position on a line of ridges and escarpments that stretched the four miles across the island. The line included, to the East: the Nishibaru Ridge, the Tanabaru Escarpment and the American named Skyline Ridge. The genius of the Japanese defense was that it had not used these higher points, most no more than 200 feet above sea level, as a straight trench-like defense, but had cleverly linked the intervening hills, pinnacles, ravines and narrow valleys into interconnecting fields of fire and minefields. Many of these strong points were closely visible to me now as bald limestone knobs, blasted and punished until there was nothing left but naked rock. American military names had been given to them for identification on target maps and in assault plans. Castle Hill, the Pinnacle, Red Hill, Tomb Hill, Triangulation Hill, Charlie, Half Moon, Horseshoe, Cactus Ridge, Sugar Loaf, all names that gave testimony to the struggle against the first real line of resistance of the Japanese 32nd Army. In two weeks of heavy and desperate fighting, General Buckner, an Infantry fighter, found it necessary to pull the

27th out of reserve and throw it into the assault, positioning this New York National Guard Division near the center of the attacking line. Casualties were heavy and the Americans, for the first time in the Pacific theatre of operations, were experiencing extremely accurate, often uncanny Japanese artillery fire. Not knowing it, they were up against Major General Kasuke Wade, perhaps the best artillery officer in the Japanese Army, commanding experienced veterans from the Chinese mainland. Concealed heavy weapons, many mounted on tracks within caves and bunkers so that they could fire and be pulled back into protective cover, decimated the American tank columns trying to penetrate the ridge line.

Since 1943 the Japanese had been fortifying the unusual East-West ridges and escarpments, which were the main geographic feature of the Southern and most heavily populated part of the island. By using the terrain and practicing concealment, they were able to dig tunnels, some nearly a mile in length and running completely through ridge lines, enabling supplies and replacements to be brought through the hills undetected to the points of combat. They were also an effective escape route back to the next line of defense.

By using connected natural and man-made caves in the limestone faces of the ridges, the Japanese were able to lay out interconnecting fields of fire and preregister their mortar and artillery rounds in preparation for an enemy that they knew would come. In addition, Okinawa provided thousands of prebuilt strong points and pillboxes in the form of ancestral burial tombs. These sacred resting places, some hundreds of years old, were built from limestone rock into hillsides. Layered over many times with mud and mortar, constantly repaired by the family, they were several feet thick. The religion dictated that the tombs be womb shaped to face the rising sun, with one small open entrance for the comings and goings of the family members. The tombs contained the bones of the spirits stored on shelves in large ceramic jars. Because they could not be effectively concealed, these tombs were limited in their tactical value, but they did make excellent mortar pits and machine gun nests. Each ridge was honeycombed with tunnels and connecting strong points, some equipped with small gauge railroads to move men and supplies rapidly from one position to another.

To make matters worse for the Americans, the two Divisions that made up the Japanese 32nd Army were well equipped with artillery and heavy automatic weapons. The 62nd Division that had defended the Shuri line, and the 24th and 44th mixed brigade from Kyushu, together with 10,000 men from the Naha Naval Base, made up the forces that had fought the final battles on the Southern part of the island. All of these units were actually equipped with heavy weapons.

Okinawa, with its protected harbor and well developed airfields, had been used as a supply distribution point for Japanese war material destined for the Philippines and for the island empire in the South Pacific. As the war began to turn against the Japanese in 1944, their shipping losses to Allied submarines were enormous, and as their bases in the South Pacific began to melt away, war material began to crowd the depots on Okinawa. General Ushijima, faced with a battle that he could not win, merely distributed guns and ammunition from the over-stocked supply to his combat troops. In some cases units had twice as many heavy weapons as their normal table of equipment would call for. Ammunition was plentiful as were the native Okinawan workers who were used to dig the defensive lines.

The Japanese regarded the Okinawan native as an inferior peasant, unworthy of anything beyond manual labor. At the same time the Japa-nese, in order to secure large support in the task of defense, filled the natives with stories of the brutality and inhuman acts that the American invaders would inflict upon their women and children. Bewildered when the war came to their island, many thousands of Okinawans chose to stay close to the Japanese Army rather than see their families raped and murdered. While others greeted the Americans as liberators and filled refugee camps with starved and sick people, far too many died with the Japanese Army in its final battles, either buried in the caves with their tormentors or victims of mass suicides on the cliffs at the farthest edge of the island to the South.

By the end of April, after three and a half weeks of bloody fighting, General Buckner had four full divisions in the five mile line. He had brought down the 6th Marines from the North after it had encountered only slight resistance from the less than 4,000 Japanese defending the heavily forested and underdeveloped upper end of the island. In addi-tion he used the First Marine, the 77th, and the 96th. He pulled the 7th Division out of the line for rest and replacements and sent the badly mauled 27th North to hold the ground previously gained by the Ma-rines.

The three and one-half weeks of an inferno had nearly stalled at the base of the Japanese second line, the Urasoe Maru Escarpment. The Americans had been able to move forward less than one mile in most places. General Ushijima's strategy was becoming very clear. He had known since 1943 or earlier that he would lose the battle but that by fighting a determined delaying action he would accomplish several things. He would cost the Americans too many casualties and might influence the U.S. announced decision to invade Japan and to force an unconditional surrender. He would disrupt the American timetable and consequently cause havoc in the enormous logistics schedule, which he knew was necessary in fighting 10,000 miles from major manpower and material supply points. And he would tie up large segments of the powerful American Navy, forced to shelter close to Okinawa in support of the 10th Army, and present a concentrated target area for the Japanese kamikaze attacks that had been launched early in April.

No one knew better than General Buckner that his respected opponent was succeeding in his strategies. Division, battalion and company commanders were strongly urged to finish off the Japanese and following a disastrous May 2nd counterattack, forced on Ushijima by his impatient junior officers, all-out American efforts were made to reach the Shuri line, mistakenly believed to be the last bastion of defense.

Once past the Urasoe Maru Escarpment the battle became, if anything, more costly and bitter for the frustrated and exhausted Americans. One 200 man company of infantry, after holding an exposed minor hilltop for 70 hours against furious counterattacks, brought only 48 men down from the hill when they were finally relieved. The relieving officer was killed just as he took command. The Shuri Line continued to hold, resisting heavy fire from the American Navy, rocket and napalm attacks from the Air Corps and determined armor and infantry assaults from the ground forces. But at last on May 21, elements of the rejoined 7th Division captured an important highway on the East Coast at Yonabura. This highway was essential to the Americans because it ran East and West across the island behind the stubbornly held Shuri Line all the way to the city of Naha on the West coast. Jubilant, General Buckner ordered a massive tank attack on this road, determined to cut off Ushijima in the Shuri Line and prevent the escape of the major portion of the Japanese Army in their natural fortress.

But before the assembled tanks could ram their way across the island, heavy rains drenched Okinawa for two weeks, cascading 12 inches of rain on the ground and allowing the alert defenders in Shuri to withdraw a major portion of their troops on night marches to the next prepared defensive line to the South. The hard roadway turned into a quagmire of mud, which could not support heavy vehicles, and in frustration and despair, the American attack was called off. Men sat in the mud under trucks and sheltered from the incessant rain, huddled under ponchos to wait out the weather.

On May 26, during the rain, Ushijima withdrew his major force from Shuri, leaving behind a small determined force of suicide troops to defend the position. But during the withdrawal there was a brief break in the weather and a Navy plane spotted the retreat column of 80 some vehicles transporting the Japanese. Joined by other fighter bombers, the subsequent aerial attack paused while command wrestled with the report that pilots counted many white robed figures on the road and were identifying them as Okinawan civilians. Finally, fearful that those dressed in white were really disguised Japanese soldiers, the order was given to continue the attack.

The rocket and napalm bombers screamed in through broken cloud cover to punish the scattering retreat column. Driven away at last by the returning bad weather, the attackers were not to know until months later that estimates of civilians killed in the strafing and bombing attack reached as high as 15,000. The incident was grim evidence of the Okinawan's confusion over who was their enemy and who was not. Three days later the rain had ended before a unit of the First Marines, jumping the 6th Marine division line, captured Shuri Castle and to the embarrassment of Army headquarters ran up a Confederate flag to commemorate the event. It was explained later that the symbol of the South was the only flag the unit had on hand, carried in the helmet liner of a Marine from South Carolina. The American flag soon replaced it.

The battle from the edge of the Kakazu Ridge to the capture of the Shuri Line, a distance of slightly more than two miles, had taken 56 days. The cost in American lives, not including the deaths to Navy personnel from the kamikaze attacks, ran into the thousands.

And the battle was not over. Ushijima entered the third and final line in the Southern most ridge, the Yaeju-dake Escarpment. Less than a mile in length, it commanded the cultivated farmland plateaus South of Naha and like its predecessors, the ridge line was a masterpiece of concealment and favored defensive positions. By now, however, the Japanese garrison was greatly reduced and burdened by the civilians who cowered with the exhausted Japanese in the caves, in fear of their future.

The Naha Airfield was still defended by a rebellious force of Navy personnel who had refused to fall back, and the Kimishi Ridge adjacent to the escarpment was heavily defended. Ushijima had managed to escape from Shuri with much of his artillery and the many caves, tunnels and chambers were well stocked with ammunition.

Except for several days in early June when a typhoon struck the island and completely stopped the American assault, the war against the caves went on all through the month of June. At last, defeated, exhausted, out of ammunition with no prospects of resupply or replacements, Ushijima ordered his remaining troops to surrender. He and his chief of staff in early morning light in the shattered forests behind the ridge on June 22 committed suicide by hari-kari in the tradition of defeated soldiers. As he took his life, this brilliant infantry tactician was never to know that his opponent, General Buckner, had been killed by a shell outburst four days before. The battle for Okinawa was declared ended. The 83 days of savage fighting had raised serious questions about the campaign among American politicians and journalists. American casualties, Army, Navy and Marines, numbered well over 75,000 counting killed, wounded, hospitalized and missing. Japanese casualties could only be estimated as being in excess of 100,000. Figures on civilian casualties could never be ascertained.

Serious fighting problems remained after the campaign was declared ended and the island secured on July 2. The pockets of bypassed

Japanese soldiers and their civilian charges were to plague the Americans who were to prepare the island for the intended invasion of Japan.

Japanese communication had broken down well before the campaign ended and thousands of armed and dangerous Japanese soldiers remained hidden in isolated caves and tunnels without knowledge that their General had committed hari-kari or that an honorable surrender had been arranged for them. It remained for the Americans, accompanied by captured Japanese officers, to comb systematically every ridge, hill, ravine and cliff trying to convince these men to abandon the battle forever. The effort, which lasted for weeks and months beyond the end of the war itself, was not always successful, leaving no alternative for the Americans but to destroy and seal shut the hiding places of these dangerous people. How many thousands of Japanese and Okinawan skeletons lie buried deep in caves on the island of Okinawa can never be realistically determined. Estimates have run as high as 20,000.

The real irony of the battle is that two weeks to the day from the declared end of the campaign, a small device placed on a raised metal framework on the sands of Alamogordo, New Mexico, was triggered and not only catapaulted the planet into the atomic age but signalled the beginning of the end of World War II.

Twenty-three days later, while infantry and tanks continued to clear Okinawa of recalcitrant Japanese soldiers, an atomic bomb was dropped on Hiroshima, forcing a quick close to the war in the Pacific.

Was the battle of Okinawa really necessary? Would the bomb itself have been enough to the end the war? Military historians, of course, say that the battle was necessary if for no other reason than to demonstrate to the Japanese that the Americans had courage, strength, and determination. Politicians and journalists are not quite so positive on the point. It only remains a moot question among the dead, the wounded, and among those whose lives would be forever changed by the battle of Okinawa.

*   *   *   *   *

Three of us sat in darkness on the bank of the narrow river behind the mess tent drinking beer out of short bottles. Slapping at mosquitoes, we talked in low voices and watched the full moon rise over the Shuri Ridge on the other side of the river. It was a large moon and it soon filled our little valley with a bright light. Stunted trees along the far side of the river cast black shadows on the brown sluggish stream, making a static pattern on the surface of the water.

Conversation gradually dwindled. There was no longer anything we could talk about that we had not covered a hundred times before. The three of us had been together for almost three years, the stories had grown old with the constant telling, and there was nothing about Okinawa to talk about. There were no towns, no women, no amorous adventures to exaggerate. There was nothing but camp life, the occasional killing and the danger that had become a form of boredom. We had learned to live in the heat and humidity, to sleep under mosquito netting, to scratch fungus spots on our feet and to drink water laced with chemicals. We had all become tanned in the open sunlight and drank anything alcoholic that we could buy or steal.

The week before, Martin and I had paid forty dollars for a bottle of Scotch whiskey that had had a broken seal on it. The seller, our despicable supply Sergeant, had tampered with the contents, lacing the half empty bottle with grain alcohol in order to make it appear to be full of Scotch. We knew it had been tampered with, but drank it anyway, sitting on the ground in the dark, numbed into unconsciousness, eventually becoming violently sick on ourselves where we sat.

Out of the shadow, Sad Ass said, "I heard that a guy in K Company drank alcohol out of tank compasses."

He waited for a response but there was none, only a gurgle in the darkness as someone emptied another beer bottle. Undeterred, Sad Ass finished his joke.

"They had to get rid of him though, he kept pointing North all the time."

There was a weary silence as we watched a leafless tree branch float slowly by on the almost motionless water. It spun in slow circles on its way to Naha and the sea. As it passed out of our sight, Johnny said in an unexpectedly loud voice. "Hey, what's that over there by that bush?"

Without much interest we followed his directions until the three of us could locate across the river what it was he was talking about.

Lying next to a bush blackened by shadow in the bright moonlight was an earth colored mound. We had not noticed it before because it had just then begun to receive the full light of the moon.

It was the body of a Japanese soldier, half submerged in the languid stream. The head and upper torso were under the surface of the water, only the back, buttocks and legs lay on the embankment. In the now very bright light we could even make out the brown rolled puttees and the curious rubberized sandals of the common soldier. Although in my travels and work on the island I had seen many dead and decomposing enemy soldiers, there was something about this lone body thirty yards away that immediately angered me. He was both an unwelcomed intrusion to my privacy and was symbolic of the causes of my frustrations at being held captive on this ugly island. It was his fault that I was here. He alone was to blame for the fact that I was not at home where I belonged.

I found myself standing, shaking in a surge of hatred toward that still figure. My arm went back and with a full swing I hurtled my half empty bottle of beer at him. The bottle struck the bank, splashing bubbles of beer back into the river. A rat scurried away from the body and a long black snake slithered across the legs and disappeared into the muddy water.

The three of us threw our remaining stack of bottles at the figure, Sad Ass scoring two thudding hits on the back.

The next day, after we reported the discovery, the body was pulled back from the water and buried in an unmarked grave next to the river. The badly decomposed corpse had apparently been there since the Japanese had abandoned the Shuri Line in late May in their retreat to the Yaeju-dake Escarpment in the Southern part of the island.

By mid September our company was still camped in the little river valley behind the Shuri Ridge. With the ending of the war we settled down into an organized camp life with a PX and movies every other night. Our job during regular working hours was concentrated on the recovery of salvagable U.S. material still remaining from the battle. This task included vehicle recovery of Amtracks, weasels, tanks and weapons. There was a surprising amount of it to be found in the ravines, hills and plateaus in the South. Large assembly depots were established to handle the hundreds of abandoned tracked vehicles that we located and either drove or towed to the nearest assembly point. We worked in teams, roaming the countryside in open weasels, a small open-tracked vehicle made for travel over snow. Much to our surprise even though many were battle damaged, we were able to restart, sometimes by merely jumping batteries, at least half of the vehicles. The work was interesting and often a challenge to negotiate a barely operating Amtrack along a torturous dirt road hanging on a cliff edge. Several times men escaped death crashing through badly damaged native bridges built across steep ditches. Some men were injured and although we were warned that snipers and bypassed Japanese soldiers still lingered in the hills, we seldom saw any moving figures during daylight hours. The feeling of danger and of being watched never left us however and once back in the hills beyond sight of anyone, there existed a stony fear. It was always a relief to come roaring out of the seemingly deserted hills onto a major travelled dusty roadway to the assembly depot.

In a frenzy to be doing something, we worked every day, soon losing track of time and arguing constantly about what day of the week it was.

Early one afternoon we stopped our weasel next to a creek on the plateau just North of the Yaejer-dake Escarpment to watch the unfamiliar sight of hundreds of birds flying to the West in cloud-like formations. Until that moment I had not actually considered Okinawan birds beyond noting that the few I had seen looked much like the starlings and sparrows of home. The sight of the great flocks of dark birds somehow had an ominous quality about it, especially considering the weather.

Normally there was a humid but steady breeze blowing across the island but on this day there was a disquieting stillness of the air that left everything encased in a thick heat. The air itself seemed compressed as though a great hand from above was pressing it toward the ground. It was difficult to breathe and we were all wet with perspiration.

By mid afternoon little cyclone-like circles of gusting winds began to blow across the island, some so strong that we had occasional difficulty with our relatively lightweight weasel. We soon left the hills and began to work our way back to camp under a peculiar canopy of an almost emerald light. By now the gusts had become a steady wind from the Southwest, rattling tree branches and sending clouds of dust through the air. The sun disappeared, replaced by a high cloud cover obscured by low racing black fingers of a streaming cloud bank.

We arrived at our camp minutes before a torrential downpour of stinging rain engulfed the ravine. The rain was cold and so heavy that visibility beyond a few feet was difficult and the dusty ground of the main compound seemed to jump in the air from the force of the water before turning itself into a quagmire of mud. Struggling into my squad tent, I was confronted with the sight of my tentmate stuffing things into duffle bags and shouting above the noise of the rain on the straining canvas of the tent. I learned that a tremendous storm, possibly a typhoon, was coming and that it was every man for himself. We were to scatter, find shelter, and wait out the storm. Finding three K-rations on my bunk, where some thoughtful person had put them in my absence, I crammed some clothing in my duffle, grabbed my helmet and rifle, made sure my canteen was full and with my pauncho streaming water, made for the hills South of the camp. I could make out figures scurrying ahead of me up the hill in all directions through the rain but I struck off for an abandoned truck, which I knew to be mired in a deep cleft-like ravine 300 yards away from the camp. Miraculously, I found the truck right away and climbed inside the relatively dry, empty cab, grateful to be out of the rain, which was now lashing horizontally across the island from the West.

The truck was a heavy-duty maintenance type used by the signal corps in stringing telephone and power lines. Box-like, it was sided by metal compartments for the storage of wire and tools. One of its rear wheels was missing, which, except for the terrain in the ravine, would have tilted the truck at an angle, instead, by some chance had securely jammed the vehicle on a fairly level keel. Except for some minor rocking back and forth in the wind, my shelter seemed safe. One of the roll up cab windows was shattered but it was on the lee side away from the wind and admitted only an occasional shower of rain.

Although by my watch it was only 6:00 p.m., it was dark outside. Taking off my rain pauncho and finding a towel in my wet duffle bag, I dried myself and put on some dry pants and socks, finally settling down in some comfort. I decided to eat one of my K-rations but discovered that of the hundreds of such boxes that I had opened during the war, I was blessed with the only one that had molded. Nothing in the box was edible and in ripping open the remaining rations I was furious to discover that the contents of all three boxes were covered with a green mold. Searching my duffle and clothes, I found a few pieces of hard candy from forgotten C-ration cans. I ate the candy and drank some water. As I did so, I was startled to see and feel a large piece of metal crash into my truck just inches from the windshield. It cartwheeled away in the wind but the impact signalled a new danger from the mounting wind. Soon after, both windshield wipers, after twisting back and forth in a mechanical agony, disappeared into the blackness. There was no light anywhere by now, only the roaring sound of the wind and the rain and the buffeting movement of the truck to mark my place in the bowels of the storm. At last the fatigue and apprehension replaced the knowledge that I needed to stay awake and I began to doze fitfully, jerking upright each time the truck was struck by debris or when it seemed to slide in the wind. Only vaguely conscious of where I was, I drifted in and out of the endless nightmare of sound and jarring blows. Once an enormous banging sound told me that part of the truck in which I sat dazed, had been blown away.

Sometime during the night my watch had stopped and it was only the sight of a greying of the windshield that told me morning had arrived. There was no respite from the storm however, and although I could not see much beyond my now cracked windshield, I could identify pieces of debris that raced around my shelter. I could also see that the heavy metal hood of the truck had been blown away.

Rummaging through the discarded ration boxes, I managed to find a piece of cheese that didn't look too bad, so with some careful carving with my knife I whittled the worst of the mold away and ate my first food in over 15 hours. It was dry, hard and tasted green but it washed down well with water. With the food and something to do, my spirits rose somewhat in spite of the constant rocking motion and the shriek of the wind. During the morning a great crash at the rear of the truck moved my shelter several feet sidewise and knocked it loose from its perch in the ravine. I was thrown against the broken window as the vehicle canted at a steep angle but it was held firmly in place against the rocks and did not continue to slide. Now the seat in the cab was close to a 45 degree angle forcing me to sit against the door with my legs in the air. After a time I managed to stuff my duffle behind me and move my legs up to the seat to form an almost comfortable couch. I soon feel asleep in this position, my head bouncing on the broken window as the storm continued. Exhausted, I slept for several hours finally being awakened by what I first thought was the close wail of a siren. Jerking awake, I saw that the broken windshield was now disintegrating and that a melon sized hole had appeared in the far corner above the steering wheel. The siren was the noise of the wind blowing across and through the hole. Alarmed, I scrambled to find something to help me keep the all important glass in place, for without the windshield my shelter would be useless and dangerous. I began with clothing, stuffing socks, underwear and finally my fatigue jacket through the violently shaking glass. I could see that the entire piece of safety glass was held in place by only three or four rapidly loosening screws. Finally closing the hole after most of my clothing had been blown away, I frantically tightened the screws with my knife. To my great relief the screws held and noise inside the cab subsided, the wind and still driving rain reduced to a train-like roar around the truck.

The day was interminable. I didn't want to sleep for fear that the windshield might go, so I simply sat there watching the color variations of the racing clouds through the sheets of rain that peppered the glass. As the day wore away, I noticed that there was less debris careening through the sky. I reasoned that by then anything to the West that could blow away had already done so.

During the night the wind began to gradually and reluctantly lose its grip on the island and by dawn the rain had stopped. The storm was over.

The truck by then was nearly on its side and I had to climb up over the driver's seat to force open the door. After 36 hours of sitting, I jumped down into inches of cold mud and water to view the badly mauled truck. Not only had the hood blown away but the heavy front fender was gone as was every compartment door on the weather side of the vehicle. If there had been tools or equipment in the compartments, they were no longer there. The enormous force of the wind had nearly disassembled the vehicle leaving only a shell behind. Waiting for some men to struggle down from the hill behind me, I gathered together what I still had left of my gear and headed for the camp area, struggling barefooted through the mud and standing water.

There was so little of our camp left that at first I thought that we had gone in the wrong direction and had missed finding the area. Only two low wooden floor platforms were standing vacantly to mark the mess tent and orderly room. A soggy jumble of canvas, cots and personal belongings lay in tatters to the East of the campgrounds, trees along the now swollen river were either gone altogether or entirely stripped of leaves and branches. In total frustration we stood together in small wordless groups under scudding black clouds looking at the wreckage of what had been our well organized encampment. Gradually we untangled what we could salvage and as the company straggled back in from the hills, we regained our vehicles and began the all important scrounging to replace materials that we had lost.

Under a clearing sky, several of us took a 6-by and headed for Naha in search of heaters, stoves and other equipment needed to rebuild our mess tent. Others went North looking for lumber and replacement tents, cots, blankets and anything else they could find or steal, preferably from the Navy or the Air Corps. Naha, already decimated by the battle, was a scene of utter desolation. Division Headquarters, located in the only standing concrete structure remaining in the city, was flooded and soaking. All previous makeshift windows had been blown out and confusion and anger were very evident among the men and officers trying to straighten out the tumbled files and soggy papers. We left the flooded compound and headed for the harbor, hoping to catch some sailors unaware. The harbor was in shambles, so wrecked that we were unable to get close enough to it to do any scrounging. The beaches and inlet were stacked with the wreckage of ships and littered with debris. Shouting SP's directed us back toward the North edge of the city before we could even stop to ask questions. We headed up Route 1, which was the main Western coast road, toward Machinato Airstrip. There at the Air Corps headquarters we learned, for the first time, that we had been through a typhoon with winds in excess of 150 miles per hour. We also discovered that there had been enough warning of the storm that most aircraft on the island had been flown to safety in Korea before the typhoon struck. The remaining aircraft lay in tangled wreckage along the single runway. Quonset huts were ripped apart and the hospitals and refugee camps were reporting deaths. It took us several days to restore our camp to an operational basis and even then we were without adequate food and water, a condition that lasted for several weeks. Okinawa was a mess, highways and roads washed away, bridges out and communications except by radio from one place on the island to another was minimal.

Nature, in its awesome power, had brought to halt a vigorous military operation for the second time in less than four months.

Several of my companions had sought refuge from the typhoon in vehicles, two had been forced into caves when their lighter trucks began to disintegrate and the rest had tales as sobering as was mine. Most men had fled to abandoned Japanese caves and tunnels on the South flank of the Shuri Ridgeline but many sat in the eerie blackness of the burial tombs and those who found themselves alone for hours with the jars of bones of unknown ancestors were less anxious to discuss the events of the storm.

Eventually we were all accounted for and except for some cuts and bruises our company survived, but we were never to completely recover our many personal belongings that had been blown away to the East, perhaps even to the sea.

*   *   *   *   *

I don't know where the four of us were going that morning, walking in single file up a narrow dirt track that lead to a small ridge line Southwest of Naha. I only knew that the heat and humidity made my eyes dance with light and that my slung rifle chafed my shoulders as I moved it back and forth to ease the pain. Head down, sweat running off my chin, I plodded along behind the rest of my heaving companions. Whenever I could, I favored my right leg that was giving me trouble again. The puncture wound I received in the Saverne Gap a thousand years before had never really healed and at times the pain and ache returned to torment me. My breath came in ragged gasps, intersticed with a rattling wheezy sound. I had first noticed the week before that I was having trouble breathing without making the noises that I heard. Visiting an aid station, a medic had speculated that I was allergic to the vegetation or dust and that I should stay quiet. He had looked at my leg wound, now puffed and red and had given me some aspirin for that.

We had almost crested the ridge when we were stopped short by the crash of a cannon shot just ahead. Cautiously we spread out across the trail and moved slowly to the ridge line to see an American Sherman just below us on the other side of the hill. A half dozen men were talking to a Japanese soldier who was standing next to the tank, which was radiating washboard heat waves from its idling rear engine. Small smoke and cordite fumes rose toward us from the 75 in the turret. We scrambled down the steep embankment off the path and joined the small group, curious to see what was happening. We were greeted with indifferent glances as an American Lieutenant continued to question the fully uniformed Japanese officer who was holding a blanket and several cartons of K-rations. Without speaking but gesturing down the narrow valley below the ridge trail, the Jap turned away from the Lieutenant and leading the way, began making his way through the cactus and scrub brush that dotted the embankment. The group, which we had joined, dutifully followed the enemy soldier, stringing themselves out in single file, rifles slung, sliding, sometimes stumbling in the rocky terrain.

The tank engine roared in protest, sending heat and dirty blue exhaust smoke into the hot morning sky as the driver swung the heavy vehicle in a sharp curve and plunged down the embankment in slow pursuit of the squad ahead of it. We followed, staying back far enough from the tank in single file to escape heat, noise and dust created by the gigantic clattering monster.

We had not gone a hundred yards when the tank stopped, its engine rumbling at idle speed. We fanned out on either side in order to see what was happening ahead. The Japanese soldier was holding his hand in the air in the universal signal to halt. The American Lieutenant left his patrol and hurried forward, immediately holding an animated discussion with the small enemy soldier. I watched, studying the physical difference between the two races. The American was easily 80 pounds heavier and at least two feet taller than the diminutive Oriental. It was suddenly clear to me that modern welfare, with its firepower and killing capabilities, had reduced all armies to equals. Blast, bullets and shrapnel made no size, racial or religious distinction when they appeared in battle.

The Japanese was pointing to the near side of the ridge, which we were following, and I could see the Lieutenant's helmet nodding in agreement as he signaled the patrol and tank to close up on his position. We followed, passing the moving tank and joining the officer and patrol. No words were spoken as the Japanese with his blanket and rations began a careful passage up the steep embankment. The tank rocked to a stop behind us and throttled down to a pulsating throb. We all watched as the Japanese disappeared on his hands and knees behind some scrub brush just 30 yards or so from where we stood. He did not reappear for almost 10 minutes but when he did, he gestured for us to join him on the hillside. Fully expecting the Lieutenant to wave the four of us away, he surprised me by including us in his orders to move up the hill, spreading us out in a small semicircle as we climbed. We arrived together around the Japanese who was shaking his head from side to side. He and the Lieutenant had a few words together as the Japanese held up seven fingers, indicating that in the small cave opening behind him, there were seven men. With a small shrug of his shoulders, the Lieutenant sent a man back to the tank with instructions to return with a satchel charge. We watched the sweating man struggle back up through the cactus and brush with his heavy load of explosives.

"We'll just do this one with the charge," said the Lieutenant in a matter-of-fact way. Within seconds he had pulled the fuse and had tossed the canvas bag into a manhole sized opening in the ground behind the scrub brush. We scattered as fast as we could but when the change went off, the jarring sensation was enough to cause some to lose balance and fall heavily down the hill. Chunks of rocks crashed around us through the choking cloud of dust that had jumped into the air when the charge went off. In a few seconds several men hurriedly accompanied both the Lieutenant and the Japanese back to where the hold had been, rifles ready.

But even from where I stood, I could see that there was nothing but a new depression on the hillside and that the hold was now filled with the rubble of dirt and rocks. Only a thin stream of smoke came from the center of the depression. I drank some warm chlorinated water from my canteen as we reassembled by the idling tank. By now the heat from the shadowless sun was becoming oppressive and the top of my steel helmet was so hot that I could not touch it with my hand.

We moved down the ravine, this time all grouped together in front of the tank, which followed us at a short distance like a faithful, but grumbling dog.

The next cave was farther up on the hill in a cliff-like protuberance with a steep overhang above it. The cave opening, this time clearly visible, resembled a frowning one-eyed man.

Again we waited while the Japanese officer, calling out words in Japanese as he approached, cautiously disappeared into the opening. He was gone a long time before he gave the signal for us to join him.

We gathered near the side of the opening, while he and the Lieutenant talked and gestured, pointing first to the cave and then to the tank that sat in the ravine about 50 yards below us. The Lieutenant kept shaking his head and striking his index finger on the chest of the Japanese. Finally the Japanese officer turned and reentered the cave, calling echoing words as he went. The Lieutenant hunkered down with his drawn pistol pointed at the entrance.

We slid into seated positions on the hillside, rifles across our knees, waiting in the heat. Trying to ignore the buzzing insects around my face, I nodded in semistupor, watching drops of sweat fall from my face onto my dust covered rifle stock. The drops made clean little spots where each splashed on the wood.

At last we could hear the Japanese coming out of the cave; he was talking to someone in a quiet cajoling voice. And when he reappeared, he was holding the hand of a very old stooped woman who was in turn clutching a baby to her breast wrapped in a dirty white towel. She was squinting and blinking against the sunlight but when she saw us a shrill wail escaped from her throat and she tried to break free from the officer but he held a tight grip on her wrist. She soon gave up the attempt to run and instead began bowing and groveling in front of the Lieutenant who smiled woodenly at her. Two men slung their rifles and helped her down the hill toward the tank. We watched as one of them continued on with her up the ravine, his arm across her shoulder, helping her through the brush. The other man came back to the cave entrance and sat heavily on the hillside.

"Jesus," he said. "The kid was dead, had been for a long, long time."

The Lieutenant finished a long discussion with the Japanese and then ordered us back to the tank where he shouted some words to the bored driver whose head stuck out of the open hatch. Within seconds the turret of the tank swung around and the 75 elevated toward the cave entrance. We moved back as the 75 began to shell the cave entrance at point-blank range. The noise, concussion and explosions of the shells as they either entered the cave or hit the cliff directly above, stunned me. I took off my helmet, fearful that it would be blown from my head from the blasts. I put my fingers in my ears and gazed in the dust clouds springing from the Sherman each time the cannon fired. After a dozen rounds or so, the Lieutenant signaled for a cease-fire and we waited for the dust to settle and for the rocks to stop falling from the cliff face. The echo from the last shell waffled through the blistering heat across the hills and valleys toward the cool sea.

Three men went back up the hill to the now demolished cave entrance, while I moved over to where the Japanese soldier sat on a rock, his head bowed staring at the boxes of K-rations that he still held in his hands. When he saw me, he smiled sadly and said in perfect English, "This is a lousy way to make a living."

At first I thought that he was a disguised American, dressed as a Japanese officer, but when I spoke to him, I was astonished to discover that he had gone to college in California and had returned to Japan before the war because he had been patriotic and he had believed that it was his sacred duty to his ancestors to fight for the Emperor. He told me this, shaking his head in disbelief that he could have been so dumb. Wounded and captured early in the Okinawa campaign, he had volunteered to try to save as many lives as he could now that the war was over. He looked up the hill to where the Americans were poking in the rubble of rocks.

"There were at least 60 gooks in that cave," he said heavily. "Women, children, old people, half a dozen crazy Japs, no food, no water, nothing," he trailed off.

After a minute he said to himself in soft passion, "Jesus, God, why can't we quit this shit!"

Convinced that the cave was sealed, we continued down the draw, stopping occasionally to blow more caves with either satchel charges or by use of the tank. By mid afternoon we had passed the ridge and found ourselves on a well traveled North-South Naha Road on the West side of the island. The patrol ended as the squad and the captured Japanese climbed on the tank and went roaring away to the South. The Lieutenant waved us a thanks and a farewell from atop the back of the Sherman.

The four of us began to work our way back to our camp about two miles away to the Northeast. Forgoing the road that was being churned into a gigantic dust cloud from the heavy traffic, we struck off across the hills looking for clumps of trees that might give us some shade on our long walk back. We were familiar enough with the terrain that with confidence, we could traverse the ridge and ravines, knowing that we could find the camp. About half way back we passed through a grove of stunted pine trees on a small plateau separated by low hillocks. There were no roads or paths to follow, so we were surprised to discover a Japanese artillery piece among the trees. We didn't know how it had gotten there but it appeared to be an inoperable antiaircraft gun, barrel pointing to the sky through the roof of trees.

Around the gun, lying where they had fallen, were the uncovered bodies of eight Japanese soldiers. Badly decomposed, all were skeletons with only the hard pieces of blackened flesh that looked like beef jerky sticking to their skulls and bones. Cases of shells and equipment lay scattered around the gun crew and off under the trees was their apparent camp. Cooking pans and personal items, ravaged now by the past rains and heat, lay in mouldering heaps around a dead camp fire. We looked for marks of strafing or shelling, but could find no signs of what had killed this gun crew.

We scrounged for souvenirs but the officer's sword and pistol were so rusty and covered with a growing mold from the leather cases that we left them in disgust. John found a moldy Japanese flag in the camp that he then stuffed in his pocket. Andy, who claimed that he was going to be a doctor when he got home, shocked me by going from body to body prying out gold teeth from the Japanese skulls. Using his bayonet, he dug out the teeth, making sharp cracking sounds as bone splintered giving way to the steel. He used his rifle butt smashing one skull to pieces in order to recover a gold bridge, shouting when he had finished that he was soon to be rich from his find.

As we left the grove, I turned to look back at the eight violated figures that lay in their windless tomb of trees. I could not account for it but after what I had seen and done that day, I felt my cheek twitching and sensed a cloying weariness settle over me.

*　*　*　*　*

I sat hurriedly on some broken stone steps next to the hilly road waiting for the dizzyness to pass. My breathing was difficult and tiny golden lights danced in the center of my eyes. I forced myself to look away toward the horizon, having learned that focusing on distant objects reduced the length of time it took for my vision to clear. I could hear my heart making a thumping noise in my throat and with a shaking hand, I removed my suddenly heavy helmet, feeling a clammy coldness across my forehead where the sweatband had been. I placed the helmet on the steps next to my rifle and continued to watch the ridge across the wide green and brown plateau, stretching out before me. Gradually I felt the strength returning to my body as the specks of fire faded away in the far corners of my eyes. I took several deep but rasping breaths noticing with relief, that I could once again see clearly the familiar knobs, hills and clumps of wreckage on the ridge. I sat for some time, forearms on my knees studying the scene in the distance. Starting at the left, I swept the ridge line, stopping to contemplate each point as I came to it. The hilltops, shattered by gunfire, the broken and burned-out American tanks, seen as rusting brown spots, each terminating at the end of scrawled track marks on the sides of the hills—exclamation marks at the ends of rambling, uncertain sentences. I looked at blackened pinnacles, scorched by napalm bombs and flame throwers, final scenes in a drama where the players, in Act III, embraced the liquid fire in a demented Oriental Gotterdamerung. Small flattened rubble marked crossroads where once stood simple peasant villages full of work, love, and laughter. Cloisters of evergreen trees, stripped of branches and needles, stood in crippled groups on the lip of the ridge, leaning together in places, seeking promises from one another.

To the far right I finally saw the sea, deep blue going to black at the edge of the earth. Riding in the harbor lay a white hospital ship, a large red cross painted triumphantly on its high side, snuggled among a flotilla of grey and anonymous vessels.

There was no sound, only the angry buzzing of insects around my face and the faint far-off surging of a fighter plane at Yonabaru, running up for takeoff. The heat from the sun on my head and face was painful, but I was gripped by a stupifying inaction so strong that I could not move to either cover my head or brush away the insects, which were after the moisture in my eyes.

My mind began to wander but with a jerk, I remembered my flying fish and then in near panic, I fought to overcome the near trance into which I could sense myself falling. With an enormous physical effort I started to lean forward in order to force myself to my feet, straining to blink my eyes against the snarling gnats.

But in so doing my vision necessarily shifted to the road under my feet and when I finally could focus on the ruts and tracks in the dried mud, a deep cry of horror came from my throat. For there, under my shoes was the crushed body of a child.

It was a small female child, seven or eight years old. She had been run down by a tank, the track marks embedded in the mud, clearly visible over the entire length of her face down spread-eagle body, her little fingers extended, clutching the mud in a final spasm.

I moved my feet, and still sitting on the steps, gazed sadly at this symbol of what the three years of war had been to me. All of it, the training and the war itself, came down to this single little girl, crushed to death on a farmer's dirt road. Her hair, matted with dried mud and blood, was blue-black and her feet were bare.

How many children had it taken I wondered? How many women and children? How many men? How many horses and cows? How many fish and tiny birds? How many worms . . . ? How many creatures had it taken to win?

I looked at the ridge again, only this time it was dimmed through tears that filled my eyes and ran silently down my cheeks. For long minutes I cried without sound for the dead child and for the lost child who was no longer within me. I sat with her until the sun, ironically, glorious in its setting, withdrew from the sky. When it had gone and I could clearly see the evening star, I rose and walked down the hill to the camp.

CHAPTER XXIII

GOING HOME

Eventually the unbearable waiting was over. After five months on the island, I received word one afternoon from Army headquarters in Naha that my accumulated points were sufficient enough to justify my discharge from the service. Curiously, I received the word without emotion and even after being promoted the next day, I found no satisfaction in hearing that I was to go home soon. I had become cynical and suspicious of anything announced by headquarters, hardened in my conviction that I would never escape the 640 square mile prison. When the Captain congratulated me on my promotion in the company street, he also casually mentioned that I was to be transferred the next day to a field artillery unit on the East side of the island near Yonabaru. The transfer was necessary for processing and transport out of the eastern Port, he explained. In spite of my suspicions, my spirits rose when I heard what he had to say and I allowed myself a very brief feeling of elation.

The unexpected transfer was a new and different twist, perhaps something was actually going to happen. The war had ended in September in the midst of rumors and delays in the final surrender arrangements and although there was little attention given to the process on Okinawa, we were engulfed in a brief period of protest and anger when it had been announced that our battalion was being sent to Korea. The move never materialized, however, so we settled down to the task of avoiding isolated and armed Japanese soldiers still holding out in the hills and of cleaning up the debris from the battle.

Our company had moved from the river ravine to a hillside North of Machinato Airstrip where we set up a uniform military tent city, complete with a roofed-over kitchen and mess tent. Some ingenious frustrated plumbers even built a shower unit with hot running water.

Days passed in weary monotony, punctuated only by regularly scheduled movies, which we viewed on a large outdoor screen in a gouged
out amphitheater nestled in a nearby ravine. It became routine to secure
something to drink and then, as a group, to mock the incredibly bad
films that we viewed over and over. We were given Sundays off and
worked an eight hour day. When we were not in the hills recovering
equipment, there were little to do but read, talk and write letters.

We did learn that two or three men from M company, located
farther down the hill from us, formed a hunting team and that on
Sundays they would hunt Japs. When the gruesome activity was discovered at battalion, the team was broken up and the hunting season declared over. The activity was stopped, not because of the senseless
killing, but because our people could be in danger or even injured.
During November and December, there was rain, even some moderately serious storms, but none ever approached the ferocity of the typhoon. A brisk trade in German souvenirs developed when nearby
units discovered that we had fought in the European theater of operations. Japanese samurai swords, of dubious manufacture, were traded
for belt buckles, swastica flags and occasionally a German pistol.

We ate, we slept, we worked and we watched carefully for the
daily posting of the names of men who were scheduled for departure.
The married family men were the first to go. There was no celebration,
only a few handshake goodbyes, sometimes a grip much harder than
it needed to be. The company began a slow dissolve as two or three at
a time would gather in class A uniforms at the orderly tent after breakfast to load their gear into a weapons carrier for the short trip to the
border. Occasionally I would watch the vehicle lurch up the dusty access road, carrying its human cargo, often solemn faces watching the
camp from the rear of the carrier. Sometimes there was an awkward
final wave to no one in particular as the truck disappeared over the
hill, the sound of its laboring engine fading away beyond sight.

The night before I was to be transferred, Johnny, Sad Ass, and Don
came by my tent as I was packing my belongings in my duffle bag.
Somehow they had obtained two sealed bottles of Scotch whiskey from
a sailor in Naha and were prepared to drink me out of the company.
We left the packing for later, walked in the dark to the hill far above the
amphitheater, and passing the bottle as we sat on the ground, became
gloriously drunk. The stars wheeled in a majestic sky and we laughed
and cried together, low voices saying words with thickened tongues
through numbed lips. Johnny passed out halfway through the second
bottle but not before he had joined in a solemn promise that the four
of us would remain friends always, that we would never lose contact
with one another and that, no matter what, we would come to one
another's aid in time of trouble.

Later, we carried Johnny down the hill to the now darkened camp, laughing whenever we dropped him and stopping now and then to be sick.

The next morning I shook a few hands, gave the finger to a no longer dangerous supply Sergeant, threw my duffle bag in the weapons carrier and left the Artillery and Fire Control Company forever. I sat in the front with the driver and did not look back as we crested the hill.

The Field Artillery Company was a ragtag camp of crooked tents strung in a haphazard manner along a ridge above Yonabaru Airfield, now deserted except for a handful of Marine Corsair fighter bombers. When I handed my transfer orders to the first Sergeant, he assigned me to a tent, gave me the chow schedule and said, "Hang around the area. We'll call you when we need you."

At first I did just that, in fact, except for hurried meals, I sat on my folding cot for two days not wanting anyone to have an excuse for not being able to find me. During that time, men came and went and I learned that the Artillery Company was no longer a field unit, it was merely being used as a holding company for men on their way home. It was the Army's way of making sure that every man showed up somewhere by name on the daily morning reports somewhere on the planet.

On the morning of the third day I was delighted when my three drunken companions showed up. They too had received orders on the same day that I had taken my leave of L Company. We sat around together for several more days before word came from the orderly room that we would board a ship together the next morning.

None of us slept well that night, convinced that the dream would die, the bubble would burst, and that something, somehow would go wrong at the last minute. Even when we crowded into bobbing LCI's, held in place by sailors alongside a wooden pier, we were silent and fearful that it would still not happen. The landing craft, fully loaded, chugged out into Buckner Bay, named after the dead General, toward a large grey troopship.

Aboard the ship, named the William A. Mann, a sister ship of the Butner, we were assigned bunks and treated with comparative respect and dignity by boarding officers and crew members. Fighting an almost ungovernable impulse to hide somewhere on the ship, we sat together, smoked, and talked in low tones so as not to attract unnecessary attention to ourselves. We were nervous when any stranger approached our group, particularly if he had orders in his hands. I myself was absolutely convinced that I would be taken off the ship at any moment and I finally withdrew into a bitter depression, silent and angry over my fate. We waited in the hold all afternoon while the ship gradually filled with happy, cheerful soldiers who did not seem to understand that a joke was being played on them, that the ship would never leave and that soon an announcement would be made over the P.A. system that we were all to get off the ship and go back to the island. I could not believe that these laughing shouting people could not see through the deception. However, as the numbers increased I took some solace in believing that I could hide in the crowd in case they came looking for just me. I was so tense late in the day that I could feel the skin creep on my arm. My legs ached from the tension of tightened muscles. There was an announcement in our hold for chow but I didn't go. I lay very still on my canvas bunk behind my duffle bag, unseen by the men pushing through the narrow aisle on their way to the mess hall.

Suddenly I was jerked awake by the throbbing of the engines in the giant ship. Virtually alone in the hold, I raced to the ladder and at two steps at a time made my way to the open deck alone to watch as our ship swung in a great slow arc on the smooth bay. We were underway. The deck was crowded but I struggled to reach the railing. There at last I gazed at Okinawa, a silhouette of blue-black against the bright evening sky. I saw the ridges and I swore then that never, in my lifetime, would I ever set foot on that island again.

I watched the long low features of Okinawa for a long time, until at last it grew so dark that I could not distinguish the shape of the island from the blackness of the sky. It was a moment I did not want to forget.

The Mann, like the Buckner, was a large ship designed for the transportation of troops and at first there was a familiarity about the structure of the holds, the latrines and the arrangement of the deck machinery that brought back the memories of the Buckner. This feeling of dread was soon dispelled, however, because there were major differences in the two voyages. I was not going to war, I was going home. Not only was the ship headed for the United States but on the first day in the open sea a friendly voice on the P.A. informed us that the ship was sailing for the San Pedro port of Los Angeles, California.

There was one other major difference, the lights.

After dinner on the second night, I went up on deck to watch the stars and to sit somewhere by myself. But when I stepped out on the deck, I was astonished to discover that the smooth sailing ship was fully lighted. Bright light spilled out from open doorways, hatches and portholes. Rigging lights blazed away in the darkness and the instant impression was that we were a moving sandlot carnival. We needed only calliope music to complete the illusion.

After a total of almost three months at sea, sailing alone, or in company with other ships in convoy, it was the first time in my life that I had ever seen a lighted ship at sea.

The effect was remarkable for the ship was no longer an anonymous part of the darkness of the night, riding on heaving black bottomless water. The ship was a statement of its own, pushing back the thickness, a self-contained unit separated from the ownership of the ocean. The lights made the night a place of cheerfulness, almost gaiety.

Other differences existed also. We were left alone, not guarded by armed Marines, and there was a friendliness from a joking crew. And the food was good and plentiful.

Concerned one morning that my breathing problem was continuing in spite of assurances that once I had left Okinawa I would be well again, I visited the sick bay for some advice and help. There an interested doctor gave me some medicine to relieve the congestion and cautioned me to watch the problem in civilian life. While I was there among the relaxed group, I noticed a young man dressed in a ship's hospital robe sitting on one of the two beds that were in the room. He was a young man with sandy, curly hair, quiet but involved as a listener to the jokes and stories being told, chuckling and smiling at the barbs and punch lines.

I learned later from an acquaintance who worked in the sick bay that his name was Larry and because he had had a nervous breakdown, he was under constant watch by the hospital staff. Because he had appeared so calm, I was surprised at the information but put it out of my mind.

Several nights later as we were approaching the coast of the United States, our P.A. system crackled and the ship's Chaplain's voice made a pleading appeal to Larry to return the hospital. "Please return, Larry, we are not going to hurt you, we want to help you," said the voice.

Several other voices joined in the search for the man but without success. Soon after the pleas and a search of the ship by serious looking crew members who passed through our compartment, the Captain announced that we were reversing our course to make a search of the sea, according to maritime law. He then asked for volunteer assistance on the decks in looking for the missing soldier.

Several of us offered to take part in the search, some out of curiosity or boredom, and some of us out of a deep unexplainable sense of loss. We steamed back over our precious course for several hours in the darkness, large arc spotlights sweeping the pearl gray water with circular pools of light, probing the surface of the choppy water like unfeeling fingertips. Eventually the spotlights were turned off and we made a wide sweeping turn to the East, to return to our original course, minus one soul.

I remained, sitting on a donkey engine cover, long after the decks were deserted, watching the sky and feeling the cold air on my face and hands. I looked to the East, in the direction in which the ship was headed, and knew that every minute was taking me back to my other life, that on the next day we would dock in San Pedro. I turned and looked back to the West, feeling a sudden grief for the youngster with the curly hair who was by now slipping slowly down and down into the sea.

When he went over the side, he must have come to the surface gasping in the cold shock of the water, only to see the great blazing ship surging away to disappear as a pinpoint of light in the distance. Perhaps, as he found himself in the darkness, paddling in spite of himself to stay on top of the cresting waves, he had regrets. He may even have changed his mind, however troubled it had been. But it had been too late, the ship was gone and there remained only the silent night and the cold water.

Surely his inevitable and lonely death was the last that I would encounter in World War II. It was an irony that it was a suicide and that I would remember it that way.

CHAPTER XXIV

DISCHARGE

I sat on the engine cover all night, facing the East, driven by some mysterious need to spend this quiet last night at sea alone with my thoughts. Driving my mind away from the great rush of joy that I felt at being close to home, I concentrated instead of thinking about my three years in the service and of the war memories—some sad, some happy—my thoughts came and went as I remembered the days of training, the humor, the stupidity, the happiness, the bitterness, the disappointments, the brutality in so many disguises, and the everlasting loneliness.

The faces and voices of the recent years drifted across my conscious thoughts, friends and false friends, each having touched me in some way. I remembered the rain, the bitter snow and cold in Europe, and the suffocating heat of the tropics. Thoughts of the humiliations, which I had endured, pressed down on me and I shuddered once in the late night wind when I remembered how close to madness I had come.

I thought of death and of those who would never experience coming home, for those whose fragile light went out on a muddy road, a snow covered open field, in an exploding crash of flame behind a row of trees. I remembered golden hair and a white blouse in a stone quarry and of two robbed and dying Americans lying on a frozen road in the Saverne Gap. And I remembered the fear. But after awhile the single visions dimmed running together into a kaleidoscope of one enormous event, the war itself.

What had died in this war? Even then I suspected that millions had perished and I concluded that the human enterprise would be reduced and set back by at least a generation, the next generation inevitably altered because of the children of dead parents who would now, never be born. The untimely and concentrated deaths of millions of people is far-reaching, it is not just personal, it has an effect on humanity itself.

And what of me? What had I learned? Would I remember the war only as a series of events, some good, some bad? Or would I remember the lessons I had learned, and more importantly would I use these lessons in readjusting to a life, which, at that moment, spread out ahead of me for an imagined eternity.

Even as a young person, I had learned that human beings live a contradiction. That on one hand there is reason, caring and compassion and yet there remains, on the other, a brutality, a studied cruelty and a disregard for others so remarkable that it barely distinguishes the intellectual human from the most savage of animal forms. To know early in life that this schism exists is to be placed on guard as an individual and to be wary of all national and international events that casually enter the multicultural life on the planet. I had learned that in the future I must pay attention to the world and to be constructively skeptical of what was reported to me by governments, including my own.

And where were the lessons that I had learned about myself? First, I had learned that I had the character to be myself. I had come to understand that I had the capacity to be patient with individuals and with circumstances. I had developed self-control under conditions that had driven others to madness and I had learned how to cope with boredom and loneliness.

I had learned to survive in conditions of despair and fear and I had seen that I had had limits when it had come to my own moments of terror. Looking back it was easy to imagine that I had demonstrated courage and leadership but sitting quietly on the ship, I honestly accepted once and for all that having emerged as a hero was not one of my unsuspected strengths. I had survived, I had limits, which I had discovered, and that was all.

I decided that never again would I take comfort for granted. I would make it a point never to be cold or wet or hungry again, that I would never stretch out under warm blankets without gratitude and that I would never regard the beauty of the world without realizing how lucky I was to be a part of it.

I had learned love and of the bonding of people under duress and I had learned that it was not in my nature to be deceptive in dealing with other people.

These were lessons learned in a crucible and forged on a young mind into a lifetime of determination. As a child and adolescent, I had lived in a secure world of parental protection, virtually unaware of life outside the sphere of warmth and love. Having seen another reality, one of harshness and ugliness, had lead me from one extreme to another. I must learn to join these extremes together as I live my life. I must seek to understand that somewhere there is a balance point, a fulcrum, and that the compromise, which will make life liveable, will filter through and be governed by the lessons that I had learned.

But as I sat there with my back against the motor cowling, I concluded with complete understanding that the most profound lesson, which I had learned, was that I was mortal. Mortality is not an easy topic when a person is young but now I knew absolutely that someday I would actually die. I had seen the coldness and capriciousness of death in many forms and knew without doubt that I had escaped it only for a period of time. In some strange way I felt some comfort in the knowledge of my mortality and I resolved that I would therefore live cheerfully and productively. I knew then that I would take the lessons of World War II, those lessons that had shaped my character, and try to make a difference in the world.

As the sky lightened to the East, I resolved that there were things, which had happened to me, that I would never allow myself to forget.

Excitably, I jumped down from the donkey engine to stand and watch the top edge of the sun appear over the horizon—a horizon, which I knew held my family, my home, my loved ones and my future. Tears came to my eyes as I realized that the very sun that I saw was the same sun, which was only then appearing over my home in Bellflower just miles ahead.

A few hours later the ship slowed and glided into the busy harbor of San Pedro. Every soldier on board was on the crowded deck as we maneuvered alongside a warehouse pier. A Navy band was playing on the pier and a large block letter billboard on the warehouse roof exclaimed, "Welcome home—well done."

Somehow the sign stunned me. I had never thought of us as having done it well, I had only thought of us as having no choice at all but to do it. Although I was touched and pleased, I had an uneasy feeling that there was something hollow, even a studied mockery, in that sign.

After a night train ride, we were held for two days at Camp Roberts near Riverside. Once in camp we were started through the process of demobilization, confined to the post, given new clothes, and fed fresh food by German POW's who manned a sumptuous chow line. The first time through the line I saw a bookish German wearing a faded African Corps cap at the end of the counter pouring fresh milk into honest china cups. I studied him as others heaped slices of beef, mashed potatoes, fresh carrots and peas and apple pie a la mode on my serving tray. I thought that he could be Franz from Camp Forrest but when he held out a cup of cold milk and smiled at me I could see that it was not the same man. I thanked him in German but as I turned away he answered me in crisp English.

Almost without exception every man became violently ill from the food. For days the latrines were crowded with groaning men trying to readjust their systems to the richness of fresh meat, vegetables and milk. While at Roberts there was no hassle and no long waits in never moving lines. We were given all the time we needed to make our phone calls and for those who were being moved to other parts of the country, time for letter writing. Our leisure time was used in animated but serious discussions about what we would do when we got home and out of uniform. Cautioned to stay near our barracks in case we were needed, we were occasionally sent for to listen to short clever lectures about returning to civilian life. One officer summed it up very well. He said, "When you get home and you're at the dinner table, try very hard not to say, pass the fucking butter."

We were also informed about the opportunity to continue our life insurance, how to handle soldier's deposits, a savings system instituted by the Armed services during the war, and how to reenlist. On the surface the reenlistment lectures were not too favorably received, although I was surprised at the number of men who, when the talk was over, moved surreptitiously to the table to take application forms.

When our newly tailored dress uniforms were ready to be picked up, each of us was given, according to the records, campaign ribbons, battle stars, earned badges and victory medals. Stripes were sown on sleeves along with overseas service bars and theatre patches. Finally, when we all looked like a civilian's impression of what a discharged soldier was supposed to look like, we were taken by train to Fort McArthur in San Pedro for the final steps in the process of being turned into an instant civilian.

For two days I was interviewed, debriefed and given a perfunctory physical examination aimed at making me seem more healthy than I had been before I entered the Army. Rumors were spread that if you reported illness or injuries you might be kept in an Army hospital for a long time. Few men, including me, reported anything but perfect health.

The interviews, conducted by serious Army counselors, delved into plans for the future and involved long conversations about previous service technical training and combat experiences.

Not wishing to upset anything, I merely reported to an apparently satisfied interviewer that I intended to return to college at the earliest opportunity.

Finally I was handed my official discharge paper to check over for errors. I held it carefully by the edges, hardly believing that I had such a precious document in my hands. There were minor errors on it but I hurriedly signed the paper, handing it back casually while assuring the clerk-typist that it was in perfect order.

Even though it was after 4:00 in the afternoon, I was told to retrieve my belongings from the barracks and to report to a certain room in the headquarters building.

When I arrived I found 20 or so men seated facing a small bespectacled Major seated at a table in front of the room. The officer soon cleared his throat, pushed back his chair and in a sincere fatherly manner addressed our group. I will never know who he was, I only knew that, at the time, he gave the best 10 minute speech that I had ever heard. His words were not words of patriotism or passion, he spoke for all of us, words of truth and honesty.

The Major first thanked us on behalf of the country for our services and our sacrifices that only we as individuals could measure. He told us quite frankly that we had often been mistreated and neglected, even brutalized by an Army system so huge and complex that individuals were, of necessity, lost within its structure. For this, he and the country were sorry. But we *had* endured and even those with physical and mental scars, could, if we fought hard, return to a peaceful and productive life. He warned us that our families and loved ones could never understand what we had been through but that our patience and understanding would help them through the adjustment.

As he talked I wondered at his wisdom and I thought to myself, "Why didn't someone explain this to me in this room when I entered the damned Army? It would have helped me to know that there was perhaps a speck of sympathy and understanding toward my personal frustrations and fears."

The Major continued in a quiet voice, thanking us again for the years of our young lives and for coming to the aid of our country in its desperate, unprepared for war against its enemies.

"Even though you hated it," he said, "you will live your lives as a generation of men who will forever be different, but who will also feel the pride of having been there when you were needed."

He stopped briefly, shuffling through the discharge papers on his tables, knowing I presumed that his remarks had touched the hearts of the men in the room. He concluded by saying that he would read our names one at a time and that when he did each man should come forward to exchange one last salute as a soldier in the Army of the United States.

When he read my name I marched forward, came to attention, looked directly at him through sudden tears and snapped him the finest salute of my service career. He congratulated me softly and handed me my signed discharge papers.

When we were seated, feeling strangely self-conscious, he said quietly, "You are all now civilians."

There was a moment of thoughtful silence as though we, as civilians, did not know what to do without instructors. He broke the silence

391

in an offhanded but calculated way, "Oh, by the way," he said, "the post commander asked me to see if you would mind policing up on your way off the post."

The room exploded in laughter, hoots and jeers as we all experienced the emotional release that he intended. Trooping out, talking and shouting back and forth louder than was necessary, we walked by the Major who thanked us one by one as we left the room.

It was already dark as I walked through the gate with my small bag of belongings. My possessions were few, my one dress uniform that I wore, and a few personal items in a kit bag. When I reached the street, curiously self-conscious about my ribbons, badges and new appearance, I turned to look back at the main gate to Fort McArthur. I don't know what I expected to see, perhaps spotlights pinpointing a flashing neon sign that read "Keim, Entrance and Exit," but in the semi-shadows of night, the gate was only two old brick pillars set rather close together. The guard who had checked my discharge papers before letting me out, seemed bored at my uncertainty and soon stepped back into the shadows and disappeared from view.

I stood alone on an empty street, having come through an important gate that I had entered exactly one thousand and twenty-nine days before. I did not have long to wait. My father drove up in his 39 Mercury sedan and parked under a light across the street. As I crossed over to him, he got out of the car and waited for me. He seemed smaller and older than I had remembered. We hesitated for a brief moment, long enough for me to see the tears glistening in his eyes, but for the first time in my life I did not wait for my father to put his arms around me, instead I put my arms around him.

EPILOGUE

And so it ends. But in a larger sense, it persists and cannot end, not for me, not for the millions of still living humans who go about their daily lives bearing the memories of World War II. Scar tissue, whether external or internal, never heals completely but remains embedded in each one as somber evidence of the events of the past. Until the very last mortal who was alive during those years passes from the face of the earth, the war will remain. When the day comes, and the last grave is dug, the war will only then become merely a thought, a curious historical event posted along humanity's path, to be studied by students and genealogists. But until that inevitable grave is dug, the war will live for what it did to change the lives of people. To have lived through the war and not to have been changed by it was not possible. Not for anyone.

And I know so very well that some day, the early morning light will probe softly into a quiet room to find me facing the final momentous truth about myself. Perhaps, at the time, I will be puzzled by a drugged mind, counting the tiny holes in the square tiles of a white accoustical ceiling in studied desperation and fighting to keep straight thoughts. I will see the blurred solemn faces and try not to understand the hushed words filtering back to me from the far corner of the room next to the brightening window. But through the swirling images and disjointed words, the end will arrive, and I will, as I must, embrace it. But before I do, I know that I will see in the corner shadows of that promised room the still young faces of my comrades from the days when I grew into what I became.

There will be a grinning Lt. Harding, anxious to tell me about his latest scheme for making money, a jovial Sgt. Sudovich, ready with a ribald joke, and Lelly, still apologizing. There will be others—Johnny, Radich, Sergeant Dow, Patterson, Senson, even Captain Smart and Lt. Bond. In front, of course, will be Don Holt, who will give me a smile and a thumbs-up sign. Among the crowded figures, I will see Mrs. Martin smile brightly, with her head tilted slightly away from the tall, dark haired Gabrielle. And there will be others to see and remember. But before my vision constricts to a single pinpoint of final flickering light, they will wave together in farewell and gently pass me beyond the memories, the lessons, and the love that each had bestowed upon me. Only then will World War II finally end.